The Old South's Modern Worlds

The Old South's Modern Worlds

Slavery, Region, and Nation in the Age of Progress

EDITED BY

L. DIANE BARNES, BRIAN SCHOEN, AND

FRANK TOWERS

OXFORD
UNIVERSITY PRESS

OXFORD
UNIVERSITY PRESS

Oxford University Press, Inc., publishes works that further
Oxford University's objective of excellence
in research, scholarship, and education.

Oxford   New York
Auckland   Cape Town   Dar es Salaam   Hong Kong   Karachi
Kuala Lumpur   Madrid   Melbourne   Mexico City   Nairobi
New Delhi   Shanghai   Taipei   Toronto

With offices in
Argentina   Austria   Brazil   Chile   Czech Republic   France   Greece
Guatemala   Hungary   Italy   Japan   Poland   Portugal   Singapore
South Korea   Switzerland   Thailand   Turkey   Ukraine   Vietnam

Copyright © 2011 by Oxford University Press, Inc.

Published by Oxford University Press, Inc.
198 Madison Avenue, New York, New York 10016

www.oup.com

Oxford is a registered trademark of Oxford University Press

Library of Congress Cataloging-in-Publication Data
The Old South's modern worlds : slavery, region, and nation in the age of progress / edited by
L. Diane Barnes, Brian Schoen, and Frank Towers.
   p.   cm.
Includes bibliographical references and index.
ISBN 978-0-19-538401-7 (hardcover : acid-free paper)—ISBN 978-0-19-538402-4
(pbk. : acid-free paper) 1. Southern States—Historiography. 2. Southern
States—History—1775–1865—Historiography. 3. Southern States—History—Study
and teaching. 4. Slavery—Southern States—Historiography. 5. Regionalism—Southern
States—Historiography. I. Barnes, L. Diane. II. Schoen, Brian. III. Towers, Frank.
F208.2.S68   2011
975—dc22   2010032534

1 3 5 7 9 8 6 4 2

Printed in the United States of America
on acid-free paper

Dedicated to
Carol and Dale Schoen, Jewel Spangler, and
Tom and Glenda Mowrey

Contents

Acknowledgments

While it is true that all historical studies require the cooperation of many individuals, this collection of essays was truly born of a collaborative effort. It began as a panel at the Victorian Association of Western Canada's conference on the Global Victorians in 2006. At that panel the three editors of this book met for the first time and had our papers critiqued by two of the chapter contributors, Larry Hudson and Marc Egnal. Our discussion over the degree to which the Old South was connected to the modern world continued in the student lounge after the panel and led to another panel, which added Diane Sommerville in the commentary role, at the annual meeting of the Society for Historians of the Early American Republic at Wooster, Massachusetts, in 2007. From these beginnings our "traveling road show" generated interest in turning the idea of a modern-connected Old South into a book showcasing newly written essays on standard topics such as cotton and slavery, as well as topics such as planter sexuality and transnational literary influences. We are very grateful to Jane Slusser, our original acquisitions editor at Oxford University Press, for seeing the merits of the collection. We also owe much to Susan Ferber, executive editor at Oxford, for her superb guidance, advice, and, above all, her patience as we moved through the course of putting the book together. During the prepublication process, we benefited from the expert advice of three anonymous readers in the proposal stage and two who read the whole manuscript. We are indebted to these scholars for their comments and especially for the questions that probed us to think deeper about many of the ideas and issues that inform the history of the Old South. These types of collections are beholden to the quality and cooperation of their contributors, and we are eternally grateful to the authors who dedicated their time and talents to this project.

A number of folks read parts of the manuscript, especially the introduction, and we would like to thank Peter Coclanis, Jewel Spangler, and Barbara Hahn for their insights. At each of our respective universities, we benefited from institutional support as well as the camaraderie of many of our colleagues and friends. At Youngstown State University, Diane Barnes received a year-long research professorship that provided some needed release time to write and edit her chapter. She also thanks colleagues Helene Sinnreich and Mehera Gerardo, who read early drafts of sections of the manuscript and provided a needed transnational critique, and Matt Alspaugh, for providing moral support and professional wisdom. Financial support from the Social Sciences and Humanities Research Council of Canada and the Faculty of Social Sciences at the University of Calgary supported the first conference where these ideas took shape. Byron Miller at the University of Calgary offered valuable comments on part of the manuscript. At Ohio University, Brian Schoen received travel funds to participate in the "road show," and he thanks his colleagues in the history department who offered intellectual and moral support.

Families often bear the brunt of time-consuming endeavors like this one. Frank Towers relied on the feedback, support, and sanity of Jewel Spangler. Diane Barnes particularly acknowledges the love and support of Ben Barnes, who rarely complained about the many hours she spent on this project. In the Schoen household, Brian thanks Kelli, Julia, and Annelise, who complied with timelines by waiting to be born after the preliminary manuscript went to readers.

Contributors

Edward L. Ayers is president and professor of history at the University of Richmond. He is the author of *The Promise of the New South: Life after Reconstruction* (1992), a finalist for the Pulitzer Prize and the National Book Award, and *In the Presence of Mine Enemies: Civil War in the Heart of America* (2003), which won the Bancroft Prize and the Beveridge Prize.

L. Diane Barnes is associate professor of history at Youngstown State University and associate editor of the Frederick Douglass Papers. She is the author of *Artisan Workers in the Upper South: Petersburg, Virginia, 1820–1865* (2008) and numerous chapters and articles. She is also editor of *Ohio History*.

Steven Deyle is associate professor of history at the University of Houston. He is the author of *Carry Me Back: The Domestic Slave Trade in American Life* (2005) and numerous articles on slavery in the American South.

Marc Egnal is professor of history at York University and author of numerous books on American history. His latest titles include *Clash of Extremes: The Economic Origins of the Civil War* (2009) and *Divergent Paths: How Culture and Institutions Have Shaped North American Growth* (1996).

Andrew K. Frank is associate professor of history at Florida State University. He is the author of *Creeks and Southerners: Biculturalism on the Early American Frontier* (2005) and several articles on southeastern Indians. He is currently completing *Those Who Camp at a Distance: The Seminoles and Indians of Florida* for the University of North Carolina Press.

Craig Thompson Friend is professor of history and director of public history at North Carolina State University. He is author of *Along the Maysville Road: The Early American Republic in the Trans-Appalachian West* (2005) and *Kentucke's Frontiers* (2010). He is editor of *Southern Masculinities: Perspectives on Manhood in the South since Reconstruction* and coeditor of *Southern Manhood: Perspectives on Masculinity in the Old South,* with Lorri Glover, and of *Family Values in the Old South,* with Anya Jabour.

Larry Hudson has a background in social history with a primary area of research on work and the African-American family under slavery. His teaching interests include the American South, the Civil War, slavery, and comparative slavery. He is currently examining alcohol usage among the enslaved in antebellum America. Publications include *"To Have and to Hold": Slave Work and Family Life in Antebellum South Carolina* (1997).

James L. Huston has taught at Oklahoma State University for thirty years and now holds the position of Regents Distinguished Professor. His most recent book is *Stephen A. Douglas and the Dilemmas of Democratic Equality* (2007). His current interest involves the intersection of national economic development, farm work, and the free-labor ideology.

Charles F. Irons is associate professor of history at Elon University in North Carolina. He has explored the rise of evangelical Protestantism and the relationship between enslaved and free evangelicals in numerous articles and a recent book, *The Origins of Proslavery Christianity: White and Black Evangelicals in Colonial and Antebellum Virginia* (2008).

Matthew Mason is associate professor of history at Brigham Young University and author of *Slavery and Politics in the Early American Republic* (2006), which was an alternate selection for the History Book Club. Along with Nicholas Mason, he edited Edward Kimber's *The History of the Life and Adventures of Mr. Anderson* (2009). He is coeditor, with John Craig Hammond, of the forthcoming volume *Contesting Slavery: The Politics of Slavery in the New American Nation.*

Michael O'Brien is professor of American intellectual history at Cambridge University. He is author of the two-volume *Conjectures Of Order: Intellectual Life and the American South, 1810–60* (2004), which won the Bancroft Prize, and numerous other works of American history.

Peter S. Onuf is Thomas Jefferson Foundation Professor of History at the University of Virginia. Trained as a colonial historian under Jack P. Greene at Johns Hopkins, Onuf has written numerous works on Thomas Jefferson and his age; in 2006 he and his brother, international-relations theorist Nicholas G. Onuf, published *Nations, Markets and War: Modern History and the American Civil War.*

Brian Schoen is author of *The Fragile Fabric of Union: Cotton, Federal Politics, and the Global Origins of the Civil War* (2009), winner of the 2010 Bennett H. Wall award, and several book chapters and articles on Southern political economy and sectionalism. He is assistant professor of history at Ohio University, where he teaches the history of the early American republic, the American South, and the Civil War and Reconstruction.

William G. Thomas is the John and Catherine Angle Chair in the Humanities and professor of history at the University of Nebraska-Lincoln. He served as director of the Virginia Center for Digital History at the University of Virginia from 1998 to 2005 and as project manager of The Valley of the Shadow: Two Communities in the American Civil War. His current work, "The Iron Way: Civil War and the Making of Modern America," examines the relationship between the railroad culture of the 1850s and 1860s and the coming, fighting, and aftermath of the American Civil War. The book's research draws on and from an accompanying digital project, *"Railroads and the Making of Modern America,"* available online at http://railroads.unl.edu (accessed October 2010).

Frank Towers teaches U.S. history at the University of Calgary in Alberta, Canada. He is the author of *The Urban South and the Coming of the Civil War* (2004) and articles and book chapters on cities, politics, and race in the antebellum South.

The Old South's Modern Worlds

Introduction: Reimagining the Old South

L. Diane Barnes, Brian Schoen, Frank Towers

The term "Old South" describes a time and a place: the fifteen states that maintained slavery from the ratification of the Constitution in 1787 to the start of the Civil War in 1861. It has also served as interpretive shorthand for seeing antebellum America as a nation torn between a backward-looking past, embodied by a static, essentialized Old South, and a forward-looking present, represented by the dynamic and diverse North. This collection of essays reconsiders that second interpretive meaning. The Old South as a place that defied the march of progress has deep roots in popular culture but also resonates through professional scholarship that measured it according to a standard of modernity defined by the North, its sectional rival, and Britain, the global superpower of its day. That comparison still has value to be sure, but it now competes with other interpretations of the Old South that avoid such sharp juxtapositions and their underlying assumptions by focusing on the region's diversity, modernity, and global interconnections.[1]

Expanding on this effort, this volume recasts the Old South not as the anti-North or as a region stuck in time, but on its own terms and as an active participant in, and even promoter of, change and progress. The essays that follow consider some of Southern history's mainstay topics, such as cotton and slavery, from fresh perspectives and explore lesser known aspects of the Southern past, such as the history of planter sexuality and the Native American encounter with modernizing trends. Taken as a whole, they reiterate the often-made point that the South contained great diversity, but contend that each of the "many Souths" was inextricably shaped by modern experience. Discussing historical actors and events in light of relevant secondary literature, they seek to give student and professional readers examples of the changing interpretation of the Old South.

An understanding of the Old South as modern-minded and globally inter-connected has emerged from studying the slave states in contexts that previ-ously drew little scholarly attention. These new contexts can be divided into two broad, interrelated areas. The first situates the national history of the United States at the center of Southern history and, in turn, considers how the Old South contributed to processes that defined the nation. Where one dominant scholarly tradition has sought to explain what made the Old South distinct from the rest of the United States, another one contemplates how Southerners contributed to national narratives and were influenced in turn by these narratives. To ask how antebellum Southerners influenced the main currents of U.S. history opens new understandings of what it meant for all Americans to celebrate the Fourth of July, seek profit, move west, join a church, and draw lines between white and black, men and women, and rich and poor. Applied within the South, those questions suggest answers that replace a regional identity often presented as dichotomous with an American one that more comfortably overlaps with it and is central to it. Putting the Old South squarely in the middle of U.S. history calls into question not only its status as an exceptional region but also as one that stood outside the currents of modern social change. As a constituent element of a modernizing nation, the Old South can more easily be comprehended as oriented toward the future rather than as stuck in the past.

The second context for reimagining the Old South is global rather than national, and it joins efforts by historians of other regions to move the United States out of an exceptionalist analytical framework and into one that integrates the nation and its regions into larger narratives of the nineteenth-century world. In the exceptionalist account of U.S. history, the Old South operated as the catch basin for those elements that did not fit easily into an understanding of America as uniquely free of the hierarchies and traditions of a premodern Old World. International and comparative studies of the nineteenth-century United States have effectively demolished the myth of American exception-alism. In turn, that reorientation of national history has cast doubt on the Old South's standing as distinctively parochial and isolated. One way to study the South's part in global trends is to investigate the transnational flows of commodities, ideas, and people between the South and the world. Such glob-ally informed histories also demonstrate the relevance for understanding

Southern history of international events such as the end of slavery in the British Empire or Asian and European competition in staple crop production. Another method, longer in use but being transformed by global history, looks beyond national borders to compare the Old South to a wider variety of places, ranging from southern and eastern Europe to Latin America. These comparisons remind historians that coerced labor, racism, and sectional identities were not exceptional to the South. Nor were Southern reading habits, consumption patterns, and immigrant flows significantly different from other contemporary cultures. As with integrating the South into the nation, placing the South in a global context casts doubt on impressions that it resisted or lagged behind in adapting to modernity.

These approaches to the South's place in nineteenth-century national and world history depart from popular narratives of the Old South and of the region's portrayal in a vast body of professional scholarship. Often associated with a traditional society at odds with the modernizing trends of its era, the term "Old South" has a history all its own. While its associations echoed the plantation myth concocted during the antebellum era, the phrase "Old South" first came into popular usage during the late 1870s as Southerners, many of whom hailed their time as a "New South," charted a variety of paths forward in the aftermath of the Civil War and Reconstruction.[2] The call for a New South referenced the immense postwar challenges to find prosperity amidst the destruction of the war and falling staple crop prices, to negotiate the meaning of race and gender after emancipation, and to redefine regional identity in the wake of the Confederacy's defeat. Diverse groups disagreed on how best to address these challenges. Despite their differences, however, late nineteenth-century observers agreed on three key points: The Old South had been defined by slavery, the Confederacy's defeat marked a fundamental break between past and present and the region was outside or at the minimum behind the modernizing trends of its times.

The boosters of a New South who promoted this last assumption about the Old South drew selectively from a variety of pre–Civil War descriptions of the region. Black and white abolitionists—though frustrated with the slave South's continued power—rightly cast the region as retrograde opponents of expanded liberty, their definition of modern progress. Economic reformers—some inside the South, others outside—alleged that Southerners' loyalty to traditional methods led them to reject new technologies and increased manufacturing. Many stressed the undeniable fact that the South had fewer markers of economic progress such as factories, railroads, and banks, than did the North and Britain. Politicians—appealing to the electorate and arming for battle against real and presumed foes—occasionally trumpeted themselves as honor-bound purists fighting external enemies and newfangled policies. Southern journalists and romantic novelists promoted regional pride by highlighting what they thought made their localities different: pastoral life and a unique appreciation for the past. Crafted for precise, often strategic, purposes in the antebellum era, narratives of a pre–Civil War Old South were treated by later writers as confirmed evidence of an exceptional society deeply committed to preserving the old rather than embracing the new.[3]

This image of the Old South as the embodiment of traditions that defy modern times has endured to the present day, with Southerners and non-Southerners alike remaining susceptible to or strategically deploying a largely fictionalized "Southern culture." Commerce offers plenty of examples. The idea helps Walt Disney World, the South's biggest tourist attraction, promote its central Florida Port Orleans Resort. "Welcome back to a time and place," their advertisement reads, "where everything seems to move a little slower and simple pleasures flourish like magnolia blossoms in the springtime."[4] Similarly, the makers of Old South pickled green beans promise "a revival of historic taste from a simpler time."[5] Popularized in novels and movies, the "Old South" conjures up a place where life was slower, community and evangelical religion mattered, and there were only two kinds of people, free Anglo-Saxon whites and enslaved African Americans.[6]

In thinking about why this image persists, literary critic Scott Romine argues that "the South still operates as a battle slogan, often in projects decompressing space and time against modernity's late encroachments."[7] Today, much as it did in the late 1800s, the conception of a premodern Old South both highlights the promise of the future by suggesting how the nation has overcome past evils and allays modern fears that fast-paced social and technological change is destroying a sense of community. Ills of today's America such as racism, violence, and persistent poverty can be isolated as either a Southern problem or explained away as unfortunate legacies of the Old South and its antimodern ways. Conversely, Americans can take "Southern comfort," not just from the whiskey that traces its origins to the mid-nineteenth-century splendor of Mississippi River towns but also from an idealized Old South where human connectedness and enduring tradition were not erased by the latest fad or disastrous downturn in the business cycle.

While rarely as one-dimensional as an advertisement, the image of the Old South as a holdout from the trends of its times has been a dominant theme in historical writing. In the early 1900s, interpretations of the Old South as a place of tradition resonated among historians who were critical of Northern industrial capitalism. For example, Ulrich B. Phillips, a prominent scholar of this era, waxed poetic about the Old South's freedom from industrial timekeepers,

contending that "the strokes of a tall clock in the hall were of little more concern than the silent shadow on the sundial outdoors."[8] From the mid-1940s
through the mid-1960s, historians influenced by victory in World War II and
the Cold War treated slavery as a historical outlier from mainstream support for
natural rights and free-market economics. This idea complemented an interpretation of U.S. history as an exception to the devastating wars and ideological
extremes of fascism and communism that beset Europe. Just as it did in popular culture, the Old South—"an alien child in a liberal family," in the words of
one historian—soaked up those elements of U.S. history that defied a narrative
of steady progress.[9]

The Vietnam War and social criticism of the 1960s leveled some weighty
intellectual challenges to Americans' self-understanding, and the civil rights
movement brought renewed focus to the study of the South and slavery. Ironically, the effort to rebut an interpretation of American history as dominated by
liberal, middle-class values drew "new" social historians to ask the same basic
questions about why the United States had diverged from European patterns.[10]
For a burgeoning number of Southern historians writing within this framework, slavery and its legacy of racism provided part of the answer. Inspired by
Marxist structuralism, historians—most famously and influentially Eugene
Genovese and Elizabeth Fox-Genovese—concluded that the South had been
born as the "bastard-child of merchant capitalism and developed as a non-cap-
italist society."[11] In arguably the most detailed and sophisticated set of plantation studies ever written, they suggested that U.S. slavery and the South were
best seen and studied through the lens of a negotiated master-slave relationship that, though cruel and fraught with tension, could be labeled "paternalist."
While sometimes qualified, subsequent work has fleshed out this argument
further suggesting that the "historically unique kind of paternalist society" that
blacks and whites created and contested in the Old South led Southern whites
towards an exceptional, tradition-driven, and evangelical-inspired understanding of the past and present.[12]

The persistence of an analytical framework that asks how the U.S. South
differed from Europe and the North has come at a price. This focus on "the
exceptional South," as historian Laura Edwards has recently observed, "still
traps historians," providing "an easy way out of difficult problems" and leaving
"comfortable historical assumptions in place. Segregating the South obviates
the need to confront the most difficult truths and contradictions in the nation's
past."[13] It has also tended towards an approach that defines the region for what
it was not, rather than for what it was.

Naturally, this interpretation has not gone unopposed. As in earlier eras,
the 1970s' and 1980s' variants on the Old South as an exception to American

progress came in for criticism. Self-described cliometricians Robert Fogel and Stanley Engerman developed a statistically driven economic argument for the productivity of slave-based agriculture as an essentially capitalist activity that generated bourgeois values and living standards at par or above those of the Northern states. Adding to the debate, Edward Pessen and Carl Degler argued that shared language, religion, politics, and history as well as innumerable economic ties made the sections more similar than different.[14] Meanwhile, social and political histories of nonelite planters, farmers, and middling Southerners emphasized the dramatic effect that commercial expansion and a liberal-capitalist mindset had in reshaping the antebellum South. Although the South was slower to modernize than the North, these historians argued, it was modernizing nonetheless. Being drawn into the market revolution brought anxiety about market downturns and soil exhaustion, but white Southerners' response—to push for slavery's expansion westward and some economic development—were meant to advance economic progress, not simply preserve noncapitalist aspects of the slave economy.[15]

The debates over slavery and capitalism in the 1970s and 1980s foreshadowed transnational and comparative themes in today's scholarship. For example, Genovese and Fox-Genovese insisted that Southern slaveholders be understood in the context of transatlantic merchant capitalism. Similarly, the first chapter of Fogel and Engerman's *Time on the Cross* considered slavery's international context. Degler's study of race and slavery in Brazil and the United States showed the possible richness of comparative histories. Moreover, present-day studies of the Old South share the earlier concern for how slavery fared in relation to the general patterns of change worldwide.[16]

Yet there are important differences between these understandings of nineteenth-century change—often summarized as modernization—and current usage. In debating the South's difference from the North, scholarship published in the 1970s and 1980s agreed on what modernization looked like, whereas more recent studies cast doubt on earlier assumptions about modernity that were built into comparisons of North and South. Previous studies saw the North as more advanced, but that judgment begs the question of what constituted "more advanced." Seeking a standard for measuring the United States, historians have (often implicitly) looked to Britain, the nineteenth-century's dominant global power, for "grand narratives of improvement and capitalist expansion."[17] In the early 1800s Britain strengthened its already powerful role in world affairs by de-emphasizing the territorial conquests and mercantilist economics that defined its eighteenth-century expansion in favor of a policy of industrial development and free trade enforced by its supremacy on the high seas. These developments were accompanied by a wave of self-proclaimed benevolent reforms that included the abolition of slavery throughout the empire in 1834. By treating Britain as the exemplar, historians have made the most visible trends in its society—empire, industrial cities, railroads and telegraphs, bourgeois gender relations and moral reform, and ultimately slavery's extinction—the standard measurements of nineteenth-century modernization for other countries. These British-cut paths through the nineteenth century are compelling comparisons both because Britain's enormous impact on the America South ensured it weighed heavily on contemporaneous minds and because enduring theories of modernization were crafted by thinkers who either lived in Britain or who took its examples as the most advanced versions of changes that were sweeping the globe.[18]

Among the theorists most often looked to were Adam Smith and Karl Marx. Despite disagreeing over capitalism's virtues, they nonetheless agreed that the system's march was inevitable and that elements not fitting the more advanced forms present in Britain were traces from earlier stages of economic development. For Smith, slave labor limited productivity, harmed capital accumulation, and made whites "unfit to get a Living by Industry."[19] Marx argued that slavery belonged to an earlier stage of "primitive accumulation" that preceded the commodification of labor through wage contracts and made the American Civil War inevitable.[20] Although his own work avoided human history, Charles Darwin's theory of evolution provided social scientists with a powerful biological metaphor for the birth, maturation, and decline of human communities.[21] Smith, Marx, Darwin, and European thinkers such as Max Weber, Emile Durkheim, and Alexis de Tocqueville disagreed sharply on what mattered most about the changes of the nineteenth century and why they had come to pass, but they shared in common developmental theories of change that used a British or near-British standard against which all other societies could be judged.

Applied to U.S. history, the North, which more closely resembled England, inevitably appeared to be the more developed section. Exemplifying this approach, prominent Civil War historian James McPherson writes: "Until 1861 . . . it was the North that was out of the mainstream, not the South. Of course the Northern states, along with Britain and a few countries in northwestern Europe, were cutting a new channel in world history that would doubtless have become the mainstream even if the American Civil War had not happened." In a world history that treats Britain and the societies most like it as the carriers of the future, the South, which fought against one of England's look-alikes, quite logically appears as a remnant of a past historical epoch.[22]

The intellectual climate of recent decades, however, has fostered doubts about the limits of any all-encompassing definition of modern social change.

In the 1970s and 1980s theorists in the humanities drew attention to the ways that language mediates, or constructs, perception of social reality and from this insight deconstructed the inherent contradictions, or disruptions, within a variety of overarching "master" narratives of human progress.[23] This new skeptical tone coincided with political and economic changes that caused historians to rethink the primacy of industrial capitalism as the leading edge of modernization. In the 1970s deindustrialization began transforming the factory districts of the northeastern United States and the British Midlands into "rust belts," casting doubt on their centrality to economic innovation.[24] The collapse of the Soviet Union in 1991 and the era of globalization that followed reinforced skepticism about a unified modernization theory. In a post–Cold War world less concerned with the struggle between capitalism and communism, the flow of goods, people, and ideas between nations seems more significant for understanding current affairs than any breaks between the traditional past and the modern present.[25]

Drawing on these influences, historians have been increasingly critical of teleological narratives because, as William Sewell argues, they attribute cause and effect not to human agency set within specific conditions, "but rather to abstract transhistorical processes leading to some future historical state."[26] This conception of a uniform chronological process encompassing all human history forces its adherents to characterize the things that do not fit a particular period—such as slavery in an age of wage labor—as anachronisms. In its place are alternative definitions of modernity that open the concept up to more general categories of experience going beyond the most visible features of change in western Europe and the northeastern U.S. and appreciating how local circumstances and transnational forces created variants of the general features of modernity.[27]

Modernity can be understood as both a matter of cultural outlook and material achievement. Modern culture gives priority to the present over the past and regards the present as elevated above and advancing beyond previous human epochs. This distinguishing feature of modernity, which historian C. A. Bayly calls "an aspiration to be 'up with the times,'" can generate an anxious pursuit of the latest fashions, most advanced technologies, and newest ideas, not merely for their own sake but also as proof of being up to date.[28] In reference to collective relationships, modernity simultaneously promotes equality and exclusivity, often expressed as racism, by treating as insiders those identified with a particular vision of human progress and shunning people perceived to stand in its way.[29] According to sociologist Zygmunt Bauman, "an era that declared achievement to be the only measure of human worth needed a theory of ascription to redeem boundary-drawing and boundary-guarding concerns under new conditions." In this way "modernity made racism possible" and elevated demand for rational, uniform systems that "[cut] out elements of the present reality that neither fit the visualized perfect reality, nor can be changed so that they do."[30]

Materialist definitions of modernity identify social organizations that rationalize human activity in order to maximize its productive capacity. Examples include open markets for land, labor, capital, and the commodities they generate; cities linked by rapid transportation and communication; sufficient levels of productivity and consumption, usually starting in agriculture, to support further improvements in production, such as manufacturing; government organized under a rational bureaucracy that protects contracts and property; a division of labor that maximizes efficiencies; and widespread literacy coupled with mass media.[31] It is tempting to boil these abstractions down to their celebrated nineteenth-century manifestations: the department store, industrial metropolis, railroad, factory, wage earner, government ministry, and penny press. Resisting that temptation allows historians to consider different, and sometimes less flattering, expressions of these modern processes and to appreciate that even conventional markers resulted from more complicated dynamics. More than simply bringing additional historical experience under the umbrella of modernity, the inclusion of unlikely players— such as the slaves and slaveholders of the Old South—in the history of modernity also reconfigures its meaning over time as something other than the inevitable unfolding of human liberty.

Two examples, one from the Old South and the other far from its shores, help to illustrate what it means to say that there were multiple paths to modernity in the nineteenth century. Between the late 1700s and the Civil War the proportion of white Southerners who fit the definition of middle class went from almost none to one in ten.[32] Helping that growth were state-funded military academies, which were nearly absent in the North but taught thousands of poorer young Southern men the bourgeois values of self-improvement and "restrained manhood." As state-run, rather than private, elite-funded institutions, these military academies helped create what historian Jennifer Green describes as "a separation between the emerging middle class and the elite" and were "a bureaucratic replacement of traditional community relationships."[33] If one works from Northern-inspired models, military academies, which were associated with a hierarchy of ranks and were created in part to staff slave-patrolling militias, were unlikely spawning grounds of the middle class.

A second example of the many routes to modernity lies beyond the borders of the United States. By 1850 the Ottoman Empire had moved away from traditional hierarchical governance driven by personal fealty towards a rational-ized bureaucracy that operated according to uniform rules that were applied horizontally across the polity by interchangeable officials. Contrary to western European states that had systematized government from the top down, how-ever, the Ottoman road to a modern nineteenth-century state flowed through local notables, the roadblocks to change in other societies. Dynastic families that had mediated between the imperial center and its subject people in places like Egypt and northern Anatolia transformed traditional privileges, like tax farming, into modern economic institutions, including private property. They created prototypes of bureaucratic uniformity through public works projects that broke down ethnic and occupational barriers in the name of community progress.[34] From a perspective that treats western Europe as the standard of modernity, military academies look like poor training grounds for egalitarian bourgeois family men, just as tax-farming landlords seem improbable stewards of modern property rights and the nation-state. Their place in the making of modernity shows how a broader definition of the term expands its reach and changes its trajectory.

More inclusive and less teleological understandings of modernity make better sense of how antebellum Southerners charted their own modern course, one that resembled British and Northern examples in some particulars, but that also was distinctly shaped by the depth of the region's commitment to liberal-capitalism and race-based slavery.[35] Antebellum Southerners under-stood their way of life to be the product of unique and dynamic modern pro-cesses, perhaps dating back to the seventeenth century but taking on new urgency in a rapidly changing nineteenth-century world. Chief among those processes were struggles over the nature and meaning of sovereignty, a height-ened sense of the individual as an agent of historical change, and expanded trade and commerce within and between vast empires and new nation-states that spanned continents. To be sure, Southerners appealed frequently to "ancient" and "medieval" societies for inspiration and occasionally for comfort in the face of these dizzying changes, but few, if any, wished to remake their society in the image of those examples. They respected traditions, but unlike their premodern ancestors they refused to be bound by them.

The essays in this volume showcase these perspectives on the Old South, joining with other scholars who, as noted at the outset, have reconsidered the region's place in national and world history. In part one, contributors use both national and world contexts to draw the Old South out of its conventional role as the North's foil and into the main currents of national and international history. Peter Onuf begins by considering the importance of American nation-alism to Southerners and of Southerners' contribution in return to national identity before the Civil War. Onuf argues that the desire for a separate Southern nation came not from an underdeveloped sense of nationalism but from an "exalted conception of themselves as American patriots" and the transatlantic-informed (and modern) belief that a distinct people could rightfully determine their own destiny. Where Onuf locates the South at the crossroads of national history, Matthew Mason places the region's political leaders in a transatlantic conversation with British moral reformers. Proslavery Southerners confronted European abolitionists to argue that slavery and the society it created provided antidotes for newly emerging ills. But instead of shunning the humanitarian initiatives that spurred British emancipation, Mason finds Southern political leaders debating how to harness the spirit of benevolence to their plans for slavery's survival. Brian Schoen's chapter develops another aspect of slaveholders' interest in global change by highlighting how a diverse planter class responded to world market conditions, a central feature of which was the emergence of competitors from the Pacific rim. Their crop-specific embrace of new technologies and labor strategies and their pursuit of specific government policies suggest that a multitude of political economies emerged in the South, one of which enabled a large number of cotton planters to feel emboldened by their perceived place at the forefront of modern agriculture.

Moving from slaveholders' efforts to shape modernity toward their own economic, political, and intellectual ends, part two considers slavery as a modernizing institution. In an examination of the internal economy of slaves, Larry Hudson shows that their "natural instincts toward economic independence and property accumulation" forced concessions from masters and that, despite the many barriers to accumulating cash and accessing markets, slaves participated in the capitalist marketplace as consumers. Recent scholarship has also emphasized that the laws that granted property rights in slaves enabled owners to use slaves themselves, as opposed to the things they produced, as sources of wealth. Steven Deyle uses the concept of the market revolution to rethink the slave trade and demonstrate how central slave traders were to the region's economy. These traders proved remarkably accepting of recent business innovations, suggesting that commodities held in slaves, as a kind of investment for future profits, were at the forefront of capitalist practices that spawned or supported life insurance, interregional markets, complex chains of credit, and cultural assumptions about modern identity that mediated sex, race, and consumerism.

If slavery was not a system that predated—or prevented—modern economic development, historians must then reconsider the common assumption that slavery would have died-out sooner or later. James Huston takes up this challenge in his thought-provoking conjectures about the future of slavery in

the border South had there been no Civil War. In speculating about an alternative future, Huston draws attention to the patterns of regional trade emerging
in the late-antebellum era. Had those trends continued, he argues, the border
South would have become a slave-based industrial economy, and slavery would
have acquired a new vitality capable of extending the system well beyond the
nineteenth century. Slavery emerges from the essays in part two as a more brutal but no less dynamic manifestation of the vast expansion of antebellum capitalism.

Such perspectives were difficult to imagine in earlier historiographies that
defined free labor markets and capitalism as coterminous, ignored culture entirely, and assumed the incompatibility of slavery and economic modernization. Yet recent critics of this all-or-nothing approach to slavery and capitalism
validate the approaches taken here. In the late 1990s historians started to
bridge the divide suggesting that capitalist structures and precapitalist ones
overlapped to explain tensions within the South.[36] More recent work has further linked slavery with modern economic processes, with one historian going
so far as to argue that the combination of property rights in humans and a
racial ideology that treated black bodies as legitimate objects of unrestrained
sexual desire meant that "slaves, along with sugar, may have been the first modern commodities."[37] Another recent commentary distinguishes a "second"
slavery that broke from its eighteenth century predecessor in terms of output,
new techniques, greater scales of production, and the "sheer mobility and
adaptability of slave labor."[38] A third commentary asks historians "to think
about the political economy of the eighteenth-and nineteenth-century Atlantic
as a single space, its dimensions defined by flows of people, money, and goods,
its nested temporalities set by interlocking (though clearly distinct) labor
regimes, cyclical rhythms of cultivation and foreign exchange, and shared standards of calculability and measurement."[39] In this integrated understanding of
slavery's place within modernity, the antebellum South—which provided
upwards of two-thirds of the world's cotton supply, owned (if slaves are included) over half of the United States' wealth, and demonstrated strong expan-
sionist impulses—must surely feature prominently. Within the United States,
territorial conquest combined with the global demand for Southern staples cat-
alyzed the removal of Native Americans and the forced westward migration of
one million enslaved African Americans from the states of the Atlantic coast to
the lower Mississippi River valley between 1800 and 1860.

This story of slavery counters interpretations of it as an archaic institution
that prevented the South from achieving the higher level of modernization
obtained by the North. Those interpretations rest not only on the absence of
slavery in the North but also on the North's greater number of conventional

markers of nineteenth-century modernity, particularly cities, railroads, and factories. In part three, contributors reconsider the Old South's experience with these long-time standard measures of modernization. Frank Towers uses a broad comparative context to understand the Old South's distinctively slave-based path to modern cities. He finds that the South resembled the North and Britain in some ways—all were at the forefront of worldwide urban growth—but, in other respects, looked more like Cuba, a fellow slave society which shared the South's pattern of urban dwellers concentrating in cities at the expense of towns. Asking whether the North's cities were bigger than the South's or vice versa, Towers argues, may tell historians less than asking how their sectional differences manifested alternative versions of the modern metropolis. In an examination of Southern railroads, William Thomas demonstrates that modern slavery incentivized a widespread transportation network, which in turn introduced other examples of modernity, including timetables and new technology, into southern life. Using Petersburg, Virginia, as a case study of industrial development in the Old South, Diane Barnes examines how Southerners incorporated an ethos of modern manufacturing into existing traditional social structures that prioritized slavery and agriculture. Together these essays avoid a sectional-scorecard approach to cities, railroads, and factories to ask how the South encountered these conventional markers of economic development on its own terms, thus creating a slavery-based road to an urban-industrial future.

Moving from bricks, steam, and metal to faith, ethnic identity, and sexuality, part four considers how national and global cultural trends manifested themselves in the Old South and, in turn, how antebellum Southerners reinterpreted cultural modernity to fit local circumstances. Black Southerners longing for freedom counted on progress, the rallying cry of those who believed that human action, usually inspired by divine providence, could create a better future. The idea of progress permeated the spirituals black Southerners sung, the narratives they wrote, and—as Charles Irons's chapter reveals—the complicated contributions they made to intraregional reform movements and biracial mission work at home and abroad. Irons shows how interracial benevolent work became the front line upon which evangelical whites and blacks pursued sometimes overlapping but often contested versions of how to achieve spiritual progress at home and in Africa. Native Americans, also victims of white notions of progress, had every reason to be skeptical of the idea of positive change, and many were. Yet, on their own terms, Native Americans, as Andrew Frank demonstrates, synthesized traditional and newer methods, trusting that collective and individual advancement was both necessary and desirable.

The modernization of Southern culture had many meanings and sometimes met unexpected foes. As it did with racial identity, modernity's emphasis on difference and exclusion drew new lines for gender identity in the South and forced a rethinking of traditional sexuality. Bringing to light the history of sexual contact between planter men, Craig Friend considers the role of sex as performance and the ways that planters such as the notorious James Henry Hammond used sex as "a way to establish power over others," whatever their gender or race. As Friend argues, the place of homosexuality in making Southern manhood is difficult to see through the modernist assumption that heterosexuality was normative everywhere and promoted in the South by the ethics of honor. Breaking from this framework, Friend joins Irons and Frank in blurring lines of difference that have long dominated the study of antebellum Southern culture.

In part five, the final set of essays offers different reactions to the broad question of the Old South's relationship to nineteenth-century modernity. In a counterpoint to other essays that look at the South in transnational and global-comparative terms, Marc Egnal reconsiders the sectional comparison that consumed the attention of antebellum Americans: how the South measured up to the North. For Egnal, the South's failure to achieve modernity on the North's terms was the critical test and the underlying cause of the Civil War. His essay offers students an alternative to the general rethinking of the Old South presented in the rest of the volume, and it is written in an effort to spark debate about the merits of moving towards transnational and global perspectives. Pivoting from Egnal's conclusions about the causes of the Civil War, Edward Ayers projects the story outward and forward in time, discussing the meaning of the Civil War and emancipation for a blood-stained nation and a global audience that watched with dismay. In so doing he reveals that many of the dynamics discussed in earlier chapters—from cotton's prominence in world markets, to the rise of nationalism, to the modernity of slavery—culminated in a cataclysmic conflict that ended legalized slavery in the United States but not the modern tensions that had sustained slavery or made the war possible. This discussion is brought full circle by Michael O'Brien in an afterword that provides context both for the critical concept of modernity and for the changing perspective on the Old South held by those who lived in it and those who more than a century and half later continue to study it. His contribution gets to the heart of questions about periodizing both Southern history and the history of modernity and about drawing borders around a region while still thinking about it in global terms.

Part five's reflections on how best to study the Old South, what its institutions left to the future, and how to think about the protean concepts of modernity and globalization bring the volume back to its original insight that thinking about the Old South as being in step with its times rather than behind them has important implications for histories of that region, the United States, and the world. For one thing we discern the Old South as not purely static or exceptional and are better able to chart how transformative change happened. We also appreciate that the region's diverse inhabitants expected and in most cases pursued additional advancement. As one Southern intellectual observed in 1837, "All worlds . . . are in one perpetual progress of organization, increase, dissolution, reproduction, change. . . .. On the existence of this mutability does our happiness, or, at least our pleasure depend."[40] Disproportionately influential in southern society, the planters and politicians who shaped national policy understood that their often tenuous control over others resulted from and depended on their ability to accept and harness change, not to deny or resist it. Like their abolitionist adversaries, they proved quite willing to selectively embrace the new and attack developments that did not comport with their vision of present and future demands. To be sure, Southerners often criticized the North for unwisely embracing new ideas that pulled people out of established relationships and threw them into transitory and ultimately empty roles. Modernity, they claimed, left Northerners (but not Southerners) prone to utopian thinking, but spiritually ignorant and unrealistic; profit-driven, but uncertain of financial security; sexually liberated, but denied the protection of marriage; and free of slavery, but bereft of the order necessary to preserve and enjoy freedom. Rather than resisting change, however, Southern leaders, encouraged their followers to join the march of progress, confident that their slave institution allowed the South to enjoy the blessings of modernity: expanded and freer commerce, democracy (for whites), cultural refinement, and (for many) spiritual fulfillment through Christ without modernity's emerging ills. At home, in national politics, and even abroad, white Southerners trumpeted their regionally distinct understanding of modernity and its socioeconomic fruits, not because they believed it rooted in the past but because they believed it well-suited for the future.

Thinking and acting within rather than outside nineteenth-century global norms, white Southerners were often successful in convincing others of the utility, if not always the justness, of their views. This perspective brings into focus how the Old South helped make America and how so much of antebellum Southern history can be understood as national history. To take one example, with the exception of the Oregon boundary dispute in 1846, the United States' major territorial acquisitions between 1788 and 1860 were made with no restriction on slavery and under the leadership of slaveholding presidents with enthusiastic support from proslavery congressmen. Like so many other features of American society, manifest destiny included arguments for the uniquely redemptive quality of slavery as practiced by the Old

South's progressive, evangelically minded masters, a vision that historian Robert Bonner has recently termed "proslavery Americanism."[41] Appreciating the power of this Southern-tinctured version of American modernity should make us all the more interested in knowing more about alternate ones that rose to challenge it.

Attention to Southerners' engagement with the trends of their times also opens up historical understanding of the ways that Southerners interacted with the wider world, drew motivation from developments far from the United States, and impacted distant lands through migration, trade, and conquest.[42] For example, Richmond's Tredegar Iron Works has long been known for things distinctively Southern: using slaves in industry and making Confederate armaments. A recent exploration of its business dealings in Cuba and other Latin American slave societies shows non-Southern contributions to Tredegar's success and the Old South's role in spreading industrial slavery across the hemisphere.[43] In both its national and international dimensions, the Old South played a formative role in creating the modern world.

In making these comparisons and appreciating the effects of global forces on the South, and vice versa, we should be reminded that modernity does not have an independent life outside of lived experiences. It exists in context. While a new emphasis on being "up with the times" was felt in China as well as New York and while trade in cotton fibers brought Indian farmers into competition with Southern planters, the process of modernization looked different depending on the local context. For wealthy, well-traveled planters like South Carolina's Manigault family, the Old South was a platform for cosmopolitanism: summers in Paris, years at a time in Philadelphia, and the best food, books, music, and company that a person of refined taste could enjoy and keep.[44] For a slave on the Manigaults' Gowrie plantation, modernity meant misery: a bad diet, a life span shortened by overwork and endemic disease, illiteracy, and shackles (both literal and figurative).[45] An Irish-born seamstress working in a Baltimore clothing factory would have known little about either the rice swamps or the wine cellars of the South Carolina Lowcountry, yet she too lived in the Old South. The different ways that these people experienced modernity and divided Southern society are too numerous to enumerate fully. Poor whites resented rich ones. Rich cotton planters resented rich sugar planters. Men followed a different ethos than women. City dwellers thought about the South in ways unfamiliar to rural folk. Protestants distrusted Catholics, especially immigrants. Whigs distrusted Democrats. Most of all, black and white Southerners shared a mutual disdain and divergence of interests that created the preconditions for secession, Civil War, and eventually emancipation. These tensions highlight how detached from reality the New South mythmakers' harmonious image of the "Old South" truly was.

Rethinking antebellum Southerners' relationship to modernity still maintains their regional identity but avoids making Southern exceptionalism the analytical start or finish. It allows us to appreciate distinctiveness, but in a way that opens up the opportunity to explore new comparisons and new forms of connectedness both within the region and outside of it, and it opens questions that did not fit comfortably within the dichotomies that have historically defined the literature of the antebellum South.

NOTES

1. In addition to the works cited below and in the conclusion, see Michael O'Brien, *Rethinking the South: Essays in Intellectual History* (Baltimore: Johns Hopkins University Press, 1988); and more recently Edward L. Ayers, *What Caused the Civil War? Reflections on the South and Southern History* (New York: W. W. Norton, 2005), 131–145; and J. William Harris, *The Making of the American South: A Short History, 1500–1877* (Malden, Mass.: Blackwell, 2006).

2. James C. Cobb, *Away Down South: A History of Southern Identity* (New York: Oxford University Press, 2005), 98; John B. Gordon, *The Old South* (Augusta, Ga.: Chronicle Publishing Co., 1887), 7, 13; John C. Reed, *The Old and New South* (New York: A. S. Barnes, 1876), 5–6; "The New South and the Old South," *The American Missionary* 5:46 (May 1892): 142.

3. Cobb, *Away Down South*, 22; Susan-Mary Grant, *North Over South: Northern Nationalism and Sectional Identity in Antebellum America* (Lawrence: University Press of Kansas, 2000), 42; William R. Taylor, *Cavalier and Yankee: The Old South and American National Character* (New York: George Braziller, 1961), 115, 133, 149; Michael O'Brien, *Conjectures of Order: Intellectual Life in the American South, 1810–1860*, 2 vols. (Chapel Hill: University of North Carolina Press, 2004), 1:127, 1:147–148, 2:598.

4. Intercot, *Walt Disney World: Inside & Out*, http://www.intercot.com/resorts/disney/riverside/default.asp (accessed October 2010).

5. Bryant Preserving Company, http://www.oldsouth.com/products.asp?id=101&;topcat=1 (accessed October 2010).

6. Gary W. Gallagher, *Causes Won, Lost, and Forgotten: How Hollywood and Popular Art Shape What We Know About the Civil War* (Chapel Hill: University of North Carolina Press, 2008), 41–90.

7. Scott Romine, *The Real South: Southern Narrative in the Age of Cultural Reproduction* (Baton Rouge: Louisiana State University Press, 2008), 9. See also Leigh Ann Duck, *The Nation's Region: Southern Modernism, Segregation, and U.S. Nationalism* (Athens: University of Georgia Press, 2006); Larry J. Griffin, "Southern Distinctiveness, Yet Again, or, Why America Still Needs the South," *Southern Cultures* 6 (Fall 2000): 47–72, esp. 68.

8. Ulrich B. Phillips, *Life and Labor in the Old South* (1929; repr., Boston: Little Brown and Company, 1963), 336. See also William E. Dodd, *The Cotton Kingdom* (New Haven, Conn.: Yale University Press, 1919); Charles A. Beard and Mary R. Beard, *The Rise of American Civilization* (New York: Macmillan, 1927).

9. Louis B. Hartz quoted in C. Vann Woodward, *The Burden of Southern History* (Baton Rouge: Louisiana State University Press, 1960), 22.

10. Daniel T. Rodgers, "Exceptionalism," in *Imagined Histories: American Historians Interpret the Past*, ed. Anthony Molho and Gordon S. Wood (Princeton, N.J.: Princeton University Press, 1998), 30.

11. Eugene D. Genovese and Elizabeth Fox-Genovese, *The Fruits of Merchant Capital* (New York: Oxford University Press, 1983), 5.

12. See especially Eugene D. Genovese, *Roll Jordan Roll: The World the Slaves Made* (New York: Random House, 1974), 4 (quotation); Genovese and Fox-Genovese, *Fruits of Merchant Capital*; Elizabeth Fox-Genovese and Eugene D. Genovese, *The Mind of the Master Class: History and Faith in the Southern Slaveholders' Worldview* (New York: Cambridge University Press, 2006).

13. Laura F. Edwards, "Southern History as U.S. History," *Journal of Southern History* 75 (August 2009): 563–564.

14. Robert W. Fogel and Stanley L. Engerman, *Time on the Cross: The Economics of American Negro Slavery* (1974; repr., New York: W. W. Norton, 1989); Edward Pessen, "How Different from Each Other Were the Antebellum North and South?" *American Historical Review* 85 (December 1980): 1119–1149, 1147; Carl Degler, *Place Over Time: The Continuity of Southern Distinctiveness* (Athens: University of Georgia Press, 1977), 93.

15. Frank L. Owsley, *Plain Folk of the Old South* (Baton Rouge: Louisiana State University Press, 1949); William L. Barney, *The Secessionist Impulse: Alabama and Mississippi in 1860* (Princeton, N.J.: Princeton University Press, 1974), 100; J. Mills Thornton, III, *Politics and Power in a Slave Society: Alabama, 1800–1860* (Baton Rouge: Louisiana State University Press, 1978); Lacy K. Ford, Jr., *The Origins of Southern Radicalism: The South Carolina Upcountry* (New York: Oxford University Press, 1988); James Oakes, *Slavery and Freedom: An Interpretation of the Old South* (New York: Knopf, 1990).

16. See Genovese and Fox-Genovese, *Fruits of Merchant Capital*; Fogel and Engerman, *Time on the Cross*, chap. 1; and Carl Degler, *Neither Black Nor White: Slavery and Race Relations in Brazil and the United States* (New York: Macmillan, 1971)

17. C. A. Bayly, "The Second British Empire," in *The Oxford History of the British Empire*, vol 5: *Historiography*, ed. Robin Winks (New York: Oxford University Press, 1999), 68.

18. Anthony Webster, *The Debate on the Rise of the British Empire* (Manchester: Manchester University Press, 2006).

19. Smith quoted in Seymour Drescher, *The Mighty Experiment: Free Labor versus Slavery in British Emancipation* (New York: Oxford University Press, 2002), 20–21.

20. For the classic application of this thesis to New World slavery, see Eric Williams, *Capitalism and Slavery* (New York: Russell and Russell, 1944). Karl Marx, *Capital: A Critique of Political Economy*, ed. Frederick Engels (1861; repr., New York: Charles H. Kerr & Company, 1906), 684 (quotation).

21. Robin I. M. Dunbar, "Evolution and the Social Sciences," *History of the Human Sciences* 20:2 (2009): 29–50, esp. 32.

22. James M. McPherson, "Antebellum Southern Exceptionalism: A New Look at an Old Question," *Civil War History* 50:4 (2004): 418–433, 433 (quotation). See also C. Vann Woodward, *The Burden of Southern History*, 3rd ed. (Baton Rouge: Louisiana State University Press, 1993), 17–22.

23. Georg G. Iggers and Q. Edward Wang with Supriya Mukherjee, *A Global History of Modern Historiography* (New York: Pearson Longman, 2008), 368–369.

24. Webster, *Debate on the Rise of the British Empire*, 145; William H. Sewell, Jr., *Logics of History: Social Theory and Social Transformation* (Chicago: University of Chicago Press, 2005), 63.

25. Nils Gilman, *Mandarins of the Future: Modernization Theory in Cold War America* (Baltimore: Johns Hopkins University Press, 2004), 253, 266–267, 272.

26. Sewell, *Logics of History*, 84. See also Mary Fulbrook, *Historical Theory* (New York: Routledge, 2002), 63.

27. S. N. Einsenstadt, "Multiple Modernities" *Daedalus* 129 (Winter 2000): 1–29.

28. C. A. Bayly, *The Birth of the Modern World, 1780–1914* (Malden, Mass.: Blackwell Publishing, 2004), 10 (quotation); Bill Ashcroft, Gareth Griffins, and Helen Tiffin, *Post-Colonial Studies: The Key Concepts* (New York: Routledge, 2000), 145; Michel Foucault, "Kant on Enlightenment and Revolution," trans. Colin Gordon, *Economy and Society* 15 (February 1986): 88–96.

29. Charles Taylor, *Modern Social Imaginaries* (Durham, N.C.: Duke University Press, 2004), 13; Zygmunt Baumnan, *Modernity and Ambivalence* (Ithaca, N.Y.: Cornell University Press, 1991); Robin Blackburn, *The Making Of New World Slavery: From the Baroque to the Modern, 1492–1800* (New York: Verso, 1997), chap. 8.

30. Zygmunt Bauman, "Modernity, Racism, Extermination," in *Theories of Race and Racism: A Reader*, ed. Les Back and John Solmos (New York: Routledge, 2000), 215.

31. Jan de Vries and Ad Van der Woude, *The First Modern Economy: Success, Failure, and Perseverance of the Dutch Economy, 1500–1815* (Cambridge: Cambridge University Press, 1997), 693; Jan de Vries, *The Industrious Revolution: Consumer Behavior and the Household Economy, 1650 to the Present* (Cambridge: Cambridge University Press, 2008), 10; Immanuel Wallerstein, *The Modern World System: Capitalist Agriculture and the Origins of the European World-Economy in the Sixteenth Century* (New York: Academic Press, 1976), 230; Daniel Walker Howe, *What Hath God Wrought: The Transformation of America, 1815–1846* (New York: Oxford University Press, 2007), 6–7.

32. Jonathan Daniel Wells, *The Origins of the Southern Middle Class, 1800–1861* (Chapel Hill: University of North Carolina Press, 2004), 8.

33. Jennifer R. Green, *Military Education and the Emerging Middle Class of the Old South* (Cambridge: Cambridge University Press, 2008), 5, 55 (quotation), 101.

34. Karen Barkey, *Empire of Difference: The Ottomans in Comparative Perspective* (Cambridge: Cambridge University Press, 2008), 256–262.

35. Oakes, *Slavery and Freedom*.

36. See, for example, Christopher Morris, "The Articulation of Two Worlds: The Master-Slave Relationship Reconsidered," *Journal of American History* 85

(December 1998): 982–1007; Jeffrey Robert Young, *Domesticating Slavery: The Master Class in Georgia and South Carolina, 1670–1837* (Chapel Hill: University of North Carolina Press, 1999).

37. Edward E. Baptist, "'Cuffy,' 'Fancy Maids,' and 'One-Eyed Men': Rape, Commodification, and the Domestic Slave Trade in the United States," *The American Historical Review* 106 (December 2001): 1619–1650, 1650 (quotation).

38. Anthony E. Kaye, "The Second Slavery: Modernity in the Nineteenth-Century South and the Atlantic World," *Journal of Southern History* 75 (August 2009): 628 (quotation); Dale W. Tomich, *Through the Prism of Slavery: Labor, Capital, and World Economy* (Oxford: Rowman and Littlefield, 2004).

39. Walter Johnson, "The Pedestal and the Veil: Rethinking the Capitalism/ Slavery Question," *Journal of the Early Republic* 24 (Summer 2004): 299–308, 304 (quotation).

40. S. A. Roszel, "Pleasurable Sensations," *Southern Literary Messenger* 3 (February 1837): 148, quoted in O'Brien, *Conjectures of Order*, 1:1.

41. Robert E. Bonner, *Mastering America: Southern Slaveholders and the Crisis of American Nationhood* (New York: Cambridge University Press, 2009), 69, 83–84. See also Nicholas Onuf and Peter Onuf, *Nations, Markets, and War: Modern History and the American Civil War* (Charlottesville: University of Virginia Press, 2006), 334.

42. Peter A. Coclanis, "Globalization before Globalization: The South and the World to 1950," in *Globalization and the American South*, ed. James C. Cobb and William Stueck (Athens: University of Georgia Press, 2005), 25; Sven Beckert, "Emancipation and Empire: Reconstructing the Worldwide Web of Cotton Production in the Age of the American Civil War," *American Historical Review* 109 (December 2004): 1405–1438.

43. Daniel Brett Rood, "Plantation Technocrats: Industrial Epistemologies: A Social History of Knowledge in the Slaveholding Atlantic World, 1830–1860" (Ph.D. diss., University of California, Irvine, 2010).

44. Daniel Kilbride, *An American Aristocracy: Southern Planters in Antebellum Philadelphia* (Columbia: University of South Carolina Press, 2006).

45. William Dusinberre, *Them Dark Days: Slavery in the American Rice Swamps* (1996; repr., Athens: University of Georgia Press, 2000), 55–57.

PART I

The South in a World of Nations

I

Antebellum Southerners and the National Idea

Peter S. Onuf

Antebellum Southerners were proud to be citizens of a powerful and expansive new nation with a "manifest destiny" to dominate the continent. Patriotic Southerners were notoriously prone to flights of spread-eagle rhetoric: with an exalted sense of their country's greatness and of their own honor, they would not be outdone in reverence for the Revolutionary fathers or devotion to the precious legacy of union. Only a few radical outliers, or "fire eaters," imagined a separate national destiny for the South before the final stages of the sectional crisis that ultimately destroyed the union. Yet the popular nationalism of the antebellum decades did not break with the descent into disunion and war. Intersectional conflict in the antebellum decades instead generated a surfeit of patriotic feelings—the revisionists' "excess of democracy"—that the federal system finally could not contain.[1]

Americans were precocious nationalists, showing the way for the rest of the "civilized," Western world. Political and military mobilization in the American Revolution set the pattern for unprecedented popular participation in public life.[2] French visitor Alexis de Tocqueville epitomized the character and consciousness of this new people in his portrait of American "democracy," offering a powerful, disquieting image of the emergent form of modern nationhood. Tocqueville was astonished by the power of public opinion in a country which by European standards hardly seemed governed at all. Citizens identified with the nation completely, reflexively rejecting "the slightest censure and insatiable in their appetite for praise."[3] For the Americans whom Tocqueville encountered in all parts of the country over the course of his travels in 1831 and 1832, "the permanence, glory, and prosperity of the nation had become sacred dogmas, and in defending their homeland they were also defending the holy city of which they were citizens."[4]

Toqueville's *Democracy in America* has been read as one of the great, canonical texts of American exceptionalism. But Tocqueville aspired to be a theorist, or diagnostician of the modern condition, who discerned broader tendencies in contemporary political development.[5] The term "democracy" is itself confusing, conflating constitution or regime type with political culture. Traveling across the country at the time of the Nullification Crisis in South Carolina, Tocqueville was well aware that the federal union was fragile and might well collapse; he also knew that the presence of "three races"—and particularly of an enslaved African-American population in the South—constituted a formidable challenge to the new nation's survival.

The present forms of government in America might well be consigned to history's dustbin, but for Toqueville there was no turning back on "democracy," the fundamental premise of equality that animated and defined American life. That "equality" sustained "liberty," Tocqueville's most cherished value, was a contingent outcome, depending on unique and fortuitous historical and geopolitical circumstances. Those circumstances might change. Indeed, Americans themselves might perversely desecrate their "holy city" by abandoning their union and with it "the permanence, glory, and prosperity of the nation." But Americans' commitment to equality—their powerful, belligerent national attachments, their sense of providential destiny—would grow even stronger in the resulting crisis.[6]

Modern democrats "want equality in liberty," Tocqueville acknowledged, "but if they cannot have it, they want it still in slavery." A nation at war demands the ultimate sacrifice, a paradoxically consensual "slavery" in which citizens forfeit their liberties and lives so that the nation can survive. Ardent patriots "will suffer poverty, servitude, and barbarity," Tocqueville concluded, "but they will not suffer aristocracy."[7] For egalitarian Americans, "aristocracy" meant both—and indistinguishably—the rule of an illegitimate, unrepresentative, privileged class and domination by a "foreign" power.

Tocqueville was the anatomist of modern nationalism. Unlike most modern students of the subject, he did not focus on France, a fraught terrain with a complicated history and unpredictable prospects. In the United States, democracy's triumph was irreversible and unassailable, the implications of the new national idea could be clinically assessed, and the future of European countries glimpsed. In his much-celebrated prophetic mode, Tocqueville predicted that the United States would be a "great nation," with Russia, its Eurasian counter-part, one of the two dominant powers.[8] Less familiar is his prophecy—or, more modestly, intimation—that the American union might fall apart, leading Americans to direct their antiaristocratic rage at one another. "The parties that threaten the Union," Tocqueville wrote, "are based not on principles"—all Americans embraced the same democratic principles—but rather "on material interests. In the various provinces of such a vast empire, those interests consti-tute not so much parties as rival nations."[9] In short, the new democratic ethos— the popular patriotism that so astonished Tocqueville—could be attached to "rival nations" and turned against itself.

This essay will seek to illuminate the contingent circumstances, as ante-bellum Southerners understood them, which made the idea of Confederate independence and nationhood compelling. "Material interests" were certainly fundamental, as Southerners' estimates of the value of their property in slaves made clear. "To surrender this $3,000,000,000 of slave property," John H. Reagan told his fellow congressmen in January 1861, would be "to dissolve so-ciety, to break up social-order, to ruin our commercial and political prospects for the future."[10] But Southerners saw themselves taking a principled stand on behalf of the liberty and equality that, they came to be convinced, were jeopar-dized by continuing union with a "rival nation." They acted according to the precepts of modern nationalism, as Tocqueville delineated them in *Democracy in America*. Their powerful national feelings, suddenly and completely detached from the federal union, were not simply an opportunistic cover for their inter-ests. To the contrary, secessionists knew that disunion would lead to a bloody war that would require them to put those interests—and their lives—at risk.

Historians are understandably skeptical about the scope and depth of Con-federate nationalism.[11] But it is a mistake to infer from the union's sudden collapse that national sentiments were tenuous and underdeveloped in ante-bellum America generally or in the South particularly.[12] Following Tocqueville's lead, I argue the opposite: It was precisely *because* of their exalted conception of themselves as American patriots that righteously aggrieved Southerners bolted the union. In doing so, they self-consciously followed the lead of an earlier generation of Anglo-American patriots who—despite their original loyalties and intentions—became Revolutionary nation-makers. Like the Revolution-aries, patriotic Southerners believed they could only fulfill their national des-tiny in a new nation freed from the corruptions of the old. Looking back on decades of bitter sectional conflict, seceding Confederates could see themselves as a distinct people with a distinctive way of life. Northerners had revealed themselves to be foreigners, intent on capturing the machinery of federal government and subjugating the South. Yankee rule threatened the future of slavery, the foundation of Southern prosperity and civilization, and thus jeopardized the union's survival—for it was slavery that made white Southerners into a distinct people, whether or not they owned slaves. This new Confederate nation became fully conscious of its own identity only as it left the union. Every nation had the right to determine its own destiny, both as the Americans had shown in 1776 and as the oppressed peoples of Europe had claimed more recently, in the failed revolutions of 1848.

Ambivalent Secessionists and Manifest Destinies

Confederate ideas of nationhood drew on a history of sectional distinctiveness and grievance; however, the secessionist outcome was not anticipated or welcomed by the vast majority of Southerners until Republican victory in 1860 signalled the imminence of Northern "aggression."[13] Throughout the antebellum period, sectional radicals who thundered against a Yankee-dominated federal government claimed to be patriotic Americans. The nullificationists of 1831–1832 thought the "interposition" of sovereign states would check "consolidationist" tendencies in the central government, thus restoring Constitutional union; John C. Calhoun later sought to save the union—or, more accurately, create a new one—by jettisoning the federal Constitution in favor of his "concurrent majority."[14] Ends and means were easily confused in such projects, but the announced intention was always to bring Americans closer together, to reinforce their union, by articulating and securing fundamental, nonnegotiable interests.

Federal politics promoted formation of sectional blocs that predictably and all too plausibly threatened to bolt the union in order to force concessions, thus putting a premium on statesmanlike "compromise" in successive crises.[15] For veterans of these crises, the secession winter of 1860–1861 seemed to reenact a familiar scenario. Perhaps another compromise was in the offing. "Secession does not necessarily destroy the Union, or rather the hope of reunion," Virginian Robert M. T. Hunter told the Senate in January 1861, weeks before resigning and heading south. It might instead "result in the establishment of some league, not merely commercial, but political, holding us together by a looser bond" that would leave "each section free to follow the law of its own genius."[16] Hunter's senatorial colleague, future Confederate president Jefferson Davis, wondered if "these two Confederacies might have relations to each other so close as to give them a united power in time of war against any foreign nation."[17]

As hostile sectional governments mobilized for war, they prayed for peace. The escalating aggravations of federal politics might abate with Southern

independence; perhaps disunion would prepare the way for peaceful coexis-
tence, if not reunion. "It would be the wonder and astonishment of the
nations," theologian James Henley Thornwell exclaimed, if "[we could] part in
peace," dividing "our common inheritance, adjust[ing] our common obligations, and, preserving, as a sacred treasure, our common principles." He concluded: "Let each set up for himself, and let the Lord bless us both. . . . [A]
course like this, heroic, sublime, glorious, would be something altogether
unexampled in the history of the world."[18] Harmonious disunion would, in
Thornwell's prayerful exhortation, represent the ultimate achievement of the
nationality Northerners and Southerners once shared.

Southern nationalism drew inspiration from American sources. The challenge for would-be nation-makers was to offer a compelling vision of the
region's future outside the union, an alternative manifest destiny that could
appeal to Southern patriots. South Carolinian William Henry Trescott echoed
and amplified providentialist themes in American nationalist rhetoric when he
argued for the "separate nationality" of each state in 1850. The union had
"redeemed a continent to the christian world . . . fertilized a wilderness, and
converted the rude force of nature into the beneficent action of a civilized agriculture," spreading "over the vast territories of this new land the laws, the
language, the literature of the Anglo-Saxon race." By developing "a population
with whom liberty is identical with law, and in training thirty-three States to
manhood," the union "has fitted them for the responsibility of independent
national life." The old union "has achieved its destiny," Trescott concluded. "Let
us achieve ours."[19]

Trescott's sequence of destinies, consigning the shared American destiny
to the past, did not capture Southerners' political imagination. However attached
they might be to parochial interests and states' rights, Southerners identified
with a more expansive conception of their national identity and destiny. Trescott
himself could not suppress the obvious contrast between the glorious achievements of the old union—a "great nation" that had profoundly changed the
world—and South Carolina's much more circumscribed prospects. Ironically,
the most precocious advocates of "separate nationality" in the South could not
escape the Old Republican logic of federalism: it was the very separateness of
the states, as the source and embodiment of "sovereignty," that made them an
effective counterforce to, or substitute for, a strong central government.

Virginian George Fitzhugh's savage indictments of "free society" in the
North played a crucial role in demystifying and thus denationalizing the federal
union, but his proposed alternative—the fulfillment of the national idea *within*
the separate states—seemed hopelessly irrelevant to most of his fellow Southerners. Fitzhugh embraced the statist and loose constructionist heresies of

Northern protectionists: "Government is the life of a nation," he asserted in
Cannibals All!, and "a constitution, strictly construed, is absolutely inconsistent
with permanent national existence."[20] True patriots should strive to "make each
State independent of the rest of the world," creating "a necessity for the exercise of all the arts, sciences, trades, professions and other pursuits that pertain
to separate nationality." For all his progressive talk, however, Fitzhugh's fundamental purpose was defensive, "to counteract the centralizing tendency of
modern improvements in locomotion and intercommunication, which naturally rob the extremities to enrich the centres of Power and of Trade."[21] Southerners certainly wanted, with Fitzhugh, to escape neocolonial dependency on
Britain or the North, but that meant participating in and controlling the benefits of "modern improvements" on an appropriate national scale.[22]

   The idea of separate state-nationality had tactical and rhetorical uses in the
political and constitutional debates of the collapsing federal union. Virginians
and South Carolinians might revel nostalgically in burnished memories of a
glorious past that fellow Southerners—including many immigrants from these
old states—would happily share.[23] Southerners might say with New Orleans
editor J. D. B. DeBow that the "Federal Government has no such elements of
strength, cohesion and conservation" as these states possessed; but it was quite
another thing to assert that "each State [is] in itself a nation."[24] Antebellum
Americans—north and south—usually spoke of the nation in the future tense,
as a "destiny" that could not be bounded by separate states.

   Southern writers found the idea of a great American nation irresistibly
appealing, even when they contemplated its destruction. Georgia jurist J. H.
Lumpkin, writing in *DeBow's Review* in 1852, epitomized Southerners' ambivalent nationalism. "This is the only nation, ancient or modern," he wrote,
"which, from the extent of her sea-coast—the exhaustless fertility of her soil—
the variety of her climate, extending through twenty degrees of latitude in the
most favored zone, and countless physical advantages, is capable of perpetuity."
Yet the most recent crisis of the union, dubiously compromised in 1850, raised
doubts about the union's survival. "Whether she is destined to it is a problem
which remains to be solved," Lumpkin concluded evasively, "and which is
wisely, perhaps, concealed in the impenetrable vigil of futurity."[25]

   Southerners did not know if the union would survive. But they did recognize that the United States collectively constituted a "great nation" with irresistible power and boundless prospects. Many loyal Southerners were therefore
reluctant to bolt the union, a Tennessee writer conceded, and so give up "the
Constitution and the Union which constitute our nationality, our glory and our
power."[26] "We have become a great nation," a New Orleans editorialist agreed,
"and we had the prospect, under a peaceful and just Government, of becoming

one of the greatest, if not the very greatest, upon the face of the globe." Yet this ascent to greatness may have been too rapid. "Our free institutions, our broad and smiling land, our great natural advantages, have made a mighty nation of us too soon, perhaps."[27]

The idea of an independent Southern nation depended on jettisoning the old idea of state rights—or separate state "nationality"—and building instead on a broadly shared conception of America's manifest destiny. Southern politicians had long complained that the Northern-dominated union drained wealth northward, thus underwriting the entire union's prosperity and power. "The revenue and resources of the Southern States," Virginian Edmund Ruffin explained in 1857, have "heretofore contributed mainly to aid Northern interests, foster Northern industry and trade, and increase Northern wealth and power," but in an independent South would "be retained and used to sustain and build up our own commerce, and cities, and general prosperity."[28] The South was a nation in embryo, unconscious of its powers, yet with "every attribute necessary to an independent and prosperous empire."[29] The union, in contrast, was no nation at all. "The theory of the nationality of the [federal] government, is, in fact," Calhoun explained, "founded on [a] fiction . . . of recent origin."[30]

For future secessionists the juxtaposition of union and nation facilitated a transvaluation of values, showing the faint of heart why "this beautiful land" should *not* "be forever one country, for one great, united, prosperous people."[31] A union that subjected wealth-producing Southern provinces to Yankee rule was unnatural and artificial, not providentially destined for greatness. "Instead of being a union that nature dictated," a contributor to the *Democratic Review* asserted, "our federal nationality . . . is a result of consummate art to unite those whom God separated, making some of them powerful and others feeble."[32] The Southern states, outside the union, were naturally "powerful." Whatever effect disunion might have on the North, a writer in *DeBow's Review* concluded, the "ultimate result . . . would be to give increased activity and impetus to every branch of Southern industry."[33] Fears that disunion would betray America's providential prospects were thus misplaced. It was the South, not the artificially united states, that had a "manifest destiny" to take a leading role in promoting the progress of civilization.

The South made the American "nation" great. An independent South, no longer paying tribute to the North, would be greater still. "If we never acquire another foot of territory for the South," James Henry Hammond enjoined his Senate colleagues in his famous "Mudsill" speech of 1858, "look at her." In the aggregate the slave states were "as large as Great Britain, France, Austria, Prussia and Spain. Is not that territory enough to make an empire that shall rule the world?" A Southern confederacy would control "the great Mississippi, a bond of union made by Nature herself," and its vast hinterland was "now the real" and would soon "be the acknowledged seat of the empire of the world." The natural dynamism of the slave-based Southern economy had been retarded by the impasse over territorial expansion. But "can you hem in such a territory as that? You talk of putting up a wall of fire around eight hundred and fifty thousand square miles so situated! How absurd."[34]

Hammond hoped that Northerners' recognition of the South's latent power—and of the likelihood that free states in the Mississippi watershed would be drawn into a new Southern confederacy—would lead to more conciliatory policies and the preservation of a union that in fact served Southern purposes. But by the secession winter, threats had become prophecies. "We have all the essential elements of a high national career," future Confederate vice president Alexander Stephens proclaimed in March 1861. Border states were holding back, still fearful "that we are too small and too weak to maintain a separate nationality." But "with such an area of territory—with such an amount of population—with a climate and soil unsurpassed by any other on the face of the earth—with such resources already at our command—with productions which control the commerce of the world—who can entertain any apprehensions as to our success, whether others join us or not."[35]

As Stephens appealed to timorous unionists in the border states, editor J. D. B. DeBow appealed to nonslaveholders. When wealth was "retained at home, to build up our towns and cities, to extend our railroads, and increase our shipping, which now goes in tariffs or other involuntary or voluntary tributes to other sections," DeBow promised, "opulence would be diffused throughout all classes, and we should become the freest, the happiest, and the most prosperous and powerful nation upon earth."[36] "The slaveholding interest is one," added Thornwell, "and it seems to us clear that the slaveholding States ought speedily to be organized under one general Government." Once Southerners recognized common interests that transcended class divisions as well as state boundaries—once they became conscious of themselves as a nation—they would find themselves to be "strong enough to maintain themselves against the world."[37] Southerners, according to Robert M. T. Hunter, "have within themselves all the capacity of empire."[38]

Southern nationalists rejected the union but not the legacy of American nationhood and manifest destiny. The more fully they articulated claims to separate nationhood the more the image of the nation they were conjuring into existence resembled the image of the nation they were abandoning. Southerners insisted that they seceded from the union on behalf of the principles their fathers had cherished: memories of the American Revolution justified yet another heroic struggle against metropolitan rule by exploited provinces. "I throw off the yoke of this Union as readily as did our ancestor the yoke of King George III," Presbyterian preacher Benjamin M. Palmer of New Orleans exclaimed, "and for causes immeasurably stronger than those pleaded in their celebrated declaration."[39] And, notwithstanding Rev. Thornwell's prayer for peace, astute observers knew that "it is utterly impossible to have a peaceable dismemberment of the confederation."[40] Bravado about their martial prowess notwithstanding, Confederates knew that Yankees would prove worthy foes: after all, Southerners and Northerners had all been good Americans. Threats of bloodshed were predicated on this recognition. If Northerners refused to let their Southern brothers go in peace, Jefferson Davis warned, "a war is to be initiated the like of which men have not seen."[41]

The recognition that the war between North and South would be a bloody one testified to the power of the national idea in antebellum America. "If the fires of civil war be kindled," a unionist editor in New Orleans predicted, "they will burn until all is consumed that is perishable, and the land become a waste over which shall brood the silence of another and hopeless desolation."[42] Of course, Southerners made the decision for war because they believed that fundamental interests and values—their "civilization"—were jeopardized by the ascendant Republicans. But they knew the war would be bitter and protracted because they recognized themselves in their enemies, as fellow Americans.

Though the rupture of the union had long been feared by anxious Southerners—even eagerly anticipated by the fire-eating few—it nonetheless came with extraordinary suddenness. Devotion to the great and rising American nation seemed so widespread that it was hard to imagine that the "centrifugal tendencies of Northern fanaticism and Southern sectionalism" could ever rip the union apart.[43] Yet American nationalism proved to be a protean force that was impossible to control. It was not so much that Southerners and Northerners had cherished incompatible conceptions of what their nation was or should be. It was rather that national feelings in all parts of the country were dangerously detached from the old and imploding federal regime and were therefore subject to mobilization in new forms and for new purposes.

War and Nationality

Southerners could only imagine their separate nationality when they were willing to make war against former fellow Americans. Threats of disunion and bloody conflict had been staples of antebellum political discourse, but were characteristically deployed to win concessions, forge compromises, and reaffirm common values. The founding fathers had created "a more perfect union" in order to restrain the "dogs of war" and rescue the states from impending anarchy. If the union was a "peace pact," disunion meant war, the betrayal of the founders' legacy.[44] The challenge for Southern nationalists was to reverse the equation, to convince Southerners that an imperfect union dominated by sectional foes was the moral equivalent of war, or worse, and that independence alone could secure lasting peace. The founders' union was the means toward ends that union no longer served. "The Union" that the founders "established does not exist," the editor of the *Charleston Mercury* insisted in July 1860: "Usurpation and encroachment have drawn into the vortex of Federal power, interests which were never intended, by the Constitution, to be embraced in its operations."[45]

Southerners' ultimate rejection of the union represented the culmination and convergence of various political and ideological developments. Most crucially, debates over commercial and foreign policy provided a broad geopolitical framework for assessing threats to vital Southern interests. During the ratification controversy, Federalists had argued that the breakup of the union would not only lead to a state of war among the states but invite foreign powers to interfere in American affairs. For Revolutionaries who cherished America's recent, hard-won independence, the prospect of foreign, counterrevolutionary interference was unthinkable, and therefore a spur to constitutional reform that would perfect the union and eliminate the threat of war. But the distinction between internal and external, domestic and foreign, proved ambiguous in subsequent decades. The French Revolution taught Americans to think of partisan foes as foreigners and to look abroad for ideological fellow travelers and prospective allies; divergent sectoral and sectional interests promoted conflicting conceptions of political economy and world order. Inevitably, regardless of the founders' warnings, precocious dissidents would violate the great American political taboo and "calculate the value of our union."[46]

As the sectional crisis deepened, more and more Southerners wondered whether union served their interests. "No one in the South can blind himself to the fact that we have no worse enemies *without*," asserted South Carolinian William Gilmore Simms, "than those which assail us from within." "Instead of protecting us," he explained, "the [federal] government becomes the instrument of our degradation and ruin."[47] By 1850, when Simms wrote, external threats had long since receded and internal threats loomed much larger. As far as the South was concerned, Trescott insisted, the North was "in fact, a foreign power."[48] In effect, the union had been turned inside out. A decade later, Alabaman Jabez Curry drew out the implications of this inversion. Rather than protecting the slave states, the union offered constitutional cover for the depredations of "a hostile, sectional party," placing "our destinies under the control of another and distinct people." He concluded: "To the slaveholding states," the federal government "is a *foreign government*, which understands not our condition, defers not to our opinions, consults not our interests, and has no sympathy with our peculiar civilization."[49]

Southerners located the South and the union in a more inclusive political and commercial system, with Britain playing a crucially ambivalent role in their political geography and historical memory. On one hand, they invoked Revolutionary Anglophobia, the touchstone of American nationalist sentiment, by equating the North with imperial Britain. On the other, they looked forward to a new commercial and political dispensation in which an independent South, no longer shackled by the union, could forge a new, more natural alliance with Britain, the great power of the modern world. Southern nationalists could thus have it both ways: by resisting the North's neocolonial dominion, they rekindled the Anglophobic spirit of 1776 even as they facilitated closer, more harmonious relations with the former mother country.

The Revolutionary analogy was pervasive in sectionalist rhetoric. "The history of our relations with the Northern States," Simms wrote, "is a precise counterpart of the case of the whole of the colonies of Great Britain, prior to 1776, with the mother country."[50] The slave states were "subjugated provinces," explained Hunter, in a "Union constructed in entire opposition to the true American spirit and American principles."[51] The British Empire was the prototype for a Yankee-dominated union, and Southern Anglophobia was exacerbated by Britain's leadership in the abolitionist crusade against Southern slavery and civilization. Yet at the same time Britain's insatiable appetite for Southern cotton pointed toward more amicable relations. Southern independence would precipitate a revolution in international relations. "In the event of a dissolution of the Union," a "Citizen of Virginia" predicted in 1850, it would be in Britain's "interest to strengthen us, and she would be bound to the Southern alliance by natural ties. . . . The dependence of four millions of her people on the South for cotton, and of many more for food, would give the slave States a powerful hold upon the good will of her Government."[52] "England [was] our natural ally," a writer in *DeBow's Review* insisted, and "would become more friendly still" when the South declared its independence. "Motives of *pounds, shillings, and pence*, if no other, would abate much in her hostility to slavery."[53]

Shifting geopolitical frameworks did not diminish nationalist sentiments in the South. But appeals to the spirit of 1776 deflected Southerners' attention away from the founders' "more perfect union" of 1787, and therefore from the great imperative of preserving peace among the states. "The Union," as Calhoun famously proclaimed in 1830, was "next to our Liberty the most dear."[54]

When union threatened liberty, however, patriotic Americans would follow the lead of Revolutionary predecessors who had risked everything to vindicate their rights. Americans had been united in their devotion to liberty in 1776. As Thomas Jefferson wrote in 1825, the Declaration of Independence was "the fundamental act of union of these states," and *this* was the union that liberty-loving Southerners cherished.[55] Far from perfecting that original union, the federal Constitution enabled loose constructionists and corrupt politicians to wage war on the "constitutional rights of the South."[56]

By the eve of secession, it was clear to Alfred Pike of Arkansas that the federal government was "the most corrupt Government on the face of the earth." The contrast between 1776 and 1861 was stark: "Great occasions and great controversies alone produce greatness in a nation," as they had when Americans broke from the empire and asserted their rights. But "when these die out, all is petty squabbling and low maneuverings," as it now was in Washington, D.C.[57] Southerners needed to recognize that the present system would "lead either to disunion or despotism," that they could either submit tamely or vindicate their rights on the battlefield. Of course the rupture of the union would lead to "injury to all," Jefferson Davis acknowledged, though "differing in degree, differing in manner." The "internal prosperity" of the Northern states would certainly suffer, but patriotic Southerners would suffer a much greater loss: "the injury to the southern States will be to their internal high pride and power which belong to the flag now representing the greatest Republic, if not the greatest Government, upon the face of the globe."[58]

Southerners' willingness to make war against their fellow Americans was the ultimate test of their patriotism, for they claimed to love their country far more than their corrupt, self-seeking Yankee counterparts. It would be much better to direct patriotic energies against a common foe, as expansion-minded Southerners urged throughout the 1850s. Virginia unionist Robert M. T. Hunter thus conjured up an inspiring vision of Americans "united once more, brothers in war, and brothers in peace, ready to take our wonted place in the front line of the mighty march of human progress, and able and willing to play for the mastery in that game of nations where the prizes are power and empire, and where victory may crown our name with eternal fame and deathless renown."[59] A great war would enable Americans to rally around Davis's "flag." But who would they fight, if not each other?

Before the 1850s Anglophobia offered a common ground for bellicose patriots, north and south. But the Texas crisis and the Mexican War (1846–1848) showed that pseudo-abolitionist Britain had no real interest in thwarting American territorial expansion or even the spread of slavery. Despite the history of British and American conflict and misunderstanding, the *Democratic Review* concluded in 1853 that no "two great empires were ever united by so many and such powerful motives of interest as the British and American."[60] Mexico provided an attractive target for another war of conquest, but Northerners failed to recognize that "to expand is the destiny of every young and growing nation" and were determined to block the annexation of more slave territory.[61] In effect, the North had taken Britain's place. Southerners no longer worried about ineffectual British abolitionism, fearing instead that Northerners would capture the federal government and launch "an unceasing crusade against our civilization," declaring "war against our property and the supremacy of the white race."[62] It was testimony to Southerners' patriotism that they were so reluctant to acknowledge that the union they cherished rendered their states "subjugated provinces" and that Northerners were their real enemies.

Southerners left the union *because* they identified so completely with the American nation and its manifest destiny. Great nations were destined to expand, "establishing in their march the way marks of progress, the altars of the reformed religion, the temples of a higher civilization, a purer liberty, and a better system of human government."[63] Yankee domination deflected America from its providential path, threatening the equality (and nationality) of slaveholding Southerners—for slavery was the "cornerstone" of Christian civilization in the South. Southerners were bound to fulfill their "providential trust," Rev. Benjamin Palmer proclaimed. They must *conserve and to perpetuate the institution of domestic slavery as now existing,* giving it "the freest scope for its natural development and extension."[64]

Slavery and Nationality

Slavery defined Southern nationality. The peculiar institution made the South "democratic" in Tocqueville's sense, securing the "equality" and racial solidarity of white Southerners while preserving "liberty" and property, the fruits of free enterprise. The racial or ethnic component that was increasingly conspicuous in nineteenth-century conceptions of nationality was particularly pronounced in the antebellum South. Southern whites defined themselves as a distinctive people both in juxtaposition to the enslaved African Americans in their midst and to the mixed populations of the urbanizing North. Slavery supposedly kept the races separate in the South, thus avoiding the promiscuous mixing that compromised American nationality and provoked a powerful nativist backlash in the 1850s. The Southern racial order promoted social peace, George Fitzhugh happily concluded: "we are not troubled with strikes, trade unions, phalasteries, communistic establishments, Mormonism, and the thousand other isms that deface and deform free society."[65] Slavery made the South more perfectly "national."

Fitizhugh's complacent account of the superiority of Southern society hinged on a critical revaluation of racial slavery. For Thomas Jefferson, John Taylor, and many other Southerners of the Revolutionary and early national period, slavery was a cancer on the body politic, an alien excrescence that jeopardized the success of the republican experiment. In their most extreme formulations, slaves were depicted as a captive nation, waiting for "a revolution of the wheel of fortune," when they would "extirpate" their masters.[66] The fear of servile insurrection—exacerbated by British recruitment of slave auxiliaries in the American Revolution and the War of 1812 and, more ominously still, by the Haitian Revolution in Saint Domingue—underscored the need for a "more perfect union." For these anxious Southerners the threat of race war was much more compelling than that of a war between the states: both made the new nation vulnerable to foreign intervention. Yet such fears did not persist. Within less than a generation of the Treaty of Ghent in 1814, which concluded the second war against Britain, Southerners began to think of slavery as a strategic asset, not as a liability.

Southerners' new thinking about slavery drew on many different sources, including emerging conceptions of racial difference in contemporaneous ethnology and anthropology. More immediately, changing geopolitical circumstances—the end of a generation of war in the North Atlantic, normalization of relations with British Canada, "pacification" of Indian country, and the rapid southwestern expansion of the unionto the lower Mississippi River valley— diminished the likelihood of external threats to the institution. The rising value of slaves reflected an increasingly effective regime of labor discipline. Slavery was now depicted by its leading advocates as a "positive good" for blacks as well as whites, an institution that could "ameliorate" the condition of human chattel even as it generated enormous wealth for planters, their fellow Southerners, and the trading world generally.[67]

The spread of Christianity in the slave quarters was both the means and the end of these ameliorative impulses.[68] "Christian morality is the natural morality in slave society," Fitzhugh asserted: unlike the anarchic and competitive "free" society of the North, "it is natural for men to love one another" in the slave South. Slavery was thus not, as Jefferson imagined, an institutionalized "state of war," but rather the best guarantee of peace.[69] Southern slavery apologists thus claimed no longer to fear servile insurrection: violent resistance, reprisals, and running away were symptomatic of the failures of individual masters, not of the institution itself. Dr. Samuel Cartwright testified to the "undoubted fact of the love" that slaves "bear their masters, similar in all respects to the love that children bear to their parents, which nothing but severity or cruelty in either case can alienate."[70]

Southerners' changing ideas about slavery paralleled—and were inextricably linked to—their changing ideas about the founding fathers' legacy of union. Dissociating the nation from an increasingly dysfunctional federal Constitutional regime, future Confederates discovered peace and love in unexpected places. Southerners idealized slaveholder paternalism, sacralizing an institution that had earned the opprobrium of the civilized world. Masters and slaves were, in sociologist Henry Hughes's awkward neologism "affamiliated." In the South "the laborer and the capitalist belong to the same family," Hughes asserted: "they have a home-association."[71] The master's household was not simply an economic unit. According to political economist Louisa McCord, "we have begun to mingle" slavery with "the graces and amenities of the highest Christian civilization." Far from compromising Southerners' claims to being a forward-looking, civilized people, the peculiar institution fostered the "most civilized and enlightened" society in the modern world.[72]

Slavery was not an archaic survival of a barbarous, despotic age. Quite to the contrary, it was the vital force that promoted the "wonderful development of this western continent," enriching the civilized world while extending the benefits of Christian civilization to benighted, naturally inferior Africans.[73] Southern nationalists unabashedly trumpeted their achievements, winning an increasingly warm reception among "civilized" Europeans who were influenced by the new science of racial difference and who recoiled from the human misery caused by modern industrial society. Senator John Reagan asked Northern Republicans to "trace the history of the African race through all the centuries of the past, in every country and every clime . . . and then come to the southern States, and compare the condition of the negroes there with their condition anywhere else, and answer me if they are not in enjoyment of more peace, more blessings, and everything that gives contentment and happiness, than any other portion of that race, bond or free, at any age or in any other portion of the world?"[74]

Southern nationalists sought to reconcile the imperatives of equality—within the union, among themselves—with the brute realities of inequality and labor exploitation on which their slave societies were founded. Nineteenth-century conceptions of national identity, emphasizing blood ties, shared historical experience, and homogenous culture, provided a crucial foundation for this enterprise. Southerners believed that independence would enable them to achieve an exalted destiny: evangelical Christianity gave pious Southerners an edifying mission to save slaves' souls; paternalists embraced idealized notions of bourgeois domesticity, drawing slave "children" into their family circle.[75]

Southern slaves were both a "distinct" and patently inferior *"nation of near 4,000,000 of people,"* Richard Keith Call proclaimed, yet at the same time constituted *"a part of the American people,"* "divided into families, and domesticated with white families." As slaves, African Americans had a destiny, with their masters, to expand across the continent. Could "the philanthropist, the Christian, the civilized man" possibly contemplate confining *"forever 4,000,000 of unoffending people within a boundary, where, from the natural increase if numbers in a few years, they must perish from famine, pestilence, and war, or drive 8,000,000 of white men into exile to avoid the same calamities"*?[76]

Neither Call nor his contemporaries imagined that slaves would drive well-armed "white men into exile." If they had, they would not have jeopardized the union and risked a war with the North, which might tip the balance of power against the master class.[77] The more likely outcome was that slaves would be "exterminated" in a genocidal bloodbath. This was one of Louisa McCord's favorite themes: "slavery . . . or extermination, seems to be the fate of the dark races." But, happily, "the universal rule of nature, by which inferior races have invariably disappeared before the advance of the superior, has, in the case of the negro, been arrested" in the South: "Instead of extermination," McCord wrote, the negro has "met protection." "Softened by Christianity and civilization, by the ties of dependence and propinquity," Southern slavery "shows us the subjection of race by race in the mildest, most humanizing form in which it is possible for this necessary subjection to exist."[78]

The word "slavery" suggested brutal despotism and degradation. Perhaps the term itself would be jettisoned as the institution took on a more benign, civilized—and civilizing—character in the Southern states. But McCord's apologetics reveal that the threat of violence ("fear" as well as "love") remained deeply embedded in her justification for this "modern" institution. The Southern nation she envisioned had a great role to play in the progress of Western civilization. If its destiny was thwarted, its enormous power would be turned against the enemy within: no longer enjoying the protection of their white families, slaves would be exterminated.

The transformation of the national idea in the antebellum South pivoted on the defense of slavery and the "civilization" it created. Until the final crisis of the union, few Southerners believed that the national identity they shared with Americans everywhere was incompatible with slavery and its "natural" expansion. After all, the "manifest destiny" of modern nations was to expand, so mobilizing the power of their peoples to promote the progress of Christian civilization. The source of this power was a passion for equality, the animating principle of what Tocqueville identified as "democracy." Equality was the predicate of nationality, the modern merging of persons with peoples. Southerners thus thought of them-selves as "Americans" and interpreted any challenge to their constitutional rights or established institutions as an assault on their national identity.

Northern abolitionists had questioned slaveholder morality for decades. By the 1850s, however, defenders of the peculiar institution had effectively neu-tralized antislavery sentiments in the South and were beginning to raise doubts and make converts elsewhere. The vast majority of Americans believed blacks were inferior, questioned the wisdom of emancipation, recognized that they profited in some way from slavery, and cherished the union: nationality was racially inflected for most Americans in the North, even for self-proclaimed enemies of the "slave power." Under these circumstances, the rapid ascen-dancy of Free-Soilers and then Republicans—Northern sectionalist parties whose electoral success depending on fostering anti-Southern sentiments—seemed particularly ominous. The threat was less that Northern opinion would be thoroughly abolitionized than that a corrupt coalition of disparate sectional interests would seek to capture the federal government and reduce the Southern states to "subjugated provinces."[79]

Southerners were astonished that so many conservative Northerners, their erstwhile allies and fellow Americans, proved so vulnerable to sectionalist appeals. Their outrage at insults to their honor was not, as so many Northerners imagined, the archaic reflex of a reactionary slave-holding "aristocracy." Republican pledges to block slavery's further expansion effectively denied that slave states were equal members of the union and therefore that Southerners were equally American. Confederates left the union *because* they had so fully embraced the democratic, egalitarian ideals of modern American nationhood. "In common decency," North-erners who betrayed those ideals should leave the union. Because they would not, "there is no alternative to the South except to withdraw for herself."[80]

The rupture of the union led to the sudden emergence of two great nations, ready to make war on one another. That outcome would not have sur-prised Tocqueville, who died in 1859, for the genius of democracy was not to guarantee or promote peace. When a people's very survival was at risk, as it seemed to be for so many Southerners in the secession winter of 1860–1861, the passion for equality could easily lead to despotic forms of rule. It was "the indestructible right of all communities to provide for their own safety and hap-piness," according to a New Orleans editorialist, and therefore to create "a new government."[81] In the case of an individual, Jabez Curry noted, "the law jus-tifies the taking of life in advance of injury, when the killer was under such apprehensions as would influence a reasonable mind." The same "rule of self-preservation applies to a people endangered."[82] Southerners must be pre-pared to make war against their Northern enemies.

But what made Southerners a distinct people, or "separate nationality"?[83] Clearly the equality principle was, to invoke the appropriate image, a double-edged sword. Democracy first made the United States a great nation, and then it destroyed the nation. Because they saw themselves as patriotic Americans, Southerners could only make nonnegotiable demands. They insisted that their fellow Americans honor the equality principle and their common nationality by recognizing the fundamental role of slavery in constituting Southern identity. Slave ownership was not merely a property right, essential to regional and national prosperity, but the legal form of a "natural," organic, providentially sanctioned relationship that defined Southerners' sense of self, family, community, and—when the union collapsed—of Confederate nationhood.[84]

NOTES

1. Roy F. Nichols, *The Disruption of American Democracy* (New York: Collier, 1967).

2. The best study of popular participation and national sentiment is David Waldstreicher, *In the Midst of Perpetual Fetes: The Making of American Nationalism, 1776–1820* (Chapel Hill: University of North Carolina Press, 1997).

3. Alexis de Tocqueville, *Democracy in America*, trans. Arthur Goldhammer (New York: Library of America, 2004), 719 (vol. 2, pt. 3, chap. 16).

4. Ibid., 106 (vol. 1, pt. 1, chap. 5).

5. I am indebted to Sheldon S. Wolin's brilliant discussion in *Tocqueville Between Two Worlds: The Making of a Political and Theoretical Life* (Princeton, N.J.: Princeton University Press, 2001).

6. Toqueville, *Democracy in America*, 106.

7. Toqueville, *Democracy in America*, 584 (vol. 2, pt. 2, chap.1).

8. Ibid., 470–476 (vol. 1, pt. 2, chap. 10).

9. Ibid., 201 (vol. 1, pt. 2, chap. 2).

10. John H. Reagan, *State of the Union. Speech . . . Delivered in the House of Representatives, January 15, 1861* (Washington, D.C., 1861), reprinted in *Southern Pamphlets on Secession, November 1860–April 1861* (hereafter cited as *So. Pamphlets*), ed. Jon L. Wakelyn (Chapel Hill: University of North Carolina Press, 1996), 146–147. For further discussion see James L. Huston, *Calculating the Value of the Union: Slavery, Property Rights, and the Economic Origins of the Civil War* (Chapel Hill: University of North Carolina Press, 2003), 27–29.

11. Gary W. Gallagher, *The Confederate War* (Cambridge, Mass.: Harvard University Press, 1997).

12. For further discussion of the conceptual history of modern nationalism, with citations to the literature, see Nicholas Onuf and Peter Onuf, *Nations, Markets, and War: Modern History and the American Civil War* (Charlottesville: University of Virginia Press, 2006).

13. I rely throughout this essay on Brian Schoen, *The Fragile Fabric of Union: Cotton, Federal Politics, and the Global Origins of the Civil War* (Baltimore: Johns

Hopkins University Press, 2009). See also Jesse T. Carpenter, *The South as a Conscious Minority, 1789–1861: A Study in Political Thought*, with a new introduction by John McCardell (1930; repr., Columbia: University of South Carolina Press, 1990); John McCardell, *The Idea of a Southern Nation: Southern Nationalists and Southern Nationalism, 1830–1860* (New York: W. W. Norton, 1979); and Eric H. Walther, *The Fire-Eaters* (Baton Rouge: Louisiana State University Press, 1992).

14. James H. Read, *Majority Rule Versus Consensus: The Political Thought of John C. Calhoun* (Lawrence: University Press of Kansas, 2009).

15. Peter B. Knupfer, *The Union As It Is: Constitutional Unionism and Sectional Compromise, 1787–1861* (Chapel Hill: University of North Carolina Press, 1991).

16. Robert M. T. Hunter, *Speech . . . on the Resolution Proposing to Retrocede the Forts . . . Delivered in the Senate of the United States, January 11, 1861* (Washington, D.C., 1861), *So. Pamphlets*, 280.

17. Jefferson Davis, *Remarks on the Special Message on Affairs in South Carolina* (Baltimore, 1861), *So. Pamphlets*, 133.

18. Rev. James Henley Thornwell, *The State of the Country* (New Orleans, 1861), *So. Pamphlets*, 178.

19. William Henry Trescott, *The Position and Course of the South* (Charleston, S.C., 1850), *So. Pamphlets*, 32.

20. George Fitzhugh, *Cannibals All!; or, Slaves Without Masters*, ed. C. Vann Woodward (1857; repr., Cambridge, Mass.: Harvard University Press, 1960), 249.

21. George Fitzhugh, *Sociology for the South: or, The Failure of Free Society* (1854; repr., New York: B. Franklin, 1965), 203.

22. Joseph J. Persky, *The Burden of Dependency: Colonial Themes in Southern Economic Thought* (Baltimore: Johns Hopkins University Press, 1992).

23. William Taylor, *Cavalier and Yankee: The Old South and American National Character* (1957; repr., Cambridge, Mass.: Harvard University Press, 1979).

24. "State Rights and State Remedies," *DeBow's Review* 25 (1858): 699; "The Union—North and South—Slave Trade and Territorial Questions—Disunion—Southern Confederacy," *DeBow's Review* 27 (1859): 561.

25. Hon. J. H. Lumpkin, "Industrial Regeneration of the South," *DeBow's Review* 12 (1852): 44. "Many of the individual members of the confederacy, especially the Middle and Southern Atlantic states, have this independent self-existent life within them," Lumpkin added. "There is scarcely a vegetable, or fruit, or cereal grain, which may not be successfully cultivated in South Carolina and Georgia" (44–45).

26. "Something for All Patriots to Read and Ponder," *Daily Nashville Patriot*, September 19, 1860, reprinted in *Southern Editorials on Secession* (hereafter cited as *So. Editorials*), ed. Dwight L. Dumond (1931; repr., Gloucester, Mass.: P. Smith, 1964), 167.

27. "An Eventful Day," *New Orleans Daily Crescent*, December 17, 1860, *So. Editorials*, 340.

28. Edmund Ruffin, "Consequences of Abolition Agitation," *DeBow's Review* 23 (1857): 604.

29. Review of *The North and the South* (pamphlet republished from the editorials of the *New York Tribune*), *Southern Quarterly Review* 11 (1855): 44.

30. John C. Calhoun, *A Discourse on the Constitution and Government of the United States* (1851), reprinted in *Union and Liberty: The Political Philosophy of John C. Calhoun*, ed. Ross Lence (Indianapolis, Ind.: Liberty Fund, 1992), 101.

31. Richard Keith Call, *Letter to John S. Littell* (Philadelphia, 1861), *So. Pamphlets*, 161. Call was the unionist governor of Florida.

32. A. B. Johnson, "The Philosophy of the American Union; Or, The Principles of its Cohesiveness," *Democratic Review* 28 (1851): 15. "The cohesiveness of the confederacy, and the circumscription of its powers, are made by nature measures of each other" (17).

33. A. Roane, "The South—In the Union or Out of It," *DeBow's Review* 29 (1860): 462.

34. James H. Hammond, "Speech on the Admission of Kansas, under the Lecompton Constitution, Delivered in the Senate of the United States, March 4, 1858" (the Mudsill Speech), excerpted in Paul Finkelman, *Defending Slavery: Proslavery Thought in the Old South. A Brief History with Documents* (Boston: Bedford/St. Martin's, 2003), 82–83.

35. Alexander H. Stephens, *Cornerstone Address* (March 21, 1861), *So. Pamphlets*, 408.

36. "The Non-Slaveholders of the South: Their Interest in the Present Controversy Identical with that of the Slaveholders," *DeBow's Review* 30 (1861): 77.

37. Rev. James Henley Thornwell, *The State of the Country* (New Orleans, 1861), *So. Pamphlets*, 175.

38. Robert M. T. Hunter, *Speech . . . on the Resolution Proposing to Retrocede the Forts . . . Delivered in the Senate of the United States, January 11, 1861* (Washington, D.C., 1861), *So. Pamphlets*, 265.

39. Rev. Benjamin Morgan Palmer, *The South: Her Peril and Her Duty* (New Orleans, 1860), *So. Pamphlets*, 73.

40. *The Daily True Delta*, December 9, 1806, *So. Editorials*, 313.

41. Jefferson Davis, *Remarks on the Special Message on Affairs in South Carolina* (Baltimore, 1861), *So. Pamphlets*, 140.

42. "What is the True Issue?" *[New Orleans] Daily Picayune*, November 4, 1860, *So. Editorials*, 218.

43. "Political Probabilities," *New Orleans Bee*, May 30, 1860, *So. Editorials*, 117.

44. David C. Hendrickson, *Peace Pact: The Lost World of the American Founding* (Lawrence: University Press of Kansas, 2003).

45. "The Union," *Charleston Mercury*, July 25, 1860, *So. Editorials*, 151.

46. Speech of Thomas Cooper (July 27, 1827), *Niles Weekly Register* (Baltimore), September 8, 1827, reprinted in *The Nullification Era: A Documentary Record*, ed. William W. Freehling (New York: Harper & Row, 1967), 25. For further discussion see Onuf and Onuf, *Nations, Markets, and War*, 247–277.

47. William Gilmore Simms, *The Southern Convention*, *Southern Quarterly Review*, n.s. 2 (September 1850): 199–208, 231–232, excerpted in *The Simms Reader: Selections from the Writings of William Gilmore Simms*, ed. John Caldwell Simms (Charlottesville: University of Virginia Press, 2001), 323.

48. William Henry Trescott, *The Position and Course of the South* (Charleston, S.C., 1850), *So. Pamphlets*, 23.

49. Jabez Lamar Monroe Curry, *The Perils and Duties of the South, Speech Delivered in Talladega, Alabama, November 26, 1860* (Washington, 1860), *So. Pamphlets*, 47.

50. Simms, *Southern Convention*, 324.

51. Robert M. T. Hunter, *Speech . . . on the Resolution Proposing to Retrocede the Forts . . . Delivered in the Senate of the United States, January 11, 1861* (Washington, D.C., 1861), *So. Pamphlets*, 272.

52. "A Citizen of Virginia" (M. R. H. Garnett), *The Union, Past and Future: How it Works and How to Save It* (Washington, D.C.: Steam Power Press of Walker & James, 1850), 22.

53. Roane, "The South—In the Union or Out of It," *DeBow's Review* 29 (1860): 462–463.

54. Calhoun quoted in Thomas Hart Benton, *Thirty Years' View: Or, A History of the Working of the American Government for Thirty Years, from 1820 to 1850*, 2 vols. (New York: D. Appleton and Company, 1854), 1:148.

55. Jefferson, minutes of the Board of Visitors, March 4, 1825, in *Thomas Jefferson Writings*, ed. Merrill D. Peterson (New York: Library of America, 1984), 479.

56. "To the Friends of the Constitution and Union," *Daily Nashville Patriot*, October 13, 1860, *So. Editorials*, 189.

57. Alfred Pike, *State or Province? Bond or Free?* (Little Rock, 1861), *So. Pamphlets*, 347.

58. Jefferson Davis, *Remarks on the Special Message on Affairs in South Carolina* (Baltimore, 1861), *So. Pamphlets*, 134.

59. Robert M. T. Hunter, *Speech . . . on the Resolution Proposing to Retrocede the Forts . . . Delivered in the Senate of the United States, January 11, 1861* (Washington, D.C., 1861), *So. Pamphlets*, 283.

60. "Foreign and Commercial Policy of the United States," *Democratic Review* 32 (1853): 7.

61. Alfred Pike, *State or Province? Bond or Free?* (Little Rock, 1861), *So. Pamphlets*, 340.

62. Jabez Lamar Monroe Curry, *Perils and Duties of the South, Speech Delivered in Talladega, Alabama, November 26, 1860* (Washington, 1860), *So. Pamphlets*, 46.

63. Richard Keith Call, *Letter to Littell* (Philadelphia, 1861), *So. Pamphlets*, 189.

64. Rev. Benjamin Morgan Palmer, *The South: Her Peril and Her Duty* (New Orleans, 1860), *So. Pamphlets*, 67.

65. Fitzhugh, *Sociology for the South*, 69. On Southern "ethnicity," see David Moltke-Hansen, "Regional Framework and Networks: Changing Identities in the Southeastern United States," in *Regional Images and Regional Realities*, ed. Lother Honnighausen (Tübingen: Stauffenburg Verlag, 2001), 149–169; and "The Rise of Southern Ethnicity," unpublished paper in author's possession.

66. Quotations from Jefferson, *Notes on the State of Virginia*, Query XVIII ("Manners"), in Peterson, *Jefferson Writings*, 289. For further discussion see my *Jefferson's Empire: The Language of American Nationhood* (Charlottesville: University of Virginia Press, 2000), 147–188.

67. I am indebted here to Christa Dierksheide, "The Amelioration of Slavery in the Anglo-American Imagination, 1780–1840" (Ph.D. diss., University of Virginia, 2008).

68. The best work on this theme is Charles F. Irons, *The Origins of Proslavery Christianity: White and Black Evangelicals in Colonial and Antebellum Virginia* (Chapel Hill: University of North Carolina Press, 2008).

69. Fitzhugh, *Cannibals All!*, 218–219. For a brilliant, deflationary account of Fitzhugh's relationship to slavery and the slave trade, see Calvin Schermerhorn, "Against All Odds: Slavery and Enslaved Families in the Making of the Antebellum Chesapeake" (Ph.D. diss., University of Virginia, 2008).

70. Samuel A. Cartwright, "Report on the Diseases and Physical Peculiarities of the Negro Race," *New Orleans Medical and Surgical Journal* 7 (May 1851): 691–714, excerpted in Paul Finkelman, *Defending Slavery: Proslavery Thought in the Old South. A Brief History with Documents* (Boston: Bedford/St. Martins, 2003), 161.

71. Henry Hughes, *Treatise on Sociology, Theoretical and Practical* (Philadelphia, 1854), 113.

72. Louisa S. McCord, *Political and Social Essays*, ed. Richard C. Lounsbury (Charlottesville: University of Virginia Press, 1995), 279, 298.

73. McCord, *Political and Social Essays*, 431.

74. John H. Reagan, *State of the Union Speech . . . Delivered in the House of Representatives, January 15, 1861* (Washington, D.C., 1861), So. Pamphlets, 146.

75. The classic study of paternalism is Eugene Genovese, *Roll, Jordan, Roll: The World the Slaves Made* (New York: Pantheon, 1974).

76. Richard Keith Call, *Letter to Littell* (Philadelphia, 1861), So. Pamphlets, 187.

77. That this is what in fact happened is the controversial contention of William W. Freehling, *The South vs. the South: How Anti-Confederate Southerners Shaped the Course of the Civil War* (New York: Oxford University Press, 2001).

78. McCord, "Diversity of the Races: Its Bearing upon Negro Slavery," *Southern Quarterly Review* (1851), and "Letter to the Duchess of Sutherland from a Lady of South Carolina," *Charleston Mercury*, August 10, 1853, reprinted in McCord, *Political and Social Essays*, 172, 407.

79. For a compelling analysis of these developments, see Michael F. Holt, *The Political Crisis of the 1850s* (New York: Wiley, 1978).

80. "The Difference," *New Orleans Daily Crescent*, January 21, 1861, So. Editorials, 407.

81. "Fundamental Principles Involved," *[New Orleans] Daily Picayune*, January 15, 1861, So. Editorials, 400.

82. Jabez Lamar Monroe Curry, *The Perils and Duties of the South, Speech Delivered in Talladega, Alabama, November 26, 1860* (Washington, 1860), So. Pamphlets, 46.

83. Alexander H. Stephens, "Cornerstone Address" (March 21, 1861), So. Pamphlets, 408.

84. I am indebted to the insights of Gary W. Gallagher, *Confederate War*.

2

A World Safe for Modernity: Antebellum Southern Proslavery Intellectuals Confront Great Britain

Matthew Mason

In place of an image of the Old South as a premodern place inhabited by provincials in full reaction against global trends, much recent scholarship interprets the Old South's planter class as cosmopolitans deeply engaged with the Atlantic world's cutting edge in all fields of thought.[1] But recent literature also highlights the centrality of one ideal to early-nineteenth-century notions of modernity—the ethic of "improvement"—that could be seen as threatening to the slave South: This ideal encompassed everything from technical marvels such as railroads and the telegraph ("internal improvements") to a dizzying array of reform causes. Both *moral* and *material* improvement became the watchwords of modernity.[2]

In an 1826 Senate debate, Virginia's John Randolph encapsulated Southern hostility especially to the moralistic embodiment of improvement, which contemporaries called the "Benevolent Empire." In the projects both domestic and foreign of the inveterate "improver" president, John Quincy Adams, Randolph detected the "meddling, obtrusive, intrusive, restless, self-dissatisfied spirit" that manifested itself "in Sunday Schools, Missionary Societies, subscriptions to Colonization Societies—taking care of the Sandwich Islanders, free negroes, and God knows who."[3] The fact that the Benevolent Empire had its seat in New and Old England did not help its image for the likes of Randolph. As both the British and the Benevolent empires grew in power, as the former abolished slavery throughout its territories in 1833, the slaveholders of the South might well be forgiven for fleeing this powerful Atlantic current.

But Southern intellectuals chose rather to confront these empires, with important consequences for Southern letters and politics. They battled British critiques of Southern slavery not only through direct replies, but also in a broad proliferation of Southern literature—poetry and fiction as well as book reviews, travel accounts, and speeches. From the mid-1830s to the mid-1840s, Southerners were particularly prolific in the "plantation romance" vein of fiction. This outburst of Southern literature added crucial building blocks to the rising edifice of proslavery polemic. Its authors romanticized the master-slave relationship, presenting it not as fiction but as drawn from life—in stark contrast with the prejudice, they argued, that produced abolitionist portrayals of slavery. Southern literature also added critiques of abolitionists, arguing that their fanatical schemes would drag civilization centuries backward. Their writings betrayed these intellectuals' ambivalence about benevolence and philanthropy, but, at least on the Atlantic stage, they evinced no ambivalence about the rightness of slavery.

Southern authors carried these arguments into politics. Southern society assured those who were willing to confront British opinion that they would merit the thanks not only of clear-sighted contemporaries but also of posterity.[4] Those who responded to the call thus saw opportunity as well as a threat in the modern world. And for all their moaning about their alienation from Southern society, antebellum Southern intellectuals enjoyed broad influence, never more so than when they defended slavery against its British critics.[5] In the short term their reward often came in the form of political office. Many Southern intellectuals became local and national politicians, ensuring that their engagement with Britain helped shape American partisan and sectional controversies, from Indian removal in the 1820s to secession in 1860–1861.

Britain was arguably more on white Southerners' minds in the long decade from 1833 to 1845 than in any other decade of the nineteenth century. Its industrial and imperial might made Britain a superpower that transfixed the world in a love-hate fashion, much as the United States does today. For their part, Americans followed Parliament and the monarchy with rapturous attention not unmixed with republican guilt.[6] The British government's actions in this decade riveted the attention of slaveholders in particular. Parliament voted on August 29, 1833, to emancipate all slaves in its West Indian colonies on August 1, 1834. This act had an enormous impact on the debate over American slavery, as scholars are beginning to appreciate.[7] In its wake British officials, who publicly averred that "Great Britain desires, and is constantly exerting herself to procure, the general abolition of slavery throughout the world," sought to procure that end in ways that irritated and outraged white Southerners.[8] They committed their government to abolishing the international slave trade, which put the United States in their crosshairs because its flag served as a protection to illicit slavers. More seriously for proslavery Southerners, British officials in the West Indies freed American slaves transported on domestic slave-trading vessels that landed in British territory. These incidents exacerbated rising fears of renewed Anglo-American warfare.[9] Finally, while white Southerners sought to annex Texas to the union, Britons crafting their nation's foreign policy declared themselves "irresistibly anxious for the abolition of slavery in Texas, for if it were abolished there, . . . the consequence would be . . . the abolition of slavery in America" as a whole.[10]

Southerners also responded angrily to accounts of their region written by British subjects who visited it in this decade. British travelers and travel accounts were not unique to this period, but these visitors possessed both an unusually high profile and newly militant antislavery convictions. Despite the latter trait, Southern readers hoped that these respected British guests would do their region justice. The likes of Harriet Martineau and Fanny Kemble produced a sensation during their visits, and their journals of their travels produced bated anticipation.[11] Southerners, however, mustered more solicitude for the visit of Charles Dickens than for any other celebrity visitor. They eagerly followed his journey and anxiously awaited what his travel account would say about America and slavery.[12] For contemporaries, these celebrated travelers epitomized British civilization, which stood for modernity and improvement. When they derided American slavery and slaveholders as barbaric, it hurt—and also produced a prolific and earnest response.

Southern intellectuals crafted their responses despite the feeling that they joined literary combat with Britons at a distinct disadvantage. They sullenly granted that, in literature, the North and especially Britain held far more cultural sway than the South. For example, South Carolinian William Gilmore Simms lamented that "we are, to all intents and purposes, a nation in bondage" to Great Britain's cultural hegemony. Even the best Southern literary figures replicated British literary modes and esteemed their own productions pale imitations of the originals.[13] Doing so exposed Southerners' "postcolonial" condition. According to Michael O'Brien, "Southerners lived at the edge of the known world"; when they approached that center, "cultural anxiety was insistent." They wondered: "Who reads a Southern book? Is someone, somewhere, laughing at us, or sneering at us?"[14] But they pressed forward anyway, even on the touchy subject of slavery.

In response to abolitionist critiques, Southern fiction writers paraded before readers a series of happy-go-lucky slaves who enjoyed deep and reciprocal attachments with their masters. Their often comical backwardness—rendered in the authors' version of black dialect—indicated that these simple people would be lost in the world without the superintending care of their white families.[15] Even in otherwise gloomy tales, such as Julia Putnam Henderson's novel *Lionel Granby*, the master-slave relationship was idyllic. The tale opened on a Virginia plantation where carefree slaves provided "the only voices which soothed the chilled solitude of the scene." When one of his slaves pledged his unending devotion to his troubled master, Granby "found in the priceless fidelity of my servant, a green spot on which my heart might rest from its storm of revenge and misanthropy."[16] While often sidelights to the central plot, these caricatures added up to a consistent and often-repeated portrayal of Southern slavery as a truly domestic institution, begging the question: Who in their right mind would seek to overturn such a benevolent social order?

Some of these authors paused mid-narrative to elucidate the implications of their tales for slavery and abolition. Knowing all too well that British critics relied heavily on the South's draconian slave laws for their depictions of Southern slavery, Henderson had Granby remonstrate that "laws are not always the truest indicators of the moral tone of society." "Slavery," he granted, "considered with reference to the laws of Virginia, is a state of penalty, degradation and suffering. Viewed in relation to its practical existence," however, "it is a condition of ease, tranquillity, and protection."[17] Henderson surely thought her position as a Southern lady enabled her to speak for Southern slavery from the domestic— as opposed to the legal, or masculine—point of view. So did Maria Georgia Milward, who peopled nostalgic stories from her youth with jaunty slave domestics. One of the blessings of her black servants' dependence on their white family, she gushed, was the "pure and benevolent satisfaction" members of the master's family derived from their "power to increase the happiness of others." Such language, especially from such authors, connected this proslavery literature to the cult of domesticity rising on both sides of the Atlantic.[18]

No Southern novelist was as didactic on the morality of slavery as was Simms. Harrison, the hero of his 1835 novel, *The Yemassee*, boasted that his slave Hector "loves me, I verily believe, as I do my mistress." After Hector's repeated acts of loyal heroism, Harrison proclaimed his intent to manumit him, but Hector expostulated, "I d—n to h—ll, maussa, ef I guine to be free!" He would meet only moral degeneracy and early death, he insisted, if Harrison cut him loose. The "deeply affected" Harrison had no answer to this rebuke of his misguided attempt to shirk his duties to this loyal savage.[19] Similarly, in Simms's *Mellichampe*, part of his Revolutionary War sequence, the slave Scipio had a lasting bond with his master, the title character. "Scipio was one of those trusty slaves to be found in almost every native southern family," Simms lectured, "who, having grown up with the children of their owners, have acquired a certain correspondence of feeling with them."[20]

Another of Simms's novelistic lectures on slavery underscored another central theme in this literature. In his Revolutionary romance *The Partisan*, in the midst of depicting saucy but loyal slaves' "indulgent bondage," Simms paused to declare that "we draw our portraits from actual life."[21] In this he echoed the likes of James Heath, who enthused that St. Leger Landon Carter's "admirable sketches" of Virginia plantation life "derive additional value from the fact that they are not the mere creations of fancy, but exact copies from nature."[22] The slave subjects were house or body servants, slave types that kept the focus on the paternalistic side of slavery, far from the bustle of the cotton fields or the horrors of the auction block.

The audience for these claims to realism became clear when Southern intellectuals rebutted British travelers' attacks on slavery as products of their prejudices rather than faithful observations. Dickens's strictures could be discounted, said one reviewer in the *Southern Literary Messenger*, because slavery was "a subject respecting which, he knows nothing, and we cannot receive his fancies as facts." Dickens relied on his wonted fictional mode, said another reviewer in the same journal, because he took only "a flying glance" at the South, "candidly confessing, that his prejudices" kept him from going any farther south than Richmond. Thus he had no recourse but to assert "as facts, things obviously false." These reviewers of Dickens's *American Notes* did not counter with their own facts about slavery; by 1843, they could expect that readers of the *Messenger* had been reading those "facts"—via fiction—for years.[23] Benjamin Blake Minor, as editor of the *Messenger*, decreed that any English traveler's treatment of American slavery comprised "a test of the liberality of his mind, and the impartiality of his judgment." Any "professed follower of Science" should be eager to pass this test.[24]

Apparently aggravated with real Britons' unwillingness to perceive the plain truth, Virginian Henry Ruffner manufactured lines for fictional travelers to speak in praise of Southern slavery in the second of two versions of his story "Judith Bensaddi." In the shorter 1828 version, the key passage carried a mildly antislavery flavor. Two charming English wayfarers told the white Virginian main character that "West Indian slavery is worse than yours; though even in its most mitigated form slavery is a bitter thing."[25] For the expanded 1839 form of the tale, Ruffner had these travelers declare that in the South "the slaves, in general, seem to be as contented and merry a set of beings as any in the world," especially compared to the "care-worn wretches" of England's laboring classes. They had learned that true benevolence towards Southern slaves would be "to leave them in the undisturbed possession of their blessings." Their new concern was that English abolitionists' malignancy towards slaveholders would lead them to embrace "a heavy indignation against the Disposer of our lot, and raise their feelings to a sublime pitch of philanthropic blasphemy."[26] These utterances spoke to the cherished Southern hope that the truth about Southern slavery would overcome the antislavery preconceptions of the best Britons.

Ruffner's fantasy allocution sounded another constant theme in this literature by warning that the philanthropy of British abolitionists was at best misguided zeal and at worst pseudo-philanthropy destructive of God's designs. Much of the Southern literature of the period was set during the Revolution, which among other things gave Southerners opportunities to instill lessons about the British and those who would cooperate with them. The British characters were mostly unprincipled, but the Loyalists figured even worse in motive and atrocity than their haughty overlords.[27] More pointedly, this literature trafficked in the old accusation that redcoats and Tories stole American slaves—certainly those slaves would never have joined them of their own free will—and sold them into slavery in the West Indies rather than freeing them as claimed.[28]

While much of this literature only implied analogies to modern-day British and American abolitionists, other sources were not shy about stating the moral of such stories. Some authors characterized British abolitionists as well-meaning but blinded by antislavery monomania to both the facts of Southern (and West Indian) slavery and the wide field for their philanthropy among the British poor.[29] Others thought even this too charitable a description for the British oligarchs who cynically devised their antislavery crusade to distract attention from their tyrannical treatment of both their own subjects and the rival United States.[30] Neither portrait was reassuring; for even when abolitionists appeared as clueless, would-be benefactors, they disregarded "the frightful evils which their blind impetuosity may produce." No matter the motive, then, "those upon whom these evils must fall" felt "an indignant resentment against the madmen who are blindly jeopardizing the peace of the country and the lives of thousands."[31] The history of British perfidy and fanaticism taught Southerners that they must awaken to the dangers. Simms, for one, declaimed that he depicted British and loyalist atrocities in South Carolina because "we should know—our sons and servants, alike, should then know—how best to avoid them."[32] An orator celebrating the sixtieth anniversary of American victory at Fort Moultrie, South Carolina, told of undaunted defenders holding out against "ruthless invaders." "The abolitionists" of 1836, he admonished, "like the British" during the Revolution, intended to "scatter wrath and desolation— . . . havoc and death, in the Eden bowers of the sunny South." The lessons of history showed that "the hawk when he pounces upon the trembling dove, has as much real genuine philanthropy at his heart, as a modern abolitionist."[33]

While many Southerners seconded this contrast between abolitionists' pretending and Southerners' "real genuine philanthropy," others were leery of the Benevolent Empire as a whole. Some were genuinely ambivalent about modern progress, but what emerged in public discussions of philanthropy and progress was less ambivalence than serious disagreement among Southern intellectuals. Various articles in the *Southern Literary Messenger*, one key host for this debate, endorsed the latest scientific theories and moral crusades such as temperance and avowed that true philosophy would restrain the extravagances of wild mobs. Americans would be "false to the great IDEA of the age" were they to fail to benefit from and add to mankind's "fields of *knowledge*." And what an age it was—"never, in the annals of this earth," exclaimed a Richmond reverend, "has it witnessed a time so interesting, so remarkable, as this!" "When," he demanded, "were there ever such great principles of truth and love and melioration, at work as at the present day?"[34] Such enthusiasm for the progress and philanthropy of modernity could have appeared in any Northern periodical dedicated to improvement.

But others were far less enthusiastic about the signs of the times. They continued a long slaveholder tradition of suspicion of "enthusiastical philosophers" who would meddle with slavery as with other alleged ills and thus make things worse.[35] "How false," insisted one writer, "are all the schemes which have been devised for universal happiness." Their projectors had too weak a grasp on the impossibility of "anything approaching perfect happiness, in this world."[36] Many other articles warned against the naivete, impiety, and hypocrisy of the professed "friend of humanity."[37] In one of Edgar Allan Poe's satirical short stories, his narrator, Signora Psyche Zenobia, set out to learn how to write an article for the celebrated *Blackwood's Edinburgh Magazine* from Mr. Blackwood himself. In Blackwood's advice to Zenobia that she submit to being eaten by bulldogs in his yard and in Zenobia's own wild swings of anger towards her farcical black servant Pompey, Poe caricatured the pseudo-philanthropic sensationalist who cared little for actual human suffering.[38] For still other critics, the problem was that philanthropists cared too much for too broad a range of human suffering to be true American patriots. One author in the *Southern Literary Messenger* griped that the consciously cosmopolitan Benevolent Empire inculcated a philanthropy which "embraces every country but its own."[39] The pages of the *Messenger* also carried frightening portraits of the French and Haitian revolutions and their Jacobin sponsors, such as Robespierre, who in a fictionalized portrait declared that he and his kind "sooner would behold this land manured with carcases and moistened with their blood, than yielding food for feudal slaves to eat."[40]

If there was anything like a majority voice in all these literary treatments of slavery, modernity, and improvement, two pieces in the *Messenger* captured it. A

Northern subscriber canceled his subscription in 1845 because the *Messenger* seemed "to despise the philanthropists of the North" and uphold the "retrograde movement in civilization" that was slavery. Pressed in this way to clarify his stance on philanthropy, Minor flatly stated that "we do not despise philanthropists of any place or age." What he opposed was "a pseudo philanthropy, that would make victims of those whom it professes to bless."[41] Another article contrasted such pseudo-benevolence with the "Patriotism of St. Paul": "He did not equivocate" in spreading the gospel, but "he did not vilify, he did not hate, revile, nor slander even his bitterest foe." As such "he was a noble model when contemplated in the character of a reformer."[42] Progress was desirable, but its reforms should be carried out by wise men. Those armed with the facts about Southern slavery, including the true nature of semibarbarous blacks under whites' tutelage, would not be inclined to tinker with such a beneficent institution. By these criteria, British abolitionists were the last people on earth who should be meddling with Southern slavery.

Southern intellectuals also engaged the British critics of slavery in direct, controversialist responses echoing the themes laid down in the literary treatments of the issue, such as the caricature of the happy slave. When writing about political economy, Southerners made political use of this literary orthodoxy by arguing that slavery was the best mode of labor-management relations, far superior to the rivalry inherent in free-labor settings—especially, of course, in Britain. Thus, for Southern slaves—"the happiest three millions of beings on whom the sun shines," according to James Henry Hammond's famous letter to English abolitionist Thomas Clarkson—emancipation would be a curse brought on them by their masters selfishly abdicating their paternal role. Seen in this light, abolitionism could only be "the work of Satan."[43]

. The romantic literature had opposed "fact" to British abolitionists' prejudices, and the controversialists piled on the facts. The bliss of Southern slavery may safely be assumed, they seemed to reason, but one could never overdo contrasting it with free labor in Britain or the North, using the latest facts and figures. This was of a piece with their eagerness to defend slavery with the latest developments in both natural and social sciences. The scientific method, they argued, showed that experiments in free labor, whether with white operatives in Britain or with blacks in the West Indies, had produced conflict and misery.[44] Armed with all this "proof," proslavery disputants reduced their debating points to mantras. "Let the philanthropist think as he may," they hammered home, but the "patriarchal character" of the master-slave relationship in the South was not imaginary—"we have seen these things." By contrast, abolitionists' exaggerated sense of Southern slavery's crimes "have no existence but in the imagination" of "those who study human nature wholly in the closet."[45]

Simms in particular sounded this theme. Responding to Martineau's critique of Southern slavery, he marshaled plain common-sense truth against what he characterized as her search for half-truths that would make her case. He cited Martineau's hardness of hearing to symbolize her limited capacity to collect true information: her senses being dulled, she had no recourse but to theoretical overgeneralization from a few superficially perceived faux facts. Her work thus stood as a testament to "how singularly obtuse the mind may become, . . . when inveterate in the pursuit of a given object, and yielded up entirely to the one controlling prejudice." He employed this tactic in response to all of Martineau's examples.[46]

One implication of these theses was that slavery comported not only with the scientific aspect of modernity, but also with the advance of civilization that constituted the spirit of the age. This interpretation inverted the characterizations of Britons who branded slavery barbarism and the thorn on the flower of American republicanism. Such assaults were manifestly untrue, said Southerners. Slavery was the bloom, not the thorn, in the garden of progress.[47] For George Fitzhugh, the vigor of Southern slavery "put the South at the lead of modern civilization."[48] Simms argued that "the slaveholders of the south, having the moral and animal guardianship of an ignorant and irresponsible people under their control, are the great moral conservators, in one powerful interest, of the entire world."[49] The slave South, in short, would hardly be left in the wake of the Atlantic vision of moral and material improvement; it was squarely in its vanguard.

Southern writers added crucial corollaries to these arguments against abolitionists. One was that, in their refusal to change course even when confronted with irrefutable evidence, British abolitionists acted from bad faith.[50] Another was that, rather than being avatars of modern civilization as they claimed, bigoted British abolitionists would drag civilization back centuries if they got their way. William Harper posited that if Southern slavery ended, "this wide and fertile region would be again restored to ancient barbarism."[51] Hammond equated British abolitionists' "crusade" against American slavery with the disastrous eleventh-century "People's Crusade" of the French monk Peter the Hermit.[52] Substituting bigoted fanaticism for the slaveholders' scientific method, British abolitionists and their American adjuncts were downright medieval.

But for all this, proslavery polemics replicated their companion literature's divided mind on the value of philanthropy as part of the modern improvement ethic. Hammond captured the ambivalence, scoffing repeatedly at "philosophers" but also asserting that American slaveholders "stand in the broadest light of the knowledge, civilization and improvement of the age."[53] To Nathaniel

Beverley Tucker, the modern world was "full of associations and combinations of men, who make it the business of their lives to regulate everything but what concerns themselves."[54] For others the problem was not philanthropy, but pseudo-philanthropy. Rather than revolt against the "saints" of the world, they hoped to see benevolence perfect itself in Southern slavery and thus fulfill "the highest wishes of saints."[55]

Forged in romantic literature and controversial works, these dogmas proved useful tools in the sectional and partisan strife Southerners waged throughout the antebellum period. Southern politicians also seemed to believe their own propaganda, which shaped their attitude toward the North as well as toward Great Britain. Southern intellectuals' influence thus reached far beyond the ivory towers and right into the heart of American politics on the eve of the Civil War.

Southern intellectuals left their fingerprints on political debates from the 1820s through the 1850s. For example, they lashed out at National Republicans and Whigs for their opposition to the forced repatriation of southeastern Indians. A "Southron," writing in the *Messenger*, echoed current proslavery arguments when he queried whether "these misguided philanthropists" who opposed Indian removal had "been taught no salutary lessons by the calamities which their interference has heaped upon the red man?"[56] In the 1830s, South Carolinian politicians cum intellectuals rehearsing familiar arguments led the charge for Congress to refuse abolitionist petitions. In these "gag-rule" debates, John C. Calhoun assured his colleagues that the South would never give slavery up because "there is and always has been in an advanced stage of wealth and civilization, a conflict between labor and capital. The condition of society in the South exempts us from the disorders and dangers resulting from this conflict." The abolitionists thus did not menace slavery, but rather the union.[57] Hammond offered a trial run of his later responses to British abolitionists. Inasmuch as slavery was "the greatest of all the great blessings which a kind Providence has bestowed upon" Southerners, both black and white, the abolitionists would find that God's designs would frustrate their "mad and savage projects." The abolitionists' "crusade" against slavery marked them as nothing short of "ignorant, infatuated barbarians."[58]

Southern intellectuals also wielded their well-honed arguments to support slavery's expansion into new territories, the core subject of antebellum sectional conflict. In their view, U.S. expansion, led by the slave states with their civilizing mission, was in the world's interests. Impertinent British meddlers in Texas were thus led on not only by "frantic benevolence" but also by their jealousy of American power.[59] Annexation of Texas as a slave state, argued one writer, would "give to freedom its fullest and fairest development" by thwarting

British designs against the American union. Britons and their Northern lap-dogs had declared "that every Southern man is outside of the pale of civilization and of humanity" as justification for their interference in Texas; but given that emancipation in the North and the West Indies "has resulted in a total failure" and that "the advancement of the [black] race, since their connection with the whites" in the United States "has been progressive," abolitionists as usual got it dead wrong. "The decisive test" of a civilized society, which the slave South passed with flying colors, was whether it conformed to "the law of amelioration—the great law of every human society." Southerners must therefore unite for annexation, which would preserve slavery from Britain's malignant interference.[60]

Despite Calhoun's confident pose during the gag-rule debates, Southern spokesmen brandished proslavery arguments largely as defensive weapons in the 1830s and 1840s. But in the 1850s they sounded much more self-assured. The British experiment with freedom in the West Indies had shown that freed-people would produce far fewer staple crops than slaves had. Meanwhile, the cotton South was an economic marvel. This encouraged breathless reasser-tions from Southern leaders in the 1850s that the slave South was the fulcrum of civilization. In the U.S. Senate in 1858, Hammond proclaimed that the Southern cotton heartland would soon "be the acknowledged seat of empire of the world," due to slave-grown cotton. The South had the advantage because its laboring class comprised a "race inferior to" its capitalists, whose "vigor, docility," and "fidelity" allowed the masters to lead out in "progress, civilization, and refinement."[61] This ebullient assessment of their place at the forefront of world civilization emboldened Southern leaders contemplating secession.[62]

If the proslavery response to the British challenge helped pull buoyant Southern intellectuals towards secession, then many Northerners' response to British critiques of slavery served as a push in the same disunionist direction. Horror at some Northerners' unwillingness, when Britons criticized Southern slavery, to privilege nationalism over their antislavery principles had long galled slaveholders and their allies.[63] As the British call became more insistent, so did Southern attention to the Northern response. Which side of the debate the bulk of Northerners would join was of enormous consequence for the future of both slavery and the union.

Some liked what they heard and sought to encourage greater assertiveness from the right element in the North. This was particularly true of Whiggish upper Southerners such as those who predominated in the *Messenger*, men and women who staked out moderate ground on slavery and worked hard to make common cause with Northerners. They, like other Southerners, scrutinized the relative sway of abolitionists and "doughfaces" (a.k.a. Northern men of Southern principles) over Northern public opinion, and they mostly proclaimed themselves

satisfied. They protested their confidence "that the honest, patriotic and intelligent among our northern brethren" (i.e., the doughfaces) "will zealously cooperate with us in stifling this meddling and pestilential spirit of fanaticism"
proceeding from its seat in England.[64] And whenever a Yankee signed up for
such duty, they rushed to praise and publicize his or her work.[65] When assault-
ing Northern abolitionists, such souls clarified that they meant "to rebuke only
the intermeddlers—not the rational and forbearing part—of the northern
people." They believed "the latter sort to be a majority there" and would not
change that by alienating them.[66] The travel account of Northerner C. Edwards
Lester was particularly useful to the *Messenger*. Traveling with a distinguished
London abolitionist who enjoined him to evade two beggar children, Lester
indignantly told his *"philanthropic* companion" that "I should give you very
little credit for all your anti-slavery philanthropy, were I a slave-owner" who
knew about this incident.[67] This scene, in which the English abolitionist played
the role of Pharisee to perfection, was irresistible ammunition. Lester's reviewer
riffed that Britain's "philanthropy is like the odor of a plant which French trav-
ellers tell of in the East: at a distance the perfume of the Veloutier fills the air
with the most exquisite fragrance—but as the plant is approached the odor
becomes intolerably suffocating and loathsome."[68] Men like Lester were welcome
allies against the British juggernaut.

Other Southerners watching the "doughface meter" thought it pointed so
far downward as to render Northern moderates powerless. Abolitionists might
seem a small minority in 1845, one writer warned, but "the History of the
French Revolution demonstrates the power which an inconsiderable number
of men may acquire when acting in concert and fired by enthusiasm." Thus it
was high time for "all northern patriots no longer to submit in silence" to the
growing abolitionist menace.[69] Many abolitionists and antislavery politicians
publicly proclaimed that they sided with Britain in its global war against slavery; for many Southerners these traitorous zealots represented the real face of
the North.[70] The article on Texas in the *Southern Quarterly Review*—which was
published in New Orleans and spoke for the Deep South more than did the
Southern Literary Messenger, published in Richmond—groused that Northerners "would prefer to see Texas a British province, than to see it a portion of this
Federal Union."[71] Simms grumbled that Martineau blatantly favored the North
over the South—something Yankees seemed to encourage rather than repel.[72]
Proslavery zealots and Deep Southerners seem to have been the most likely to
take a dim view of the reliability and efficacy of the doughfaces.[73] But many
writers in the *Messenger* shared this sense of betrayal by Yankees. "That any
portion of our people should cooperate with" Great Britain's designs against
slavery and their own country, raged one particularly peeved Virginian, "is an

instance of wickedness, or infatuation, unmatched in the history of man-kind."[74] A "Southron" lambasted Yankee abolitionists for having "permitted themselves to become the agents of foreign agitators."[75]

The Anglo-American aspect of slavery politics had ratcheted up the already high North-South tension over slavery. It had revealed the secret of Yankees' souls. Doughfaces seemed powerless against a rising Northern majority that would fight alongside Britain in the struggle between slavery and nominal free-dom. In 1838 a "Southron" spoke in nationalist terms of how the union as well as slavery was at stake; but by 1860, many Southerners had concluded that political union with the antislavery variant of the Benevolent Empire was untenable.

The British voice in the debate also gave Southern intellectuals an apoca-lyptic global vision that raised the already high stakes of the debate. Seen in this way, "it is not the narrow question of Abolitionism or Slavery," James Henley Thornwell summed. It was rather "a question as broad as the interests of the human race."[76] When moderates on slavery in domestic politics considered the issue from a global perspective, they took much more strident positions. A doctor writing in the *Messenger*, for instance, refused to call slavery good or bad, but asserted that the American slaves' lot was superior to that of English laborers and that Caribbean emancipation had produced "evil results." He hoped no other Atlantic power would join in "the madness of the times" and free additional slaves.[77] It was not only that defending slavery involved a des-perate struggle against the old imperial enemy and current world hegemon. Responding to British antagonists also convinced Southern opinion leaders that they manned the crucial bastion of civilization fending off the fanatical barbarians at the gates.

NOTES

1. Bertram Wyatt-Brown, "Modernizing Southern Slavery: The Proslavery Argument Reinterpreted," in *Region, Race, and Reconstruction: Essays in Honor of C. Vann Woodward*, ed. J. Morgan Kousser and James M. McPherson (New York: Oxford University Press, 1982), 27–49; Eugene D. Genovese, *The Slaveholders' Dilemma: Freedom and Progress in Southern Conservative Thought, 1820–1860* (Columbia: Univer-sity of South Carolina Press, 1992); Jeffrey Robert Young, *Domesticating Slavery: The Master Class in Georgia and South Carolina, 1670–1837* (Chapel Hill: University of North Carolina Press, 1999); William Kauffman Scarborough, *Masters of the Big House: Elite Slaveholders of the Mid-Nineteenth Century South* (Baton Rouge: Louisiana State University Press, 2003), esp. 28–44, 65–89; Timothy M. Roberts, "'Revolutions Have Become the Bloody Toy of the Multitude': European Revolutions, the South, and the Crisis of 1850," *Journal of the Early Republic* 25 (Summer 2005): 259–283; Christopher

A. Luse, "Slavery's Champions Stood at Odds: Polygenesis and the Defense of Slavery," *Civil War History* 53 (December 2007): 379–412; Steven Heath Mitton, "The Free World Confronted: The Problem of Slavery and Progress in American Foreign Relations, 1833–1844" (Ph.D. diss., Louisiana State University, 2005); Edward Bartlett Rugemer, *The Problem of Emancipation: The Caribbean Roots of the American Civil War* (Baton Rouge: Louisiana State University Press, 2008); Brian Schoen, *The Fragile Fabric of Union: Cotton, Federal Politics, and the Global Origins of the Civil War* (Baltimore: Johns Hopkins University Press, 2009); and esp. Michael O'Brien, *Conjectures of Order: Intellectual Life and the American South, 1810–1860*, 2 vols. (Chapel Hill: University of North Carolina Press, 2004); and Elizabeth Fox-Genovese and Eugene D. Genovese, *The Mind of the Master Class: History and Faith in the Southern Slaveholders' Worldview* (Cambridge: Cambridge University Press, 2005). For the older interpretation, see William Sumner Jenkins, *Pro-Slavery Thought in the Old South* (1935; repr., Gloucester, Mass.: Peter Smith, 1960); W. J. Cash, *The Mind of the South* (New York: Alfred A. Knopf, 1941); Louis Hartz, *The Liberal Tradition in America: An Interpretation of American Political Thought Since the Revolution* (New York: Harcourt, Brace, 1955), 145–200; Clement Eaton, *The Mind of the Old South* (Baton Rouge: Louisiana State University Press, 1964); David Donald, "The Proslavery Argument Reconsidered," *Journal of Southern History* 37 (February 1971): 3–18; Lewis P. Simpson, *The Dispossessed Garden: Pastoral and History in Southern Literature* (Athens: University of Georgia Press, 1975), 14–64.

2. Daniel Walker Howe, *What Hath God Wrought: The Transformation of America, 1815–1848* (New York: Oxford University Press, 2007), 244. For Southerners' view of "benevolence," see Fox-Genovese and Genovese, *Mind of the Master Class*, 543–546.

3. *Register of Debates in Congress* (Washington, D.C.: Gales and Seaton, 1825–1837), 19th Congress, 1st sess., 402.

4. John Pendleton Kennedy, *Horse-Shoe Robinson. A Tale of the Tory Ascendency*, rev. ed. (1835; repr., Philadelphia: J. B. Lippincott and Co., 1860), 134–137; *Southern Literary Messenger* (Richmond) (hereafter cited as *SLM*) 1 (January 1835): 227–231; *SLM* 1 (April 1835): 405–421; *SLM* 2 (April 1836): 339; *SLM* 2 (October 1836): 722; *SLM* 2 (November 1836): 761–765; *SLM* 9 (December 1843): 736–737; William Harper, *Memoir on Slavery* (Charleston, S.C., 1838), reprinted in *The Ideology of Slavery: Proslavery Thought in the Antebellum South, 1830–1860*, ed. Drew Gilpin Faust (Baton Rouge: Louisiana State University Press, 1981), 80–81.

5. Drew Gilpin Faust, *A Sacred Circle: The Dilemma of the Intellectual in the Old South, 1840–1860* (Baltimore: Johns Hopkins University Press, 1977), tends to take griping Southern intellectuals at their word. For intellectuals' influence, see Wyatt-Brown, "Modernizing Southern Slavery," 27–28; Genovese, *Slaveholders' Dilemma*, 1–2, 14; O'Brien, *Conjectures of Order*, 1: 388–392.

6. *SLM* 1 (March 1835): 366–369; *SLM* 1 (August 1835): 699; *SLM* 1 (September 1835): 756; *SLM* 2 (July 1836): 471–476, 504–505, 507–511; *SLM* 2 (August 1836): 547–549; *SLM* 2 (September 1836): 636–644; *SLM* 3 (May 1837): 309–314; *SLM* 3 (June 1837): 337–338; *SLM* 4 (March 1838): 152; *SLM* 6 (January 1840): 21–22, 53.

7. See esp. Mitton, "Free World Confronted"; Rugemer, *Problem of Emancipation*. For Southern Anglophobia, see Joseph A. Fry, *Dixie Looks Abroad: The South and U.S. Foreign Relations, 1789–1973* (Baton Rouge: Louisiana State University Press, 2002), 8–74.

8. Lord Aberdeen to Richard Pakenham, February 26, 1843, quoted in *Congressional Globe* (Washington, D.C.: Blair & Rives, 1844), 28th Congress, 1st sess., 448, 481.

9. Rugemer, *Problem of Emancipation*, 197–204; Mitton, "Free World Confronted," 22–109; Don E. Fehrenbacher, *The Slaveholding Republic: An Account of the United States Government's Relations to Slavery* (New York: Oxford University Press, 2001), 104–111, 157–172.

10. *Congressional Globe* (Washington, D.C.: Blair & Rives, 1844), 28th Congress, 1st sess., 448.

11. *SLM* 1 (February 1835): 319; *SLM* 1 (May 1835): 524.

12. *SLM* 5 (October 1839): 704; *SLM* 2 (November 1836): 787; *SLM* 9 (January 1843): 60; *[Charlestown] Virginia Free Press*, November 4, 1841; *[Washington, D.C.] Daily National Intelligencer*, November 9, 1841, and January 12, February 25, 1842; *Daily [St. Louis] Missouri Republican*, November 10, 1841; *[Raleigh, N.C.] Register*, February 25, May 13, 1842; *[Columbia] South Carolina Temperance Advocate*, March 3, 1842; Fox-Genovese and Genovese, *Mind of the Master Class*, 138–139, 736–737; Edgar Allan Poe, *Essays and Reviews* (New York: Library of America, 1984), 13, 155, 160, 179–180, 189, 204–244, 313–314, 325, 812, 1316–1317, 1358–1359.

13. Mary C. Sims Oliphant et al., eds. *The Letters of William Gilmore Simms*, 5 vols. (Columbia: University of South Carolina Press, 1954), 1:201–206. See also William R. Taylor, *Cavalier and Yankee: The Old South and American National Character* (1957; repr., Garden City, N.Y.: Anchor Books, 1963), 156–181; Poe, *Essays and Reviews*, 95–350; Michael Allen, *Poe and the British Magazine Tradition* (New York: Oxford University Press, 1969).

14. O'Brien, *Conjectures of Order*, 1: 2–7, 41–45.

15. See William Gilmore Simms, *Guy Rivers: A Tale of Georgia*, rev. ed. (1834; New York: Lovell, Coryell & Co., n.d.), 55–56, 493–495; Simms, *The Kinsmen: or the Black Riders of the Congaree*, 2 vols. (Philadelphia: Lea and Blanchard, 1841), 2:132–134; Kennedy, *Horse-Shoe Robinson*, esp. 405–407, 434; [T. T. Tabb,] *Rose-Hill; A Tale of the Old Dominion, By A Virginian* (Philadelphia: Key and Biddle, 1835), esp. 102–107, 131–132; William A. Caruthers, *The Knights of the Horseshoe: A Traditionary Tale of the Cocked Hat Gentry in the Old Dominion* (1845; repr., New York: A. L. Burt Company, n.d.), 12, 21–27, 31, 68–69, 96–97, 106, 135–137, 180–181, 196, 369–370, 427; *SLM* 1 (December 1834): 181–183; *SLM* 2 (July 1836): 462; *SLM* 3 (April 1837): 233–234; *SLM* 4 (March 1838): 160–162; *SLM* 4 (October 1838): 653–654; *SLM* 5 (June 1839): 375–379; *SLM* 6 (July 1840): 505–514.

16. *SLM* 1 (May 1835): 516–518; *SLM* 2 (February 1836): 162; *SLM* 2 (March 1836): 254; *SLM* 4 (January 1838): 24. For Henderson's authorship, see David K. Jackson, *The Contributors and Contributions to* The Southern Literary Messenger *(1834–1864)* (Charlottesville, Va.: The Historical Publishing Company, 1936), 3.

17. *SLM* 1 (June 1835): 542–543.

18. *SLM* 7 (January 1841): 37–48; *SLM* 7 (February 1841): 119. For more on Southern women and plantation fiction, see Elizabeth R. Varon, *We Mean to Be Counted: White Women and Politics in Antebellum Virginia* (Chapel Hill: University of North Carolina Press, 1998), chap. 4.

19. William Gilmore Simms, *The Yemassee: A Romance of Carolina*, rev. ed. (1835; repr., New York: J. S. Redfield, 1853), 47–51, 79–81, 121–122, 142–147, 254–255, 344–348, 354, 415–418, 429–430, 437–438, 441, 443, 453.

20. William Gilmore Simms, *Mellichampe: A Legend of the Santee*, rev. ed. (1836; repr., New York: J. S. Redfield, 1854), 98–105, 113, 116, 234–238, 301–302, 333–426.

21. William Gilmore Simms, *The Partisan: A Romance of the Revolution*, rev. ed. (1835; New York: J. S. Redfield, 1853), 73, 76, 98, 110–111, 141, 148, 227, 246, 255–256, 349–351, 363–368, 416–418, 424–427, 498.

22. *SLM* 1 (December 1834): 191. For Carter's authorship, see Jackson, *Contributors and Contributions*, 1.

23. *SLM* 9 (January 1843): 58–62; *SLM* 2 (January 1836): 121–122; *SLM* 3 (May 1837): 281; *SLM* 4 (May 1838): 341; *SLM* 6 (January 1840): 72–85; *SLM* 7 (April 1841): 253–276; *SLM* 9 (November 1843): 704; *SLM* 10 (February 1844): 124–125; *SLM* 11 (February 1845): 127; *SLM* 11 (April 1845): 254–255; *[New Orleans] Southern Quarterly Review* 3 (January 1843): 166–181, and 7 (April 1845): 335.

24. *SLM* 11 (November 1845): 699.

25. *The [Philadelphia] Souvenir* 2 (July 23, 1828): 25. See also J. Michael Pemberton, ed., *Judith Bensaddi, A Tale; and Seclusaval, Or the Sequel to the Tale of Judith Bensaddi* (Baton Rouge: Louisiana State University Press, 1984), 1–29.

26. *SLM* 5 (July 1839): 471–474.

27. Simms, *Partisan*, 13–17, 48, 53; Simms, *Mellichampe*, passim; Simms, *Kinsmen*, esp. 1:66; Kennedy, *Horse-Shoe Robinson*, esp. xiii–xiv, 48–53.

28. Simms, *Partisan*, 132, 142, 147, 151; Simms, *Kinsmen*, 1:174–175, 2:181; *SLM* 7 (December 1841): 860.

29. *SLM* 1 (November 1834): 82–83; *SLM* 2 (March 1836): 254–256; *SLM* 2 (May 1836): 352–353; *SLM* 5 (June 1839): 381.

30. *SLM* 7 (April 1841): 253–276; *SLM* 8 (April 1842): 289–301; *SLM* 8 (June 1842): 381–396.

31. *SLM* 1 (July 1835): 650–651.

32. Simms, *Partisan*, x.

33. Cited in Patricia Roberts-Miller, *Fanatical Schemes: Proslavery Rhetoric and the Tragedy of Consensus* (Tuscaloosa: University of Alabama Press, 2009), 61–64.

34. *SLM* 1 (April 1835): 405–421; *SLM* 2 (October 1836): 761–765; *SLM* 5 (June 1839): 393–394; *SLM* 6 (January 1840): 25; *SLM* 6 (May 1840): 388–391; *SLM* 6 (September 1840): 651–652; *SLM* 7 (December 1841): 848–850; *SLM* 8 (March 1842): 209–211; *SLM* 8 (July 1842): 439–444; *SLM* 9 (December 1843): 745–746.

35. Jenkins, *Pro-Slavery Thought*, 43, 58–65, 68–69; *SLM* 2 (July 1836): 462; Rugemer, *Problem of Emancipation*, 43–53; Larry E. Tise, *Proslavery: A History of the Defense of Slavery in America, 1701–1840* (Athens: University of Georgia Press, 1987),

29; Young, *Domesticating Slavery*, 158; Matthew Mason, *Slavery and Politics in the Early American Republic* (Chapel Hill: University of North Carolina Press, 2006), 103–104, 124, 158, 162, 164–171, 176, 197, 201–204, 236.

36. *SLM* 6 (July 1840): 503.

37. *SLM* 4 (March 1838): 203–204; *SLM* 5 (April 1839): 296; *SLM* 5 (November 1839): 725; *SLM* 6 (December 1840): 840–841; *SLM* 11 (May 1845): 323–326; *SLM* 11 (September 1845): 513–528; *SLM* 11 (October 1845): 646.

38. Edgar Allan Poe, "How to Write a Blackwood Article" (1838), in *Complete Stories and Poems of Edgar Allan Poe* (Garden City, N.Y.: Doubleday & Co., 1966), 320–334.

39. *SLM* 11 (April 1845): 211.

40. "The Death of Robespierre," *SLM* 2 (April 1836): 304–309; see also *SLM* 1 (February 1835): 309; *SLM* 7 (September 1841): 609–619; *SLM* 9 (March 1843): 136–144; *SLM* 10 (June 1844): 357–359.

41. *SLM* 11 (January 1845): 61–62.

42. *SLM* 8 (August 1842): 524–527.

43. *SLM* 1 (January 1835): 227–231; *SLM* 2 (March 1836): 261–282; *SLM* 5 (October 1839): 677–687, esp. 687; *SLM* 8 (July 1842): 446–447; Simms, *Slavery in America*, 26–28, 49; James Henry Hammond, *Letter . . . to the Free Church of Glasgow*, in James Henry Hammond, *Selections from the Letters and Speeches of the Hon. James H. Hammond* (New York: J.F. Trow & Co., 1866), 105–113; "Hammond's Letters on Slavery" (1845), in *The Pro-slavery Argument as Maintained by the Most Distinguished Authors of the Southern States* (Charleston, S.C.: Walker, Richards & Co., 1852), 103–140, 142–149; George Fitzhugh, *Sociology for the South* (1854), in *Slavery Defended: The Views of the Old South*, ed. Eric L. McKitrick, (Englewood Cliffs, N.J.: Prentice-Hall, 1963), 44–49; Edward A. Pollard, *Black Diamonds Gathered in the Darkey Homes of the South* (1859), in McKitrick, *Slavery Defended*, 162–168.

44. *SLM* 5 (September 1839): 616–620; *SLM* 9 (June 1843): 340–352; *SLM* 9 (December 1843): 736–744; *SLM* 10 (March 1844): 178–181; Faust, *Ideology of Slavery*, 237–271; Schoen, *Fragile Fabric*, chap. 3.

45. *SLM* 2 (April 1836): 338–339; *SLM* 4 (December 1838): 737–739; *SLM* 7 (November 1841): 774; *SLM* 6 (March 1840): 193; *SLM* 10 (June 1844): 329–339; Hammond, *Letter . . . to the Free Church of Glasgow*, 5; "Hammond's Letters on Slavery," 100, 130–139, 152–155, 160–161.

46. Simms, *Slavery in America*, 20, 28.

47. I take this analogy from Henderson's "Lionel Granby"; *SLM* 2 (February 1836): 255.

48. George Fitzhugh, "Southern Thought" (1857) and "Southern Thought Again" (1857), in Faust, *Ideology of Slavery*, 272–299.

49. Simms, *Slavery in America*, 60–84. See also "Appendix," in *Pro-Slavery Argument*, 276–285; *SLM* 2 (March 1836): 261–282; 7 (November 1841): 774; 10 (August 1844): 480; Faust, *Ideology of Slavery*, 270–271; O'Brien, *Conjectures of Order*, 2: 940–942, 965, 979–981; McKitrick, ed., *Slavery Defended*, 69–85, 111–120; John C.

Calhoun, "Disquisition on Government," in *The Works of John C. Calhoun*, 6 vols. (New York: D. Appleton and Co., 1854), 1:52–59.

50. See, for example, *SLM* 8 (March 8, 1842): 234–236; *SLM* 9 (June 1843): 350–352; Fitzhugh, "Southern Thought" (1857), in Faust, *Ideology of Slavery*, 299.

51. Harper, *Memoir on Slavery*, 130.

52. "Hammond's Letters on Slavery," 103. For another allusion to Peter the Hermit, see *SLM* 4 (September 1838): 549.

53. "Hammond's Letters on Slavery," 149–151, 162–163; Hammond, *Letter . . . to the Free Church of Glasgow*, 4, 6–7.

54. *SLM* 1 (January 1835): 228, 231; *SLM* 10 (June 1844): 329–339.

55. *SLM* 3 (March 1840): 193–200; Faust, *Ideology of Slavery*, 166, 237–238.

56. *SLM* 4 (September 1838): 552–555. See also *SLM* 11 (April 1845): 202–211.

57. Clyde N. Wilson, ed., *The Papers of John C. Calhoun*, 28 vols. (Columbia: University of South Carolina Press, 1959–2003), 13:391–397.

58. *Congressional Globe* (Washington, D.C.: Blair & Rives, 1834–1873), 24th Congress, 1st sess., 611–615.

59. *SLM* 4 (September 1838): 545–560; *SLM* 10 (May 1844): 315–326; *SLM* 10 (June 1844): 383–384; *SLM* 10 (October 1844): 577–591.

60. *Southern Quarterly Review* 12 (October 1844): 483–520.

61. *Congressional Globe* (Washington, D.C.: Blair & Rives, 1834–1873), 35th Congress, 1st sess., 961–962.

62. See also Rugemer, *Problem of Emancipation*, 260–264; O'Brien, *Conjectures of Order*, 2: 991–992, 1067; Fry, *Dixie Looks Abroad*, 65–75; and esp. Schoen, *Fragile Fabric*, 10, chap. 5; Mitton, "Free World Confronted," xiii, 1–19, 114–193.

63. Matthew Mason, "The Battle of the Slaveholding Liberators: Great Britain, the United States, and Slavery in the Early Nineteenth Century," *William and Mary Quarterly*, 3rd series, 59 (July 2002): 665–696.

64. *SLM* 7 (April 1841): 271; *SLM* 4 (October 1838): 609; *SLM* 10 (January 1844): 2.

65. *SLM* 2 (January 1836): 122–123; *SLM* 2 (June 1836): 433–434; *SLM* 2 (July 1836): 511–512; *SLM* 2 (August 1836): 556; *SLM* 3 (May 1837): 281; *SLM* 7 (April 1841): 314–315.

66. *SLM* 4 (March 1838): 165. See also *SLM* 1 (November 1834): 87–88; *SLM* 1 (December 1834): 166–167; *SLM* 1 (February 1835): 273, 322–323; *SLM* 1 (April 1835): 426; *SLM* 3 (July 1837): 412–416; *SLM* 3 (December 1837): 764; *SLM* 6 (November 1840): 763.

67. C. Edwards Lester, *The Glory and the Shame of England*, 2 vols. (New York: Harper and Brothers, 1842), 1:98–125.

68. *SLM* 7 (December 1841): 875. See also *SLM* 9 (August 1843): 506–507.

69. *SLM* 11 (August 1845): 464.

70. Rugemer, *Problem of Emancipation*, 91, 137–138, 151, 183–184, 193, 222–257, 285; Mitton, "Free World Confronted," 44–46, 113–114, 120.

71. *Southern Quarterly Review* 12 (October 1844): 503, 516.

72. Simms, *Slavery in America*, 11, 22–25, 30–31, 39. See also *SLM* 4 (May 1838): 341.

73. Genovese, *Slaveholders' Dilemma*, 101–107; Faust, *Ideology of Slavery*, 281.

74. *SLM* 8 (March 1842): 236. See also *SLM* 10 (May 1844): 323–324; *SLM* 11 (May 1845): 326.

75. *SLM* 4 (September 1838): 545–560.

76. Quoted in Fox-Genovese and Genovese, *Mind of the Master Class*, 407.

77. *SLM* 10 (May 1844): 268–275.

3

The Burdens and Opportunities of Interdependence: The Political Economies of the Planter Class

Brian Schoen

Southern planters, like most inhabitants of the modern world, relied on a vast network of people for their economic livelihoods. That reliance began at home where they managed the day-to-day operations of plantations, ranging from the planning to the picking, processing, and eventual selling of staple products. Success or failure depended on a planter's choices and the cooperation, forced or not, of slaves whose own capacity for thought and willingness to work either created income or ensured debt. In idealistic moments planters liked to think of their plantation and laborers as large, harmonious households and themselves as "paternalists" (or in some cases "maternalists") vigilantly guarding the boundaries of their "peculiar" domestic sphere from the harshness of a rapidly changing world around them. Historians have long rejected the claims of planter benevolence but until recently have been remarkably accepting of the boundaries implied by this domestic metaphor.

Under our high-resolution microscopes, the "world of the plantation" (think of all that often-used phrase connotes) has remained a more or less distinct unit, permeating its influence outwards to all aspects of Southern life but little altered by broader dynamics. Too often, external markets appear as constants and broader events and developments as epiphenomenal. Planters emerge as either passive and hopelessly "dependent," or as reactionaries whose responses only confirm their peculiarity and lack of comfort with modern nineteenth-century processes. This tendency has been particularly acute among economists and historians who, whether inspired by Marxism, classical economics, or twentieth-century developmental theories, undervalue and homogenize agrarian pursuits while interpreting the slave South primarily for what it was not (the industrial North) rather than for what it was. Such segregation and essentialization of the antebellum plantation has undervalued and grossly oversimplified the role that outside processes had in substantively reshaping the lives of planters and slaves.[1] The complicated "worlds" that masters and slaves created on plantations, large and small, were central features of Southern antebellum society, but this chapter joins recent scholarship to argue that they were anything but isolated, organic, antimodern, or homogeneous.

Increasingly strong scholarly undercurrents, many derived from placing the antebellum South in a broader comparative context, have demonstrated modern tendencies amongst planters. For example, close examinations of planters' exhaustive accounting logs and letters reveal their obsession with gains and losses, early embrace of clock time, and subscriptions to agricultural journals and commercial newsletters, reminding us that their homes were also modern businesses, often on a grand and very brutal scale. The size and scope of larger operations, including the estimated 46,000 planters who in 1860 possessed upwards of twenty slaves, almost certainly approximated Northern factories or merchant houses more closely than urban artisan shops or family farms. They and the nearly 127,000 smaller planters who owned between six and nineteen slaves remained deeply enmeshed in local labor markets, contracting extra labor when needed and hiring out their own when possible. Planters were the primary buyers and sellers in a complicated domestic slave trade. They invested in factories, railroads, neighbors' farms, and commercial ventures. As with most entrepreneurial activities of the age, some investments succeeded, many others failed.[2]

Ultimately, however, planters' profits and the sustainability of their slave society depended on successfully navigating ever-changing global commodity markets, where they faced three interrelated developments transforming the world economy between 1750 and 1850. First, industrial revolutions reorganized household consumption patterns and created new finance and trade networks, generally advantaging Europeans and especially the British whose legal structures, financial institutions, and imperial reach gave them a comparative edge over non-Europeans. Second, political independence movements in the Western Hemisphere broke down mercantilist systems, albeit haltingly and unevenly, forcing European powers to look for trade outside of their landed empires. Conversely, patriotic North and South Americans, previously wed to European empires, now passed duties, tariffs, taxes, and signed reciprocity agreements of their own, all calculated to enhance their own comparative advantage within domestic and international markets. Third, while a competitive imperial world remained, European powers shifted tactics by selectively pursuing freer trade and enhancing their formal and informal empires in Asia and Africa. This deeper reach eastward and southward, by Great Britain in particular, transformed a semiautonomous eighteenth-century Atlantic world into a truly international nineteenth-century one.[3]

These seismic shifts had immense ramifications for Southern planters, who proved essential to the first, proudly participated in the second, and responded with varying degrees of success to the third. Most welcomed their place within the global economy and all constantly worked to improve it, closely studying overseas developments for clues about how new enterprises, colonization schemes, and wars would join older mercantilist policies to affect prices and market share for their particular crops. Planters saw—depending on trade conditions—reasons to be both optimistic and concerned about their place within this evolving world economy. Indeed, by responding to and exploiting international demand for their diverse staple products and by regulating race-based slavery with brutal efficiency, Southern planters lined their pockets and gave their region considerable local, national, and even, many believed, global power. Those desires required that planters be constantly aware of and engaged with an economic world best described as modern because of its increasingly complex division of labor, inherent dynamism, global nature, and assumption of material progress.

Historians have often judged the South harshly for having considerably more capital invested in supposedly archaic slave-grown agriculture than in progress-minded manufacturing or commercial activities. Yet in a nineteenth-century world in which agriculture generated far more jobs and commerce than did industry, the South emerged as one of the most profitable, scientific, and exacting agricultural economies the world had yet seen. They did so, however, not as a monolithic class, but profoundly aware of each crop's unique market orientations, labor demands, technological requirements, and policy needs. There was, in short, no single planter political economy but rather multiple pathways towards modern agricultural practices with varying results.[4]

This brief examination of these "many Souths" suggests the need to reconsider how we approach and understand the plantation South and slavery's place within the modern world. First, as useful as Atlantic history has been, the emergence of Asia as a competitive market in the mid-nineteenth century requires that historians of the South's diverse agricultural economies think in truly global terms, with an eye towards developments in the Pacific rim. Second, it echoes Anthony Kaye's recent assertion that "in the new techniques and increased scale of production and adaptability of slave labor the second slavery was, in a word, modern."[5] It seems increasingly clear that slavery advanced, rather than hindered, Southern agricultural development, allowing planters to concentrate and move labor across a vast continent. For example, contrary to their image as economically backward, cotton planters proved remarkably successful at deploying their political power and adapting their crop and slavery to meet the modern global marketplace. That they were also the most numerous and most committed slaveholders forces us to reconsider the relationship between slave-based agriculture and modernity. Third, planters' global awareness and appreciation for crop-specific demands reveal a level of pragmatism, diversity, and economic deftness too often neglected in studies of the South's most powerful class. Evolving conditions forced considerable changes within a Southern political economy generally seen as static and, consequently, studied without acknowledgment of how crop differentiation affected political and ideological commitments. A closer look at antebellum planters' particular interests and market orientations demonstrates that a variety of crop-determined "political economies" coexisted and competed in the South, explaining a variety of approaches to national economic policy, slavery, and ultimately secession.

Meeting the Market

The new world economic order emerging in the late eighteenth and early nineteenth centuries presented very real challenges to American growers of traditional colonial crops, such as tobacco and Lowcountry rice, but created new opportunities for entrepreneurs willing to risk experimenting with commercial variants of crops newer to North America—cotton, sugar, and to a lesser extent hemp. The post-Revolutionary order proved especially difficult for tobacco planters long-plagued by depressed markets and, in eastern states, land exhaustion. Newly applied British navigation acts, the continuation of French monopolies, and war in the Atlantic further limited demand through 1815. Lower prices led more than a few tobacco growers to shift land to wheat production or to abandon the business altogether, many pursuing wealth in newly developed southwestern cotton fields. After a brief postwar boom, tobacco planters' troubles returned in the 1820s, as increased competition from operations (many by nonslaveholders) in Kentucky, western North Carolina, and Tennessee resulted in overproduction and lower prices.[6]

Consequently, when Virginia, still the leading tobacco-producing state, seriously debated ending slavery after Nat Turner's 1830 rebellion, they did so under a cloud of economic uncertainty. Although stridently contending that "every plan of emancipation and deportation which we can possibly conceive, is *totally* impracticable," William and Mary professor Thomas Dew's proslavery response remained defensive, calling into question slavery's long-term profitability.[7] In 1832 a narrow majority of Virginians decided slavery could not be efficaciously ended, but planters had to expend extra effort to prove the long-term profitability of a commodity doubly damned by reformers for the slave system growing it and for its poor health effects. As one 1860 report on the tobacco trade lamented, the "reformers of the world seemed to have converged their batteries" and abandoned the tobacco "cultivator and consumer . . . to the anthemas [sic.] of an ultra moralism, and the exactions of needy or oppressive governments" who restricted consumer access by levying heavy discrimination duties on the noxious weed.[8]

Nutritious rice could not be so easily attacked on moral grounds, yet shifting market realities suggested that rice planters' golden era had also passed. Unlike tobacco, which required relatively few hands, the rigors of growing rice in swampy terrain limited its cultivation to Lowcountry planters capable of mobilizing labor on a grand scale, leaving few Georgia or Carolina rice grandees doubting slavery's desirability. Although the dominant grain in other areas of the world, rice competed in Europe and the Western Hemisphere with wheat, potatoes, and corn for a place on working families' dinner tables. Worldwide demand steadily increased in the post-1815 period, but American planters were poorly positioned to take advantage. Instead, Europe's peacetime protection of native grains and the accelerated, at times violent, incorporation of Southeast Asian rice-producing regions into the global economy placed U.S. rice planters in a significantly weakened position. Already by the 1830s the Dutch colony of Java and the British colonies of Burma and Bengal undercut U.S. prices in northern European ports, reducing North America's share of the British market from 98 percent in the 1780s to 20.5 percent. The decline continued through the 1850s, when U.S. planters had to ask Congress for protective tariffs against Asian competition. Rice planters still made a reasonably good living, but Asian rice's ascendance combined with increased self-sufficiency (and sweet potato production) in post-emancipationist colonies and newly independent Latin American nations left rice planters on the periphery of global markets and less dominant within their own.[9]

Whereas Lowcountry rice producers faced relative global decline, upper South hemp growers struggled to find a place in national markets dominated by outsiders. Growers of hemp, which was used to make bagging for cotton, cheap cloth, rope, and cordage, benefited from the ideally suited soil and climate of Kentucky and Missouri as well as from Atlantic wars, but struggled to compete when open commerce returned in 1815. The young nation's postwar shipping business surged, but sailors preferred stronger Russian-made cordage, even at higher prices. This preference led American shipbuilders and U.S. Navy officials, who believed American methods weakened the final product, to torpedo planters' efforts to receive tariff protection. With hemp used largely for bagging cotton and prices thus overly dependent on raw cotton prices, growers struggled to find alternate domestic markets, urging Congress for higher duties against Baltic competitors and for internal improvements to link their fields and factories to eastern markets. Congress acquiesced in the 1820s, but that and a revived cotton trade in the mid-1830s brought only temporary relief. In the 1840s, the rapid expansion of the jute and abaca (also known as Manila hemp) trade from India and the Philippines pushed global hemp prices even lower.[10]

Sugar planters, concentrated in southeast Louisiana and small in number due to the considerable capital investment necessary, began the century with a bleak forecast, but the emancipation of slaves elsewhere provided them new opportunities. At the close of the eighteenth century, British and French colonies led by Jamaica, Barbados, and especially Saint Domingue controlled over 75 percent of international sugar production, with North American producers statistically insignificant. Violence associated with the Haitian Revolution in Saint Domingue precipitated a "dramatic transformation of the world sugar industry" that inaugurated several decades of "British hegemony."[11] Emancipation in 1834, however, dropped British West Indian production by over 13,000 metric tons, and those colonies' market share fell from 47.4 percent at the end of the 1810s to 24.8 percent by the early 1840s. Cuban slave owners primarily benefited, but American planters greatly expanded their foothold in domestic markets that tariff protection had created in the 1820s. Largely due to their embrace of new technologies and flexible approaches to slave labor, U.S. sugar growers raised their total production from 161 million pounds in 1837 to 900 million pounds in 1854, claiming a quarter of total world production.[12]

Cotton planters emerged as the largest and—because of the crop's profitability and toll on the soil—most broadly dispersed group of Southern agrarians. Their rise was an improbable one, especially because it relied on trade with sworn British enemies whose vast empire and commercial connections provided them a number of potential alternative suppliers. An early boom in the late 1790s, however, demonstrated the crop's viability, especially the luxury long-staple Sea Island variety, and helped lift South Carolina's and Georgia's economies out of their post-Revolutionary funk. War with Britain, cotton's chief consumer, threatened the nascent international trade, but peace in the North Atlantic after 1815 opened up a second boom, eventually stretching production of short-staple varieties from the Carolina Upcountry, across the Deep South states of Georgia, Alabama, and Mississippi, and into the trans-Mississippi regions of Louisiana, Arkansas, and Texas. By the 1830s U.S. cotton made up over half of the value of all national exports and provided well over half of the world's total production, including over three-fourths of the raw cotton imported into Britain. These facts led British manufacturers, politicians, and antislavery humanitarians to fret about their overdependence on a Southern slavocracy and to redouble their efforts to grow supplies in India.[13]

Cotton barons were not passive recipients of this strategically important position. On the contrary, both as individual economic actors who optimized output and as a collective political interest that entered the fray in major national controversies, including Indian removal and slavery's expansion, cotton planters worked to create and protect their status. Though occasionally upset about fluctuating prices and their reliance on Northern merchants and financiers, they eagerly accepted global interdependence and after 1816 argued for ever-freer trade, largely because contemporary accounts suggested that global demand for raw cotton generally outpaced supply.[14] The crop's centrality for international trade and the sheer number and wide distribution of republican-minded growers gave cotton planters a degree of political power unprecedented amongst other agricultural interests in the South or, for that matter, the world. Explaining their and other Southern planters' relative success (or lack thereof) requires not just understanding the market conditions they faced, but also how they micromanaged the resources necessary to meet them.

Mastering the Field as Innovators and Organizers

Profits and a determination to catch up with or keep ahead of global competitors provided powerful incentives to experiment with new seeds, mechanization, and labor practices. Being successful abroad, in short, required being creative risk takers at home. For planters of most crops, this meant investment in technology; but new scholarship indicates that often-overlooked biological innovations proved just as critical as mechanical ones for successful agricultural development. Rather than undermining slavery, these innovations reinforced the region's economic and psychological commitment to an institution that provided planters the capital, mobility, and control necessary to ensure a central place in global commodities markets.

New technologies were a gamble, and planters had to weigh the pros and cons of experimentation. Hemp planters generally found extra labor expenses more cost effective than new tools and machines, believing, as one journalist noted in 1859, that "a stout negro man, with a good hand brake, a fair task before him, and prompt pay for his overwork, . . . has a decided preference, if not a complete monopoly" on breaking and cleaning Kentucky hemp.[15] Planters of other crops, however, strategically invented and deployed technology. Confronting rising sugar and slave prices, Louisiana planters invested massive capital in new technologies such as a steam-exhaust vacuum technique perfected by a Louisiana-born and Paris-trained free black, Norbert Rillieux, that increased production of a purer (and therefore higher-priced) sugar with less fuel. To transport cane to and from these sophisticated mills, planters built elaborate systems of conveyor belts and mechanized cane carriers that are perhaps best described as "prototypes of the modern line-production system."[16] Tobacco planters also resorted to new technologies, hoping to make their commodity's quality attractive enough to overcome European tariffs. After 1830 planters adopted improved flues and thermometers for better-cured leaves and used new flavoring techniques to promote brand loyalty. Such innovations, which often blurred the lines between agricultural and industrial production, allowed them to remain dominant in the global smoking and snuff business.[17]

Even some rice planters, generally known for resisting change, compensated for lower prices with higher output by turning to steam-powered machinery to save the labor of manually pounding and thrashing rice. In 1833 Roswell King installed a steam-powered pounding machine on Butler Island off the coast of Georgia, which he and local planters purportedly kept running for over twelve hours a day. By the 1840s, steam-powered thrashers further quickened the process, leading planters like Charles Manigault to express "great relief" and "pride" in the "triumphal performance" of the "iron Beater" they had entrusted to enslaved millers and artisans. These changes—along with close supervision by his son, a Yale graduate recently returned from the Far East and Latin America—helped Manigault net handsome profits despite a depressed market and incompetent overseer.[18]

Although such expensive machines often remained concentrated in the hands of the wealthiest planters, their rental to credit-strapped small planters and yeomen proliferated their usage. That these and other less-costly devices were commonplace across the plantation South reflected a willingness to embrace innovation not qualitatively different from northwestern farmers who purchased plows and mechanical reapers. Joyce Chaplin, in her path-breaking study of eighteenth-century lower South agriculture, was thus right to see planters as "cautious denizens of the modern age," but wrong to conclude that they increasingly retreated from it after 1815.[19] Especially as slave prices peaked in the late antebellum period, slave owners realized it was in their interest to purchase labor-saving devices, less to replace the slaves they owned than to more effectively deploy them towards cultivation-centered tasks not yet profitably mechanized.

Indeed technological advancements actually increased demand for new land and slave labor on cotton plantations. Continually improving cotton gins, created more by white and black Southern experimentation than by Eli Whitney's "Yankee" ingenuity, greatly accelerated the price and quantity of slaves destined for fields in the Deep South. The biggest labor-saving and production-enhancing development in the cotton South came not from mechanization but from planters' successful seed hybridization. In 1846, South Carolina planter Whitemarsh Seabrook identified at least fifteen subvarieties of Sea Island cotton. Crossbreeding had an even greater impact inland where the mixing of native and Mexican varieties in the 1820s, most famously Mississippi planters Dr. Rush Nutt's Petit Gulf seed and Henry Vick's One Hundred seed, created cotton plants that ripened earlier, had higher lint-to-seed yields, and produced a bigger, more easily picked bulb. Because seeds were not generally patented, their use spread and begat new experiments. A close study of 142 cotton plantations suggests that these new varieties (especially well-suited for fresh southwestern lands) more than quadrupled the per-day picking efficiency of slaves between 1801 and 1862. Further aiding productivity, southwestern planters relied heavily on allegedly more docile female field hands, who cost two-thirds the price of their male counterparts but proved to be at least as effective pickers. This productivity and a price spike in the 1850s provided wealthier planters the need and the means to install more efficient and expensive steam-powered gins and balers.[20]

Planters who experimented with new seeds, tinkered with Rillieux's techniques, or purchased more advanced tobacco flues were validated in (and proud of) the recognition they received at annual county and state fairs and at national and international exhibits. Cotton growers, in particular, could boast about being at the forefront of their field and celebrate the *New York Times* observation that no exhibit at the New York Great Exhibition in 1853 "exercised greater influence upon the civilized world" than the improved Sea Island and Petit Gulf varieties.[21] Self-promotion in a modern age, however, came at the cost of emulation and increased competition. As such, the *Southern Quarterly Review* was flattered and concerned with a British Foreign Office attempt to bring Southern planters to East India, noting that the introduction of superior Southern techniques among an entire Indian people "in a state of slavery" would present the U.S. planter with a worthy challenge.[22]

This anxiety, made all the more real given the history of European protectionism, reinforced the need to embrace the most scientific management of slaves possible. Former Louisiana slave Charley Williams vividly remembered his and other masters' regulatory predilections: "When the day began to crack, the whole plantation break out with all kinds of noises . . . and you can hear a old bell donging way on some plantation a mile or two off, and then more bells at other places and maybe a horn. . . . All we knew was go and come by the bells and horns! Old ram horn blow to send us all to the field."[23] As Mark Smith has shown, the need to increase slavery's productivity and maximize profits made Southern planters among the most eager purchasers of watches and arguably the first agrarians to transition away from "natural" time to "clock time."[24]

Timepieces alone could not ensure that slaves would live up to planters' expectations, however, and planters famously struggled to balance coercion and reward. The lash, or its threat, joined other fear-inducing strategies, ranging from public humiliation and limited rations to the sale of a loved one, along a gamut of psychological and physical horrors employed on the plantation. Recent scholarship on slavery complicates other aspects of the traditional picture, however, suggesting that older bifurcations of slave organization into "gang" and "task" systems fail to reveal the diversity of labor strategies. Driven by market calculations, seasonal patterns, and fear of slave resistance, cotton planters, for example, blended gang and task methods and tailored specific jobs towards the strengths of individual slaves or groups of slaves.[25]

The extent of slaves' de facto property ownership and slave society's "internal economy," though partly resulting from theft, also indicate that many of the South's "labor lords" recognized the value of compensating slaves in goods or cash to incentivize quality and, especially during the busy harvest time, extra work.[26] Individual or collective garden plots were perhaps the most commonly offered rewards. An equally revealing tactic, however, was the use of "overwork," or incentive systems that paid slaves in cash, goods, or privileges for extra time worked and which according to Richard Follett, "fused a manipulative management style with an idealized notion of the master-slave relationship." The overwork system was a central feature of hemp and sugar plantations, especially at the height of harvesting and processing time. Profit-seeking planters who engaged in this practice seemed willing to risk giving slaves more autonomy and a peek at the real value of their labor, subtly using such opportunities (and the threat of their abolition) to compel the labor necessary to increase their bottom line.[27]

The efficiency and implications of slave labor, especially when compared with freer labor practices in the North and in Europe, will remain debated. Yet comparisons with free-labor options available in the South indicate slavery's economic effectiveness, as studies of Virginia's wheat industry suggest. During the 1850s output per laborer on slave plantations in Virginia's Piedmont region increased with each additional slave; it was twice and in some instances nearly four times higher than on free-labor farms. While the expansion of wheat into new northwestern states had reduced the South's per capita share of the national business from 35 to 29 percent between 1839 and 1859, a Virginia wheat renaissance allowed it to surpass Pennsylvania and lead the nation in overall production.[28] Such efficiency suggests that Northern Free-Soilers' fears of slavery spreading into the Great Plains were not ill-founded.

While intranational judgments certainly informed U.S. planters' world-view, they also placed great value in global commercial statistics, drawing their own comparisons to overseas competitors. Hemp growers had readily available evidence that free labor, in northern Europe and in Southeast Asia, produced ample amounts of higher-quality hemp at cheaper prices, perhaps explaining their less rigid commitment to slavery's permanency. Rice planters could have drawn the same conclusion but persisted in their fatalistic belief that only coercion could maintain and harvest rice in the Lowcountry. Tobacco planters found comfort in the fact that their leaves remained the preferred choice of middle- and upper-class Europeans.

Deep South sugar and cotton planters found even less reason to question slavery's alleged superiority. Sugar planters had directly benefited from emancipation on Francophone and Anglophone Caribbean islands. Cotton planters, aware of free labor competition in India and Africa, eagerly highlighted that their continued dominance had forced a dependent status on European powers, who admitted as much when they virtually ended efforts at discrimination in the 1840s. That Brazil, the second largest slaveholding region, had been the second-leading cotton producer in the 1830s and that Cuba, with its 350,000 slaves, emerged as the leading sugar-producing region by mid-century only confirmed Deep South planters' predisposition to see slavery as a structural strength rather than weakness. The measurable drop in the market share of postslavery societies together with Africa's limited growth—though actually evidence of self-initiative and resistance to the brutal plantation system— appeared to racist U.S. tobacco, sugar, and cotton planters (and many European merchants) as proof of slavery's success at getting allegedly "lazy" persons of color to cultivate tropical and semitropical crops on a massive scale.

Whatever effects slavery had on the region's embrace of large-scale manufacturing, its effectiveness in agro-industrial pursuits are not easily disputed. Planters' legally protected right to command people as property allowed them to transport labor wherever it seemed most profitable and to organize it, more or less, as they saw fit. Investors in labor, land, and (when

needed) technology, Southern planters had a degree of microeconomic control that other nineteenth-century capitalists would have envied.[29] Unfortunately for them, however, antebellum planters were neither as dominant, nor
necessarily as united, in the national political arena as has occasionally been
assumed.

Planters' Political Economies

Once appreciated, the market behavior, modern practices, and diversity of
Southern planters force us to reconsider deeply held assumptions about how
they viewed government activism and federal protection—policy preferences
too often interpreted as markers of a "modern" mindset. While older histories
asserted that planters feared an activist state, some newer ones increasingly
contend that planters desired a stronger state. In reality the degree of government activism sought depended on which level of government and for what
purpose. Nearly every planter proved willing to empower local, state, and (as
the debates over abolitionist mailings and the fugitive slave acts reveal) even
national officials with the policing powers necessary to preserve slavery.[30] Their
commitment to use government to deprive slaves of liberty (and conversely
their fear that Northern officials might use it to liberate them) did not mean
that planters envisioned no positive role for the state in creating economic
opportunity, especially at the state or local level.

As John Majewski has recently shown, Southern desire to optimize agricultural production led planters and reformers to seek a greater role for state governments in resource management and subsidizing agricultural surveys,
journals and colleges. They hoped that these state-sponsored efforts would
ameliorate the highly acidic and comparatively malnourished soil, the region's
chief agricultural problem and one not solved until commercially available fer-
tilizers became widely available later in the century. Southern planters more
heavily and successfully relied upon state and local governments to plan and
pay for internal improvement projects aimed at linking fields to commercial
ports and towns. Of the nearly quarter billion dollars estimated to have been
invested in Southern railroads prior to 1860, 57 percent came from public
sources, compared to a nationwide average of between 25 and 30 percent.
Though planters invested considerable time and private capital in these transportation projects, the smaller amount of private commercial capital available
in the South required them to turn to activist states to pursue their modernizing agenda. The political challenge planters faced was convincing nonslave-
holding majorities that such enterprises were worth precious tax dollars.[31]

A brief examination of tariff and commercial policies indicates that support for federal government activism in the economic realm varied considerably depending on a crop's particular market circumstances. In the case of Southern planters, as the earlier discussion of rice planters indicates, pragmatism generally prevailed over dogmatism. At one time or another, Southern planters of all crops benefited—or sought to benefit—from federal commercial regulation. This was especially true early on as Jeffersonians pursued discriminatory duties against foreign shipping, largely hoping to curtail European mercantilist policies. What varied was the depth and trajectory of their support for fostering a post-1815 nation-centered home market, the relative forgetfulness of earlier federal assistance, and the degree to which different planter groups could harmonize interest and a free-trade ideology trumpeted by many contemporaries as the modern ideal.

Different market orientations regularly pitted planters against one another in political combat. Throughout the antebellum era, upper South hemp growers remained heavily dependent on the national market and increasingly hopeful that they would find new consumers of rope and ropewalks in the burgeoning urban towns and cities in the North and West. Yet their fervent advocacy of an American system to support that effort drew the ire of cotton planters, their main consumers, who saw tariffs on hemp bagging as a shameless attempt to ensure a monopoly. Until the 1850s, Louisiana sugar and cotton planters waged a fierce intrastate political battle over the relative merits of protectionism. Adding to the drama was the fact that, especially after the 1830s, many economic reformers, as well as the South's emerging middle class of artisans and manufacturers, believed protective tariffs would assist their own businesses and nascent manufacturing.[32]

Planters' competing views of how the national economy benefited (or failed to benefit) the antebellum South's agrarian interests proffer important, though not determinative, insights into the political dynamics surrounding the political crisis of the 1850s and secession. Though tobacco planters had been vocal opponents of protectionism in the 1820s, by the mid-1840s continued frustration with their treatment in international circles led them to conclude that they needed help from the national government. In 1844 the Virginia state Whig convention pledged to campaign in support of the tariff of 1842, and Piedmont resident William Rives became one of the party's most forceful advocates for raising duties to force better commercial terms within the global economy.[33] This policy preference along with a more diversified manufacturing base kept tobacco farmers and planters open to the beneficial possibilities of federal economic policy and more supportive of the Whig platform, helping to explain that party's endurance within Virginia, Kentucky, and North Carolina. This commitment also led tobacco farmers—along with their hemp-growing neighbors—to express anger at what one 1860 petitioner called the "indifference" with which cotton planters and "other agricultural interests of the United States, content with a free market for their own productions, look . . . upon the burdens imposed upon this friendless staple." The "victim[s] of domestic neglect and of foreign injustice," tobacco planters split blame between New York speculators, free-trading cotton planters, and European protectionists. Neither national nor international political economy provided much optimism or clarity for tobacco planters heading into the secession winter.[34]

Sugar planters, especially well acquainted with the utility of tariffs, partially sympathized. Yet unlike tobacco, global sugar consumption continued to accelerate in the nineteenth century, and international and domestic developments had made growers less dependent on protection or desirous of commercial retaliation. American sugar planters knew they were in the ascendance, explaining perhaps why many coveted Cuba's advanced sugar plantations despite the competition that annexation would introduce into U.S. markets. Indeed, sugar planters and the politicians representing them showed a heightened sense of concern about Northern Free-Soil advances, which informed their understanding of politics. They thus faced the same difficult choices that tobacco planters did in the presidential election of 1860 and in state elections held after Lincoln's victory to consider secession from the union. Understanding the unique tensions facing sugar planters clarifies why their counties of residence disproportionately went for John Bell's Constitutional Unionist ticket in the presidential balloting and then experienced a particularly sharp decrease in voting participation during the following winter's secession elections. Economically optimistic but politically disheartened, sugar planters chose to stay home, suggesting either political paralysis or, as likely, tempered enthusiasm for Southern political independence.[35]

By the 1850s Southern cotton planters had come to a quite different understanding of how the international and national political economies worked, or could work, for them. Despite insisting upon a three-cent per pound duty on raw cotton in the 1790s and relying heavily on the military prowess of the federal government to remove Native Americans and survey and settle the lower Mississippi River valley, they firmly believed protective tariffs would undermine their interests at just the time that Britain and other European powers were welcoming freer trade of American cotton. After the annexation of Mexican lands (especially Texas in 1845) and the passage of the freer-trade Walker Tariff (1846), cotton planters brimmed with confidence. Not dependent on the national market and having experienced severe historical amnesia, many came to view the federal government's activities as hindering their economic development.

Consequently, as the sectional crisis deepened, cotton—a commodity that Constitutional Unionists (many of them former "Cotton Whigs") and Northern Democrats hoped could preserve the union—actually increased the political capital of secessionists, who turned cotton's alleged regal status into an advertisement not only for why the South should secede but for why doing so would benefit the region's economic interest by freeing it from overdependence on Northern merchants.[36]

Cotton planters received timely, if unintended, validation from sources outside the South, perhaps most influentially Thomas Kettell's 1860 unionist appeal, *Southern Wealth and Northern Profits*. Already Kettell, perhaps the nation's most prominent political economist, had delighted the Southern readership of *DeBow's Review* by claiming that cotton "enveloped the commercial world, and bound the fortunes of American slaves so firmly to human progress, that civilization may also be said to depend upon the continual servitude of blacks in America."[37] With the United States facing possible disunion, he now offered a damning attack on Northern antislavery sentiment and financial policy, arguing that slave labor was more advantageous than free labor, that the South's industrial revolution was well underway, and that as a result of her monopolistic position in the raw cotton supply "the South is the master of the position." Quoting European sources emphasizing Europe's dependence on the "slave States of America," Kettell inadvertently elevated secessionists' faith that Europe would allow interest rather than morality to dictate action, even if Republican-controlled Congresses and Republican presidents might not. As his title suggests, he also provided them a catalog of explanations for how the North had purportedly milked Southern agriculturalists of hundreds of millions of dollars.[38]

Secessionists could not have said it better, and they confidently asserted that interdependent European economic partners would offer direct trade and recognition to a confederacy of cotton states. South Carolina cotton planters and merchants like John Townsend and Robert Gourdin showed the way, sweeping up hapless rice planters and more ambivalent white yeomanry into a secessionist furor that culminated in disunion in December 1860. Kindred spirits—in particular, cotton planters from younger plantation regions in Mississippi, Alabama, Texas, Florida, and (after some debate) Georgia and Louisiana—quickly joined the cause. Upper South residents—many tobacco, hemp, and wheat growers—hesitated until the firing of Fort Sumter and Lincoln's response forced their hands.

Crop orientation and international commerce, to be sure, were far from the only—and likely not the determinative—factors leading to secession. They do, however, warrant closer study for those seeking to better explain the contours of antebellum party politics and understand why some slaveholders preferred staying in the union while others did not. Similarly, competing understandings of which policies would best modernize the South's economy carried over into the new Confederacy, where the free-trade propensities of some planters and the semiprotectionist tendencies of others, joined by important pockets of real and would-be industrialists, created remarkable political tension.[39] Though planters remained exceedingly united in their commitment to preserving a nation premised on slavery and defeating the North, the task of balancing the various commercial, manufacturing, and diverse agricultural needs of the aspiring nation practically paralyzed the C.S.A's ability to pursue a constructive— and diplomatically useful—financial and commercial policy. Ironically and fortunately, the war that Southern planters fought to protect and extend their slave-driven pathways to agricultural advancement created the very conditions for destroying them through emancipation. The economic effects of that protracted conflict and its unintended results reverberated throughout an interdependent world economy, both demonstrating the centrality of slavery and the South to international trade and leaving planters, merchants, manufacturers, and officials of various governments fretting over what regional and global progress would look like in a post-emancipation world.[40]

NOTES

1. See, for example, Eugene D. Genovese, *The World the Slaveholders Made: Two Essays in Interpretation* (New York: Pantheon Books, 1969); Erskine Clarke, *Dwelling Place: A Plantation Epic* (New Haven, Conn.: Yale University Press, 2005).

2. For summaries of new scholarship seeking to deprovincialize the South, see Peter Kolchin, "The South and the World," and Anthony Kaye, "The Second Slavery: Modernity in the Nineteenth-Century South and the Atlantic World," *Journal of Southern History* 75 (August 2009): 565–580 and 627–650, respectively; Mark Smith, *Debating Slavery: Economy and Society in the Antebellum American South* (New York: Cambridge University Press, 1999). Planter numbers from the 1860 census as interpreted in James Huston, *Calculating the Value of Union: Slavery, Property Rights, and the Economic Origins of the Civil War* (Chapel Hill: University of North Carolina Press, 2003), 36, 293n22. See also Jacob Metzer, "Rational Management, Modern Business Practices, and Economies of Scale in the Antebellum Southern Plantations," *Explorations in Economic History* 12 (April 1975): 123–150; Stanley Engerman, *Slavery, Emancipation, and Freedom: Comparative Perspectives* (Baton Rouge: Louisiana State University Press, 2007); William Fogel, *Without Consent or Contract: The Rise and Fall of American Slavery* (New York: W. W. Norton, 1989); William Kauffman Scarborough, *Masters of the Big House: Elite Slaveholders of the Mid-Nineteenth-Century South* (Baton Rouge: Louisiana State University Press, 2006).

3. See Christopher Bayly, *The Birth of the Modern World, 1780–1914* (Malden, Mass.: Blackwell Publishing, 2004), chap. 2; Kenneth Pomeranz, *The Great Divergence:*

China, Europe and the Making of the Modern World Economy (Princeton, N.J.: Princeton University Press, 2000).

4. Studies of planters would be well-served to follow the lead of historians of slavery, including Ira Berlin and Philip D. Morgan, *Cultivation and Culture: Labor and the Shaping of Slave Life in the Americas* (Charlottesville: University of Virginia Press, 1993). The effort here adds to James Oakes's emphasis on class-based differences among slaveholders in *Ruling Race: A History of American Slaveholders* (1982; New York: W. W. Norton, 1998), while also suggesting the desirability of revisiting Lewis Gray's *History of Agriculture in the Southern United States to 1860* (1933; repr., Gloucester, Mass.: Peter Smith, 1958).

5. Kaye, "Second Slavery," 627–228.

6. Joseph Clarke Robert, *The Tobacco Kingdom: Plantation, Market, and Factory in Virginia and North Carolina, 1800–1860* (1938; repr., Gloucester, Mass.: Peter Smith, 1965), 132–160.

7. Thomas Roderick Dew, "On Slavery," in *The Proslavery Argument as Maintained by . . .* (Philadelphia: Lippincott, Grambo, & Co, 1853), 292. See also Michael O'Brien, *Conjectures of Order: Intellectual Life and the American South, 1810–1860*, 2 vols. (Chapel Hill: University of North Carolina Press, 2004), 2:942–946.

8. House Select Committee, "Tobacco Trade," 36th Congress, 1st sess., H. Rep. 667 (1860), 1.

9. Peter A. Coclanis, *The Shadow of a Dream: Economic Life and Death in the South Carolina Low Country, 1670–1920* (New York: Oxford University Press, 1989), 133–136, and "Distant Thunder: The Creation of a World Market in Rice and the Transformations It Wrought," *American Historical Review* 98 (October 1993): 1050–1078, esp. 1058–1059.

10. Baltic and Russian producers used a special snow-rotting technique believed to create a stronger rope. A lack of clear or official grading also may have hindered U.S. hemp producers' ability to compete from well-graded European and Asian crops. James F. Hopkins, *A History of the Hemp Industry in Kentucky* (1951; repr., Lexington: University Press of Kentucky, 1998), esp. chap. 3.

11. Dale W. Tomich, *Slavery in the Circuit of Sugar: Martinique and the World Economy, 1830–1848* (Baltimore: Johns Hopkins University Press, 1990), 21.

12. Tomich, *Circuit of Sugar*, 15 (table 1.1); Richard Follett, *The Sugar Masters: Planters and Slaves in Louisiana's Cane World, 1820–1860* (Baton Rouge: Louisiana State University Press, 2005), 21–22; Wendy Woloson, *Refined Tastes: Sugar, Confectionary, and Consumers in Nineteenth-Century America* (Baltimore: Johns Hopkins University Press, 2002).

13. On cotton and its spread, see Brian Schoen, *The Fragile Fabric of Union: Cotton, Federal Politics, and the Global Origins of the Civil War* (Baltimore: Johns Hopkins University Press, 2009), chap. 1; Adam Rothman, *Slave Country: American Expansion and the Origins of the Deep South* (Cambridge, Mass.: Harvard University Press, 2005); James David Miller, *South by Southwest: Planter Emigration and Identity in the Slave South* (Charlottesville: University of Virginia Press, 2002). For statistics and global perspective, see Stuart Bruchey, *Cotton and the Growth of the American Economy,*

1790–1860: Sources and Readings (New York: Harcourt, Brace & World, Inc., 1967), table 3.K; Louis Billington, "British Humanitarians and American Cotton, 1840–1860," *Journal of American Studies* 11 (1977): 313–334.

14. James A. Mann, *The Cotton Trade of Great Britain: Its Rise, Progress, & Present Extent* (1860; repr., London: Frank Cass & Co, 1968), 40 (table 1).

15. *Kentucky Farmer* 1 (1859): 138, cited in Hopkins, *Hemp Industry*, 60.

16. Follett, *Sugar Masters*, 33–34, 102 (quotation), 122; John Alfred Heitmann, *The Modernization of the Louisiana Sugar Industry, 1830–1910* (Baton Rouge: Louisiana State University Press, 1987), 8–48.

17. Julia A. King, "Tobacco, Innovation, and Economic Persistence in Nineteenth-Century Southern Maryland," *Agricultural History* 71 (Spring 1997): 207–236; Barbara Hahn, "Making Tobacco Bright: Information, Institutions, and Industrialization in the Creation of an Agricultural Commodity, 1617–1937" (Ph.D. diss., University of North Carolina, 2006), 54–104.

18. William Dusinberre, *Them Dark Days: Slavery in the American Rice Swamps* (Athens: University of Georgia Press, 2000), 9; Charles Manigault to James Haynes, January 1, 1847, in *Life and Labor on Argyle Island*, ed. James M. Clifton (Savannah, Ga.: The Beehive Press, 1978), xxxvi–xli, 44–45 (quotation).

19. Joyce Chaplin, *An Anxious Pursuit: Agricultural Innovation and Modernity in the Lower South, 1730–1815* (Chapel Hill: University of North Carolina Press, 1996), 357.

20. Angela Lakwete, *Inventing the Cotton Gin: Machine and Myth in Antebellum America* (Baltimore: Johns Hopkins University Press, 2003). On seed hybridization, see Alan Olmstead and Paul Rhode, *Creating Abundance: Biological Innovation and American Agricultural Development* (New York: Cambridge University Press, 2008), and "Biological Innovation and Productivity Growth in the Antebellum Cotton Economy," National Bureau of Economic Research (NBER) Working Paper 14142 (2008); Chaplin, *Anxious Pursuit*, 221. On labor, see Gavin Wright, *Slavery and American Economic Development* (Baton Rouge: Louisiana State University Press, 2006), 105–112; Daniel S. Dupre, *Transforming the Cotton Frontier: Madison County, Alabama, 1800–1840* (Baton Rouge: Louisiana State University Press, 1997); Schoen, *Fragile Fabric*.

21. *New York Times*, July 26, 1853, cited in Olmstead and Rhode, "Biological Innovation," 17.

22. "East Indian Cotton," *Southern Quarterly Review* 1 (April 1842): 457–459. See Schoen, *Fragile Fabric*.

23. Cited in Keumsoo Hong, "The Geography of Time and Labor in the Late Antebellum American Rural South: *Fine-de*-Servitude Time Consciousness, Contested Labor, and Plantation Capitalism," *International Review of Social History* 46 (2001): 4n.

24. Mark M. Smith, "Old South Time in Comparative Perspective," *American Historical Review* 101 (1996): 1432–1469.

25. Steven F. Miller, "Plantation Labor Organization and Slave Life on the Cotton Frontier: The Alabama-Mississippi Black Belt, 1815–1840," in Berlin and Morgan, *Cultivation and Culture*, 199; John Hebron Moore, *The Emergence of the Cotton Kingdom in the Old Southwest: Mississippi, 1770–1860* (Baton Rouge: Louisiana State University Press, 1988), 78–80, 95–98.

26. See Larry E. Hudson, Jr.'s contribution to this volume and essays in Ira Berlin and Philip D. Morgan, eds., *The Slaves' Economy: Independent Production by Slaves in the Americas* (Portland Or.: Frank Cass, 1991).

27. Follet, *Sugar Masters*, 5 (quotation), 140–142, 196–210.

28. James Irwin, "Exploring the Affinity of Wheat and Slavery in the Virginia Piedmont," *Explorations in Economic History* 25 (Fall 1988): 298.

29. On the importance of slavery as a property right, see Wright, *Slavery and American Economic Development*, 83–122; Huston, *Calculating the Value of Union*.

30. Sally E. Hadden, *Slave Patrols: Law and Violence in Virginia and the Carolinas* (Cambridge, Mass.: Harvard University Press, 2001), esp. 105–166.

31. John Majewski, *Modernizing the Slave Economy: The Economic Vision of the Confederate Nation* (Chapel Hill: University of North Carolina Press, 2009), esp. 32–38; Milton Heath, "Public Railroad Construction and the Development of Private Enterprise in the South before 1861," *Journal of Economic History*, supplement 10 (1950): 41, and *Constructive Liberalism: The Role of the State in Economic Development in Georgia* (Cambridge, Mass.: Harvard University Press, 1954), 239–53; J. Mills Thornton III, *Politics and Power in a Slave Society: Alabama, 1800–1860* (Baton Rouge: Louisiana State University Press, 1978); Tom Downey, *Planting a Capitalist South: Masters, Merchants, and Manufacturers in the Southern Interior, 1790–1860* (Baton Rouge: Louisiana State University Press, 2006); James A. Ward, "A New Look at Antebellum Southern Railroad Development," *Journal of Southern History* 39 (August 1973): 409–420.

32. Edward Stanwood, *American Tariff Controversies in the Nineteenth Century* (Boston: Houghton, Mifflin, 1903), passim.

33. Michael Holt, *The Rise and Fall of the American Whig Party: Jacksonian Politics and the Onset of the Civil War* (New York: Oxford University Press, 1999), 167. For one of many examples, see "Tobacco Trade with Europe," 30th Congress, 1st sess., H. Rep. 810 (1848).

34. House Select Committee, "Tobacco Trade," 36th Congress, 1st sess., H. Rep. 667 (1860), 1; Robert, *Tobacco Kingdom*, 155–157, 227–233.

35. Peyton McCray, Clark Miller, and Dale Baum, "Class and Party in the Secession Crisis: Voting Behavior in the Deep South, 1856–1861," *Journal of Interdisciplinary History* 8 (Winter 1978): 452, 456; Charles P. Roland "Louisiana and Secession," *Louisiana History* 19 (Autumn 1978): 389–399.

36. Schoen, *Fragile Fabric*, 237–259.

37. "The Future of the South," *DeBow's Review* 21 (September 1856): 308–323.

38. Thomas Prentice Kettell, *Southern Wealth and Northern Profits*, ed. Fletcher Green (1860; repr., Tuscaloosa: University of Alabama Press, 1965), 32, 34.

39. Richard Franklin Bensel, *Yankee Leviathan: The Origins of Central State Authority in America, 1859–1877* (New York: Cambridge University Press, 1990), 175–176.

40. Sven Beckert, "Emancipation and Empire: Reconstructing the Worldwide Web of Cotton Production in the Age of the American Civil War," *American Historical Review* 109:5 (December 2004): 1405–1438.

PART II

Slavery in a Modernizing Society

4

"A Disposition to Work": Rural Enslaved Laborers on the Eve of the Civil War

Larry E. Hudson, Jr.

"any child, white or black, of ordinary capacity, may be taught, in a few weeks, to be expert in any part of a cotton factory. . . ."
—William Gregg, 1845[1]

A still-popular explanation for the lack of industrial development in the pre–Civil War South is that the mass of enslaved agricultural workers, devoid of any talent for industrial employment, confined the region to traditional labor systems with only minor excursions into economic diversity and industrial development. For some time historians have linked the South's labor system with a persistent premodern economic outlook. More recently, however, a more focused examination of the work and economic activities of enslaved agricultural workers on the eve of the Civil War has revealed a distinct bent toward the modern, suggesting that the absence of a modern-minded workforce provides an unsatisfactory explanation for the South's industrial underdevelopment.[2] Over the last decade or two the scholarship on Southern slavery has revealed not only an abundance of examples of industrial activity on antebellum farms and plantations, but also a noticeable commercial savvy among enslaved workers who participated in an informal or "internal economy": the trading and selling of surplus goods they had produced for themselves in small gardens provided by their owners.[3]

Having succeeded to a remarkable extent in encouraging their workers to "grab a stake" in slavery, masters fought a losing battle to curtail burgeoning entrepreneurship that went from cabin to cabin and throughout the wider cabin community as bondmen and bondwomen expanded the terrain of work and mastered new tasks on farms and plantations and in villages, towns, and cities.[4] By the eve of the Civil War, the South's enslaved workers had or were acquiring the economic and market skills necessary to advance their interests in a slowly modernizing South.[5] Constituting an increasingly flexible labor force eager to acquire new skills and opportunities, these laborers are more usefully examined as a distinct and growing group of Southerners who embraced modernization. Historians need no longer confine their search to a few exceptional instances; recent scholarly focus on the activities of enslaved workers suggests that the distance—geographical, economical, and social—between skilled and unskilled workers and between town and country was shrinking as more and more enslaved people, taking advantage of diverse work opportunities, found a way into an expanding internal economy. Increasingly sophisticated and incorporating more and more people, goods, and services, the internal economy extended the reach of individuals and cabin communities sufficiently to narrow if not completely erase economic and cultural differences between rural and urban settings, as well as between skilled and unskilled workers. As David Goldfield has shown, the boundary between city and country was indeed "permeable."[6]

Studies of enslaved workers and the internal economy, in raising important questions about slaves' role or potential role in the pace of Old South modernization, have shaken the old image of the South. Despite this, there remains a tendency to identify any industrial activity in the South as exceptional, and the image of agricultural "slave gangs" remains the norm. Given such preconceptions, the thousands of enslaved agricultural workers who made the transition to industrial work have puzzled contemporaries and scholars alike. It has become standard to focus on exceptional individuals, groups, and places while seldom seeking to locate their broader social and economic contexts.[7] Historians of the South have tended to disaggregate the cabin community and its values, separating them by town and country, class and status, despite the fact that such neat divides—sometimes imposed for practical reasons—did not always exist. For even quarters on the most isolated plantations, such as some plantations of central Georgia, could establish and maintain significant economic and social connections with towns and cities.[8] Rather than exceptionalizing outstanding accomplishments by enslaved workers, for example, we would do better to consider enslaved workers on some kind of blurred continuum from artisans and skilled workers (who hired out their time) to the spiritless gang workers (who labored with little respite and few positive incentives). In the broad middle, of course, lay the vast majority whose labor was organized within a task-and-garden system that encouraged the production of extra provisions for themselves.[9]

Over the last two decades the working life of the South's enslaved workers has garnered a good deal of attention, with particular interest in the operation of a task-and-garden system. In its most sophisticated configuration, plantation managers would assign each worker a measured amount of work for a given period of time, usually a working day; once the task was completed the worker was at liberty to tend to his or her small garden, on which the family cultivated a variety of foodstuffs. In addition, provision gardens, which ranged in size from small areas around their cabins to five or more acres in remote corners of the plantation, supplemented the workers' food allowance and provided surplus that could be traded or sold. Although a primary feature on South Carolina and Georgia rice plantations, the practice of tasking spread well beyond the rice-producing regions of the South and encompassed a wide variety of labor activities on the plantation.[10] At its most successful, the task-and-garden system came to represent an acceptance on the part of both enslaver and enslaved of a degree of trust and mutual responsibility. Treating the workers as individuals and giving them responsibility for a particular piece of land, the task system did not require the close supervision usually associated with forced gang labor. Tasked workers were not only expected to complete their assignment, they were expected to do it well. In turn, owners were obliged to respect the workers' "nonwork" time—indeed, this time "became sacrosanct," and the workers' right to use this time as they saw fit (within certain parameters) was duly acknowledged by planters.[11]

The popularity of the task-and-garden system among planters, coupled with the material and spiritual rewards the workers could reap from the system, facilitated its spread to other crops and other regions. The task-and-garden system was, however, only the most sophisticated expression of pervasive work-and-garden-systems under which enslaved workers of all classes and regions were encouraged to work efficiently for their owners first and then for themselves as time became available. As a general rule, enslaved workers throughout the South were allowed time each week to work their own gardens. In addition, former bondsmen recalled having worked "extra" hours on neighboring farms and plantations for which they were paid. Thus, a growing number of enslaved workers were provided, in a variety of ways, with the opportunity to produce food surpluses and earn cash for themselves and their families.[12] The accumulation of food surpluses was the primary means by which enslaved people entered the internal economy, wherein they could engage in the increasingly sophisticated trading of goods and services—commercial activities that expanded to include their fellows in a widening economic and social network of cabin communities, connecting an expanding group of people, enslaved and free, white and black, rural and urban.

The production of extra work performed by ordinary workers was the currency that fueled the underground economy—with all its associated rewards and risks. Armed with a few pounds of cotton, rice, or corn, grown in a cabin garden, the least skilled worker could enter the internal economy and trade his or her goods for a desired item that might otherwise remain out of reach. Importantly, John Campbell writes: "As market participants—who produced, sold and purchased their own property—slaves temporarily experienced one of the central attributes of freedom: the purchase and sale of labor power and the enjoyment of its fruits." Here, then, was a potent challenge to the traditional ways of the rural South—a first, and necessary, step toward modernity. As Joseph Reidy makes clear, by trading a portion of their own produce beyond the plantation, "slaves crossed the boundary into the corrupting world of commerce that most masters wished to keep impermeable." In so doing, they satisfied not only "a variety of material and psychological needs," they also challenged the ideological and legal tenets on which Southern slavery rested. Contained in these numerous, small, bold acts of resistance was an inherent opposition to an oppressive system, under which the enslaved workers' natural instincts toward economic independence and property accumulation were thwarted or, at best, forcefully restricted. Agricultural workers who participated in the internal economy, in challenging the region's dominant values, displayed to their fellows the kind of economic and social value system requisite for workers in a modern (free) society. Furthermore, in discriminating which goods they chose to trade with white Southerners, "some slaves evinced sophisticated market behavior," suggests Jeff Forret, "carefully calculating which items were best suited for trade." To become successful traders in the internal economy, these market participants, with little or no formal training, acquired what Kathleen Mary Hilliard describes as "consumer skills": numeracy, marketing pricing, and debt and credit negotiation.[13]

Emphasizing the work and commercial activities of enslaved people, scholars have challenged many previously held assumptions; there remains a tendency, however, to focus on certain groups, such as those hired out as skilled industrial workers. In contradistinction to the vast majority of the enslaved, these (largely) urban workers reaped economic and psychological rewards denied to their rural fellows and appear, somehow, unconnected with the inhabitants and values of rural cabin communities.[14] It is now abundantly clear, however, that whatever benefits were available to enslaved people on the eve of the Civil War, they were not neatly located within one particular class to the exclusion of all others. Furthermore, as Forret argues, the success of the few at one end of a broad spectrum—the skilled and those who hired their labor—might be shared by the whole as the "sale of their labor enabled all members of the slave community . . . to face their masters as equals in a market shorn of racial, social, and class hierarchies."[15] An enslaved population—knit together by family, race, class, and a common need to restrict its economic and political communication to the trusted among its own—produced a growing black community with expanding geographical boundaries and, as Susan O'Donovan suggests, "the efficacy and power of the networks of subterranean communication that linked quarter to field to workshop." Writing in 1862, Georgia planter Richard F. Lyon described black networks that no doubt were in operation long before the outbreak of war, but which only became visible once the plantation order came under military attack. As Lyon wrote to Georgia governor Joseph E. Brown: "A negro or negroes from any part of the state . . . will meet in Savannah, where the negroes & traitorous white men are in constant communication . . . the negroes there are as fully informed . . . an opportunity will thus be afforded them of talking with one another of their wants & wishes. . . ."[16] The enslaved used their networks of communication and exchange to distribute benefits gained by the skilled elite to the larger slave community. By the eve of Civil War, there were, among the enslaved population, clear indications of a positive disposition to work in order to obtain increased access to an expanding internal economy. At several junctures and on a variety of terrains, some more visible than others, the behavior of the enslaved reflected a decidedly modern outlook as they negotiated their way through the rigors of property accumulation and participation in an increasingly sophisticated internal economy.[17]

Whether or not an individual was a full participant in this clandestine world of the enslaved, it no doubt provided a worldview and ways of understanding self, family, and community different from those typically encouraged by plantation masters. As enslaved people moved from place to place, new ideas and economic and social techniques likely returned with them and filtered into the community. It is not surprising, then, that plantation managers feared "strange Negroes"—never sure what they might bring with them—and took care to keep corrupting influences out of the home place. However, the very demands of plantation management made it virtually impossible for owners to quarantine their enslaved workers from strange, unfamiliar people and ideas. Armed only with the weapon of gossip, then, hired workers and others exposed to more industrial style working relationships with temporary white managers could easily reconfigure work relationships back on the plantation. If, as Charles Dew demonstrates, enslaved ironworkers knowing full well that they could "get the ear of [the] master" by pleading "ironmaster brutality," it seems that in industrial work situations, as well as on farms and plantations, the "slaves' wishes . . . counted for something."[18]

The two scholars most responsible for the recent focus on the labor and economic activities of rural bondmen, Ira Berlin and Philip Morgan, describe work as a double-edged sword for the enslaved, but of crucial importance, as it provided all kinds of positive benefits, the like of which has only recently been explored with any depth and sensitivity. What is now clear is that slaves' broader, and increasingly varied, work experiences shaped the way the enslaved viewed the many terrains on which they labored. For enslaved people throughout the South, work was full of economic, social, and psychological meaning. Placing the world of work of the enslaved at the center helps to better understand the institution itself, as well as the African-American experience under slavery. The cultural and psychological relevancy of the work the enslaved performed for themselves has been elevated above that performed for their owners alone. Increasingly, scholars focus their attention on the emotionally liberating aspects of the enslaved workers' own labor and commercial activities. As Lawrence McDonnell asserts, for example, "few incidents of slave life rivaled market relations for political and psychological meaning. Commodity exchange and property accumulation, however trivial . . . transformed real relations . . . within the slave community itself." Similarly, Roderick McDonald found that their participation in the internal economy "proved cathartic. . . . The dimensions of independence, responsibility, and decision making inherent in the system would, in themselves, have held rewards. . . . [I]t was a source of satisfaction."[19]

This chapter argues in part against the exceptionalization of both the South and enslaved Southerners.[20] It is clear that occupational training was systematically denied rural slaves; only about 6 percent of adult male slaves held occupations above those of agricultural worker. When one considers the social status accrued to the skilled worker from grateful owners, one begins to see a scholarly pattern: exceptionalize those who fared well and critique the vast majority. Clearly an individual was better placed to combat the evils of slavery armed with some skills and specialized know-how, but it is a distortion to suggest that this small group alone had the wherewithal to advance and protect its interests. The concern here is that many scholars have emphasized those singular, consciousness-raising, commercial-exchange experiences—as if they were only rare "moments," fragile and fleeting—with little sense of their broader and cumulative affects on the individual, group, and community. Given that these emotionally powerful moments often extended beyond the individual actors, we should avoid exceptionalizing them at the expense of the larger group. This chapter follows the more recent, alternative scholarly approach and seeks to examine the enslaved on their own terrain and, wherever possible, on their own terms. In this regard, it acknowledges the advice of the late John Blassingame and, more recently, Michael Johnson, who warned against the tendency to create and reinforce artificial divisions among the enslaved people, often self-servingly imposed by slaveholders. Dylan Penningroth has added his plea for an examination of black lives on black terms.[21]

By the eve of the Civil War, measured by the growing number of enslaved people who were involved in diverse work on farms, plantations, shops and factories across the South—from agricultural laborers confined to field work, to nonskilled workers who hired themselves out daily or annually, to fully skilled workers—enslaved workers participated in a Southern economy that was, sometimes reluctantly, acquiring elements of a modern mentality.[22] Much of this change is revealed in the expanding range of enslaved work experiences, and the resulting shift in their attitude to performing work that promised some tangible economic and social reward.

The constant movement of its members, and a growing participation in the internal economy, brought into the cabin community a steady flow of new commodities, new people, and (with them) new ways of thinking about and responding to enslavement.[23] Inasmuch as the more mobile individuals on the plantation (skilled artisans, coachmen, wagoners, messengers) moved between different social spaces, they not only were conduits and purveyors of the ideas, values, and behaviors prevalent in urban settings, but also were themselves concrete evidence of the immediate rewards of industrial work, providing powerful endorsements of the strategies necessary to aspire to similar positions on farms or in towns. Not surprisingly, in his exhaustive study of the mortality schedules of the 1860 U.S. federal census manuscripts, Michael Johnson concludes: "[D]espite skilled slaves' more desirable and rewarding work, the thousands of slave narratives contain no evidence that field hands resented the prerogatives of skilled craftsmen—in vivid contrast to field hands' views of house servants. The narratives' silence about uppity or unworthy skilled slaves suggests that field hands saw craftsmen as more attractive models of behavior than house servants who were expected to bow and scrape."[24]

Hiring and other economic opportunities pursued by the enslaved were often only small steps toward freedom. Those who held any realistic hope of self-purchase had to command incomes sizable enough to persuade owners to enter into arrangements that might bring about that desired end. While artisans and some hired workers could shape their working conditions and enjoy some control over their income—and even accumulate quite considerable sums of money—for the vast majority of enslaved workers, the goal was not self-purchase, but merely the acquisition of desired goods and services and the emotional satisfaction that came with the process that led to their procurement.[25]

As such, a primary result for enslaved people of laboring within work-and-garden systems and participating in an internal economy was an emotional means to improve the quality of their daily lives and so combat the more debilitating aspects of their enslavement. Not surprisingly, then, cabin communities encouraged their members to grab any opportunity to diversify their work routines, learn new skills, and increase their work options. These enslaved workers were predisposed to respond positively to new work opportunities—the more sophisticated, the better.

On cotton farms and plantations there were clear signs of excursions into the industrial sphere. The economic activities of South Carolina's Michael Gramling, a cotton planter who owned thirty-eight bondmen and women, demonstrates the close proximity and easy combination of agricultural and industrial enterprise—as well as the willingness, even desire, of the enslaved to embrace new work experiences. In producing "mudsills" for the local railroad, Gramling's enslaved workers, with some ease, made the transition from agricultural to industrial work. For a felled tree that measured thirty-six feet long by seven inches wide and sixteen inches across the stump, Gramling was paid "at 2 cents the running foot." He delegated this task to two of his workers, Anthony and Tom. The former would be tasked "15 pieces a week" and the latter would be tasked only 12 pieces. "I make this difference," Gramling explained, "because Tom has never hewn before and Anthony has."[26] Like many other masters, Gramling held little fear of industrialization and willingly embraced modernization (manifested in this case by the rationalization of labor time into piece rates), if only on his terms—economic development, "plantation style."

Gramling's encounter with the modern provides only a small-scale example of the ease with which Southern planters could incorporate industrial activities into the rhythm of plantation life. On a much larger scale, Richmond's William Weaver combined his iron-making operations and farming operations, resulting in a "constant interchange of slave labor between industrial and agricultural tasks." Dew suggests that this was the pattern at "furnaces and forges throughout the South." A similar arrangement existed in other industries, most noticeably in textiles. As E. M. Lander pointed out over half a century ago, cotton mills, typically established on or near the plantations, "were financed and run by local planters and merchants, many of whom were large slaveholders." As such, industrialization was more likely to flourish when it accommodated agriculture and was organized as an appendage to and in tandem with the plantation system. Diversification of this kind encountered little opposition from the Southern nationalists and Whigs, who saw no danger in industrialization so long as it remained subordinate to the plantation system.[27]

As important as were the financial rewards that came to rural workers who, like Gramling's Anthony and Tom, performed industrial tasks for the railroad, another significant benefit was the opportunity to interact with others, enslaved and free, who resided in nearby towns and cities. As David Goldfield's study of Richmond's railroads suggests, although many of the bondmen who were owned or employed by the railroad companies worked in the countryside, "they lived in and contributed to the life of the city."[28]

The disposition to work, visible among a growing number of enslaved people on Southern farms and plantations, did not emerge from financial and social rewards alone; a crucial factor was the cabin community's ability to reward productive members and to punish those who spurned opportunities to increase their occupational skills. There are numerous examples of parents and grandparents passing along occupational skills, literacy, and numeracy; some even managed to bequeath their accumulated wealth.[29]

The case of Edward Brown and William Drayton illustrates how some enslaved families and communities provided a social environment that encouraged hard work and property accumulation. Brown, a young man under slavery, had been left a mule by his grandfather and had "used the mule as his own property for two or three years before he left to join the Union Army." Drayton's father had died and "left me the means with which I bought the Jenny mule." His father had entrusted "the means and property he left for his children" to his oldest brother, and Drayton had purchased the mule on the advice of his uncle and paid in three installments: the first was $100 in gold and silver, then a second payment of $50 "all in silver," and a final payment of $100 in "state bank bills."[30] As stunning as might be the extent of property ownership among this family, their attitude towards work, wealth accumulation, and provision for the future are, if nothing else, modern. As rural workers in Beaufort, South Carolina, the actions of the Browns suggests that such modern outlook and behavior among the enslaved were not limited to artisans, skilled, or hired-out industrial workers.

As eager as planters were to find new ways of profiting from their enslaved workers, the enslaved too had an eye to their own economic interests. If the South was to diversify its agriculture and develop more manufacturing, it would require technical flexibility from both enslaver and enslaved. Antebellum masters, however, seemed unclear as to what exactly they desired from their enslaved workers: dependency, talent, versatility, obedience, or merely sufficient flexibility to respond to management's dictates. Renowned agricultural reformer Edmund Ruffin of Virginia was determined to realize the South's independence. Ruffin, however, seems to have been intellectually incapable of recognizing the abilities of his black labor force, which had been trained according to his precise instructions. His biographer suggests that once slavery "became a closed issue," despite overwhelming evidence to the contrary, some planters were unable to accept that their black laborers had the capacity and willingness to learn the new techniques that agricultural reform demanded. Experimenting with a compli- cated fertilization system, Ruffin could not believe that Jem Sykes, his highly competent black foreman, could take responsibility for the new tasks at hand, much less display what were quite basic cognitive skills. He was taken aback to learn that Sykes had had the wherewithal to identify and acknowledge the improvements Ruffin's reforms had brought to the plantation. While gratified that Sykes gave him the credit for the increased productiveness of the planta- tion, Ruffin was nonetheless surprised that "the slave had the wit to do so." He noted that he "did not expect a negro, even one of superior intelligence as he is, to look back to causes so remote, & of such slow & and gradual action." Here was the major obstacle in the way of Southern diversification and improve- ment—a Southern racist mind-set from which naturally followed an inability to "see" black intellectual and mental capacity, and the determination that "slavery was necessary to make blacks work."[31] Of course, planters like Ruffin were not unique; and, in all fairness to them, enslaved people often deliberately hid their skills and talents from a white world unaccustomed to black people straying too far from their traditionally assigned, intellectually subordinate roles.

A short account of slavery written in the 1920s by Susan Bradford Eppes, the daughter of a former slaveholder, reveals the concealed talents of several enslaved people and the kinds of work they performed on a regular basis under white supervision—work that often went unrecognized, unacknowledged, and unrewarded. Eppes recounted the story of Henry Fort, who had worked as "stoker for the engineer" in the mill. Once the white workers had enlisted in the Confederacy, the expectation was that the mill would have to close. Henry, however, asked permission to "fire up." He was told that it would be of no use to "fire up without an engineer," to which Henry replied that he had been "a'studyin' an' a'studyin' on dat ingin' a long time—an' I kin run her jis' as well as John Grady." Furthermore, the stoker informed "Marse Ned," "me an' Mac an' Peter kin run dat whole concern if you will keep the books an' will let us pick out de helpers we wants." According to Eppes, Master Ned was both "surprised and pleased, but also somewhat doubtful." Questioned as to their ability to run the mill, Henry repeated that he ran the engine as well as the white engineer, John Grady, adding that Peter "is run the saw fur Wheeler when you didn't know nuthin' erbout it—an Mac is jis' as good a miller as you want to see." Mrs. Eppes reported that the "new force was put on, to their great joy, and barring a few, a very few, mistakes, all went well."[32] For whatever rea- son, many white Southerners found it difficult to concede that black, enslaved labor could be "as well adapted to mechanical employment as to agriculture."[33] Despite these attitudes, we can only imagine the satisfaction felt by Henry, Mac, and Peter at their ability to "run dat whole concern." Both these examples reveal the desire and ability of the enslaved to perform complicated industrial tasks, as well as the lengths to which many had to go in order to convince their owners that, as a racial group and as individuals, they had the mental capacity and predisposition to perform a wide range of agricultural and industrial tasks. As John Blassingame suggests, many would have looked to and found the recognition and reward for their skills and talents in their own community—both the quarters and the broader cabin community.

An increasingly diverse work life and its associated benefits triggered a mind-set that included a disposition to work and a value system in antebellum cabin communities that elevated those who worked hard and provided much-needed goods and services for their families and the community at large. As enslaved workers took advantage of opportunities to expand the range and quality of their working lives and acquire new skills, these cabin communities took on features of the larger, slaveholders' world. On the ever-changing landscape of work and labor, enslaved men and women in cabin communities all across the rural South displayed an economic and social mind-set that was decidedly modern in its benign rebellion against traditionalism as well as in its pragmatism.

In the last decades before the Civil War, few enslaved people were in a position to purchase themselves and/or their family members. As such, it serves no useful purpose to gauge their economic success solely on markers such as the ability to self-purchase. Far more significant was the multilayered meanings that certain kinds of work held for the enslaved as individuals and as a community. As Christopher Morris has suggested, by serving the economic interests of their owners, the enslaved not only took steps toward advancing their own interests, but they also embraced some of the language and practices, if not the underlying values, prevalent in the public world of their owners. For example, ex-slave Albert Todd recalled that "work was a religion we was taught." In many regards, the enslaved were instinctively and often deliberately modern. The values of the marketplace, absent interference from disgruntled white slaveholders, offered to the enslaved the promise of self-realization, if not freedom; even if the poorest enslaved person stumbled into the commercial arena, he or she would have found a means to participate as equal members in an exchange of goods and services and, as a consequence, to experience the associated psychological benefits. Without these opportunities, short of violent rebellion, the enslaved population would have been ill-equipped to pursue their own economic and social interests.[34]

Much of the recent scholarship provides evidence of a disposition among enslaved plantation workers to work themselves away from, if not out of, slavery's worst elements. As such, decades before the outbreak of the Civil War, these people were well prepared to make the transition to a more diversified agriculture on home farms and plantations and to industrial labor in the South's factories and mines. Not surprisingly, and in large part as a result of this disposition to labor, there was little delay in the Confederacy's ability to rev-up its industrial machine.[35]

Most slaveowners (and not a few scholars today) were convinced that "illegal" goods fueled the internal economy. As their commercial activity became increasingly sophisticated, the internal economy expanded and attracted more "clients." Whatever their background or location, these people could exploit their work opportunities to participate in an economy that promised a widening variety of rewards.[36] Of course, not everyone who traded goods did so with honestly acquired items. In the absence of legal access to a stake in the internal economy, some were tempted to use other methods. Not surprisingly, the line between honest work and illegal behavior was sometimes blurred.[37]

Antebellum court trial records reveal a clandestine world that exposes much about the values and desires of enslaved men and women.[38] The latter group, though too often excluded from discussions of "skilled" workers and similarly under-represented in the antebellum court records, nevertheless, also engaged in the internal economy to improve their economic and social position. For example, women armed with tailoring skill could provide extra income for themselves and their families. Trial records also reveal the extent to which the internal economy rested on a principle of free-market transactions—here, work was directly exchanged for compensation. Daniel and Abram, charged in Spartanburg with stealing two bushels of wheat from Reverend Thomas Curtin and two more from their master, explained how they transported the wheat to the house of Sally and how Daniel "sold her a part of it for sewing." The theft of property provided Daniel with the means to pay Sally for her skills—he traded the wheat for her work. The exchange, here as elsewhere, is a direct, commercial transaction: Daniel "sold" her a part of the stolen wheat "for sewing." No doubt other women, like Sally, provided a crucial service in the internal economy by transforming an easily recognizable item into a more nondescript but more valuable commodity.[39] The creation of widely valued commodities delivered not only cash but also pride and satisfaction for those who made and sold them. These psychic rewards of the internal economy were embedded elements of a modern consciousness that not only fuelled the internal economy, but also shaped the attitude of the enslaved to their own work—and the very idea of work itself as a means to a desired end. The male's everyday need for what might be termed "female skills"—sewing, tailoring, and doc-toring—rendered women like Sally a far greater presence in the cabin community and its internal economy than their white counterparts in the formal economy.[40] This pattern helps explain the complementary, egalitarian character of marriages among the enslaved, described by Deborah Gray White, wherein the male and female roles were "different yet so critical to slave survival that they were of equal necessity." To participate in the internal economy, Sally relied upon these opportunities to market her skills so as to increase her income.[41]

The steady expansion of the antebellum South's economy and the many attempts at agricultural diversification demanded that the enslaved labor force take on new jobs, skills, and responsibilities. In turn, work as artisans, domestic servants, teamsters, and the like offered slaves opportunities and with it a broader "vision" of the world around them—a world that ever expanded as members took on new responsibilities. The more skilled slaves became, the more likely they were to be hired out, further exposing them to a larger, changing world.

Southern slaveholders, bombarded both externally and internally by a rapidly modernizing world, had the difficult task of monitoring and controlling economic and social changes while trying to keep from their enslaved populations those ideas and habits that threatened the authority of the so-called master class. In general, they failed as the ideas and practices which, through these newly skilled and modern-minded workers, infused the internal economy, and argued powerfully argued against human inequality and slavery. On the eve of the Civil War, for the vast majority of the enslaved, the overwhelming disposition was to work. From the Brown family who looked to the future and bequeathed funds to their descendants, or to the majority who looked to more immediate realization of their extra efforts via their internal economy, the enslaved were positively disposed to labor demands placed before them, so long as they promised some economic and social reward. If there was an obstacle to the spread of market culture throughout the South, it was the region's political and intellectual elite, not the enslaved.

NOTES

1. William Gregg, *Essays on Domestic Industry or, An Inquiry into the Expediency of Establishing Cotton Manufactures in South Carolina* (Charleston, S.C.: Burges & James, 1845), 21.

2. Winfred B. Moore, Jr., Joseph F. Tripp, and Lyon G. Tyler, eds., *Developing Dixie: Modernization in a Traditional Society* (New York: Greenwood Press, 1988), 31–44.

3. Betty Wood, *Women's Work, Men's Work: The Informal Slave Economies of Lowcountry Georgia* (Athens: University of Georgia Press, 1995), 2.

4. Lawrence T. McDonnell, "Money Knows No Master: Market Relations and the American Slave Community," in Moore, Tripp, and Tyler, *Developing Dixie*, 31–44; Roderick McDonald, *The Economy and Material Culture of Slaves: Goods and Chattels on the Plantations of Jamaica and Louisiana* (Baton Rouge: Louisiana State University Press, 1993), 79. On the various incentives used to instill in the enslaved workers a "Protestant ethic," see Robert William Fogel and Stanley L. Engerman, *Time on the Cross: The Economics of American Negro Slavery* (Boston: Little, Brown, 1974), 147. The "cabin community" lay at the heart of the broader neighborhood community in which enslaved people interacted socially and economically with one another, as well as with free black and white people. It was, as John Blassingame described, the major source of values such as mutual cooperation, service to the community, and respect for family and place. The cabin community was the very pulse of the expanding neighborhood described so well by Anthony Kaye. See Blassingame, *The Slave Community: Plantation Life in the Antebellum South* (Oxford: Oxford University Press, 1979); Anthony Kaye, *Joining Places: Slave Neighborhoods in the Old South* (Chapel Hill: University of North Carolina Press, 2007).

5. Kathleen Mary Hilliard, "Spending in Black and White: Race, Slavery and Consumer Values in the Antebellum South" (Ph.D. diss., University of South Carolina, 2006); David E. Paterson, "Slavery, Slaves, and Cash in a Georgia Village, 1825–1865," *Journal of Southern History* 75 (November 2009): 879–930.

6. David Goldfield, *Region, Race and Cities: Interpreting the Urban South* (Baton Rouge: Louisiana State University Press, 1997), 106; Kaye, *Joining Places*, 151.

7. Shearer Davis Bowman, "Industrialization and Economic Development in the South," in *Global Perspective on Industrial Transformation in the American South*, ed. Susanna Delfino and Michele Gillespie (Columbia: University of Missouri Press, 2005), 84; Charles B. Dew, "Disciplining Slave Ironworkers in the Antebellum South: Coercion, Conciliation, and Accommodation," *American Historical Review* 79 (April 1974): 393–418; Midori Takagi, *"Rearing Wolves to Our Own Destruction": Slavery in Richmond, Virginia, 1782–1865* (Charlottesville: University of Virginia Press, 1999).

8. Paterson, "Slavery, Slaves, and Cash," 884; Susan O'Donovan, *Becoming Free in the Cotton South* (Cambridge, Mass.: Harvard University Press, 2007).

9. Paterson, "Slavery, Slaves, and Cash," 928. See also Ira Berlin and Philip Morgan, eds., *Cultivation and Culture: Labor and the Shaping of Slave Life in the Americas* (Charlottesville: University of Virginia Press, 1993), 1–48; Larry E. Hudson, Jr., *"To Have and to Hold": Slave Work and Family Life in Antebellum South Carolina* (Athens: University of Georgia Press, 1997).

10. Philip D. Morgan, "Work and Culture: The Task System and the World of Low Country Blacks, 1700 to 1860," *William and Mary Quarterly* 39 (October 1982): 566, 575. See also Hudson, *"To Have and to Hold,"* chap. 2; Marie Jenkins Schwartz, *Birthing a Slave: Motherhood and Medicine in the Antebellum South* (Cambridge, Mass.: Harvard University Press, 2006), 12.

11. John Campbell, "As 'A Kind of Freeman'?: Slaves' Market-Related Activities in the South Carolina Upcountry, 1800–1860," in *The Slaves' Economy: Independent Production by Slaves in the Americas*, ed. Ira Berlin and Philip D. Morgan (London: Frank Cass, 1991), 162, 146.

12. McDonald, *Economy and Material Culture*; Richard Follett, *The Sugar Masters: Planters and Slaves in Louisiana's Cane World, 1820–1860* (Baton Rouge: Louisiana State University Press, 2005), 120–123; Sharla M. Fett, *Working Cures: Healing, Health, and Power on Southern Slave Plantations* (Chapel Hill: University of North Carolina Press, 2002); Berlin and Morgan, *Cultivation and Culture*, 1–48; Hudson, *"To Have and to Hold."*

13. Campbell, "As 'A Kind of Freeman'?" 131; Joseph P. Reidy, "Obligation and Right: Patterns of Labor, Subsistence and Exchange in the Cotton Belt of Georgia, 1790–1860," in Berlin and Morgan, *Slaves' Economy*, 154;. Jeff Forret, "Slaves, Poor Whites and the Underground Economy of the Rural Carolinas," *Journal of Southern History* 70 (November 2004): 792, 803; Hilliard, "Spending in Black and White," 85, 89.

14. James C. Cobb, *Industrialization and Southern Society, 1877–1984* (Lexington: University Press of Kentucky, 1984), 8; Claudia Goldin, *Urban Slavery in the American South, 1820–1860: A Quantitative History* (Chicago: University of Chicago Press, 1976), 121. Goldin identifies a close correlation between increasing demand for agricultural slaves and a decline in the urban population.

15. Jeff Forret, *Race Relations at the Margins: Slaves and Poor Whites in the Antebellum Southern Countryside* (Baton Rouge: Louisiana State University Press, 2006), 199.

16. Lyon quoted in O'Donovan, *Becoming Free*, 80.

17. According to Charles Ball, enslaved people looked for opportunities to leave their owner's fields to find paid work opportunities elsewhere, especially on Sundays. Charles Ball, *Fifty Years In Chains* (New York: Dover Publications, 1970), 166, 187,272, 275; John Campbell, "As 'A Kind of Freeman'?: Slaves' Market-Related Activities in the South Carolina Upcountry, 1800-1860," in Ira Berlin and Philip D. Morgan, eds., *The Slaves' Economy: Independent Production by Slaves in the Americas* (London: Frank Cass, 1991), 131, 134, 135; and Christopher Morris, "The Articulation of Two Worlds: The Master-Slave Relationship Reconsidered," *Journal of American History* 85 (1998): 982–1007.

18. See Berlin and Morgan, *Slaves' Economy*, 1; McDonnell, "Money Knows no Master," 79; Follett, *The Sugar Masters*, 199. My concern here is that McDonnell and others tend to identify those consciousness raising commercial exchanges moments, but often only as "moments" fragile and fleeting with little sense of their broader and cumulative affects on the group and the community. Given that these emotionally powerful moments could extend beyond the individual actors we should avoid exceptionalizing them and the individuals involved at the expense of the larger group. As Morris makes clear, "the interests of masters and slaves often overlapped and reciprocated." See Morris, "The Articulation of Two Worlds, 986.

19. McDonald, *Economy and Material Culture*, 79; Berlin and Morgan, *Slaves' Economy*, 1; McDonnell, "Money Knows No Master," 79; Follett, *Sugar Masters*, 199.

20. This tendency is evident in the work of Roger Ransom and Richard Sutch, *One Kind of Freedom: The Economic Consequences of Emancipation* (New York: Cambridge University Press, 1977), 15. More recently, see John Majewski, *Modernizing a Slave Economy: The Economic Vision of the Confederate Nation* (Chapel Hill: University of North Carolina Press, 2009), 155–156.

21. John Blassingame, "Status and Social Structure in the Slave Community: Evidence From New Sources," in *Perspectives and Irony in American Slavery*, ed. Harry P. Owens, (Jackson: University Press of Mississippi, 1976), 137–188; Michael P. Johnson, "Work, Culture, and the Slave Community: Slave Occupations in the Cotton Belt in 1860," *Labor History* 27 (Summer 1986): 325–355; Dylan Penningroth, *The Claims of Kinfolk: African American Property and Community in the Nineteenth-Century South* (Chapel Hill: University of North Carolina Press, 2003), 7.

22. See, for example, David L. Carlton and Peter A. Coclanis, *The South, the Nation, and the World: Perspectives on Southern Economic Development* (Charlottesville: University of Virginia Press, 2003).

23. Anthony E. Kaye, "'In the Neighborhood': Towards a Human Geography of U.S. Slave Society," *Southern Spaces*, September 3, 2008, http://southernspaces. org/2008/neighborhood-towards-human-geography-us-slave-society (accessed October 2010).

24. Johnson, "Work, Culture, and the Slave Community," 348.

25. Jonathan D. Martin, *Divided Mastery: Slave Hiring in the American South* (Cambridge, Mass.: Harvard University Press, 2004); Dew, "Disciplining Slave Ironworkers," 393–418.

26. Michael Gramling, Plantation Journal, entry for March 1846, South Carolin-iana Library, University of South Carolina, Columbia. Susie King Taylor, *A Black Woman's Civil War Memoirs: Reminiscences of My Life in Camp with the 33rd U.S. Colored Troops, late 1st South Carolina Volunteers* (1902; repr., New York: Arno Press, 1968), 176. Evidence from the economic activities of the enslaved from the sugar regions is in Follett, *Sugar Masters*, 122, 123; McDonald, *Economy and Material Culture*, 60.

27. Industrialization and the use of skilled black workers were widely embraced when Southern planters merely extended the geography of the plantation economy to incorporate and invest in industrial activities. See E. M. Lander, "Slave Labor in South Carolina Cotton Mills," *Journal of Negro History* 38 (April 1953): 161–173, 164; Charles B. Dew, *Bond of Iron: Master and Slave at Buffalo Forge* (New York: W. W. Norton, 1995), 30. For a more recent example, see Majewski, *Modernizing a Slave Economy*, 107.

28. Dew, "Disciplining Slave Ironworkers," 396. See also Goldfield, *Region, Race and Cities*, 108.

29. Hilliard, "Spending in Black and White," 85, 89.

30. Testimonies of William Izzard, claim no. 10096 (1876), and E. Brown, claim no. 21768 (1876), Southern Claims Commission, Approved Claims, 1871–1880, Records of the Accounting Officers of the Department of the Treasury, record group 217, boxes 236–244, National Archives, Washington, D.C. See also Ira Berlin et al., *Freedom: A Documentary History of Emancipation, 1861–1867*, series 1, vol. 1: *The Destruction of Slavery* (Cambridge: Cambridge University Press, 1985), 140–141.

31. William M. Mathew, *Edmund Ruffin and the Crisis of Slavery in the Old South* (Athens: University of Georgia Press, 1988), 57, 59, 206, 181; Eugene D. Genovese, *The Political Economy of Slavery: Studies in the Economy and Society of the Slave South* (New York: Pantheon Books, 1965).

32. Susan Bradford Eppes (Mrs. Nicholas Ware Eppes), *The Negro of the Old South: A Bit of Period History* (Chicago: Joseph G. Branch, 1925), 108–109.

33. Robert R. Russell, "The General Effects of Slavery upon Southern Economic Progress," *Journal of Southern History* 4 (February 1938): 48. See also Dew, *Bond of Iron*.

34. Christopher Morris, "The Articulation of Two Worlds: The Master-Slave Relationship Reconsidered," *Journal of American History* 85 (December 1998): 982–1007; Johnson, "Work, Culture, and the Slave Community," 325 (Todd quoted); Takagi, *"Rearing Wolves to Our Own Destruction,"* 2.

35. Morgan, "Work and Culture"; Hudson, *"To Have and to Hold"*; Bruce Levine, *Confederate Emancipation: Southern Plans to Free and Arm the Slaves During the Civil War* (New York: Oxford University Press, 2006), 62.

36. See Larry E. Hudson Jr., "'All that Cash': Work and Status in the Slave Quarters," in *Working Toward Freedom: Slave Society and Domestic Economy in the American South*, ed. Larry E. Hudson Jr. (Rochester, N.Y.: University of Rochester Press, 1994), 77–94. Peter Berger seems to have anticipated these outcomes; as he noted, modernity has a tendency to fundamentally uproot "beliefs, values, and even the emotional texture of life." See Berger, *Facing Up to Modernity: Excursions in Society, Politics, and Religion* (New York: Basic Books, 1977), 107.

37. Alex Lichtenstein, "'That Disposition to Theft with which They Have Been Branded': Moral Economy, Slave Management, and the Law," *Journal of Social History* 21 (Spring 1988): 413–440; McDonnell, "Money Knows No Master," 31–44; Eugene D. Genovese, *Roll, Jordan, Roll: The World the Slaves Made* (New York: Pantheon Books, 1974), 608.

38. Anderson Magistrates and Freeholders Court, case 176, December 30, 1845, South Carolina Department of Archives and History, Columbia. For the operation and organization of the Magistrates and Freeholders Court, see Philip Racine, "The Spartanburg District Magistrates and Freeholders Court, 1824–1865," *South Carolina Historical Magazine* 87 (October 1986): 197–212.

39. Spartanburg Magistrates and Freeholders Court, case 102, September 3, 1849, South Carolina Department of Archives and History, Columbia.

42. For distinctions between "informal" and "formal" economies, see Wood, *Women's Work, Men's Work*, 2–3.

41. Fett, *Working Cures*; Blassingame, "Status and Social Structure," 151; Anne Firor Scott, *The Southern Lady: From Pedestal to Politics, 1830–1930* (Chicago: University of Chicago Press, 1970); Diana Ramey Berry, *"Swing the Sickle for the Harvest is Ripe":* *Gender and Slavery in Antebellum Georgia* (Urbana: University of Illinois Press, 2007); Deborah Gray White, *"Ar'n't I a Woman?": Female Slaves in the Plantation South* (New York: W. W. Norton, 1985), 158.

5

Rethinking the Slave Trade: Slave Traders and the Market Revolution in the South

Steven Deyle

After arriving in South Carolina via an overland coffle of slaves in chains, the former slave Charles Ball recalled how "in the State of Maryland, my master had been called a *negro buyer, or Georgia trader*, sometimes a *negro driver*; but here, I found that he was elevated to the rank of merchant, and a merchant of the first order too; for it was very clear that in the opinion of the landlord, no branch of trade was more honourable than the traffic in us poor slaves." Moreover, according to the person who housed them, Ball's trader was "a public benefactor, and entitled to the respect and gratitude of every friend of the South."[1]

There was much truth in this South Carolinian landlord's viewpoint, at least as far as the white South was concerned. Many slave traders were merchants of the first order, who possessed important marketing skills that most slave owners found useful. Few were the slaveholders who did not seek the aid of these businessmen at least once when necessary. Slave traders likewise provided an important service to the region by introducing elements of the nation's emerging market economy into Southern society. Often encompassed under the umbrella term, "market revolution," the first half of the nineteenth century witnessed a major transformation in American life, with advances in transportation, communications, and industry, as well as the creation of new regional and national markets. One of the most important engines driving this development in the South was the new domestic slave trade and its creation of a region-wide market in slaves. As with the market revolution in the North, this traffic, and especially the men who operated it, helped to encourage market activity in all subregions of the South and make speculation in commodities a greater part of people's everyday lives.[2]

It is hard to overemphasize the crucial role that slave traders played in the economic development of the South. Most important, they infused a significant amount of capital into the Southern economy each year. Between 1820 and 1860, interregional slave traders averaged roughly $11 million worth of sales each year. To conduct their businesses, they relied upon an array of supporting personnel, such as bankers, factorage houses, lawyers, doctors, clothiers, provisioners, blacksmiths, insurance companies, and shipping agents. This ancillary activity drew more people into the marketplace and pumped at least another $1.5 million into the Southern economy each year. In the four decades preceding the Civil War, the interregional slave trade generated, on average, more than $12.5 million worth of business each year (and roughly $18 million each year during the 1850s). Furthermore, unlike the money that came from the production of cotton, which only flowed into certain subregions of the South, the cash associated with the slave trade poured into every county in the slaveholding states.[3]

Many of the men who made their living by buying and selling slaves also ventured into other aspects of the new market economy. While it was common for slave traders to work as farmers or planters during the off-season, a large number of them engaged in other business activities, such as owning general stores and buying and selling other types of commodities. Not only did they speculate in humans, but slave traders bought and sold real estate, livestock, bonds, and all types of stock, including bank, railroad, telegraph, insurance, and manufacturing. The versatility of such men can be seen in the report that the credit agency R. G. Dun & Co. gave of the South Carolinian Thomas Weatherly, calling him "quite a bold speculator. Besides merchandise he deals in slaves, Kentucky horses, mules and swine" and "is decidedly a man of bus[iness] talents."[4]

Many of the more successful slave traders likewise played leading roles in diversifying market development in the South. In New Orleans, the former butcher turned leading slave auctioneer Joseph Beard was a part-owner of the *New Orleans Commercial Bulletin*, the city's foremost commercial newspaper. Others promoted internal improvements. In North Carolina, the former slave trader Joseph Totten became the president of a local turnpike company; in Virginia, Francis Rives used his slave-trading wealth and political influence to build and manage railroads. Some even became important entrepreneurs and venture capitalists. By the time of his death in 1853, the South Carolinian and former slave trader John Springs III had one of the more extensive investment portfolios in the nation. Among other things, he was an early investor in the largest textile mill in the South.[5]

In no Southern city did slave traders play a more prominent role in supporting the new market economy than Charleston, South Carolina. During the 1850s, traders Thomas Ryan, Thomas Gadsden, Philip Porcher, and T. S. Heyward all served as directors or vice presidents of banks; Porcher also served as a director of the Santee Canal Company. Traders Louis DeSaussure and Alonzo White served as directors of the Charleston Gas Light Company. The economic success of slave traders likewise allowed them to play a major role in the city's social and benevolent societies. Porcher and DeSaussure were stewards at the Charleston Jockey Club, and fellow trader Ziba Oakes was a prominent Mason and Odd Fellow. He served on both the Committee of Charity and the Committee of the Cemetery for the city's Masonic Grand Lodge, as well as being the Grand Treasurer for his local lodge; in addition, he was an officer for the city's Grand Lodge of the Independent Order of Odd Fellows.[6]

This image of modern, entrepreneurial businessmen and prominent social figures is not the one that comes to mind when most people today think of Southern slave traders. The common stereotype is that of the fictional trader Dan Haley in Harriet Beecher Stowe's *Uncle Tom's Cabin* (1852). As Stowe portrayed him, Haley was an uncouth and unprincipled man who, according to one character, "would sell his own mother at a good per centage—not wishing the old woman any harm either." This caricature of slave traders as unscrupulous peddlers had acceptance in both the antebellum North and South. For Northerners, the slave trader came to symbolize all of the evils associated with the Southern slave system, especially turning of human beings into property, or things, that could be bought and sold at will. Therefore, these men, along with the domestic slave trade in general, played an important role in the abolitionist attack against slavery.[7]

Southern slave owners likewise expressed their abhorrence of this individual, at least in the abstract. Their professed contempt for the slave trader, however, had more to do with the need to defend their slave system to the outside world than with any real uneasiness about the transactions they performed. During the nineteenth century most Southern slave owners saw their human property as valuable commodities and willingly bought and sold tens of thousands of these people each year. They also frequently employed the services of professional slave traders to help them increase their profits. Still, to defend their system from abolitionist attacks, especially those concerning the buying and selling of slaves, Southern slaveholders created a stereotyped slave trader, a fantasized individual, whom they could blame for these sales. This supposedly manipulative social outcast became the perfect scapegoat for all of the system's ills. Slave owners liked to present the view that they themselves were loving paternalists who never parted with their black families (slaves); however, since a certain number of sales could not be denied, they claimed that a handful of bad apples (slave traders) sometimes forced them to part with their people against their will. Luckily, according to the slave owners, these evil slave traders were always few in number and only marginal to the Southern slave system. They were likewise of the lowest social classes and shunned by polite society.[8]

Unfortunately, the prevalence of this stereotype, as well as the deplorable nature of this business, has continued to influence our view of the men who worked in this trade. Moreover, our tendency to speak of the slave trader in generic terms perpetuates the idea that these men were somehow all the same. By doing so, we continue our own misleading stereotype about these men. In fact, slave traders were not all the same. They came from all parts of the South and from all social classes in society, from the wealthiest, oldest families to the most hardscrabble backgrounds on the western frontier. It is also impossible to describe their "typical" work activities. Some had offices in cities, others were itinerants who drifted from place to place, and many worked as brokers, auctioneers, financiers, or slave hirers. Simply put, slave traders were as varied as the "typical" merchant. Subsequently, their place in Southern society was based not on their occupation, but mostly on their social class. There is no denying that there were thousands of men who fit the stereotype as depicted by Harriet Beecher Stowe. Many of these men were of the lower classes, some even swindlers and outright criminals. Naturally, they were looked down upon by most respectable people in Southern society. But there were also men, like the individuals in Charleston, who traveled in the uppermost circles of their communities. While these latter individuals constituted only a tiny fraction of the people who made their living from the slave trade, they always remained their industry's leaders. This proved true not only in the number of slaves they handled each year but also in their introduction into the trade of modern business practices. They were among their region's pioneers in market development; smaller and midsized traders who strived to be successful adapted their commercial innovations.[9]

Therefore, instead of fitting a misleading if comforting stereotype, slave traders varied considerably and included many individuals who were leading advocates for the new business practices and values associated with the market revolution. These men created a region-wide market, connecting those areas of the upper South that had a surplus of slaves with those parts of the lower South where slaves were more in demand. They took advantage of all the new innovations in transportation and communications, and introduced many of the new business practices that were revolutionizing American society at the time.

These included developing complex, urban-based enterprises; improving accounting techniques for recording profits; and classifying slaves of differing ages, sexes, and abilities into standardized commodities for easier purchase and retail. They stimulated sales through their creative marketing practices and customer service. Most important, their effective use of advertising not only sold thousands of men, women, and children each year but also helped to increase the desire for, and dependence upon, cash in Southern society. Their successful business activity encouraged even more Southerners to speculate in this valuable commodity, providing them with capital to expand their investments in other markets.[10]

The slave-trading firm that best exemplified these new market values and proved to be the most successful in implementing them was Franklin & Armfield. Founded by Isaac Franklin and John Armfield in 1828, by the time the elder Franklin retired in 1835 their company and its affiliates had become one of the largest business operations of any kind in the South, far surpassing all but the largest cotton or sugar plantations in annual revenue. While their actual income is impossible to know, in 1834 the firm held $400,000 in accounts receivable, an especially high figure considering that most slave traders liked to sell for cash or easily convertible paper. At the time of Franklin's retirement, Armfield was said to be worth $500,000, and contemporaries referred to Franklin as a millionaire, which was probably true.[11]

Like other large businesses in the new market economy, the firm understood the importance of trustworthiness in attracting customers. Franklin & Armfield established elaborate urban offices at both ends of its operation. Armfield controlled the purchasing of slaves in Alexandria, which at that time was still in the District of Columbia. He then shipped the slaves to Franklin, who did the selling in New Orleans, Louisiana, and in Natchez, Mississippi, the two most important slave-trading centers in the lower Mississippi River valley. By making themselves permanent members of their communities, these traders developed confidence in their customers, who subsequently felt more comfortable bringing them their business.[12]

Franklin & Armfield's most entrepreneurial business innovation involved purchasing and operating its own vessels in the coastal trade. In the beginning, the company provided shipping service on boats initially owned by others. The firm, however, quickly recognized the financial advantages of owning its own vessels and reinvested its profits to purchase three brigs: the *Tribune*, the *Uncas*, and the self-titled *Isaac Franklin*, which it had constructed expressly for this trade. Eliminating the middlemen not only cut the partners' charges for shipping but also gave them an advantage in the buying market. The money that was saved on transportation allowed Franklin &

Armfield to offer more for its purchases than did its competitors and still make a profit.[13]

One major reason for Franklin & Armfield's success was its adaptation of a shipping innovation that was transforming business practice in the North; the firm offered the relatively new service of "packet lines." The first American packet line was the Black Ball Line, which began regular service between New York City and Liverpool in 1818. Franklin & Armfield was one of the first businesses in the South to offer this service, beginning in 1833. Unlike the method of previous vessels, which did not sail until they had a full cargo, a packet line was guaranteed to sail at a specified date, whether it was full or not. Naturally, this led to some cut in profits since few of the company's boats sailed full. The *Tribune* was capable of holding up to 180 slaves (100 men and 80 women), but most of the firm's ships left port with only 75–100 on board. Rarely did the cargo exceed 150. But the partners made up for this loss in revenue by attracting more customers with their reliable shipping schedules.[14]

Franklin & Armfield also drew customers for its packets with effective advertising. Notices reassured patrons that its boats were "all vessels of the first class, commanded by experienced and accommodating officers" and that every effort would be "used to promote the interest of shippers and comfort of passengers." The success of Franklin & Armfield's packet service can be seen in the rapid growth of its fleet, as well as in the increased frequency with which the ships sailed. In 1833, its advertisements stated that its boats would leave Alexandria "every thirty days throughout the shipping season," which began in October and lasted until April. Two years later, the partners moved their schedule to start service on September 1 and announced that one of their *"Alexandria and New Orleans Packets"* would "leave this port on the 1st and 15th of each month throughout the season."[15]

As with other expanding American businesses during the market revolution, Franklin & Armfield maintained a series of complex business relationships to help run their extensive enterprise. Isaac Franklin's nephew James Franklin was brought in to assist his uncle in the two main selling markets. At the other end, Armfield supervised a wide network of purchasing agents. By 1833, in addition to several part-time buyers, the company had set up permanent agents in Richmond, Warrenton, and Fredericksburg, Virginia, and in Frederick, Baltimore, Annapolis, Easton, and Port Tobacco, Maryland. Most of these buyers worked on commission. To further increase its purchasing ability, Franklin & Armfield formed a subsidiary-like company with one of its agents, Rice Ballard. This new company was a branch of the larger firm, in which Ballard purchased slaves in Richmond (employing agents of his own) and then sold them through Franklin in the southwest under the name of Franklin,

Ballard & Co. After Franklin's retirement in 1835, the firm reorganized with Ballard moving to Natchez to take on the selling responsibilities until the company eventually dissolved in 1841.[16]

While few slave traders matched the success of Franklin & Armfield, most mirrored their adaptation of the new business practices associated with the nation's market transformation. Especially important were new shipping innovations brought about by the transportation revolution. Although most did not possess their own ships, some traders working near the port cities of the Chesapeake, who had previously transported their slaves to the lower South by overland coffle, found it more convenient to ship their human cargo on ocean-going vessels owned by others in the coastal trade. For traders in the lower Mississippi River valley, the most significant development was the arrival of steamboats during the 1820s. Most large traders in that region, such as John White from Missouri, used these vessels to transport the hundreds of Missouri, Kentucky, and Virginia slaves that they and their agents bought each year to Louisiana and other states in the Deep South. But numerous small-scale traders also made their journeys on steamboats, often stopping in riverbank towns along the way to sell their human goods.[17]

By the 1840s and 1850s, many speculators had also begun transporting their slaves on the region's emerging railroad lines. This advance in technology proved a real boon to slave traders, as it cut both costs and travel time. On Southern trains, slaves rode for half price (the same as children), and most trains carried a "nigger car," which often doubled as the freight or baggage car. One indication of the effect that railroads had on slashing shipping times can be found in the message a trader in southern Virginia sent to his partner in Alabama. Despite having to travel to Richmond first, Philip Thomas could still expect that "in 8 days after I leave home I will be in Montgomery with a fresh lot of negroes." This was almost one-third the time it took via the coastal trade and at least six weeks faster than the premodern and inefficient overland coffle. One month later, Thomas noted that he made the return trip home from Montgomery to Richmond in just fifty-five hours.[18]

Slave traders likewise capitalized on the latest developments in communication, in particular the telegraph, invented in 1844. One of the biggest problems for American businesses before this advancement was the delay in conveying information to associates in other locations. Companies had to depend upon the speed and reliability of the mail or personal couriers, which could often take days, if not weeks, to relay important information. This proved especially troublesome for region-wide businesses like the slave trade, where profits depended upon knowing the latest prices in both the buying and selling markets. As a result, interregional traders continually corresponded with one another to obtain this information and complained when it was not provided to them on time. As one North Carolina trader admonished his partner in New Orleans: "Write often as the times is Criticle & it depends on the prices you get to Govern me in buying."[19]

As telegraph lines spread across the South, slave traders jumped at the opportunity to use this invention to confirm the receipt of letters or money, to inform their partners of their whereabouts, and to decide whether or not to buy another lot and at what price. It even allowed them to assess the profitability of specific purchases. After informing his partner in Alabama of some field hands for sale, one Virginia trader wanted to know if they would turn a profit at their asking price, adding, if so "Telegraph me and I will buy them, if not do not Telegraph and I will understand not to buy." While the availability of the telegraph was limited to those areas with telegraph offices, which naturally benefited the larger urban firms, all traders made use of it whenever possible.[20]

In addition to taking advantage of all the new innovations in transportation and communication, slave traders employed modern accounting practices to record their transactions. Unlike the majority of planters, who merely kept lists of local debts and credits, many slave traders adopted the relatively new method of double-entry bookkeeping for the most accurate accounts. While this technique had been around for centuries, it gained wide acceptance among American businessmen during the early nineteenth century, and Southern speculators proved no exception. In fact, they often paid careful attention to these records. The Savannah dealer William Parker once complained that he had "Been Busy all day looking after 2 cents in the Balance of my Ledger." They also made sure their employees followed suit, and more than one agent had to promise his boss that he would "keep a strict account of all your loosses & Proffitts."[21]

Southern slave traders likewise made frequent use of the financial instruments of the new market economy. Most important, they constantly sought funding from banks to finance their operations and extended their own network of credit to customers. Most speculators preferred to sell their slaves for cash, in part to pay off their own loans but also to avoid the difficulties of collection. Typical was the trader in Mississippi who did "not expect to be able to collect more than 1/3 or 1/2" of his notes. Yet by necessity they were often forced to accept promissory notes if they wanted to make sufficient sales. As one Alabama trader advised, "A good note with interest ought not to be refused." Some traders even capitalized on this practice. Bernard Kendig of New Orleans became quite successful through his liberal credit policies, as did Walter Campbell, another dealer in that city, who began his early advertisements under the heading "Long Credit Sale of Negroes." Speculators then used the cash and commercial paper that they received to pay off their own loans and to obtain more credit to acquire the cash to purchase more slaves.[22]

Furthermore, slave traders had to have a good understanding of the nation's money markets. At a time when the country's main form of currency consisted of discounted bank notes, they had to keep track of the comparative value of the various drafts, in order to deal in those with the greatest acceptability. For that reason, whenever possible, they favored paper from major Northern banks, which generally held its value better nationally than that from local Southern banks. As one Nashville trader remarked after sending his partner some sight drafts on a New York bank, "They are the best funds and safe to Remit." To be successful, then, Southern slave traders needed to follow not only the price of cotton but all of the nation's financial markets as well. Commenting on this occupational habit, a Memphis newspaper noted that one local trader did not speak much about his personal life, but became "very animated on the subjects of dollars, negroes and cotton."[23]

Southern speculators also protected themselves against unexpected loss by taking out insurance policies on the men and women in their stock. A number of traders bought policies when shipping slaves to the Deep South by sea. Others insured against losses when transporting their cargos down American rivers. While marine insurance had been around for a long time, some traders also began protecting themselves against losses caused by sickness and disease. They took out life insurance policies on their slaves, a relatively new financial instrument that had become popular in the South by the 1840s, an indication of how valuable slave property had become by that time. After noting that it was "very sickly here among negroes, 1 or 2 dies every day," the Richmond trader Philip Thomas informed his partner that he was "having all I by [buy] insured." A few even used this protection as a selling point. After announcing his arrival in Natchez with 100 slaves from Virginia and Tennessee, R. H. Elam added that "there is also a Life Insurance on them for twelve months, with policies transferable."[24]

As participants in a long-distance commodity market, where profits were dependent upon prices in divergent parts of the South, speculators likewise needed a way to communicate with their colleagues about the state of one another's markets. Like other brokers in the new market economy, slave traders had to categorize their human merchandise so they could accurately compare their information. Usually this was done by sorting people into classes, such as first-, second-, or third-rate men and women, with boys and girls normally divided according to age or height. One Richmond firm, D. M. Pulliam & Co., even broke the market into twenty different categories, with everything from "No. 1 MEN, Extra" down to "Scrubs," a term that traders used to refer to the elderly, diseased, physically handicapped, or other hard-to-sell individuals.[25]

Finally, Southern speculators made extensive use of advertising to market and purchase their human commodities. One reason for slave traders' success in the exporting states was their heavy reliance upon cash when acquiring their merchandise. In a world where most business transactions were conducted on credit, slave traders were one of the few groups in the South who dealt primarily in cash. Consequently, that became their main selling point. Throughout the upper South, traders filled the newspapers with long-running, bold-type advertisements that blared this point home. "CASH FOR NEGROES" or "NEGROES WANTED" were the most common headings, but the more innovative dealers grabbed readers' attention with phrases like "WHO WANTS CASH!" "HIGHEST CASH PRICE" or simply "CASH! CASH!! CASH!!!"[26]

While all traders stressed the promise of cash when advertising for slaves, they also needed to make their notices stand out from those of their competitors. One dealer on the Eastern Shore of Maryland emphasized his reliability, assuring customers that he was "permanently settled in this market, and at all times will give the highest cash prices." Virtually all traders claimed to offer the highest prices. One St. Louis dealer, Thomas Dickens, played upon these assertions, warning potential sellers to "test the market by giving every buyer a *chance*, and not rely upon advertisements that profess to pay more than others. We *know* that we can and *will* pay as high prices as any other person or persons." The majority of traders likewise pledged responses to all inquiries. In Missouri, the St. Louis firm of Blakey & McAfee was even "prepared to visit persons wanting to sell in any part of the State."[27]

Upon arrival in the lower South, successful traders employed creative advertising to sell their slaves. Almost all notices began with bold-type headings, such as "SLAVES FOR SALE" or "NEW ARRIVAL OF NEGROES." As in the upper South, there were those who tried to stand out with headings like "COME ONE AND ALL WHO WANT NEGROES" and "GREAT EXCITEMENT!! FOUR HUNDRED SLAVES EXPECTED TO ARRIVE BY FIRST NOVEMBER." Others took a simpler but equally effective approach, blaring "SLAVES! SLAVES!! SLAVES!!!" or "NEGROES! NEGROES! MORE NEGROES!"[28]

In their notices, speculators did everything they could to attract business. Like in the exporting states, some stressed their reliability and trustworthiness. Joseph Bruin of New Orleans emphasized that he had been "a regular trader in this city for the last twenty six years." Others in the market went out of their way to accommodate customers. Womack & Martin offered to save patrons a trip, suggesting that "planters wishing to purchase can have their orders filled upon advantageous terms without coming to the city, should they prefer to do so." Conversely, John Smith took his slaves to the planters, advertising that he would "be at Donaldsonville, La., on September 20th, with 100 likely Virginia and Carolina NEGROES." And there were always some who appealed to buyers' pocketbooks. In Natchez, R. H. Elam operated "on the principle that a 'quick penny is better than a slow shilling,'" while the Nashville dealer Reese Porter claimed that he would "sell so cheap you will hardly know the difference between buying and hiring."[29]

Attracting potential customers with good advertising was one thing; getting them to buy was another matter. Or, as one experienced dealer in Savannah put it: "Buyers are like horses, you can offer the bucket *but* can't *make them drink*." Therefore, traders also needed to be good salesmen and work their customers to make a sale. This aspect of the business was best expressed by the former slave Charles Ball, who noted that the speculator who bought him "regarded the southern planters as no less the subjects of trade and speculation, than the slaves he sold to them." Some traders did this by offering special arrangements. In the upper South, they persuaded owners to sell by paying cash during the summer months and letting them keep their slaves until after the crop had been harvested in the fall. Or, they let buyers take an individual home on trial before actually purchasing. Others worked their customers by befriending them with charm and alcohol. Frederick Douglass described the traders he saw in Maryland as "generally well dressed men, and very captivating in their manners. Ever ready to drink, to treat, and to gamble." The former slave William Wells Brown observed that the speculator he worked for "always put up at the best hotel, and kept his wines in his room, for the accommodation of those who called to negotiate with him for the purchase of slaves."[30]

For many slave traders, especially those at the lower end of the trade, working their customers also involved outright trickery and deception. As the former slave John Brown noted, "There are 'nigger jockeys' as well as horse jockeys, and as many tricks are played off to sell a bad or an unsound 'nigger,' as there are to palm off a diseased horse." The most common tactics were fixing up older individuals to look young and outfitting slaves in new clothes. Almost all traders believed that their merchandise would "sell much better for being well dressed," and this was usually the case but not always. At least one man had to inform his client that he "dressed up your negroes and made them look their best but could not screw them up any higher."[31] While such practices might be expected, other traders engaged in much less socially acceptable acts and pawned off individuals with known health problems as sound. One trader in Richmond considered purchasing a "naked headed girl" at a discount, believing that he could "put a fals set of hair on her and sell her for as mutch as if she had it growing." Another buyer in Alabama came home with his new purchase only to find *"that the fellow had no toes on his feet."* The seller had "cunningly stuffed" cotton in the front of the man's shoes "for show."[32]

Because of the reputation that slave traders had for engaging in such unsavory practices, a number of dealers used creative advertising to help improve their public image as honest businessmen. Nathan Bedford Forrest assured customers in Memphis that "that which we promise or say, we guarantee," while, in New Orleans, Thomas Foster made it clear that he conducted his "business in a proper and Strictly Moral manner." Even in tiny Lumpkin, Georgia, J. F. Moses advertised that "being a regular trader to this market he has nothing to gain by misrepresentation, and will, therefore, warrant every negro sold to come up to the bill, squarely and completely." Many speculators also listed references in their advertisements. When the firm of Mosely & Spragins opened a new slave depot in Alexandria, Louisiana, they let it be known that they had "been trading in the Mississippi market for a number of years—and can give the most satisfactory New Orleans references as to their responsibility and character." While most mentioned only local firms, some stressed their national reputation, such as the New Orleans dealer Seneca Bennet, who listed men in Baltimore, Mobile, Norfolk, Charleston, and New Orleans in his notice.[33]

Leading traders consciously strove to project a positive image in their day-to-day dealings with the public. They dressed and conducted themselves in a professional manner. A visitor to John Armfield's office called him "a man of fine personal appearance, and of engaging and graceful manners," while a former Northerner living in Natchez described Isaac Franklin as "a man of gentlemanly address, as are many of these merchants, and not the ferocious, Captain Kidd looking fellows, we Yankees have been apt to imagine them." One visitor to Richmond even noted that the slave auctioneer he met there was "a most respectable-looking person" and "so far as dress is concerned, he might pass for a clergyman or church-warden." Many traders also knew the importance of good customer service. Several were thanked by their clients for their "promptness and Punctuality," and, at least according to his court testimony, one agent working in a New Orleans depot had been instructed by his employer "never to misrepresent negroes and to exchange them any time rather than go to a law suit."[34]

As a result of this public-relations effort, most of the leading slave traders managed to create a reputation of honor and respect. One visitor to Alexandria noted that John Armfield "bears a good character, and is considered a charitable man," while another traveler to that city believed that Armfield had "acquired the confidence of all the neighboring country, by his resolute efforts to prevent kidnapping, and by his honorable mode of dealing." This same reliable observer had earlier visited Austin Woolfolk, a leading dealer in Baltimore, remarking that "the business is conducted by him, and by the other regular traders, in such a manner, that there is never any suspicion of unfairness in regard to their mode of acquiring slaves. In this respect, at least, their business is conducted in an honorable manner." It is important to remember that the vast majority of speculators were not leading traders, nor did they have the same resources or abilities to create such positive public images. In fact, many could have cared less about what others thought of them. Yet, the most successful and market-savvy traders all knew the importance of effective advertising, to promote both their businesses and themselves.[35]

Therefore, while there were plenty of Southern slave traders who fit the commonly held stereotype of such men, there were also many others who resembled modern businessmen. They knew that hard work, a willingness to take risks, and mastery over a new set of commercial skills were the surest way to financial success in the increasingly market-driven American economy. The motivations that attracted these men to the slave trade were not so different from those that drew other men into the business world in the North. They recognized that changes in transportation and communications had revolutionized the way that business could now be conducted. The scale at which their enterprises operated also demanded new practices, like modern accounting techniques and standardization of commodities for easier purchase and retail. They understood the importance of creative marketing tools, especially the effective use of advertising, to increase the demand for their goods and services. And they took pride in their abilities as good salesmen.

Of course, the product these men were selling was not textiles or shoes but enslaved human beings. That is a fact that should never be forgotten. The impact that this trade had on the men and women who were its commodities was unconscionable and the devastating effects it had on them (and the nation) would linger for generations. For Americans today, such traffic seems impossible to understand. Yet, it is important to remember that this country had always held slaves; as property, they had always been bought and sold. The explosion of economic activity that transformed the nation in the early republic affected all forms of property, including slaves. Therefore, it should come as no surprise that this development also led to a heightened commodification of that property and to more effective and pervasive speculation in that commodity by both professional traders and slave owners alike. It was all part of the market revolution that modernized American society in the first half of the nineteenth century.

NOTES

1. Charles Ball, *Slavery in the United States: A Narrative of the Life and Adventures of Charles Ball, a Black Man* (New York: J. S. Taylor, 1837), 86–87.

2. For works discussing the role that slave traders played in promoting the Southern economy, see Edmund L. Drago, ed., *Broke by the War: Letters of a Slave Trader* (Columbia: University of South Carolina Press, 1991), 9; Steven Deyle, *Carry Me Back: The Domestic Slave Trade in American Life* (New York: Oxford University Press, 2005), chap. 4. For other works on the domestic slave trade, see Frederic Bancroft, *Slave Trading in the Old South* (1931; repr., New York: Unger, 1959); Michael Tadman, *Speculators and Slaves: Masters, Traders, and Slaves in the Old South* (Madison: University of Wisconsin Press, 1989); Walter Johnson, *Soul by Soul: Life Inside the Antebellum Slave Market* (Cambridge, Mass.: Harvard University Press, 1999); Robert H. Gudmestad, *A Troublesome Commerce: The Transformation of the Interstate Slave Trade* (Baton Rouge: Louisiana State University Press, 2003). For newer work being done on the domestic slave trade, see the essays in Walter Johnson, ed., *The Chattel Principle: Internal Slave Trades in the Americas* (New Haven, Conn.: Yale University Press, 2004).

3. For a full discussion of the determination of these estimates, see Deyle, *Carry Me Back*, 139–140.

4. Dun & Co. report from the early 1850s, quoted in Michael Tadman, "The Hidden History of Slave Trading in Antebellum South Carolina: John Springs III and Other 'Gentlemen Dealing in Slaves,'" *South Carolina Historical Magazine* 97 (January 1996): 17.

5. Tadman, *Speculators and Slaves*, 192–199; Richard Tansey, "Bernard Kendig and the New Orleans Slave Trade," *Louisiana History* 23 (Spring 1982): 168–169; receipt, July 24, 1855, Totten Papers, North Carolina State Archives, Raleigh (hereafter cited as NCSA); Tadman, "Hidden History of Slave Trading," 6–29; Lacy K. Ford, "The Tale of Two Entrepreneurs in the Old South: John Springs III and Hiram Hutchison of the South Carolina Upcountry," *South Carolina Historical Magazine* 95 (July 1994): 198–224.

6. *The Charleston City and General Business Directory for 1855* (Charleston, S.C.: David Gazlay, 1855), appendix:19–34; Mears & Trunbull, *The Charleston Directory Containing the Names of the Inhabitants, a Subscribers' Business Directory, Street Maps of the City, with an Appendix, of Much Useful Information* (Charleston, S.C.: Walker, Evans, 1859), 250–251, 275; *Directory of the City of Charleston, to which is added a Business Directory, 1860* (Charleston, S.C.: Ferslew, 1860), 33–36.

7. Harriet Beecher Stowe, *Uncle Tom's Cabin; or, Life among the Lowly*, ed. Ann Douglas (1852; repr., New York: Penguin, 1981), 86.

8. Deyle, *Carry Me Back*, chaps. 6–7.

9. Ibid., chap. 4.

10. For a sampling of works exploring other types of market development in the antebellum South, see Jonathan D. Martin, *Divided Mastery: Slave Hiring in the Antebellum South* (Cambridge, Mass.: Harvard University Press, 2004); Jonathan Daniel Wells, *The Origins of the Southern Middle Class, 1800–1861* (Chapel Hill: University of North Carolina Press, 2004); Frank J. Byrne, *Becoming Bourgeois: Merchant Culture in the South, 1820–1865* (Lexington: University Press of Kentucky, 2006); Tom Downey, *Planting a Capitalist South: Masters, Merchants, and Manufacturers in the Southern Interior, 1790–1860* (Baton Rouge: Louisiana State University Press, 2006); and L. Diane Barnes, *Artisan Workers in the Upper South: Petersburg, Virginia, 1820–1865* (Baton Rouge: Louisiana State University Press, 2008).

11. Isaac Franklin to R. C. Ballard, March 10, 1834, Rice C. Ballard Papers, Southern Historical Collection, University of North Carolina, Chapel Hill; Deyle, *Carry Me Back*, chap. 4.

12. Wendell H. Stephenson, *Isaac Franklin: Slave Trader and Planter of the Old South* (Baton Rouge: Louisiana State University Press, 1938), chaps. 2–3; Isabel Howell, "John Armfield, Slave-Trader," *Tennessee Historical Quarterly* 2 (March 1943): 3–29; Gudmestad, *Troublesome Commerce*, chap. 1.

13. *[Alexandria] Phenix Gazette*, October 8, 1828, December 11, 1829, December 18, 1830, February 25, 1831, November 3, 1831, February 15, 1833, April 16, 1833, October 5, 1833, and July 14, 1835; *[Washington, D.C.] National Intelligencer* November 7, 1836, and February 18, 1837.

14. *[Alexandria] Phenix Gazette*, January 4, 1833. For a good account of the transforming effect that packet lines had on the American economy, especially in the North, see George R. Taylor, *The Transportation Revolution, 1815–1860* (New York: Rinehart, 1951), 104–107.

15. *[Alexandria] Phenix Gazette*, October 5, 1833, and July 14, 1835.

16. *[Alexandria] Phenix Gazette*, August 27, 1833. When the firm reorganized in 1835, it took the names Armfield, Franklin & Co. (in Alexandria) and Ballard, Franklin & Co., (in New Orleans and Natchez). Both firms dissolved on November 10, 1841. Articles of Agreement, March 15, 1831, and July 10, 1835, Rice C. Ballard Papers, Southern Historical Collection, University of North Carolina, Chapel Hill; Stephenson, *Isaac Franklin*, 67.

17. John R. White, Slave Record Book (1846–1860), Chinn Collection, Missouri Historical Society, St. Louis; William Wells Brown, *Narrative of William W. Brown, a Fugitive Slave* (Boston: Anti-Slavery Office, 1847), chap. 6.

18. Philip Thomas to William Finney, October 6 and November 8, 1859, Finney Papers, Perkins Library, Duke University, Durham, N.C. (hereafter cited as DU); Eugene Alvarez, *Travel on Southern Antebellum Railroads, 1828–1860* (Tuscaloosa: University of Alabama Press, 1974), 118, 134–137.

19. G. W. Barnes to T. Freeman, November 16, 1839, Slave Trade Papers, Boston Public Library.

20. Philip Thomas to William Finney, January 24, 1859, Finney Papers, DU.

21. Entry for January 2, 1860, Parker Diary, Hargrett Rare Book and Manuscript Library, University of Georgia, Athens; G. W. Eutsler to [Elias Ferguson], August 16, 1856, Ferguson Papers, NCSA; Patricia C. Cohen, *A Calculating People: The Spread of Numeracy in Early America* (Chicago: University of Chicago Press, 1982), 176.

22. Joseph Meek to Samuel Logan, October 9, 1836, Meek Papers, Virginia Historical Society, Richmond; John Forsyth to Henderson Forsyth, February 19, 1837, Forsyth Papers, DU; Tansey, "Bernard Kendig," 166–167; *[New Orleans] Daily Picayune*, December 4, 1853.

23. Joseph Meek to Samuel Logan, March 19, 1835, Meek Papers, Virginia Historical Society, Richmond; *Memphis Appeal*, December 4, 1857.

24. Thomas to William Finney, January 24, 1859, Finney Papers, DU; *[Vidalia, La.] Concordia Intelligencer*, November 26, 1853. For a general discussion of life

insurance and slaves, but not including policies taken out by slave traders, see Sharon A. Murphy, "Securing Human Property: Slavery, Life Insurance, and Industrialization in the Upper South," *Journal of the Early Republic* 25 (Winter 2005): 615–652.

25. D. M. Pulliam & Co., circular, September 1, 1857, Bond Papers, NCSA.

26. *Cambridge [Md.] Chronicle*, February 1, 1834; *Lexington Observer and Reporter*, December 1, 1855; *Cambridge [Md.] Chronicle*, May 23, 1833. For a discussion of the role that merchants advertising cash played in promoting consumerism in the North, see Mary P. Ryan, *Cradle of the Middle Class: The Family in Oneida County, New York, 1790–1865* (New York: Cambridge University Press, 1981), 9.

27. *Centreville [Md.] Times and Eastern-Shore Public Advertiser*, May 4, 1833; *Missouri Democrat*, July 28, 1854; *Missouri Republican*, January 23, 1852.

28. *[Montgomery, Ala.] Confederation*, August 31, 1859; *[New Orleans] Daily Picayune*, October 12, 1859; *[Natchez] Mississippi Free Trader*, February 1, 1859; *[New Orleans] Delta*, January 18, 1857.

29. *[New Orleans] Daily Picayune*, September 19, 1860, July 30, 1853, September 19, 1858, and January 14, 1857; *[Nashville] Republican Banner*, December 24, 1856.

30. Joseph Bryan to Ellison S. Keitt, April 20, 1860, Black History Collection, Library of Congress, Washington, D.C. (hereafter cited as DLC); Ball, *Slavery in the United States*, 93; Douglass, "Speech of July 5, 1852," in *Frederick Douglass Papers*, ed. John W. Blassingame, 5 vols. (New Haven, Conn.: Yale University Press, 1979–1992), 2:374; Brown, *Narrative of William W. Brown*, 53.

31. John Brown, *Slave Life in Georgia: A Narrative of the Life, Sufferings, and Escape of John Brown, a Fugitive Slave*, ed. F. N. Boney (1855; repr., Savannah, Ga.: Beehive Press, 1972), 99; Ethan A. Andrews, *Slavery and the Domestic Slave-Trade in the United States* (Boston: Light and Stearns, 1836), 150; James H. Taylor to Franklin H. Elmore, January 30, 1836, Elmore Papers, DLC.

32. Elias W. Ferguson to [G. W. Eutsler], August 13, 1856, Ferguson Papers, NCSA; John W. Walker to Chapley R. Wellborne, September 20, 1818, Walker Papers, Alabama Department of Archives and History, Montgomery.

33. *Memphis Avalanche*, November 23, 1859; unknown New Orleans paper quoted in *[Boston] Liberator*, November 24, 1854; Moses handbill, November 14, 1859, reproduced in Bertram W. Korn, *Jews and Negro Slavery in the Old South, 1789–1865* (Elkins Park, Pa.: Reform Congregation Keneseth Israel, 1961), 22; *[Alexandria] Louisiana Democrat*, November 16, 1859; *[New Orleans] Daily Picayune*, May 27, 1838.

34. Andrews, *Domestic Slave-Trade*, 136; Joseph H. Ingraham, *The South-west, by a Yankee*, 2 vols. (1835; repr., New York: Negro Universities Press, 1968), 2:245; William Chambers, *Things as They Are in America* (1854; New York: Negro Universities Press, 1968), 284–285; R. O. Harris to E. H. Stokes, December 20, 1862, Chase Papers, DLC; testimony of James K. Blakeney, *Kock & McCall v. Slatter*, no. 1748, 5 La. Ann. 739, (1850), University of New Orleans, Long Library.

35. Edward S. Abdy, *Journal of a Residence and Tour in the United States of North America, from April, 1833, to October, 1834*, 3 vols. (London: J. Murray, 1835), 2:180; Andrews, *Domestic Slave-Trade*, 150, 80.

6

The Pregnant Economies of the Border South, 1840–1860: Virginia, Kentucky, Tennessee, and the Possibilities of Slave-Labor Expansion

James L. Huston

In the sectional conflict, the border states of Delaware, Maryland, Virginia, Kentucky, Tennessee, Missouri, and Arkansas have been the abandoned children of scholarship, writers instead having paid most attention to the plantation states. Neglect of the border South's economic evolution has led investigators to overlook possible economic developments that might have had serious consequences for the non-slave states. This chapter will propose that in the cases of Kentucky and Virginia, and possibly Tennessee, economic development was taking a particularly modern route of urbanization and industrialization that did not at all preclude slave labor but which probably enhanced the border states' demand for slaves.

The reason for reevaluating the border states has much to do with current trends in the historiography dealing with the origins of the Civil War. Recent scholarship questions the rationality of, and hence the motivation behind, the hostile Northern reaction to the slavery issue; some scholars now doubt whether the institution of slavery could have exerted any negative influence on the Yankee way of life. Since 1960, historians have explained Northern anguish over the expansion of slavery in terms of Northern dread of the "slave power"—the control of Congress by slaveholders that produced laws favorable to slave society and inimical to free society—and in terms of free-labor ideology. The present viewpoint is tending to argue that slavery simply could not compete with the free-labor economy of the North, so no real economic antagonism existed. Politically the free states had a two-thirds population majority, and the states entering the union after 1860 (all agree) would be nonslave states; in other words, the imbalance between the North and the South was growing, and so the slave power, if it existed at all, would inevitably be overwhelmed and rendered impotent. Finally, the program of the slave power, never explicitly defined in its details, hardly caused the North any real damage; the North entered a period of vast prosperity between 1830 and 1860, the supposed height of the slave power. In the place of these explanations for the Northern reaction to the issue of slavery, historians have been pursuing two alternatives: First, the battle between North and South was really over an economic program of tariffs, banks, and internal improvements. Second, and probably most prominent, the facet of slavery upsetting Northerners was its morality—slavery increasingly appeared an immoral institution at odds with the Bible and Northern evangelicalism. Scholars are, seemingly, turning to the topics of values and morality to comprehend sectional hostilities—topics based on emotions rather than reason.[1]

Thus, historians who hold that slavery had severely negative consequences for the North must now make their case anew.[2] One argument for slavery's potentially deleterious influence on the North is economic: an expanding Southern economy could have moved slaves out of plantation agriculture and into craft and industrial labor. If slave labor were sufficiently cheaper than free labor, then slave-labor products out of the South could have entered the North, deranging its economy and its society.[3] This latter possibility is the subject of this chapter.

The literature on the border states has altered in the last twenty years, casting the inhabitants of the region as more Northern in their economic and political values than those of the Deep South.[4] Nonetheless, economic studies of the border South have not proliferated, and, except for studies of the subregion of Appalachia, one generally has to rely on an older historiography. While most scholars have recorded economic improvement in the area between 1840 and 1860, they have come to two general conclusions: First, slavery retarded economic growth because the institution created "thin" markets that produced weak demand for nonagricultural goods. Second, the border states were abandoning slavery by the interstate slave trade, selling their slaves to meet the voracious demand of the plantation states. By some accounts, the border states' long-term trend of selling slaves was destined to turn those lands into free states, finally resulting in the border states' having no ties to the remaining slaveholding states and thereby politically weakening these slave states. Realization of this possibility, according to Stephen Deyle, generated bitterness between representatives of the Deep South and the border South.[5]

This chapter will look at the evolution of the economies of Virginia, Tennessee, and Kentucky from 1840 to 1860. The presentation has three components: the creation of a market setting for economic growth based on regional alliances, the calculation of economic growth per capita, and, finally, the potential for cessation of the interstate slave trade and perhaps even its reversal. The essential point is that economic development in the border slave states could easily have expanded employment of slave labor over a wide array of occupations—a possibility that contained deleterious consequences for Northern society because it could disrupt Northern growth by enabling slave-labor products to outcompete free-labor products. The information for this analysis is almost completely derived from the published U.S. federal census reports and is largely numerical.[6]

The Potential Regional Market of the South

The great motor of American economic growth in the nineteenth century was not individual states but the fusing of the economic activities of the New England region, the Mid-Atlantic region (New York, New Jersey, and Pennsylvania), and the Great Lakes region. This alliance became the economic engine of the nation between 1840 and 1930; the Great Lakes supplied agricultural and mineral products to the eastern United States and beyond, while the New England and Mid-Atlantic regions provided investment capital and manufactured goods.[7] The technology enabling that economic alliance was the railroad; the obvious tendency of railroad construction between 1840 and 1860 was to build east to west.

While the east-west alignment of railroad mileage in the North has dominated economic discussion of the national economy, the alignment of Southern railroads has been overlooked or slighted. Just as the Northerners were creating a larger market area by producing a transportation system that operated east to west, Southerners were also developing a larger market area by constructing their railroad system between the border states and plantation states. By the census year of 1850, the entire South had perhaps only 2,100 miles of track completed; by 1860, they had added 7,400 more miles, the bulk of it coming between 1855 and 1860. Southern railroads had manifest deficiencies: they were built more cheaply than Northern lines, they carried less passengers and freight, they lacked skilled labor to maintain them, they were not financial successes, and they ran through unpopulated areas. But as a counterpoint, the Southern railroad network by 1860 was just forming and had only assumed a skeletal shape; Southerners had built their own railroads and owned them; and, moreover, the problems of Southern railroads were hardly novel. Early Northern railroads had many of the same problems, and it took Northerners nearly two decades to overcome them. By benefiting from the Northern experience, Southern railroads might have performed much better in the next decade, had the Civil War not intervened.[8]

The potentials of this internal railroad network need to be spelled out in market terms. The geographical differences were important; the border South had the minerals for economic advancement—lead, coal, iron, and petroleum—whereas the Deep South did not. But the Deep South grew the famous staple crops that the border South mostly could not—cotton, sugar, and rice. Whether the plantation states could grow enough corn, wheat, and other staple crops to feed its own population has been a vexed question in the economic-history literature, but no one doubts the ability of the border states, especially Virginia and Maryland, to produce a surplus of the food crops and to ship them to the cotton states and to overseas markets. The Deep South lacked manufacturing, whereas manufacturing was taking hold and expanding in the border South. Finally, there was a population imbalance, with the border states possessing 7.28 million (including North Carolina, Delaware, and Arkansas) while the plantation states had 4.96 million. Moreover, the border South was experiencing a surge in urban population, indicating the continual growth of nonagricultural activities. Between 1840 and 1860, the percentage of population that was urban (defined here as centers with a population above 2,000 people) grew in Kentucky from 4.5 to 11.1 percent (to 16.3 percent in 1880) and in Virginia from 1.0 to 8.9 percent (to 11.7 percent in 1880); in the same period, however, Tennessee remained an overwhelmingly rural state, with urban population growing only from 0.7 to 1.5 percent (but leaping to 8.8 percent in 1880).[9]

The importance of these resource and occupational imbalances needs to be underscored in terms of market activity. Trade does not occur between regions producing the same product unless there are significant price differentials. Trade occurs where one region has surpluses in products and resources that another region has deficits in. This is why Southern trade routes made little sense in an east-to-west direction; in the Deep South, eastern and western Deep Southerners were growing the same products. The imbalances in resources and outputs in the South lay in the respective subregions of the border South and the plantation South. Trade between these two regions was already well established before the advent of the railroad; but the iron horse was magnifying the possibilities of this Southern trade such that—had there been no Civil War—it might have mimicked, probably with less power, Northern trade between New England and the Mid-Atlantic, on the one hand, and the Great Lakes, on the other. One other aspect of the rising Southern railroad network made a vast augmentation of internal Southern trade possible: in 1860, the network had no links to the North. Only at four points did Southern railroads "touch" the Ohio River: Cairo, Evansville, New Albany-Jeffersonville, and Cincinnati. In 1860, the internal market system of the South was fairly isolated from the North.[10]

Income and Wealth in Kentucky, Tennessee, and Virginia

One way to see how the border states of Kentucky, Tennessee, and Virginia were economically evolving is to estimate state income and per capita income in the various census years. These are, of course, estimates and should be taken as such. However, I devised a methodology and consistently applied it to the census data gathered for 1839, 1849, 1859, and 1879 in order to trace a pattern over time. Because the methodology is consistent for each census year, the pattern over time should be reliable even if the estimates in any given year are not. I created this procedure because the literature lacks these kinds of numbers. For state gross domestic product and state per capita income, there are no figures until 1929, when the Census Bureau began publishing them in *The Statistical Abstract of the United States*.[11]

The results of my calculations are given in table 6.1. Some commentary on methodology is absolutely necessary, although the discussion here will be limited. Important discrepancies—often overlooked—exist between the censuses of 1840, 1850, and 1860. The census of 1840 enumerated people employed in the occupational categories of mining, agriculture, commerce, manufacturing and trade, navigation, learned professions, and engineers; the censuses of 1850 and 1860 dropped that aggregation (it was not picked up until the census of 1880, when the directors created four categories: agriculture, trade and transportation, manufacturing, and professions and services). To calculate the income derived respectively from commerce, professions, and services, I manipulated the occupational listings for 1850 and 1860 to fit into these categories. This procedure showed that the total occupations for 1840 outnumbered the occupations for 1850 and that the number of farmers was much larger in 1840 than in either 1850 or 1860. It becomes apparent—for this is the only way to explain these counts of farming population—that, in 1840, census enumerators included slaves in their occupational totals. Thus all the occupational categories for the census of 1840 include slaves.

This proves a dilemma for handling the censuses of 1850 and 1860, because it is apparent that census enumerators in these years excluded slaves from the occupational categories that could be categorized as agricultural. Evaluating

TABLE 6.1. Kentucky, Tennessee, and Virginia state income, 1839–1879.

Income in Kentucky, Tennessee, and Virginia, 1839–1879, by occupational category (millions of U.S. dollars)

	Kentucky				Tennessee				Virginia			
	1839	1849	1859	1879	1839	1849	1859	1879	1839	1849	1859	1879
Agriculture	28.7	35.5	59.6	67.0	27.4	40.5	66.9	63.3	45.0	44.7	68.7	64.2
Rent	0.7	1.0	1.1	2.0	0.7	1.0	1.2	1.6	1.1	1.4	1.7	2.6
Slave trade	0.5	1.5	1.7	—	0.0	0.0	2.0	—	3.2	4.0	4.6	—
Commerce	2.4	3.4	5.8	14.2	1.3	3.3	4.6	9.9	6.1	5.1	6.9	15.5
Professions	1.4	5.3	7.2	12.3	1.3	3.6	6.2	9.5	1.7	5.5	8.7	15.0
Services												
a. General	0.8	2.0	3.4	21.2	0.6	1.1	2.3	19.3	1.5	3.4	4.8	39.8
b. Women	—	—	1.3	6.5	—	—	1.2	5.5	—	—	2.5	10.1
c. Labor	—	—	—	12.6	—	—	—	14.3	—	—	—	27.9
Transportation	—	0.3	0.7	2.5	—	0.2	0.5	2.0	0.1	0.3	0.2	0.0
Manufactures	5.8	9.5	15.6	29.0	4.0	4.6	8.6	13.2	17.2	11.5	19.8	27.7
Slave hires	—	5.3	6.4	—	—	6.0	7.9	—	—	11.8	14.0	—
Total income	40.3	63.8	102.8	167.3	35.3	60.1	101.4	138.6	75.9	87.7	131.9	202.8
Total income (millions of 1879 U.S. dollars)	42.4	75.1	107.1	167.3	37.2	70.7	105.6	138.6	79.9	103.2	137.4	202.8

TABLE 6.2. Per capita income in Kentucky, Tennessee, and Virginia, 1839-1879 (in constant 1879 dollars).

	Kentucky				Tennessee				Virginia			
	1839	1849	1859	1879	1839	1849	1859	1879	1839	1849	1859	1879
(1) Entire population (slaves, free)	54.4	76.4	92.6	101.5	44.9	70.5	95.1	89.9	64.4	72.6	86.1	95.2
(2) White population	71.9	98.7	116.5	121.5	58.0	93.4	127.2	121.7	107.8	115.3	131.2	137.6

Sources for Table 6.1 and 6.2: Compendium . . . of the Sixth Census; Seventh Census; Eighth Census, vol. 2: Agriculture; Preliminary Report on the Eighth Census; and Tenth Census, vol. 3: Agriculture. For price information, I divided the total value of each agricultural category, as listed in Gallman, "Commodity Output, 1839–1899," 46–48 (table A-2), by the total outputs in the census. Slave trade figures and prices from Michael Tadman, *Speculators and Slaves: Masters, Traders, and Slaves in the Old South* (Madison: University of Wisconsin Press, 1989), 12 (table 2.1), 116 (chart). Income from commerce, professions, and services was based on the annual income of common labor—calculated at $250 in 1840, $250 in 1850, $285 in 1860, and $310 in 1880, using wages from Stanley Lebergott, *Manpower in Economic Growth: The American Record Since 1800* (New York: McGraw Hill, 1964), table A-25, 255–315. Commerce was calculated as four times common labor; professions as 2.5 times common labor; services as equal to common labor for general services and unspecified labor, but as one-half of common labor for women. Theodore F. Marburg, "Income Originating in Trade, 1799–1869," and Harold Barger, "Income Originating in Trade, 1869–1929," in *Trends in the American Economy in the Nineteenth Century*, Studies in Income and Wealth 24 (New York: Princeton University Press, 1960), 321–323 and 329–330, respectively. Figures for 1840 derived from Ezra Seaman, *Essays on the Progress of Nations, In Productive Industry, Civilization, Population, and Wealth* . . . (New York: Baker and Scribner, 1846), 144–148, 217–218, 441–442.

income on the basis of people in an occupational category thereby means the estimates for 1840 will greatly outnumber those for 1850 and 1860. To compensate, I took 20 percent of the total slave population in the three border states, calling this occupational category "slave hires," and multiplied it times the common labor annual earnings estimate. The 20 percent figure is derived by estimating that roughly 80 percent of the adult slaves in the border states were probably engaged in agriculture.[12]

This particular puzzle leads to another conundrum concerning the estimate for service income, especially in the census years of 1860 and 1880. This estimate is derived by multiplying the population in the services category by the estimated common labor annual wage. The services category does not appear in the 1840 census, where service occupations were evidently lodged in commerce and professions. To make a rational assessment of the numbers engaged in services, professions, and merchandising in 1840, I allowed only one-fourth of the people listed in commerce and professions to belong to those categories; the other three-fourths were placed in a services category. However, it is worth remarking that a surge in both professions and services occurred after 1850; for these occupational categories, table 6.3 shows a dramatic increase in numbers in 1860 and 1880, which reveals something about the evolution of these border economies.

TABLE 6.3. Population and Occupations of Kentucky, Tennessee, and Virginia, 1839-1879 (in thousands).

	Kentucky				Tennessee				Virginia			
	1839	1849	1859	1879	1839	1849	1859	1879	1839	1849	1859	1879
Population Total	780	982	1156	1649	829	1002	1110	1542	1240	1422	1596	2131
White	590	761	919	1377	641	757	827	1139	741	895	1047	1473
Slave	182	211	225	—	183	239	276	—	449	473	491	—
Farmers	198	115	150	321	228	119	132	294	319	170	208	362
Total Farms	66.8	74.8	83.7	106.5	67.7	72.7	77.7	105.7	68.6	77.0	86.5	181.2
Manufactures	23.5	21.5	21.3	61.5	17.9	12.0	12.5	36.1	56.1	29.2	36.2	94.3
Merchants	4.5	4.7	7.1	25.6	1.3	3.3	4.1	8.0	6.1	5.1	6.1	12.5
Professions	2.3	8.5	10.1	15.9	2.1	5.7	8.7	12.3	2.8	8.9	12.2	19.4
Services												
(a) General	3.1	8.2	11.9	68.5	2.3	4.2	8.0	62.3	5.9	13.5	16.7	128.4
(b) Women	—	0.2	9.0	41.9	—	0.3	8.3	35.3	—	0.1	17.7	65.0
(c) Labor	—	—	—	40.8	—	—	—	46.0	—	—	—	90.0
Total Occupations	229	191	257	520	251	168	252	448	390	227	297	670

Sources and definitions: A list of occupations usually exists in the volume of population or in the *Compendium* of the censuses for 1850, 1860, and 1880. For *farming:* dairymen, drivers, farmers, farm laborers, fruiterers, gardners and nurserymen, milkmen, overseers, and planters. Laborers or common laborers were not accounted for in my estimates. For *commerce:* bankers, bank officers, booksellers, brokers, cattle dealers, coal dealers, commission merchants, dealers, flour dealers, ice dealers, insurance officers, marketmen, merchants, paper dealers, pork dealers, produce dealers, provision dealers, speculators, traders, wine dealers, and wood dealers. For *professions:* actors, architects, artists, chemists, clergy, engineers, daugerrotypists, dancers, dentists, editors, judges, lawyers, musicians, music teachers, music sellers, newsmen, officers, opticians, peddlers, physicians, piano tuners, professors, reporters, superintendents, surgeons, surveyors, teachers, telegraph operators, undertakers, U.S. officers. For *services, general:* auctioneers, bakers, barbers, barkeepers and saloonkeeprs, boarding house owners, boatmen, book sellers, canal men, carters, clerks, collectors, draughtsmen, drovers, druggists, expressmen, fishermen, florists, gatekeepers, grocers, innkeepers, livery stable owners, locksmiths, mariners, oystermen, pilots, plumbers, railroadmen, roofers, ship carpenters, steamboatmen, tailors, teamsters, watchmen. For *services, women:* domestics, midwives, seamstresses, servants. For *services, labor,* the category of labor was unspecified, except in the personal services column of the 1880 census. For the results of the 1880 census, the categories listed under commerce and fisheries were divided into fourths: one-fourth became the total for the category of commerce in tables 6.1 and 6.2, and three-fourths became the total for services. To the services column was added three-fourths of the sum of professions and military service, and the remainder became the category of professions. The 1880 occupations were recalculated to match categories of the other censuses.

Note: Numbers do not sum to the total occupations because the category of "common labor" or "laborer" was not assigned to one of the occupational divisions.

By the results in table 6.1, Kentucky, Tennessee, and Virginia were by no means economic sluggards. The per capita income growth rates were quite high between 1840 and 1860 (Kentucky, 2.7 percent; Tennessee, 3.8 percent; and Virginia, 1.5 percent). Just as important, however, was the observable movement of these states away from purely agrarian economies to more diversified ones. Commercial, professional, and personal service occupations rose impressively between 1850 and 1860 (see table 6.3) as did income from manufacturing. Indeed, from the numbers generated by this study, Kentucky looked in 1860 to be in an especially promising position.[13] One concludes that these states, and probably Maryland and Missouri, would have greatly benefited from the completion of a railroad network solidifying a Southern regional market. They were already on the path to a diversified economy, and the opening up of market forces in the form of a greater market area would have only goaded more powerfully their incipient moves into commerce and manufacturing.

Stopping the Flow of the Interstate Slave Trade

Among the truisms oft repeated about the border slave states is that they were in danger of becoming nonslave states due to the sale of slaves to the plantation states. Certainly there is some truth to the statement: Delaware and Maryland were depleting their stock of slaves. However, the outflow of slaves from Virginia and Kentucky to the southwest was not enough to eliminate the institution in those states. In fact, a simple look at the population totals for slaves (table 6.3) shows that the absolute number of slaves was increasing. Moreover, the depletion interpretation overlooks other possibilities. Between 1840 and 1860, border state slaveholders sold slaves to the cotton areas because prices of slaves rose to mountainous heights, reaching $1,800 for a prime field hand in 1859. Under such conditions, it was hardly surprising that slaves were sold to the Deep South instead of being put directly to work. The border South likely expanded the use of free labor in manufacturing, using hired-out slaves on occasion, because it made more economic sense to sell valuable slaves to the cotton lords and to use "free labor" at home. But there was a catch to this arrangement.

Studies on antebellum wages have proliferated since 1960, and scholars have firmly established that in many instances Southern wages were higher than their Northern counterparts. One way to approach the vexatious subject of wages by using the census reports is to locate Southern counties with some industrial activity and examine the capital invested, the number of people employed, and the total wages paid in certain industries. Most enterprises hired a variety of people earning different wages, but an average wage can be calculated to show generally how expensive labor was in manufacturing. Such results are given in table 6.4 for a number of enterprises in Kentucky, Tennessee, and Virginia counties in 1860. For a contrast, table 6.4 also provides some summary information on the same industries in some of the most heavily industrialized northern counties. Table 6.4 highlights the obvious fact that Southern manufacturing was in its infancy. Compared to Northern enterprises, Southern ones were small and not especially prominent in Southern life.[14] In terms of wages, however, it does appear that by 1860 Southern workers in manufacturing establishments did generally receive higher average wages.[15]

A prominent fear of abolitionists and political antislavery leaders was the possibility that slavery could expand beyond staple-crop production, enter manufacturing, depress wages, and ruin Northern society by eliminating an egalitarianism obtained through economic mobility.[16] Northerners constantly depicted economic activities in the South as a competition between free labor and slave labor, with slave labor winning because it unfairly reduced wages. Kentucky abolitionist Cassius M. Clay put the matter as forthrightly as anyone: "It is an evil to the free laborer, by forcing him by the laws of competition, supply and demand, to work for the wages of the slave—food and shelter." Northerners shared this dread and did not confine it to the controversy over slavery's expansion into the territories. George M. Weston, a Maine Democrat, wrote a tract entitled *Southern Slavery Reduces Northern Wages*. In it he warned Northerners to be wary of the day when population density forced slaves into factories: "such a contingency is neither distant nor improbable, and it behooves the North to look the approaching evil fairly in the face." The editor of the Springfield, Illinois, *State Journal*, thought that Southern policy intended for "slaves being brought in[to] competition with free white laborers every where." New York senator William H. Seward seconded this apprehension: speaking in 1856, he said, "Only grant now that this great end of the slaveholders can be attained [protection of slave property nationwide], and you will need no argument to prove that African slaves will be found in the ports, not merely of New York, New Orleans, and Philadelphia, and in the fields of Kansas and Nebraska, but even in the ports of Oswego, Rochester, and Buffalo."[17]

Manufacturing entrepreneurs in the border states had by 1860 become accustomed to using slaves in their endeavors. Slaves were prominent in coal and iron factories in Virginia and Kentucky, in hemp manufacturing in Kentucky, in tobacco establishments in Maryland and Virginia, and in a number of skilled trades. During the 1850s, slaves were also profitably employed in wheat cultivation. Individuals acquainted with slavery in the border states knew the institution's adaptability to numerous economic pursuits, and they had no

TABLE 6.4. Average wages in manufacturing concerns, 1860, North vs. South, by selected states and counties.

	Cast iron		Bar iron		Machinery		Cotton textiles		Boots and shoes		Carriages		Furniture	
	Employees[a]	Wages[b]	Employees	Wages	Employees	Wage	Employees	Wage	Employees	Wage	Employees	Wage	Employees	Wage
Border South states and counties														
Tennessee														
Knox	30	$600	—	—	—	—	—	—	5	$300	2.5	$353	8	$525
Davidson	9	$447	—	—	111	$269	—	—	23	$210	—	$691	—	—
Shelby	3	$520	—	—	80	$450	—	—	5	$369	17	$406	—	—
Kentucky														
Fayette	—	—	—	—	7	$277	80	$120	8	$399	11	$439	35	$480
Jefferson	50	$446	120	$650	—	—	6	$207	2	$439	9	$461	14	$404
Kenton	—	—	220	$491	3	$480	—	—	3	$329	18	$389	2	$390
Virginia														
Henrico	17	$394	800	$384	53	$332	20	$240	8	$300	11	$362	11	$333
Brooke	12	$300	—	—	—	—	88	$146	2	$240	3	$252	4	$240
Ohio	17	$332	210	$213	—	—	—	—	—	—	—	—	15	$450
Northern states and counties														
New York														
Albany	71	$333	—	—	23	$339	310	$166	7	$287	20	$358	40	$258
Pennsylvania														
Schuylkill	26	$402	77	$385	27	$292	—	—	3	$280	7	$303	4	$287
Massachusetts														
Middlesex	47	$403	15	$360	45	$356	685	$204	51	$303	6	$395	23	$370
Essex	13	$332	12	$350	8	$400	444	$204	63	$225	7	$335	6	$395

Source: Eighth Census, vol. 3: Manufactures.

[a]Columns labeled "employees" represent the number of employees per firm.

[b]Columns labeled "wages" represent total wages divided by the number of employees per firm.

trouble in postulating that if profits from agriculture plunged, slaves could be profitably transferred into manufacturing. Thus Representative Thomas H. Bayly of Virginia warned Northerners not to stop the slaveholding states from agricultural expansion; if necessary, slaves could be placed in industry—"less skill is required; the operative in the factory is little more than an animated part of the machinery; slaves are fully equal to it."[18]

How a collision between free labor and slave labor in manufacturing could arise, and thus fuel northern paranoia, can be illustrated by weighing slave costs against free-labor wage rates. Estimates of the annual earnings of slaves range from a maintenance cost of $48 (Fogel and Engerman) and $63 (Ransom and Sutch), to $200 for slaves in manufacturing (Bateman and Weiss.) Perhaps the safest range for the annual cost of a slave (roughly speaking, the slave's wage rate) is $150 to $200.[19] Consider the annual cost to a manufacturer purchasing a slave, a prime field hand. Assume that a financial market existed in the South to purchase slaves on a mortgage basis the way Northerners bought farms: an eight-year mortgage at 12 percent interest.[20] Table 6.5 shows how the cost of a slave on a mortgage basis might appear to a manufacturer, depending on what the actual maintenance cost of a slave was. In summary:

- For a purchase price of $1,800, the annual loan payment is $351.00 ($29.26 monthly).
- For a purchase price of $1,120, the annual loan payment is $195.00 ($16.26 monthly).
- For a purchase price of $540, the annual loan payment is $117.00 ($9.76 monthly).
- For a purchase price of $490, the annual loan payment is $97.56 ($8.13 monthly).

The point of this exercise is that in terms of antebellum prices, it hardly is any wonder that few slaves were used in manufacturing. At the high prices slaves were commanding, the effective wage rate of slaves under almost any maintenance cost was too high. But if the price of slaves fell down from $1,800 to around $1,200, then the slave laborer became a viable alternative to a free laborer—in some occupations. Wherever free workers earned over $375, a slave laborer was a cheaper form of labor. And if the price of slaves decreased further, to the point where a $50-per-year gap emerged between the wage of a free worker and a slave worker, then the cost considerations were entirely in favor of purchasing a slave (see table 6.5).

A special feature of this comparison is a rebuttal to those who argue that slavery consumed capital and retarded Southern economic development

TABLE 6.5. Potential total cost (wage) of a slave to a manufacturer, by alternative maintenance costs.

Annual maintenance cost[a] of a slave

	(A) $50	(B) $75	(C) $100	(D) $150	(E) $200	(F) $250
(1) Purchase price: $1,800						
Annual loan payment	$351	$351	$351	$351	$351	$351
Total annual cost (wage)	$401	$426	$451	$501	$551	$601
(2) Purchase price: $1,100						
Annual loan payment	$195	$195	$195	$195	$195	$195
Total annual cost (wage)	$245	$270	$295	$345	$395	$445
(3) Purchase price: $540						
Annual loan payment	$117	$117	$117	$117	$117	$117
Total annual cost (wage)	$167	$192	$217	$267	$317	$367
(4) Purchase price: $490						
Annual loan payment	$98	$98	$98	$98	$98	$98
Total annual cost (wage)	$148	$173	$198	$248	$298	$348

[a]Maintenance cost can be considered as the payment made to the slave not only to keep him or her healthy but also sufficiently satisfied (indifferent) to do the job satisfactorily without engaging in destructive behaviors and overt revolution.

because it diverted investment away from improving capital stock and placed it into purchasing humans. This example demonstrates that, given the difference between the cost of a slave bought on a mortgage arrangement and the wages paid to free labor, the manufacturer would have had *more* money to invest in machinery when he or she purchased a slave than if he or she used free labor.[21] For example, take an entrepreneur with $1,000 to engage in some activity who, ignoring all other considerations, had to divide his or her money between hiring one laborer and spending the rest on tools, implements, and machines. Say the wage rate for free labor was $300 to $350 a year—which leaves $650 to $700 to purchase machinery. If the price of cotton plummeted such that the price of a prime field hand fell, for instance, to $540, then the effective wage of a slave (being the cost of purchase and maintenance) might have been between $217 and $317 annually for eight years (the period of the mortgage payments).

Thus if the entrepreneur purchased a slave, his investment costs would be about $217 to $317 for labor (a slave) and $683 to $783 for capital goods—he or she would have saved $33 to $133 in labor costs by using slave labor and then could have applied those funds elsewhere. In short, the entrepreneur would have been left with more money to invest in machinery and equipment if he or she had used slave labor instead of free labor—the reverse of the old argument. Under these particular conditions—the existence of a financial market that allows mortgage financing on slaves, high wages for free labor, and low slave prices—not only would the purchase of slaves result in savings in wage costs, but it would also free up money to spend on capital stock. This discussion, however, leaves unresolved the other debatable aspect about free labor versus slave labor: whether the productivity and the quality of work performed by slaves was the same as free laborers. However, it is also worth noting that the way free labor could have won the competition would have been by lowering its wage rate—and that was exactly the fear that Northerners expressed about the impact of slavery on a free-market economy.

The preceding illustration is given primarily to convince modern readers that a potential substitution of slaves for free laborers existed. Antebellum entrepreneurs probably would not have gone through a lengthy calculation as given above to determine exactly the point at which it made sense to employ slaves at home rather than to ship them for sale at New Orleans. They would not have to. The price of free labor would be known, the maintenance cost of a slave would be known, and the price of a prime field hand in New Orleans would be known. That was sufficient information for a slaveholder to decide whether to put a slave into the interstate slave trade or to hire the slave out locally.

The pertinent question then becomes whether slave prices could have plunged after 1860 so as to entice border South entrepreneurs to purchase slaves for manufacturing enterprises. In his work on the interstate slave trade, Michael Tadman graphs some relationships between the price of cotton and the price of slaves. When the price of cotton ranged around 11 cents per pound, slave prices seemed to average $1,600 for a prime field hand; when the price was 9 cents per pound, the price for a prime field hand averaged about $775; and when the price of cotton fell to 7 cents per pound, the average field hand price dropped to about $700.[22] At these lower prices for cotton, the value of slaves would have dropped to the range where their purchase by manufacturers made sense—they could profit from substituting slave labor for free labor (see table 6.4).

The downward plunge of cotton prices was in the offing, although the exact timing has been distorted by the American Civil War. Gavin Wright has convincingly shown that cotton demand, which had been high between 1815 and 1860, was destined to fall by two-thirds after 1868 or 1869. With demand for textiles falling, the price of cotton would fall as well. The bicentennial edition of *Historical Statistics* shows prices for one pound of cotton starting in 1876 at 9.71 cents, falling in the next year to 8.53 cents per pound. After a small upward spike in 1881, the price of cotton then remained under 9.20 cents per pound until 1897.[23] One assumes that the price of slaves, had slavery not ended due to the war, would have fallen as well; that is, if the relations in Tadman's graph have any sway beyond the time period around which they were constructed, prices for a prime slave hand would have fallen to $750–$850. At that price, entrepreneurs could have purchased slaves by a mortgage financial arrangement that would have lowered their annual wage bill. Thus, Southern manufacturers in the 1870s and 1880s might well have stopped exporting slaves to the cotton South; indeed, the possibility existed that border South entrepreneurs might have repurchased slaves from the West, thus reversing the direction of the interstate slave trade.

In the potential pattern of events depicted in this chapter, certain developments were going to happen and are not conjectural. Railroads enhance trade and economic growth so long as population centers of sufficient size could be linked together. Southern manufacturing wages for white artisans were high relative to the North. Cotton prices were going to fall dramatically after 1870 due to a slowing world demand for cotton. Lower cotton prices would have lowered the price of slaves. A repetition of the economic conditions of the 1840s was likely to occur in the 1870s and 1880s. After the Panic of 1837, when cotton prices were low, Southern entrepreneurs established the basic manufacturing structure of the South. The recovery of cotton prices in the 1850s turned Southerners away from investing in industry and back to investing in cotton. It is no stretch of the imagination to think that should cotton prices have plummeted in the 1870s, the same pattern of the 1840s would have reemerged—a diversion of resources and capital out of agriculture and into manufacturing. The one major assumption governing this exercise is the existence of a market rationality among border South economic actors, that they would have responded to changes in market prices.[24]

The potential scenario is this, then: The Southern states were coalescing into an internal market area that reinforced an already strong trade linkage between the border South and the cotton South. An enlarged market area would have given a considerable stimulus to an already modernizing border-state economy: more manufacturing, more urbanization, and more services. Because prices for cotton were destined to fall within a few years after 1860, slave prices were also likely to fall. And when prices of slaves fell far enough, it would have made sense to replace free labor with slave labor—unless free labor agreed to lower wages. As slave labor expanded into manufacturing, sending products made by slave labor into the free North became a possibility. Then the North would have faced what many had always dreaded: the direct competition between free labor and slave labor. And in the free market, cheap labor always wins. Northerners' fears about the possibilities of an expanding Southern economy that could distort and injure the Northern economy were not figments of their imagination or an irrationality supported by evangelical spiritualism. In a national market setting where one region had access to illegitimate cheap labor because of certain state laws (the laws of slavery), it made sense to be deeply suspicious of slavery and slavery's potential to harm Northern society and its economic underpinnings.

Postscript about Per Capita Income Estimates

One of the more fascinating results that research into the postbellum South has disclosed has been a backward plunge of per capita income between 1860 and 1880. Explaining that retrogression has led to conflicting interpretations.[25] But these analyses about the postbellum South depend heavily on the regional income estimates of Richard Easterlin, and there may be a problem with those numbers.

This chapter has produced income estimates for Kentucky, Tennessee, and Virginia that diverge enormously from Easterlin's. To be explicit, the first divergence is the calculation of annual growth of per capita income from 1860 to 1880: Robert Fogel computes, using modified Easterlin figures, an annual growth rate of –00.4 percent (for the Southern Atlantic region), while data presented in this chapter yields growth rates of +00.5 percent for Kentucky, +00.05 percent for Virginia, and –00.03 percent for Tennessee.[26] The second divergence is enormous: the calculations of state per capita income for these states are somewhat different from Easterlin's estimates for 1840 but are astronomically different for 1880; for example, this chapter gives a per capita income in 1879 of $167.30 for Kentucky, $138.60 for Tennessee, and $202.80 for Virginia (and West Virginia). Easterlin's estimates are, respectively, $66.00, $43.00, and $79.00 (and $30.00 for West Virginia).[27] This is a most unsettling comparison.

The source of the difference between the estimates in this chapter and Easterlin's is not difficult to find. Easterlin's estimates exclude the services category; his estimates are based on commodity production.[28] The estimates in this chapter

TABLE 6.6. Differences in ratio of occupations to total population, 1840–1880.

A. *Occupations as percentage of total population*

	1840	1850	1860	1880
Kentucky				
Census occupations as percentage of total population	29.3	19.4	22.3	31.5
One-half slave percentage of population	—	11.2	10.2	—
Total	29.3	30.8	32.5	31.5
Tennessee				
Census occupations as percentage of total population	30.3	16.8	19.5	29.1
One-half slave percentage of population	—	12.3	12.8	—
Total	30.3	29.1	32.3	29.1
Virginia				
Census occupations as percentage of total population	31.1	16.0	18.6	31.5
One-half slave percentage of population	—	18.6	17.2	—
Total	31.1	34.6	35.8	31.5

B. *Easterlin's Agricultural and Nonagricultural Labor Force as a Percentage of Total Population*

	1840	1880
Kentucky	29.0	25.2
Tennessee	29.9	21.2
Virginia	31.0	25.0

Source: Computed from information provided in table 6.2 of this chapter and Easterlin, "Interregional Income Differences," 98 (table A-1), 100 (table A-2).

include people in commerce, services, and professions; in 1840 the services sector did not weigh mightily in the economies of these states, but this was not the case after 1850. Moreover, services may not have been sizeable in the Deep South, but they were in the border South. By excluding them, one reduces significantly the proportion of people engaged in economic activity (see table 6.6). Inclusion of those engaged in the "services" sector of the economy in per capita income estimates underscores the fact that the economic trajectory of the border South may have been markedly different from that of the plantation South. In table 6.6, part B, it is clear that the Easterlin's income estimates are based on a much smaller proportion of the population in 1880 than in 1840, thus raising the question of how meaningful these figures are for calculating regional growth over those years. This subject requires attention because a host of explanations about economic growth in the Deep South from 1865 to 1900—and even more so for the border South from 1865 to 1900—may be deeply flawed. Other processes, such as interregional competition, may have had more to do with border South economic stagnation than the extinction of slavery and the rise of sharecropping.[29]

NOTES

1. This interpretation is in embryonic form and does not exist as I have written it; I have stitched this explanation by extrapolating some of the views I have seen in the following works: Michael F. Holt, *The Fate of Their Country: Politicians, Slavery Extension, and the Coming of the Civil War* (New York: Hill and Wang, 2004); Richard W. Carwardine, *Evangelicals and Politics in Antebellum America* (New Haven, Conn.: Yale University Press, 1993); Edward L. Ayers, *In the Presence of Mine Enemies: War in the Heart of America, 1859–1865* (New York: W. W. Norton, 2003). A resurrection of the economic program being the cause of sectional animosities is the theme of Marc Egnal, *Clash of Extremes: The Economic Origins of the Civil War* (New York: Hill and Wang, 2009). For current scholarship on the slave power, see Leonard L. Richards, *The Slave Power: The Free North and Southern Domination, 1780–1860* (Baton Rouge: Louisiana State University Press, 2000). On the free labor ideology, consult Eric Foner, *Free Soil, Free Labor, Free Men: The Ideology of the Republican Party Before the Civil War*, 2d ed. (New York: Oxford University Press, 1995). Most historians will note that the current trend in Civil War historiography is a return to the revisionist analysis; see James G. Randall, "The Blundering Generation," *Mississippi Valley Historical Review* 27 (June 1940): 3–28.

2. Younger scholars of the early republic seem more interested in detailing how slavery affected the republic: Robert Pierce Forbes, *The Missouri Compromise and Its Aftermath: Slavery and the Meaning of America* (Chapel Hill: University of North Carolina Press, 2007); Robin Einhorn, *American Taxation, American Slavery* (Chicago: University of Chicago Press, 2006).

3. See James L. Huston, *Calculating the Value of the Union: Slavery, Property Rights, and the Economic Origins of the Civil War* (Chapel Hill: University of North Carolina Press, 2003), chap. 3.

4. William G. Shade, *Democratizing the Old Dominion: Virginia and the Second Party System, 1824–1861* (Charlottesville: University of Virginia Press, 1996), chaps. 1, 8; Ayers, *In the Presence of Mine Enemies*, 87–99, 148–149; William W. Freehling, *The South vs. the South: How Anti-Confederate Southerners Shaped the Course of the Civil War* (New York: Oxford University Press, 2001), 3–5, 50–54, 61; Christopher J. Olsen, *Political Culture and Secession in Mississippi: Masculinity, Honor, and the Antiparty Tradition, 1830–1860* (New York: Oxford University Press, 2000), 8; Jonathan Daniel Wells, *The Origins of the Southern Middle Class, 1800–1861* (Chapel Hill: University of North Carolina Press, 2004); Frank Towers, *The Urban South and the Coming of the Civil War* (Charlottesville: University of Virginia Press, 2004).

5. This note will only give a superficial overview of works on the border South economy: Clement Eaton, *History of the Old South*, 2nd ed. (New York: Macmillan, 1966), 213–229; Emory Q. Hawk, *Economic History of the South* (New York: Prentice-

Hall, 1934), 266–278, 285–286, 295–307; Avery O. Craven, *Soil Exhaustion as a Factor in the Agricultural History of Virginia and Maryland, 1606–1860* (Urbana: University of Illinois Press, 1925), 128–163; Blanche Henry Clark, *The Tennessee Yeomen, 1840–1860* (Nashville: Vanderbilt University Press, 1942), 7–46, 110–133, 141–161; Robert Tracy McKenzie, *One South or Many? Plantation Belt and Upcountry in Civil War–Era Tennessee* (Cambridge: Cambridge University Press, 1994); Kenneth W. Noe, "Appalachia before Mr. Peabody: Some Recent Literature on the Southern Mountain Region," *Virginia Magazine of History and Biography* 110 (2002): 5–34; John Majewski, *A House Dividing: Economic Development in Pennsylvania and Virginia Before the Civil War* (Cambridge: Cambridge University Press, 2000); Carville Earle, *Geographical Inquiry and American Historical Problems* (Stanford, Calif.: Stanford University Press, 1992), chap. 3; Charles B. Dew, *Ironmaker to the Confederacy: Joseph R. Anderson and the Tredegar Iron Works* (New Haven, Conn.: Yale University Press, 1966), 32–37; Ronald L. Lewis, *Coal, Iron, and Slaves: Industrial Slavery in Maryland and Virginia, 1715–1865* (Westport, Conn.: Greenwood Press, 1979); Robert S. Starobin, *Industrial Slavery in the Old South* (New York: Oxford University Press, 1970); William W. Freehling, *The Road to Disunion*, vol. 2: *Secessionists Triumphant, 1854–1861* (New York: Oxford University Press, 2007), 13–16; Stephen Deyle, *Carry Me Back: The Domestic Slave Trade in American Life* (New York: Oxford University Press, 2005), chap. 3.

6. U.S. Bureau of the Census, *Compendium of the Enumeration of the Inhabitants and Statistics of the United States . . . from the Returns of the Sixth Census* (Washington, D.C.: Thomas Allen, 1841); U.S. Bureau of the Census, *The Seventh Census of the United States, 1850* (Washington, D.C.: Robert Armstrong, 1853); U.S. Bureau of the Census, *Statistical View of the United States . . . being a Compendium of the Seventh Census* (Washington. D.C.: Beverly Tucker, 1854); U.S. Bureau of the Census, *The Eighth Census*, vol. 1: *Population of the United States in 1860* (Washington, D.C.: GPO, 1864); U.S. Bureau of the Census, *The Eighth Census*, vol. 2: *Agriculture of the United States in 1860* (Washington, D.C.: GPO, 1864); U.S. Bureau of the Census, *The Eighth Census*, vol. 3: *Manufactures of the United States in 1860* (Washington: GPO, 1865); U.S. Bureau of the Census, *The Eighth Census*, vol. 4: *Statistics of the United States (including Mortality, Property, &c.) in 1860* (Washington, D.C.: GPO, 1866); U.S. Bureau of the Census, *Preliminary Report on the Eighth Census, 1860* (Washington, D.C.: GPO, 1862); U.S. Bureau of the Census, *Tenth Census of the United States, June 1, 1880*, vol. 1: *Statistics of the Population of the United States* (Washington, D.C.: GPO, 1883); U.S. Bureau of the Census, *Tenth Census of the United States*, vol. 2: *Report on the Manufactures of the United States* (Washington, D.C.: GPO, 1883); U.S. Bureau of the Census, *Tenth Census of the United States*, vol. 3: *Report on the Productions of Agriculture* (Washington, D.C.: GPO, 1883); U.S. Bureau of the Census, *Tenth Census of the United States*, vol. 4: *Report on the Agencies of Transportation* (Washington, D.C.: GPO, 1883); U.S. Bureau of the Census, *Compendium of the Tenth Census*, rev. ed., 2 vols. (Washington, D.C.: GPO, 1885); U.S. Bureau of the Census, *Tenth Census of the United States*, vol. 20: *Report on the Statistics of Wages in Manufacturing Industries* (Washington, D.C.: GPO, 1886).

7. On geography and economic regions, see D. W. Meinig, *The Shaping of America: A Geographical Perspective on 500 Years of History*, vols. 2 and 3 (1993; repr.,

New Haven, Conn.: Yale University Press, 1998), 2:330–48, 2:388–427, 2:494, 3:217–224, 3:240–242; Ronald R. Boyce, *The Bases of Economic Geography*, 2nd ed. (New York: Holt, Rinehard and Winston, 1978), 13–18, 102–105. The regional alliance was early elaborated upon by Douglass C. North, *The Economic Growth of the United States, 1790–1860* (New York: W. W. Norton, 1961).

8. John F. Stover, *Iron Road to the West: American Railroads in the 1850s* (New York: Columbia University Press, 1978), 10, 12, 60–92; Stover, *The Railroads of the South 1865–1900: A Study in Finance and Control* (Chapel Hill: University of North Carolina Press, 1955), chap. 1. The above summary agrees with the recent work of Aaron W. Marrs, *Railroads in the Old South: Pursuing Progress in a Slave Society* (Baltimore: Johns Hopkins University Press, 2009).

9. Sources from the census listing principal cities in the 1840 census and from the sections on county populations and cities in the other censuses. *Compendium . . . of the Sixth Census; Seventh Census; Eighth Census*, vol. 1: *Population; Tenth Census*, vol. 1: *Population*. Almost all this material is now accessible on the Internet, made available by the U.S. Census Bureau.

10. Stover, *Iron Road to the West*, 177. Resources of the border South taken from Paul H. Bergeron, Stephen V. Ash, and Jeanette Keith, *Tennesseans and Their History* (Knoxville: University of Tennessee Press, 1999), 116–118; Craven, *Soil Exhaustion*, 128–163; Hawk, *Economic History of the South*, 265–337; Dew, *Ironmaker to the Confederacy*, 32–37. The lack of population centers was the major hindrance to Southern economic growth; see Roger L. Ransom, *The Confederate States of America: What Might Have Been* (New York: W. W. Norton, 2005), 173–176.

11. Robert E. Gallman, "Commodity Output, 1839–1899," in *Trends in the American Economy in the Nineteenth Century*, Studies in Income and Wealth 24 (Princeton, N.J.: Princeton University Press, 1960), 13–71; and Gallman, "Gross National Product in the United States, 1834–1909," in *Output, Employment, and Productivity in the United States After 1800*, Studies in Income and Wealth 30 (New York: National Bureau of Economic Research, 1966), 3–75. Richard Easterlin produced state income estimates for 1840, 1880, and 1900. My preference would be to use figures by professional economists for this study, but the crucial year of 1860 is missing. Instead of giving state totals, as he did for 1840 and 1880, Easterlin estimated the 1860 totals by regions, not by states. Easterlin used regions defined by the Census Bureau in 1910 that obliterated the distinction between border states and plantation states. For this reason, I have produced my own estimates. Regional divisions portrayed graphically in Richard A. Easterlin, "Regional Income Trends, 1840–1950," in *The Reinterpretation of American Economic History*, ed. Robert W. Fogel and Stanley L. Engerman (New York: Harper and Row, 1971), 39; the same division is used by Robert William Fogel, *Without Consent or Contract: The Rise and Fall of American Slavery* (New York: W. W. Norton, 1989), 84–89.

12. See Starobin, *Industrial Slavery*; Lewis, *Coal, Iron, and Slaves*. Ezra C. Seaman estimated national income in 1840, and he noted the value of the slave trade to the border South. Whether Seaman incorporated this into his final tallies is not clear. See Seaman, *Essays on the Progress of Nations, In Productive Industry, Civiliza-*

tion, Population, and Wealth (New York: Baker and Scribner, 1846), 144–148, 217–218, 441–442.

13. Unfortunately, the accuracy of these figures cannot be tested because of lack of state income and wealth estimates for 1850 and 1860. For comparison of per capita income growth rates 1840–1860, Robert Fogel calculates 1.4 percent for the nation and 1.7 percent for the northeastern states. See Fogel, *Without Consent or Contract*, 88.

14. Computed from *Eighth Census*, vol. 3: *Manufactures*.

15. On Southern wages, see Fogel, *Without Consent or Contract*, 88, 110–111; Robert A. Margo, *Wages and Labor Markets in the United States, 1820–1860* (Chicago: University of Chicago Press, 2000), 5; Gavin Wright, *Old South, New South: Revolutions in the Southern Economy Since the Civil War* (New York: Basic Books, 1986), 27–29; Wright, *Slavery and American Economic Development* (Baton Rouge: Louisiana State University Press, 2006), 71.

16. This is the free-labor ideology. See Foner, *Free Soil, Free Labor, Free Men*, chap. 1; Huston, *Calculating the Value of the Union*, chap. 3.

17. Horace Greeley, ed., *The Writings of Cassius Marcellus Clay, Including Speeches and Addresses* (1848; repr. New York: New York Universities Press, 1969), 205; George M. Weston, *Southern Slavery Reduces Northern Wages* (Washington, D.C.: Republican Association, 1856), 2; *Daily [Springfield] Illinois State Journal*, September 29, 1857; William H. Seward, *Immigrant White Free Labor, or Imported Black African Slave Labor: Speech of William H. Seward at Oswego, New York, November 3, 1856* (Washington, D.C.: Buell and Blanchard, 1857), 4. For a full treatment, consult Huston, *Calculating the Value of the Union*, chap. 3.

18. Quote of Thomas H. Bayly, February 11, 1847, in *Congressional Globe* (Washington, D.C.: Blair & Rives, 1834–1873), 29th Congress, 2d sess., appendix, 393. Also see editorials of the *[Richmond] Whig*, May 8, 1849, and the *[Louisville] Daily Journal*, July 20, 1849. On the use of slaves in border-state factories, consult Dew, *Ironmaker to the Confederacy*; Lewis, *Coal, Iron, and Slaves*; Marion B. Lucas, *A History of Blacks in Kentucky: From Slavery to Segregation, 1760–1891*, 2nd ed. (Lexington: Kentucky Historical Society, 2003), 7–11, 101–107; Richard C. Wade, *Slavery in the Cities: The South, 1820–1860* (New York: Oxford University Press, 1967), 23–48; Starobin, *Industrial Slavery*; Marrs, *Railroads in the Old South*, 6–8, 57–66; James R. Irwin, "Exploring the Affinity of Wheat and Slavery in the Virginia Piedmont," *Explorations in Economic History* 25 (July 1988): 295–322.

19. Robert W. Fogel and Stanley L. Engerman, *Time on the Cross: The Economics of American Negro Slavery* (Boston: Little, Brown, 1974), 77, 78,151–152; Roger L. Ransom and Richard Sutch, *One Kind of Freedom: The Economic Consequences of Emancipation*, 2nd ed. (Cambridge: Cambridge University Press, 2001), 210 (table A.4); Fred Bateman and Thomas Weiss, *A Deplorable Scarcity: The Failure of Industrialization in the Slave Economy* (Chapel Hill: University of North Carolina Press, 1981), 86–87. Starobin and Lewis figured that slaves made about one-third the wages paid to free labor, putting the remuneration at $100 to $150; Starobin, *Industrial Slavery*, 157–158; Lewis, *Coal, Iron, and Slaves*, 194. Folmsbee, Corlew, and Mitchell wrote that skilled slaves could earn in Tennessee about $200 per year, while

unskilled slaves obtained $80 to $100 per year; Stanley J. Folmsbee, Robert E. Corlew, and Enoch L. Mitchell, *Tennessee: A Short History* (Knoxville: University of Tennessee Press, 1969), 220.

20. The mortgage loan repayments were taken from *Monthly Interest Amortization Tables, Covering Interest Rates of 5% to 28.75%, Loan Amounts of $50 to $160,000, Terms up to 40 Years* (Chicago: Contemporary Books, n.d.), 58.

21. On the misallocation of investment money, see Wright, *Slavery and American Economic Development*, 61.

22. Michael Tadman, *Speculators and Slaves: Masters, Traders, and Slaves in the Old South* (Madison: University of Wisconsin Press, 1989), 116.

23. Gavin Wright, "Slavery and the Cotton Boom," *Explorations in Economic History* 12 (October 1975): 439; U.S. Bureau of the Census, *Historical Statistics of the United States* (Washington, D.C.: GPO, 1975), 518.

24. On the impact of railroads economically, although this example is east to west, see Kenneth W. Noe, *Southwest Virginia's Railroad: Modernization and the Sectional Crisis* (Urbana: University of Illinois Press, 1994), 28–85. On Southern economic evolution in the 1830s and 1840s, see William J. Cooper, Jr., and Thomas E. Terrill, *The American South*, vol. 1, 3rd ed. (New York: McGraw-Hill, 2002), 305–308; on the advanced financing practices involved with antebellum slavery, see Richard Holcombe Kilbourne, *Debt, Investment, Slaves: Credit Relations in East Feliciana Parish, Louisiana, 1825–1885* (Tuscaloosa: University of Alabama Press, 1995).

25. Ransom and Sutch, *One Kind of Freedom*, xiii–xxvi, 40–41, chaps. 6–9; Fogel, *Without Consent or Contract*, 89–102; Wright, *Old South, New South*, chap. 1. For interpretations about Reconstruction and the economic status of the postwar South generally, consult Peter A. Coclanis and Scott Marler, "The Economics of Reconstruction," in *A Companion to the Civil War and Reconstruction*, ed. Lacy K. Ford (Malden, Mass: Blackwell, 2005), 344–364.

26. Fogel, *Without Consent or Contract*, 88–89 (tables 2 and 3); see also Stanley L. Engerman, "The Economic Impact of the Civil War," in Fogel and Engerman, *Reinterpretation of American Economic History*, 369–379.

27. Easterlin, "Interregional Income Differences," 98 (table A-1), 100 (table A-2).

28. Ibid., appendix B, 105–106, 126, 130.

29. See Kenneth Noe, "Appalachia's Civil War Genesis: Southwest Virginia as Depicted by Northern and Southern Writers, 1825–1865," *West Virginia History* 50 (1991): 102–104; Daniel W. Crofts, "Late Antebellum Virginia Reconsidered," *Virginia Magazine of History and Biography* 107 (1999): 255, 260–262; W. David Lewis, "Joseph Bryan and the Virginia Connection in the Industrial Development of Northern Alabama," *Virginia Magazine of History and Biography* 98 (1990): 613; Paul Salstrom, "Subsistence-Barter-and-Borrow Systems: An Approach to West Virginia's Economic History," *West Virginia History* 51 (1992): 46–49.

PART III

Material Progress and Its Discontents

7

The Southern Path to Modern Cities: Urbanization in the Slave States

Frank Towers

> Our theme is a city—a great Southern importing, exporting,
> and manufacturing city . . . where we can . . . open facilities
> for direct communication with foreign countries, and
> establish all those collateral sources of wealth, utility,
> and adornment, which are the usual concomitants of a
> metropolis. . . . Without a city of this kind, the South can
> never develop her commercial resources nor attain that
> eminent position to which those vast resources would
> otherwise exalt her.[1]

In *The Impending Crisis of the South*, an influential attack on slavery published in 1857, Hinton Helper asserted that the South's lack of a "great" city blocked economic development and denied it international prestige. Helper's criticism reflected his experience in cities, Northern and Southern. Raised in central North Carolina towns by middle-class manufacturers, Helper clerked at the store of a slaveholding planter/ industrialist. In 1850, Gold Rush tales lured Helper west via New York and other free-state cities, where he saw poor men enjoy opportunities unavailable back home. Helper was prevented from including this observation in a book about his travels because his publisher feared offending Southern readers. Infuriated, Helper wrote his full-length indictment of slavery while living in Baltimore, Maryland, the South's largest city. There he witnessed proslavery mobbing of Republican Party meetings, even as city manufacturers seemingly vindicated

Republican free-labor ideas by employing over 17,000 wage workers but almost no slaves, whose local presence was fading. The latter trend convinced Helper that among Southern cities Baltimore was "greatest because freest" from slavery's "pestilential atmosphere" within which "an aspect of most melancholy inactivity and dilapidation broods over every city and town."[2] Notwithstanding this observation, Helper's own life, which included patronage from a modernizing slaveholder and experience in a proslavery industrial port, suggests that the urban South did, in fact, possess the "usual concomitants of a metropolis" but in a form that Helper and sympathetic readers disliked.

A "great city," as Helper understood it, was measured by the giant metropoles of his day, New York and London, and their example continues to influence interpretations of Old South urbanization. While urbanization had other features, the North and England were clearly ahead of the South in urban population, a basic measurement of city building. In 1860, the North possessed thirty-four cities with more than 20,000 residents, while the South had only eleven; one in four Northerners lived in a community of more than 2,500 people (the U.S. census definition of urban) compared to only one in ten Southerners; and the largest Northern city was five times the size of the largest Southern one. England was even farther ahead. In 1850, it had become majority urban and had ten times the South's urban population, a number that London alone doubled.[3]

To explain the South's lower proportion of urban residence, historians have followed Helper in portraying Southern cities as stunted versions of the modern metropolitan centers that transformed the North. For example, David Goldfield regards the South as "part of the modern urban nation," but a lesser one that, because of rural folkways and slaveholder economics, "by 1860 . . . was lagging farther behind northern urbanization than at any previous time American history." These arguments work from a developmental model of social history that posits growth from infancy to maturity. Applied to cities, societies travel the same road from rural to urban but some move faster than others. Accordingly, slavery acted as a "handicap" on the South that caused it to lag behind the North in urban modernity.[4]

This scholarship mischaracterizes antebellum Southern urban history as either opposed to change or trailing behind more advanced societies. At issue is urbanization, a flexible historical process that does not treat commercial-industrial metropoles like New York and London as the essential measure of a city. Urbanization refers to a proportional increase in the urban-over-rural population and qualitative change within cities marked by "differentiation, standardization, [and] change in the quality of social relations. . . ." City growth promotes innovation and fosters urban trade networks of goods, information, and people—changes that, in turn, promote "relationships that cross the boundaries of kinship, locality, and traditional alliances."[5] Conceiving of the slave states as lagging behind the North loses sight of the ways that the Old South met the standards of urbanization but did so on terms that suited its commitment to slavery. That perspective can be lost if the urban South is considered solely in comparison to standards of city size and industrial output set by the eastern Northern states and England. Southern cities were smaller than Northern ones, but by the same token Northern cities were smaller than those in other parts of the world. For example, mid-nineteenth-century New York is rarely characterized as a less-modern version of Beijing, even though the latter had 60 percent more people than the former. To understand how Old South city-building was caught up in the currents of modernity, this essay makes comparisons beyond the North and looks anew at the differences slavery made for urbanization.

Southern cities grew rapidly, combined industry and trade, built railroads and telegraphs, attracted a heterogeneous population, standardized public spaces, and allowed for social mobility and political openness. Yet each of these steps bore the marks of slavery. The results were something different than an immature version of the North and England. By comparison, Southern urbanites typically lived in bigger cities. And their cities were more comprehensively policed, and more culturally diverse. On the other hand, Southern cities had less industry, less democracy, and fewer public services than their free-labor peers. For someone like Helper, who hated slavery and valued political openness, the urban North was a better place. However, to say—as Helper and like-minded observers did—that Northern cities were also more modern ignores the features of Old South urbanization that worked their way into the fabric of post–Civil War cities, Rather than a retrograde stage of urbanization, antebellum Southern cities represented one of several ways that the forces of population growth, communications revolution, and mass production remade urban life in the nineteenth century.

How Fast and How Many?

Judged by the rate of urban population growth, the antebellum South stood in the vanguard of its contemporaries in the Americas and Europe. To measure the rate of net urbanization—how much faster cities grew than rural places— the comparative rate of urban increase divides growth rates for cities and towns by the total population's rate of change. This method corrects the distortion of fast growth rates for societies with few city dwellers by measuring urban change against a society's total population change.[6] As shown in table 7.1, the Old

South stood just behind the northeastern United States in net urbanization. Although the South was still overwhelmingly rural in 1850, its quickening city growth, which steadily gave cities more people and prominence in Southern life, put it in the camp of urbanizers like the North-east states and England.

TABLE 7.1.   Comparative rates of urban increase, 1800–1850.

Place	Urban population, 1800	Total population, 1800	Urban population, 1850 (percentage change, 1800–1850)	Total population, 1850 (percentage change, 1800–1850)	Comparative urban rate of increase[#]
U.S. North-east[*]	244,579	2,635,626	2,319,671 (848%)	8,626,851 (227%)	3.73
U.S. South	78,000	2,622,850	823,100 (955%)	9,593,700 (266%)	3.59
Europe (without Russia)	24,200,000	154,000,000	45,300,000 (87%)	203,000,000 (32%)	2.74
England	2,648,700	8,829,000	9,034,704 (241%)	17,926,000 (103%)	2.34
France	5,637,500	27,500,000	6,354,845 (62%)	35,780,000 (30%)	2.05
U.S. North-central	0 (2,500)	51,006	418,830 (16,653%)[+]	4,721,526 (9,157%)	1.82
Sweden	229,000	2,118,000	352,000 (54%)	3,131,000 (48%)	1.12
Latin America	2,900,000	20,000,000	4,300,000 (48%)	33,000,000 (65%)	0.74

Source: Data comes from Paul Bairoch, Cities and Economic Development: From the Dawn of History to the Present (Chicago: University of Chicago Press, 1991), 423; John M. Merriman, ed., French Cities in the Nineteenth Century, (London: Hutchinson, 1982), 14; Andrew Lees and Lynn Hollen Lees, Cities and the Making of Modern Europe, 1750–1914 (New York: Cambridge University Press, 2007), 5; David B. Grigg, Population Growth and Agrarian Change: An Historical Perspective (New York: Cambridge University Press, 1980), 169, 226. Lower limit of U.S. urban is 2,500 people; Europe, 2,000; Latin America, 5,000.

Note: For method see Jan De Vries, "Problems in the Measurement, Description, and Analysis of Historical Urbanization," in Urbanization in History: A Process of Dynamic Interactions ed. Ad van der Woude, Akira Hayami, and Jan De Vries (New York: Oxford University Press, 1995), 47; Leonard P. Curry, "Urbanization and Urbanism in the Old South: A Comparative View," Journal of Southern History 40 (February 1974): 50.

The comparative rate of urban increase is determined by dividing the rate of change for the urban population by the rate of change for the total population.
* The Pennsylvania-Ohio border divides North-east from North-central. Pacific Coast states excluded. U.S. North-east states include Connecticut, Maine, Massachusetts, New Hampshire, New Jersey, New York, Pennsylvania, Rhode Island, and Vermont. U.S. North-central states include Illinois, Indiana, Iowa, Michigan, Minnesota, Ohio, and Wisconsin.
+ Because North-central's 1800 urban population is zero, it cannot be divided into the 1850 regional urban population. Therefore, the equivalent of the minimum urban unit, 2,500 people, is used as a stand-in for zero. Showing the proximity of that number to the actual early republic population of the North-central states, in the 1810 federal census their total urban population was 2,540.

The rapidly urbanizing South differed fundamentally from other highly rural societies like Sweden or Latin America that experienced static or declining net urbanization. The rural character of these societies signified continuity with a predominantly rural past. In the South, the comparatively small share of urbanites in its mid-century population belied a demographic transition from country to city that broke with the region's eighteenth-century past. The South's higher rate of urban growth as a percent of total population growth also diverged from the North-central states, where the boom in agriculture made rural population rise at a pace more in balance with their impressive urban increase. As time passed residents of each section of the nation would find the other's pattern of city building disturbingly unlike their own experience.

During a steamboat passage from Cairo, Illinois, to New Orleans in 1857, Alabama-bred writer Daniel Hundley met "an old gentleman from New-York" habituated to his city's "continuous hum and noise." Traveling southward, the man grew so agitated by the "vast solitude" of the lower Mississippi River that he burst out "WHERE'S YOUR TOWNS?"[7] This question reflected how differently urbanization in the slave states appeared to a resident of the free states. While the South's growth rates resembled those of the North-east and England, its distribution of urbanites between large cities and smaller towns better resembled a Latin American slave society. The North as a whole and England stood out not only for New York and London but also for their numerous smaller towns. In 1851, England's vast urban edifice included 563 places of 5,000 or more people, and instead of London "the typical British urban dweller lived in a small town."[8] Meanwhile, the typical Southern urbanite lived in a city of at least 20,000, an experience more familiar to residents of other New World slave societies.

The share of urbanites living in large cities, for which comparable data are available, stands in as a measure of town-to-city ratios. In 1860, 65 percent of urban Southerners lived in the section's ten largest cities.[9] Outside the South, the ten largest U.S. cities had many more residents, but they accounted for only half of the non-Southern urban population. The North's lower concentration of big-city residents resembled the pattern for other Atlantic rim nations that lacked slavery, such as Sweden (49 percent), England (40 percent), and France (39 percent). Furthermore, urban population dispersal looked alike in free societies that urbanized rapidly, like the North, or slowly, as did Sweden. Only the sugar-planting, slave island of Cuba, with three-fourths of its urban population resident in large cities, surpassed the South.[10]

The importance of property rights in slaves helps explain the South's cities-without-towns pattern of urbanization. Contrasting the investment strategies of Northern "landlords" and Southern slaveholding "laborlords," Gavin

Wright shows how Northern town building met the needs of land promoters who had to provide public amenities such as roads, schools, and markets to attract laborers who would buy land. Slaveholders, on the other hand, had the capital and coercive power to take their labor to new plantations. Having invested in labor and land instead of land by itself, slaveholders did not need the towns that free workers demanded.[11]

Although slaves were more concentrated in the lower South, slavery's negative impact on town building was evident everywhere that the institution was legal. In 1824, a British traveler wrote that "in New York . . . villages were rising up in various places. . . . But in Virginia how dismal was the look of things! Few, very few villages attracted the eye. From Richmond to Charlottesville, a distance of eighty miles, there was hardly one deserving the name. . . ."[12] A decade later, aboard an Ohio River boat, Frenchman Alexis de Tocqueville noticed "the population is sparse" in slave Kentucky, while "the confused hum emanating from the right bank [in free Ohio] proclaims from afar the presence of industry."[13] Like Hundley's associate, free-labor visitors' equation of few towns with failed urbanization reveals more about expectations derived from their homelands than about the South, where urban dwellers were more likely to live in cities.

Because Ohio had many more people than Kentucky, a more telling test of Tocqueville's riverboat observation is Indiana, another of Kentucky's free-state neighbors. In 1860 these states had nearly the same size and percentage of urban residents but very different distributions of cities and towns. Villages of a few hundred to 2,500 people littered Indiana but were scarce in Kentucky, whereas Kentucky doubled Indiana's population in cities of 10,000 or more. Arguably, concentration in cities gave Kentucky urbanites a more cosmopolitan experience than did the diffusion of Hoosiers in towns.

The same trend held for the sections at large. As the size of the urban unit increased, the South narrowed its gap with the North. In 1860, the ratio of Northerners to Southerners living in towns of less than 2,500 people was 6:1; for places of 2,500 or more, the ratio fell to 4:1; and for cities over 20,000, it dropped to 3:1. At no point did the South achieve parity with the North, but it got closer near the top of the urban scale. As discussed below, slavery as practiced in the highly commercialized economy of the Old South stimulated urban growth—but a particular kind that favored cities over towns. What appeared to free-labor observers as a sign of social decay was, in fact, a different kind of urbanization, one in which cities shot up without a network of small towns, much like tree trunks without branches.[14] Notwithstanding explanations of the comparative lack of towns in the antebellum South as products of a rural mind-set or poor soils, the rapid growth of towns after slavery

ended strongly indicates that the labor laws of the Old South more than anything else shaped its path to building modern cities.[15]

Significantly, the Southern subregion with the most pronounced cities-
without-towns growth pattern, the seven cotton-growing states of the lower
South, also had the highest share of slaves (one-half) in its rural population. In
1860, the lower South housed a smaller proportion of the South's small-town
residents (one-fourth) than of its 20,000-plus city dwellers (one-third), and it
had a higher rate of urban residence than the upper South states of Arkansas,
North Carolina, Tennessee, and Virginia, despite having fewer towns proportional to population. In Georgia, small towns dotted small-farming Piedmont
counties, but in "the coastal savannahs and swamps of the southeast, villages
were relatively few." Not surprisingly, "the latter area boasted the highest concentration of slaves in the state and the greatest commitment to commercial
agriculture."[16] Rather than an innate antiurbanism, the scarcity of Southern
towns was a symptom, or expression, of the ways that slavery influenced land-
development strategies. As explained above, slaveholding planters—the wealthiest rural Southerners—had less incentive than Northern land speculators to
invest in town-building public works aimed at attracting free labor to their
lands. Furthermore, enslaved workers were less able to stimulate town growth
than were free workers because slaves were not paid a wage and therefore had
less cash to spend in local stores, which were the primary economic enterprise
in most small towns.

Cities in Society: Urban Networks

In addition to implying failed urbanization, the South's comparative absence of
towns also informs the argument that "no southern *system* of cities developed"
and that the urban South was a "'colonial' outlier of the northeastern regional
city-system."[17] Sometimes called "urban network," city-systems refer to connections that cities share with one another. Like comparisons of city size, the
"colonial outlier" assessment of the South's city-system captures a real difference between the sections. The North had a denser urban network that in many
respects, particularly international trade, subordinated the South to its primary
city, New York. Nevertheless, concluding from these facts that the South either
lacked an urban network or relied on New York to mediate between its cities
hides connections that bound Southern urbanites to one another and to the
wider urban world.

The South's urban networks are hard to see if viewed through a theoretical
framework that treats large-scale manufacturing as an essential component of

modern city-systems. Formulated during modernization theory's heyday in the Cold War era, the classic city-system model regarded industrial innovations, like improved plows, as catalysts that "released" capital and labor from agriculture and redirected them to cities possessing an "agglomeration" of factors necessary for further production. Cities that cross a resource "threshold" experienced an industrial "takeoff" that compounded into additional growth and drew smaller urban places into their network.[18]

As critics note, however, flows of investment capital—the driver behind factories and commerce—are only one of many exchanges between cities. Movements of labor, ideas, and political power do not always coincide with capital flows because "networks are always partial and cannot, and are not, simply mapped straight onto a messy and complex world."[19] For example, New Orleans was subordinate to New York City in global cotton commerce and in intellectual life, but it was the center of the domestic slave trade and, along with Richmond and Charleston, a leader in the genre of proslavery polemics.

Furthermore, industry was not a prerequisite for building cities and towns. Europe's first net increase in urban populations occurred in Britain and the Netherlands in the seventeenth and eighteenth centuries, before the factory system came to dominate either country. Instead of being caused by industry, urban growth responded to a change in rural culture that went from seeking only subsistence to a new consumerism that created demand for more goods. This change, which occurred independent of labor-saving technology like better plows, created more jobs in cities to meet rural demand. "Only in a fully developed market economy with country dwellers strongly conscious of a desire to acquire urban goods and services," writes E. A. Wrigley, "were there the kinds of incentives to improve agricultural practices that could underwrite urban growth by providing the flow of food for people and organic raw materials for industry." In short, the country had to change before the city could grow.[20] This pattern of rural consumption driving the expansion of cities and towns held for the antebellum South, but slavery altered the pattern from the free-labor archetype.

To explain that pattern: After the 1750s, planters in the Southern colonies raised their personal consumption, which aided urban growth.[21] Thereafter rural Southerners' consumer demand sufficiently exceeded the level of subsistence to make cities grow. Not only did planters buy luxuries like books, clocks, and fine clothing, but recent studies demonstrate that even in areas with bad soils and transportation, like Appalachia, small farmers concentrated on cash crops and avidly bought town goods.[22] As Larry Hudson shows in this volume, slaves participated in the market,[23] but bondage restricted the amount of cash they could spend and barred them from urban amenities like schools and banks, thereby diminishing rural resources for small-town development. The South urbanized in a heavily commercialized slave society, where the limits on slave labor's ability to purchase urban goods and services kept the region's rate of urbanization below that of the northeast, where free farm labor had more disposable income. For the same reason, the South's urban growth rate fell behind the North-central states in the 1820s, when improved transportation and a steady influx of farmers boosted the role of marketing and manufacturing in North-central cities.[24]

Slavery's impact on consumption also manifested itself in the behavior of planters, which favored the development of a few cities over numerous small towns. In the village of Gallatin, Mississippi, merchant Samuel Aby built a thriving business with local cotton growers but moved to New Orleans when a proposed "Rail Road from N. O. to Jackson" threatened to bypass Gallatin and "ruin our trade here." Confident that his "great many friends amongst the planters . . . will doubtless transact all their business in N. Orleans through him," Aby retained rural customers who preferred long-distance shipping rather than buying direct at the cost of building up Gallatin, which never registered enough population to appear in antebellum census records.[25]

On top of cutting costs, moving to a major port improved Aby's access to new trends and products preferred by wealthy country consumers. More generally, cities connected Southerners to goods, people, and ideas from around the world. Leading merchants, editors, booksellers, and authors clustered in cities, as did theater troupes, visual artists, and architects. City dwellers discussed the ideas generated by these professionals in lyceums and debating societies that fed what one historian calls the "desire to rethink southern ideas and institutions."[26] To better experience these cosmopolitan trends, planters often maintained dual residences in town and country. Illustrating these plantation-city ties, in 1850 John Rutherfoord, who lived in Richmond, wrote to his father, a politician running the family estate in the Virginia Piedmont, to convey news about state government, promise to fulfill his father's request for "the best buggy that Richmond can furnish," and criticize "the lonely and dreary life you lead in the country. . . ."[27] The Rutherfoords' links to Richmond typified a rural relationship to urban services that favored cities over small towns because cities had a much higher density of the commercial and cultural amenities that planters desired.

The Rutherfoords' correspondence hints dually at an identification with a universalist cosmopolitanism—that is, rather than get by with local gossip and handicrafts, they wanted the news and the goods of the world—and a rootedness in the particular setting of the slave South. This dual perspective found expression in a description of English cities written in 1853 by William Henry

Trescot, an American diplomat from Charleston, South Carolina. Correspond-
ing to his wife about London, Trescot exclaimed "what magnificent streets and
buildings! Nothing however, strikes me as strange—even the soldiers seem like
so many militia companies on parade—with a difference." Although that passage did not elaborate the "difference," Trescot generally approved of the contrast between London and his home. He praised the "abundance of room for
light air" in public squares, the "superb avenues and room for thousands not to
crowd each other," and went so far as to call London "the perfection of this
world's civilization." Yet Trescott did not want to stay there. Like many Americans abroad, he felt shut out of London's social life, which he described as
"nearly always frivolous and often vicious." Moreover, as a slaveholder dedicated to white supremacy, Trescot was unnerved by London's blurring of racial
boundaries. He expressed less surprise at his hosts' antislavery opinions—
Americans were well aware of British abolitionism—than at their respectful
treatment of persons of African descent. This discomfort was manifest in
Trescot's account of a visit to the U.S. embassy by Liberian President Joseph
Jenkins Roberts, who, like many of Liberia's elite, was a free black immigrant
from the United States. Trescot described Roberts as "the most elaborately
dressed man I have seen in London" who, in response to white "servants
bowing very politely," carried himself "with a dignified complacency." Of all the
sights London had to offer, it was the ability of Roberts, a black man who might
have been attacked for a similar display in his Virginia birthplace, to be treated
as an equal in elite circles that left Trescot "standing in gaping wonderment."
In London, Trescot recognized improvements on familiar features of his native
Charleston, but he also identified differences that provoked him to assert his
affiliation with a separate, unique country and section, one ultimately defined
by the practice of racial slavery. Many urban Southerners shared this defense of
distinctiveness, but they, like Trescot, also reveled in their connections with the
cities of the world.[28]

Perhaps the best illustration of the ways that Southern urban networks
went beyond the nation's borders is immigration. In 1860, 34 percent of people
in Southern cities of 20,000 or more were born abroad as compared to 39 percent in comparable Northern places. However, the higher percentage of blacks
in the urban South (15 percent) than the North (2 percent) meant that immigrants comprised the same share of whites (two-fifths) in each section's cities.
The urban South had a smaller proportion of native-born whites (51 percent)
than the urban North (59 percent); of those, 10–15 percent were Northern
migrants, such that a majority of whites hailed from outside the slave states. By
these demographics the urban South was more culturally diverse than the
urban North and much more so than contemporary London, where the largest

immigrant contingent, the nearby Irish, accounted for only 4.6 percent of its people. The urban South's cultural pluralism not only confounds another measure of its supposed lag behind the North, it also reveals the intercity networks that slave states shared with foreign ports.[29]

If Southern cities' interconnections and industry seem weak compared to the North, a comparison with Latin America throws into relief the basic strength of Southern city building. Although not the prime cause of initial city growth, manufacturing usually increased along with urban networks. In 1860 the U.S. South achieved levels of industrial production three and four times above what Brazil mustered a quarter-century later. Most Southern industry was urban, and all Southern cities had growing manufacturing sectors. In railroad track, which connected cities, the South dwarfed the almost nonexistent networks of Brazil and Argentina: In 1860, Southern tracks totaled 9,165 miles, which connected the region's major cities to each other across vast distances; Brazil had only 70 miles. Likewise, in 1855, the Argentine capital of Buenos Aires was fed by only 6 miles of track.[30]

Latin American cities' weak links to the countryside owed much to "the tendency for export production to be based on relatively self-sufficient economies within plantations, haciendas, or mines," which soaked up rural demand that spurred urbanization in the non-self-sufficient rural South.[31] Contrasting rural mind-sets in his 1853 history of Mexico, Baltimore's Brantz Mayer wrote that "the planter . . . is usually in our own country to be envied for the peculiar privileges which his station affords him. But in Mexico, the position and education of the planter . . . are altogether different from those of the North American . . . ," because, among other reasons, hacendados did not "enjoy equal facilities of intercommunication between the cities or rural districts of Mexico."[32] Along with very weak rural demand, the below-subsistence wages paid in some Latin American cities curtailed consumption in the towns themselves. After Ecuador's separation from Spain in 1820, investors in the port of Guayaquil tried to manufacture for local customers only to find that "the poor were unable to buy even tobacco." By comparison, markets and consumerism were more pervasive in the rural Old South; as a result, the slave states had faster growing and more densely networked cities.[33]

Some Latin American cities succeeded in creating strong urban networks. For example, Havana, Cuba, which rivaled Baltimore's Civil War–era population, completed Latin America's first railroad in 1838, adopted the telegraph in 1851, and hosted a thriving tobacco industry that employed over 15,000 workers. Of course, Cuba, like the U.S. South, was a slave society, and the two "shared markets, technologies, and a bedrock reliance on a coercive labor system marked by brutality."[34] Cities in Cuba and the U.S. South grew faster than their countrysides because of well-developed urban networks that supplied rural consumer demand. Similarly, both places differed from the pattern of free-labor urbanization by concentrating urban dwellers in cities at the expense of towns. Understood in a global comparative context, the Old South built urban networks typical of commercialized slave societies.

Could Slavery Survive without Cities?

Although slavery did not prevent urbanization, slaves' presence in large cities was declining. Between 1840 and 1860, the South's ten largest cities added nearly half a million whites but almost no slaves, lowering the proportion of slaves from 19 to 8 percent of the total population. In his chapter in this volume, Marc Egnal regards this proportional decline as evidence of the "weakening grip of slavery on the Southern cities." This trend and Egnal's counterpoint raise an important question about Old South urbanization: could slavery survive in its growing cities? Historian Richard Wade answered in the negative by exploring how urban life's everyday freedoms acted like "corrosive acids" on slave discipline. For Wade and others, "the cause of slavery's difficulty in the city was the nature of urban society itself."[35] Unquestionably, cities challenged slaveholder authority, but few have asked this question in reverse: could the South's version of chattel slavery have survived *without* cities? An overview of the topic suggests that the answer is no.

Cities played a "crucial role" in the slave trade that sold one million bond-people from the seaboard states to the southwest and approximately two million more within state lines.[36] Urban places offered slave traders access to credit from banks, security from jails, food and clothing (as well as whips and chains) from provisioners, and, most of all, markets and customers. One-time slave Frederick Douglass thought his move from country to city "opened the gateway" to freedom, but for countless others going to town brought one of slavery's worst features: forced separation from family. Recalling the sale of "little Joe, the cook's son," Elizabeth Keckley, a slave in southern Virginia, wrote that "his mother was kept in ignorance of the transaction, but her suspicions were aroused. When her son started for Petersburg in the wagon, the truth began to dawn upon her mind, and she pleaded piteously that her boy should not be taken from her."[37]

If transported to a county seat, slaves waited in jail for shipment or sale. In cities they went to "depots" and auction houses operated by traders, often, as in Richmond, a short walk from the principal hotels and businesses.[38] In their campaign to outlaw slave sales in Washington, D.C., which occurred within sight of the capitol, antislavery Northerners protested a commonplace feature of the urban South that generated outsized profits. On the eve of the Civil War, slave sales amounted to $8 million for New Orleans, $4 million each for Charleston and Richmond, and $2 million for Natchez, Mississippi, which had only 6,000 residents.[39]

The slave trade also used the South's urban network to direct the flow of interstate traffic following the cotton boom. Trading networks moved human cargo between Lexington and Louisville in Kentucky to Memphis and Natchez on the lower Mississippi, and from Alexandria, Danville, and Norfolk on Virginia's Chesapeake coast to the ports of the lower South and New Orleans. Border South towns, even those with few slaves, were vital sale and shipment points. In St. Joseph's, Missouri, perched on slavery's northwestern frontier and home to only 170 slaves out of 8,932 people, English immigrant Elise Isely remembered seeing "a negro woman sold from a scaffolding built beside the street. . . . Right past my uncle's house drove the slaver, while the woman screamed in bitterest anguish."[40] Similarly, Wheeling, Virginia, which had only forty-four slaves in 1850, "grew into a major regional slave-trading hub" because of its location at the northernmost point where slaves could be traded legally on the Ohio River, and hence the entire Mississippi watercourse.[41] In the 1850s the slave population of the four border states increased by 10 percent, notwithstanding mass sales southward. Even if border cities themselves had few enslaved residents, slave traders needed them to conduct commerce in human chattels.

In a role analogous to a research-and-development laboratory for slaveholders, cities spawned most of the adaptations cited as keys to slavery's chances for persisting past 1865 had the Civil War not intervened. The practice of slave hiring—that is, leasing a slave to an employer for a fixed period—began in Charleston, South Carolina, in the first half of the eighteenth century, as local masters sought to maximize profits by meeting rising demand for domestic service and artisan labor. The Chesapeake region adopted hiring only after its towns grew in the late 1700s. Along with hiring, urban masters pioneered "term slavery," whereby slaves exchanged work and cash for postdated manumission.[42]

Factory slave labor occurred in cities because unlike mining and lumbering, only cities had the agglomeration of capital, markets, and service that mass production required. As James Huston argues, the comparatively small number of enslaved industrial workers owed more to wage rates than to problems of factory discipline. If cotton prices fell, the tobacco mills of Petersburg and iron foundries of Richmond offered slaveholders ready prototypes for making factory hands of field workers.[43]

Increases in slave hiring, dangerous industrial work, and rising slave prices spurred another urban innovation: slave life insurance. On an 1851 visit to Richmond, a British traveler noted that "a good man will fetch $800. Some I saw had been hired at seventy-five dollars a year, and are therefore generally a very good investment." The increasing profits of urban slavery encouraged owners to insure hired slaves' lives against risky industrial work. A recent study finds that "the proportion of life insurance policies on the lives of urban slaves in the Upper South approximated that of white male northeasterners by the mid-1850s." Significantly, the pioneering firm in slave insurance was headquartered in Baltimore, the South's most industrial city and an early site for slave hiring.[44]

The problem of urban slave discipline, often cited as the reason that cities undermined slavery, prompted the South's early development of paid policing. In 1805, New Orleans, newly arrived in the union, organized a "city guard" that ran like a military company and funded itself with a tax on slaveholders, a reflection of its role in suppressing revolt. Charleston, Savannah, Richmond, and Mobile also established paid police well before 1845, when New York City became the first Northern municipality to do so. In 1837, Charleston had the largest paid force of any American city, even though it ranked tenth in total population.[45]

The racial component of law enforcement stood out in Southern city statute books. Curfews, passes, badges, and bans on access to liquor, weapons, and public assembly all aimed at preventing revolt. Racial bars on high-paying occupations and access to public markets reserved the best economic opportunities for whites. Even seemingly inconsequential behavior could be outlawed if officials thought it threatened racial hierarchy; for example, New Orleans and Richmond, among other cities, banned African-American public smoking because the right to blow smoke in another's face carried a "connotation of equality and social presence." For some settlements, the need for paid police who could perform these multiple tasks of white supremacy motivated their initial request for municipal incorporation. Slave jails and markets created a slavery-influenced urban landscape in the South that included forts like Charleston's Citadel, built in the wake of an 1822 insurrection panic, and a concern for street designs that facilitated surveillance of the black population. Slavery's impact on law enforcement gave the urban South a greater militarized police presence than existed in the urban North.[46]

The Urban South's Unstable Politics

In light of slavery's need for cities, its supporters had reason to worry about the late-antebellum surge in urban free labor. As noted above, by 1860, Southern-born whites were outnumbered in the cities by a heterogeneous mix of African Americans, European immigrants, and Northern whites whose loyalty to slaveholders was questionable. African Americans, free or slave, were closely policed and could not vote, but white men could, and where their numbers were large enough they elected municipal governments that pushed against the wishes of rural planters and their urban allies. Although white workers challenged aspects of the slave regime across the urban South, they had more difficulty gaining political control in smaller cities, such as Richmond, Charleston, Savannah, and Mobile, that had higher percentages of disfranchised workers in labor forces that were 40–50 percent African American as well as higher proportions of women and nonnaturalized immigrant men.[47]

In the 1850s voters in the three largest slave-state cities, Baltimore, New Orleans, and St. Louis, elected governments at odds with the increasingly solid Democratic South. In Baltimore and New Orleans, the anti-immigrant but proslavery American or Know-Nothing Party ran things, whereas St. Louis openly defied the planters by electing Republicans who opposed slavery's expansion. American-born white labor backed the Know-Nothings because they promised to provide public works jobs for the unemployed, combat immigrant influence, and disrupt patron-client relationships that employers had used to keep wages low and labor docile. By expanding government spending and patronage, and by encouraging working-class gangs to intimidate Democratic voters, Southern Know-Nothings experimented with machine politics that flourished later in the century. Know-Nothings made sure to avow their support for slavery, but they angered planters nonetheless when Baltimore congressman Henry Winter Davis voted for a Republican speaker of the House of Representatives and when New Orleans Know-Nothings attacked Democratic candidate P. G. T. Beauregard for hiring slaves on a federal construction project.[48]

Proslavery publicists such as George Fitzhugh and J. D. B. DeBow promoted urbanization as key to Southern self-sufficiency and often praised particular cities like Richmond as "a subject of just pride throughout all the Southern States" that would "lead off in every matter that concerns the honor and security of the South,"[49] but these same writers worried about the increasing power of white workers in big-city politics and the trend they set for smaller cities. Commenting on the local rise of free labor, the *Charleston Mercury* warned that "the process of disintegration has commenced. . . . [White workers] may acquire the power to determine municipal elections; they will inexorably use it; and thus this town of Charleston, at the very heart of slavery, may become a fortress of democratic power against it."[50] These comments reflected the outlook of the Democratic Party, which by the late 1850s controlled most Southern state governments. Democrats achieved state and regional dominance because slaveholders, who dominated rural Southern politics, increasingly demanded a united front to fight Northern antislavery. City governments run by worker-supported opposition parties were a dangerous challenge to this new orthodoxy.

Proslavery politicians did not want to end urbanization but instead sought to control urban democracy. In Baltimore and New Orleans, reform movements emerged in 1857 bankrolled by urban businessmen and planters influential in state government. Officially nonpartisan so as to attract ex-Whig businessmen, Democrats allied to the party's Southern leadership dominated these organizations. To overcome Know-Nothing police and gangs, reformers relied on state troops, federal patronage workers, and volunteer militia like Baltimore's newly created Maryland Guard, a 300-plus unit of the sons of pro-Democratic merchants. State government also helped. In 1859, the Maryland legislature took over Baltimore's police and courts. The next year, police arrested gang members and kept the polls clear for reformers to win election on a campaign promising law, order, and "the suppression of partisan government altogether." New Orleans Know-Nothings survived by a combination of street muscle and an alliance to a dissident Democratic faction that thwarted a legislative takeover of city functions. Ominously for secessionists, St. Louis Republicans stopped nonpartisan reform in its tracks. In each city, foes of the machine were friends of secession, while the opposition's rank-and-file backed the union and, during the Civil War, fulfilled proslavery fears by spearheading state-level emancipation movements.[51]

The Civil War ended proslavery municipal reform as well as the broader process of Old South urbanization, but echoes of the urban Old South reverberated after 1865 in machine politics, racial segregation, ethnic heterogeneity, heavily armed and quasi-militarized police, the cities' eclipse of small towns, and the contract-labor networks that built the West. None of these aspects of modern U.S. urban history is directly and solely traceable to the Old South— New York's paid police differed from Charleston's, antebellum Northerners had their own struggles over machine politics, contract labor was not enslaved— but neither are they completely free of that history. The South's brand of proslavery urbanization existed within, not outside of, the United States and just as Northern influences disrupted secessionists' urban dreams, so too did elements of slaveholders' blueprint for urban America find their way into the cities remade by the Civil War.

NOTES

In common usage "city," "town," and "village" signify a large-to-small gradient in size but have no fixed population values. For clarity, this essay classifies a city as a concentration over 10,000 people; a town as 2,500–10,000; and a village or small town as under 2,500.

1. Hinton Rowan Helper, *The Impending Crisis of the South: How to Meet It* (New York: Burdick Bros., 1857), 333.

2. Ibid., 56, 215; David Brown, "Attacking Slavery from Within: The Making of *The Impending Crisis of the South*," *Journal of Southern History* 70 (August 2004): 546–549, 560, 562–563; Frank Towers, *The Urban South and the Coming of the Civil War* (Charlottesville: University of Virginia Press, 2004), 22.

3. Lynn Hollen Lees, "Urban Networks," in *The Cambridge Urban History of Britain*, vol. 3: *1840–1950*, ed. Martin Daunton (Cambridge: Cambridge University Press, 2000), 70. Unless otherwise specified, population numbers for U.S. cities come from Joseph C. G. Kennedy, *Population of the United States in 1860* (Washington, D.C.: GPO, 1864); U.S. Bureau of the Census, *Population of the 100 Largest Cities and Other Urban Places in the United States: 1790 to 1990*, comp. Campbell Gibson, Population Division Working Paper 27 (Washington, D.C.: U.S. Bureau of the Census 1998); Michael R. Haines, "State Populations," in *Historical Statistics of the United States: Earliest Times to the Present: Millennial Edition*, vol. 1, part A: *Population*, ed. Susan B. Carter et al. (New York: Cambridge University Press, 2006), 180–374.

4. David Goldfield, *Region, Race, and Cities: Interpreting the Urban South* (Baton Rouge: Louisiana State University Press, 1997), 235; David R. Goldfield, *Cotton Fields and Skyscrapers: Southern City and Region* (1982; repr., Baltimore: Johns Hopkins University Press, 1989), 64; David L. Carlton, "Antebellum Southern Urbanization," in *The South, the Nation, and the World: Perspectives on Southern Economic Development*, ed. David L. Carlton and Peter A. Coclanis (Charlottesville: University of Virginia Press, 2003), 42 (2nd quotation). Also see Peter Kolchin, *A Sphinx on the American Land: The Nineteenth-Century South in Comparative Perspective* (Baton Rouge: Louisiana State University Press, 2003), 26–27; James M. McPherson, *Ordeal by Fire: The Civil War and Reconstruction* (Boston: McGraw Hill, 2001), 28, 35; Robert William Fogel, *Without Consent or Contract: The Rise and Fall of American Slavery* (New York: W. W. Norton, 1989), 307.

5. Jan De Vries, "Problems in the Measurement, Description, and Analysis of Historical Urbanization," in *Urbanization in History: A Process of Dynamic Interactions*, ed. Ad van der Woude, Akira Hayami, and Jan De Vries (New York: Oxford University Press, 1995), 44.

6. Ibid., 47; Leonard P. Curry, "Urbanization and Urbanism in the Old South: A Comparative View," *Journal of Southern History* 40 (February 1974): 50.

7. Daniel R. Hundley, *Social Relations in Our Southern States* (New York: Henry B. Price, 1860), 26.

8. Lees, "Urban Networks," 67–68.

9. In 1860, these cities were Baltimore, New Orleans, St. Louis, Louisville, Washington, Charleston, Richmond, Mobile, Memphis, and Savannah.

10. John M. Merriman, *French Cities in the Nineteenth Century* (New York: Holmes and Meier, 1981), 14; Richard M. Morse, "Cuba," in *The Urban Development of Latin America, 1750–1920*, ed. Richard M. Morse, with Michael L. Coniff and John Wibel

(Stanford, Calif.: Center for Latin American Studies, Stanford University, 1971), 78; Sergio Diaz-Briquets, "Cuba," in *Latin American Urbanization: Historical Profiles of Major Cities* ed. Gerald M. Greenfield (Westport, Conn.: Greenwood Press, 1994), 177. For Swedish cities see http://www2.historia.su.se/urbanhistory/cybcity/nedladd/befolkn_mac/befolkning_1860_mac.txt (accessed October 2010).

11. Gavin Wright, *Slavery and American Economic Development* (Baton Rouge: Louisiana State University Press, 2006), 66–68.

12. Isaac Candler, *A Summary View of America: Comprising a Description of the Face of the Country, and of Several of the Principal Cities* (London: T. Cadell, 1824), 251.

13. Alexis de Tocqueville, *Democracy in America*, trans. Arthur Goldhammer (New York: Library of America, 2004), 399.

14. Data interpolated from Michael J. Fishman, "Population of Counties, Towns, and Cities in the United States, 1850 and 1860" (computer file), (Chicago: University of Chicago, Center for Population Economics [producer], 1990; Ann Arbor, Mich.: Inter-university Consortium for Political and Social Research [distributor], 1990). Fishman used Kennedy, *United States in 1860*, which presents disproportionately high urban populations for some states. Carter et al., *Historical Statistics of the United States*, has been used to adjust errors.

15. Goldfield, *Cotton Fields and Skyscrapers*, 4; John Majewski, *Modernizing a Slave Economy: The Economic Vision of the Confederate Nation* (Chapel Hill: University of North Carolina Press, 2009), 25, 41. For town growth after 1865, see Gavin Wright, *Old South, New South: Revolutions in the Southern Economy Since the Civil War* (New York: Basic Books, 1986), 39–42, and Edward L. Ayers, *The Promise of the South: Life after Reconstruction* (New York: Oxford University Press, 1992), 20.

16. Darrett B. Rutman with Anita H. Rutman, *Small Worlds, Large Questions: Explorations in Early American Social History, 1600–1850* (Charlottesville: University of Virginia Press, 1994), 251–252.

17. Carlton, "Antebellum Southern Urbanization," 38–39 (first quotation); Alan Pred, *Urban Growth and City Systems in the United States, 1840–1860* (Cambridge, Mass.: Harvard University Press, 1980), 115–116 (second quotation); John Majewski, *A House Dividing: Economic Development in Pennsylvania and Virginia Before the Civil War* (New York: Cambridge University Press, 2000), 166; Goldfield, *Cotton Fields and Skyscrapers*, 64–65.

18. Pred, *Urban Growth and City-Systems*, 8; Alan Pred, "Industrialization, Initial Advantage, and American Metropolitan Growth," *Geographical Review* 55 (April 1965): 168; Eric E. Lampard, "Historical Contours of Contemporary Urban Society: A Comparative View," *Journal of Contemporary History* 4 (July 1969): 17.

19. Richard G. Smith, "World City Actor Networks," *Progress in Human Geography* 27 (February 2003): 32 (quotation); Ben Derudder, "On Conceptual Confusion in Empirical Analyses of a Transnational Urban Network," *Urban Studies* 43 (October 2006): 2027–2046.

20. E. A. Wrigley, *Poverty, Progress, and Population* (New York: Cambridge University Press, 2004), 267.

21. Peter A. Coclanis, "Global Perspectives on the Early Economic History of South Carolina," *South Carolina Historical Magazine* 106:2–3 (2006): 130–146.

22. J. William Harris, *The Making of the American South: A Short History, 1500–1877* (Malden, Mass.: Blackwell, 2006), 99.

23. Sources in Hudson's chapter and Kathleen Mary Hilliard, "Spending in Black and White: Race, Slavery and Consumer Values in the Antebellum South" (Ph.D. diss., University of South Carolina, 2006), 8, 17–39.

24. "Growth rate" measures simple urban population increase rather than how fast cities grew compared to total population growth, the metric used in table 7.1. On that score the South was far ahead of the North-central states for the period 1800–1850. Richard Wade, *The Urban Frontier: The Rise of Western Cities, 1790–1830* (1959; repr., Urbana, Ill.: Illini Books, 1996), 193.

25. Samuel Aby to Charles Aby, July 1, 1853, and Charles Aby to Mrs. Jonas Aby, June 20, 1855, Aby Family Papers, Mississippi Department of Archives and History, Jackson.

26. Jonathan D. Wells, *The Origins of the Southern Middle Class, 1800–1861* (Chapel Hill: University of North Carolina Press, 2004), 96; Gregg D. Kimball, *American City, Southern Place: A Cultural History of Antebellum Richmond* (Athens: University of Georgia Press, 2000), 105.

27. John Rutherfoord to John Coles Rutherfoord, July 4, 1850, John Rutherfoord Papers, Rare Book, Manuscript, and Special Collections Library, Duke University, Durham, N.C.

28. William Henry Trescott to Eliza Trescot, January 28, February 15, and 16,and April 4, 1853, William Henry Trescot Papers, South Caroliniana Library, University of South Carolina, Columbia.

29. Dennis C. Rousey, "Aliens in the WASP Nest: Ethnocultural Diversity in the Antebellum Urban South," *Journal of American History* 79 (June 1992): 156; Dennis C. Rousey, "Friends and Foes of Slavery: Foreigners and Northerners in the Old South," *Journal of Social History* 35 (Winter 2001): 374.

30. Majewski, *Modernizing a Slave Economy*, 174; Richard Graham, "Slavery and Economic Development: Brazil and the United States South in the Nineteenth Century," *Comparative Studies in Society and History* 23 (October 1981): 626, 631; Richard E. Boyer and Keith A. Davies, *Urbanization in 19th Century Latin America: Statistics and Sources*, supplement to *The Statistical Abstract of Latin America* (Los Angeles: Latin American Center, UCLA, 1973), 7, 9.

31. Bryan R. Roberts, *The Making of Citizens: Cities of Peasants Revisited* (New York: Arnold, 1995), 38.

32. Brantz Mayer, *Mexico; Aztec, Spanish and Republican* (Hartford: S. Drake, 1853), 34–35.

33. Camilla Townsend, *Tales of Two Cities: Race and Economic Culture in Early Republican North and South America* (Austin: University of Texas Press, 2000), 92.

34. Rebecca J. Scott, *Degrees of Freedom: Louisiana and Cuba after Slavery* (Cambridge, Mass.: Harvard University Press, 2005), 27; Joan Casanovas, *Bread or Bullets!*

Urban Labor and Spanish Colonialism in Cuba, 1850–1898 (Pittsburgh: University of Pittsburgh Press, 1998), 25–27, 31.

35. Richard C. Wade, *Slavery in the Cities: The South, 1820–1860* (New York: Oxford University Press, 1964), 246. Claudia Dale Goldin, *Urban Slavery in the American South, 1820–1860* (Chicago: University of Chicago Press, 1976); Barbara Jeanne Fields, *Slavery and Freedom on the Middle Ground: Maryland During the Nineteenth Century* (New Haven, Conn.: Yale University Press, 1986), chap. 3.

36. Steven Deyle, *Carry Me Back: The Domestic Slave Trade in American Life* (New York: Oxford University Press, 2005), 149.

37. Frederick Douglass, *Narrative of the Life of Frederick Douglass, an American Slave* (Boston: Anti-Slavery Office, 1845), 31; Elizabeth Keckley, *Behind the Scenes, or, Thirty Years a Slave, and Four Years in the White House* (New York: G. W. Carleton, 1868), 28–29.

38. Deyle, *Carry Me Back*, 115; Kimball, *American City, Southern Place*, 157.

39. Deyle, *Carry Me Back*, 4, 149, 155; Jonathan D. Martin, *Divided Mastery: Slave Hiring in the American South* (Cambridge, Mass.: Harvard University Press, 2004), 30.

40. Elise Dubach Isely and Bliss Isely, *Sunbonnet Days* (Caldwell, Idaho: Caxton Printers, 1935), 115–116.

41. Wilma A. Dunaway, "Put in Master's Pocket: Cotton Expansion and Interstate Slave Trading in the Mountain South," in *Appalachians and Race: The Mountain South from Slavery to Segregation*, ed. John C. Inscoe (Lexington: University Press of Kentucky, 2000), 117–118.

42. Martin, *Divided Mastery*, 22, 32; T. Stephen Whitman, *The Price of Freedom: Slavery and Manumission in Baltimore and Early National Maryland* (Lexington: University Press of Kentucky, 1997), 93–118.

43. Robert S. Starobin, *Industrial Slavery in the Old South* (New York: Oxford University Press, 1970), 11; James L. Huston, *Calculating the Value of the Union: Slavery, Property Rights, and the Economic Origins of the Civil War* (Chapel Hill: University of North Carolina Press, 2003), 100.

44. George M. Dixon, *Transatlantic Rambles: or, A Record of Twelve Months' Travel in the United States, Cuba, and the Brazils* (London: George Bell, 1851), 54 (first quotation); Sharon Ann Murphy, "Securing Human Property: Slavery, Life Insurance, and Industrialization in the Upper South," *Journal of the Early Republic* 25 (Winter 2005): 618 (second quotation).

45. Dennis C. Rousey, *Policing the Southern City: New Orleans, 1805–1889* (Baton Rouge: Louisiana State University Press, 1996), 13–19, 38; Sally E. Hadden, *Slave Patrols: Law and Violence in Virginia and the Carolinas* (Cambridge, Mass.: Harvard University Press, 2001), 52–56; Robert C. Wadman and William Thomas Allison, *To Protect and to Serve: A History of Police in America* (Upper Saddle River, N.J.: Pearson, 2003), 35.

46. Dell Upton, *Another City: Urban Life and Urban Spaces in the New American Republic* (New Haven, Conn.: Yale University Press, 2008), 329 (quotation); Tom Downey, *Planting a Capitalist South: Masters, Merchants, and Manufacturers in the Southern Interior, 1790–1860* (Baton Rouge: Louisiana State University Press, 2006),

170; Wade, *Slavery in the Cities*, 266–268; Lisa C. Tolbert, *Constructing Townscapes: Space and Society in Antebellum Tennessee* (Chapel Hill: University of North Carolina Press, 1999), 259n16.

47. Towers, *Urban South*, 23, 56; Jacqueline Jones, *Saving Savannah: The City and the Civil War* (New York: Alfred A. Knopf, 2008), 103; William A. Link, *The Roots of Secession: Slavery and Politics in Antebellum Virginia* (Chapel Hill: University of North Carolina Press, 2003), 88.

48. Towers, *Urban South*, 101, 146.

49. "The Cities of the South," *DeBow's Review* 28:2 (August 1860): 187.

50. Towers, *Urban South*, 34–35 (quotation); Blaine A. Brownell, "The Idea of the City in the American South," in *The Pursuit Of Urban History*, ed. Derek Fraser and Anthony Sutcliffe (London: Edward Arnold, 1983), 144.

51. Towers, *Urban South*, 155, 158, 171–172.

8

"Swerve Me?": The South, Railroads, and the Rush to Modernity

William G. Thomas

"Swerve me? The path to my fixed purpose is laid with iron rails, whereon my soul is grooved to run. Over unsounded gorges, through the rifled hearts of mountains, under torrents' beds, unerringly I rush! Naught's an obstacle, naught's an angle to the iron way!"
—Herman Melville, *Moby Dick* (1851)

Let us begin with a simple railroad timetable from the 1850s. Railroad companies printed timetables on cards of varying sizes, posted them at depots, and reproduced them in handbills and in newspaper advertisements. With their long lists of arrival and departure times, mileages, and routes, the railroad timetables stood apart from many printed broadsides and pamphlets at the time because they did more than print text—they offered readers the opportunity to rehearse their movement between parts of the South and to calculate their time, distance, and route. The tables were like nothing else in the newspapers for nineteenth-century readers, eventually comparable only to financial market information and commodity prices in their complexity and detail. These abstractions of time and space represented an important break in how Americans, North and South, thought of time, geography, and themselves.

The timetable acted as a translation, a mediator, and a symbol. It signified, among other things, progress, freedom, escape, history, order, movement, mobility, control, and the future. As a means to assess one's position on a rapidly changing network, the timetable was useful but imperfect. Railroads rarely ran on time in the North or the South, and stops along the route were dropped and missed routinely.

Like the tackle on a whaling ship, however, the railroad timetable held together a set of associations, some physical and some abstract. Towns, depots, and cities were linked together on the printed paper and brought into a practiced relationship as the trains ran between them, continually rehearsing the timetable. The timetable was an important, if silent and often forgotten, agent in the social world of nineteenth-century America, devised for a singular purpose, but used for many different applications.[1]

All sorts of people consulted the timetables in the South—more than we had previously realized, including slaves, women, free blacks, businessmen, planters, merchants, and politicians. The technology of the timetable, indeed of the railroad, proved widely adaptable. As it turned out, people of all classes and races shaped and adapted the railroad to their own interests. In this respect the railroad and its timetables, as well as its locomotives, rails, roadbeds, water stations, passenger depots, bridges, and tunnels, played active roles in the South in ways we have ignored. They comprised profoundly important connections between the material and social worlds and offered enormously diverse possibilities for the South in the decades before the Civil War.[2]

Frederick Douglass's escape from slavery, to take a dramatic example, was brought into movement by a railroad timetable. Although he kept the exact means of his escape from slavery secret for nearly forty years, we know that Douglass consulted the Philadelphia, Wilmington, and Baltimore Railroad timetable on September 3, 1838, to plot his escape. Timing his arrival at the depot and his boarding of the northbound train with the precise time of its departure, Douglass carefully avoided any unnecessary exposure on the platform.[3]

White Southerners associated the railroad technologies with political power, urban development, and regional identity. The experience of these years in the South, therefore, was full of awkwardness and promise, as everywhere the modern coexisted side-by-side with the premodern, and new connections between the material and social worlds were made.

Slavery was the most obvious example. Many Northerners considered the institution a sign of backwardness, a glaring stain on the tapestry of American progress. Watching slavery from afar, some Northerners held out hope that America's technological progress would be joined someday by moral and material progress and slavery would be ended. Frederick Douglass had great confidence in the ability of technological progress to change the moral landscape and eventually to destroy slavery. Even some white Southerners predicted that modern advances might consign slavery to the margins of history. William

H. Ruffner, president of Washington College in Virginia, issued a stirring pamphlet against slavery's expansion in 1847 and questioned whether slavery could long endure or bring material progress to the South. Ruffner argued that "the atmosphere of free States" was enough to slow slavery's deleterious effects. He boldly proclaimed that slavery "infected" Virginia, weakening and ultimately crippling its material and cultural progress. For this he was forced to resign in disgrace.[4]

Despite Ruffner's doubts, slavery proved quite adaptive to the modern age. Slave labor was used to build thousands of miles of railroads in the South. As in the North, this work went forward with crude technology and in stark contrast to the highly complex steam locomotive engines that would run on the finished tracks. To lay the tracks, workers wielded picks and shovels, axes and wheelbarrows, mules and carts. Even more surprising, Southern railroads were quick to begin purchasing slaves to help operate their lines once the hard labor of construction was finished. The modern technologies, it seemed, might extend slavery rather than rendering it obsolete, despite the fervent hopes and prayers of some Northerners and of those enslaved.

Historians have often dismissed Southern railroad development before the Civil War as antithetical to the plantation system of the South and indicative of the region's limited priorities. Because slavery encouraged local production of cheap goods and low consumer demand, they contend, rails carried cash crops to market, but brought little back into the plantation. Furthermore, the Southern railroads were built with different gauges (width) of track, and few of them were connected, therefore to talk of a railroad "system" in the South is a fiction. Built to carry light loads, the argument goes, Southern railroads could not withstand the heavy hauling of the war, and they broke down quickly. Southern railroad management was inefficient, fractious, and ill suited to large-scale business operations, critics have charged, and because Southern roads were laid with track produced in England or the North and operated with locomotives built and fitted out in shops also outside of the South, the network, such as it was, could not be maintained in the war. One historian has summarized that, "because southern railroads relied so heavily on individual states, a 'South' simply did not cohere before the Civil War."[5]

When we look closely at the South's railroad culture, its experience with railroads, and the wide-ranging associations that railroads signified for Southerners, however, a different picture emerges. The South's experimentation with and investment in railroads and other technologies, it turns out, was consistent with the rest of the nation. In retrospect, the South's self-reliance, industry, and adaptation to technologies appear surprisingly robust. The South's business and railroad leaders spoke in a language of expansion familiar to the North, and they faced many of the same obstacles to financing, constructing, and running their operations. Increasingly, despite the rhetoric of national unification that accompanied the railroads, regional networks coalesced in the North and South with distinctive alignments that knit together the slaveholding states. The expansion of railroads accentuated the divergent regional identities that were already taking shape in the rush of modernizing development before the Civil War.

Reshaping Slavery

On at least three levels slavery and modern railroad development in the South were fused in a relationship of profound social consequence. First, by 1860 Southern railroads became some of the largest slaveholding and slave-employing entities in the South, marking for Southerners, black and white, a consistent pattern: advanced technologies and modern development did not appear incompatible with slavery but instead inextricably linked with the institution. As early as 1841, the chairman of the board of the Louisville, Cincinnati and Charleston Railroad proposed a resolution that the directors "purchase for the service of the Rail-road, from fifty to sixty male Slaves between the ages of sixteen and thirty." It was adopted without argument or amendment.[6]

By 1860 the South Carolina Rail Road Company held 90 slaves and was among the top 200 slaveholders in the city of Charleston (out of over 2,800 total slaveholders). In rural Autauwga County, Alabama, the South and North Rail Road with 121 slaves was the largest slaveholder in the county. In Baldwin County, Alabama, the Northern Rail Road held 41 slaves, and ranked among the top 25 slaveholders in the county. Although many slaveholders in the South held similarly large numbers of slaves, and some planters held many more than these companies, the railroad companies as a group in the 1850s employed over 10,000 slaves in the South and individually amassed holdings in slaves that rivaled the largest planters in the region.[7]

Railroad directors and officers also personally held slaves. They pursued the new technological opportunities of railroading from within their position in the slaveholding elite. In Virginia, among the directors and corporate officers of the state's fifteen railroad companies in 1859, 87 out of 112 held slaves. Those that did not were head engineers or superintendents, men who worked directly for the companies, often at the start of their careers. The average number of slaves held by the Virginia corporate directors was twenty. Some held over ninety, and many held over fifty. The list of directors in Virginia, furthermore, included many of the top slaveholding families in the state with extensive, large-scale plantations. Virginia's fifteen railroad presidents, despite the demands of running these new systems, included eight slaveholders, four of whom held over thirty slaves. The lower officers held slaves, too. D. S. Walton, the engineer on the Richmond and York River Railroad, held two slaves. Every class of company ownership and senior management, moreover, from engineer to president, secretary, treasurer, superintendent, and director, included slaveholders.[8]

Second, the extension of railroads gave white Southern slaveholders the means to dramatically enhance their property rights in slaves. The growing rail and telegraphic networks enhanced the slave trade; indeed, these technologies shaped the slave trade into a modern, information and time-sensitive market by the late 1850s. In addition, the networks gave white Southern slaveholders the ability to expand slavery into the western borderlands at a scale and speed that had important consequences for the ways they thought about their region and its growth.[9]

Third, and similarly, the railroads brought formerly distant regions into unexpectedly close proximity as New England free-labor, antislavery, and abolition advocates were much nearer to Kansas in 1856 than ever before. Along the borders, including some of the fastest-growing slaveholding counties in the South, slavery was no longer a distant threat to Northerners but instead a visible presence three or four depot stops away. Slavery's strongholds were measurable in minutes on a railroad timetable from places in the free North.

The reverse was also true, of course, and the free-labor society of the North was reachable in minutes from the South at several points along the border. The modernizing effects of the railroads and telegraphs did not point in a single direction for the South. Instead, they sustained all sorts of models for how the Southern states might progress and slavery might adapt. The Baltimore and Ohio Railroad (B & O) oriented its entire operation toward free labor, employing no slaves and hiring some free blacks on its payroll. None of the directors of its subsidiary line in Virginia held slaves. Although the company never took a stand on slavery per se in the growing sectional crisis, the B & O's great celebratory banquet in 1857 featured speeches and toasts to the Union from the abolitionist governor of Ohio, Salmon P. Chase, who praised the loyalty of the western states and by implication a free-labor society. Indeed, one B & O director toasted that the railroads would effectively "republicanize a people" by leveling class distinctions and providing equal access to mobility and modern progress. With its position skirting the border, however, the B & O became the sole exception in the South in its commitment to free labor and in its orientation to the free west. For the rest of the South, railroads advanced everywhere with slavery.[10]

If we look at the progress of the South in the 1850s and halt our gaze short of the Civil War, we begin to see just how rapidly and thoroughly the region's technology was becoming associated with its civilization. When *The Railroad Advocate*, for example, a trade journal published out of New York, wanted to assess the state of Southern railroads in 1855, the editor, Zerah Colburn, sent a special correspondent on a tour of the South. Colburn's correspondent reported a South brimming with modern development, a region that had harnessed slaves to the most advanced technologies of the day. He found the Seaboard and Roanoke, a road Frederick Law Olmsted traveled a year later, to be "well managed" and "well constructed." The locomotives were built by the nation's finest manufacturer, and the shops were equipped with "the best tools." The entire enterprise was impressive. On the North Carolina Central, a road over 200 miles long, without a grade exceeding 50 feet, and laid with the best 60 pound iron rails available, he discovered "one of the best constructed [roads] in the country." Its locomotives were deemed the most "beautiful machines in the country."

When Colburn's traveler arrived in Savannah, Georgia, moreover, the railroad station there stunned him. "To say that Savannah, Georgia, is likely to have the most complete and elegant railroad station in the country (besides being one of the very largest) may be a matter of some surprise to northern and western railroad men," he reported. The building was 800 feet long and 63 feet wide, designed in a modern style and rivaled only by a few railroad stations in the nation, the ones in Boston and Baltimore. The road was equipped with engines exhibited at the New York Crystal Palace Exhibition. The yards included six parallel tracks, with over three miles of railroad, a remarkably large and extensive facility. The shops held the best workbenches and lathes in the business, "the best we've seen."[11]

All of these railroads were both worked and made possible by slave labor. According to Colburn's journal, Southern railroads had achieved through slavery an extraordinary level of quality construction at half the cost of Northern and Western railroads. And the low cost of construction through the use of slaves prompted "astonishment in more northern communities." At a cost of $15,000 per mile to construct, the Southern railroads had achieved staggering efficiency, and Colburn praised the slaveholding railroad stockholder who let his slaves work "at cost" and who "looks for his profits not to what he can make *out* of the road but to what the road can, when in operation, make *for* him." Northern and Western roads often cost twice as much to build, averaging by most estimates at the time between $30,000 and $35,000 per mile.[12] There was much to admire about these Southern efficiencies, Colburn found himself admitting: no contractors scamming the roads for high profits, no inflated costs and padding of contracts, no secretive promoters keeping the public at arm's length while they engineered a boondoggle.

In 1855, then, the South's railroads, at least according to a leading Northern-based industry journal, appeared the envy of the nation, built at a level of efficiency that no Northern line could manage and equipped at the very highest levels of quality. The notion that Southern roads were all laid with "strap rail," Colburn noted, was wrong, because all of these had been replaced with "heavy T rail." The "best engineering talent . . . in the world" was in the South building railroads. Led by its public men, the white South had sidestepped the financial scheming and shenanigans that afflicted Northern lines, according to Colburn. And slavery was a big part of the explanation for the region's success.

If railroad companies were buying slaves by the dozens, and leasing them by the hundreds, they were also shipping them from one part of the South to another as part of a modernized slave-trading system and market. With the growth of railroads and telegraphs in the South, slave trading took on the characteristics of other markets: time-sensitive information, networks of buyers, rapid transit, and national reach. Slaveholders and slave traders increasingly used and adapted these technologies. Slave sales shifted in the 1850s from a localized courthouse trade to a wider railroad-and-telegraph-enabled trade. Up-to-the-minute information, telegraphed from markets all over the South, affected the sales and prospects of traders. Browning, Moore, & Co., one of the largest slave traders in Richmond, Virginia, negotiated deals by telegraph, maintained close contact with the railroads, and shipped slaves out to buyers on the railroad network all over the South. So did Moore & Dawson, another Richmond slave-trading firm. One of their agents in Baltimore wired, "if I buy them I am going to . . . take the negroes and carry them by first train to Richmond." His expense sheet listed not only the prices he paid for the slaves but clothing expenses, the house commission, and the train tickets "on negroes from Baltimore to Richmond." Buyers used the telegraphs to deliver instructions for credit and used the railroads for quick delivery: "bring the negroes on immediately" meant load them on the trains as soon as possible. "I can be down tomorrow with five (5) Negroes," one seller from Lynchburg wired the Richmond firm.[13]

In this context many white Southerners began to argue that the competition with the North had entered a new phase with the arrival of railroads, telegraphs, and steamships. When the Virginia Board of Public Works and the Blue Ridge Railroad began building a tunnel through the mountains of western Virginia, the project became symbolic of the South's resurgent development and the region's attempt to conquer the natural barriers to regional unity. As one of the most challenging engineering feats of the day, the tunnel drew national attention because it would be the longest tunnel in the United States. As a means to unify Virginia and the South, the tunnel served a wider purpose, a small step on the path of Southern modern economy and political independence.

The project, moreover, would link together the older Virginia Tidewater region with the more recently settled western parts of the state. Virginia seemed in many respects to be a microcosm of the South. There was, it turned out, nothing inevitable about mountainous geography and free labor. Slavery pushed into the mountains and valleys of western Virginia throughout the 1850s, often along the lines established by the railroads. The Blue Ridge tunnel, then, was strategically positioned to orient western Virginia into the dominant, slavery-based network of the state and to satisfy the long-standing grievances of westerners that they had been denied adequate transportation and support.[14]

In 1851 the Virginia Board of Public Works engaged one of nation's most distinguished engineers, Claudius Crozet, to design and build the line through the mountains. Born in France and a man of wide military and engineering experience, Crozet served as the chief civil engineer for the board. He planned and surveyed the state's development of canals, turnpikes, bridges, and railroads. By 1850 he was one of the leading engineers in the world and had written widely used textbooks and treatises.[15]

Slavery figured prominently in every aspect of the operation. Crozet hired contractors who brought hundreds of Irish workers to the Blue Ridge Mountains and housed them in "shanties." White Irish laborers were put to work almost exclusively on the tunnel, the most dangerous job. In the early phases of the project, though, Crozet secured permission from the board to use enslaved labor to lay the tracks and build the roadbed, and hundreds of black slaves worked along the line. After a series of strikes, however, and after the price of white labor jumped higher in 1853–1854, Crozet moved to hire black slaves for the tunnel. Slaveholders set limits on when, where, and under what conditions slaves might work, and Crozet found that he could hire slaves only for drilling in the tunnel but not for "blasting." "Fifty negroes in the Tunnel," he explained, "will relieve the white hands, and enable us to have a full force at the drills." The board, at Crozet's urging, took out insurance policies on slaves hired in the tunnel. When two slaves were killed in the operation, Crozet attempted to deflect the board's liability onto the Virginia Central Railroad, which owned the tracks leading to the tunnel. The attorney general of Virginia, however, determined that the board was liable and should compensate the slaveholders at fair market value. Affidavits were taken from white men who had known the slaves and who estimated their value. The state paid the slaveholders.[16]

When Southern railroads could not buy or lease slaves, they turned to other means. One ready source of labor was in state prisons. Virginia authorized the hiring of slave prisoners to companies in 1858 in its "Act Providing for the Employment of Negro Convicts on Public Works." The governor of Virginia, John Letcher, negotiated the contracts with railroads, and in 1860 he sent over one hundred men and sixteen women to work on the Covington & Ohio Railroad (C & O). The C & O was the state's premier project to follow the Blue Ridge tunnel and break through the Allegheny Mountains to the Ohio River valley. Another symbolic effort to reshape the South, the C & O project had been praised by George Fitzhugh in the dedication of his widely read treatise defending slavery, *Cannibals All! Or Slaves Without Masters*. The slaves sent to work there found themselves pitched into the largest construction project in the state. In 1861 with the onset of war, the project was abandoned, but in 1863 Virginia's engineers recommended restarting it and supplying the necessary labor again by using convicts.[17]

For slaveholders, too, the prospect of hiring out their slaves to the railroads was financially attractive, and few passed up the opportunity. Once slaves were sent to the railroad, however, it might be months before they returned. One ex-slave from Athens, Georgia, Paul Smith, recalled that his father had worked on the first railroad in the state. When the family's slaveholder died, the administrator of the estate "hired out most all" of the slaves to work on the railroad. The slaveholder's wife had little say in the matter, and "it was a long time 'fore she could get 'em back home."[18]

In the 1850s railroads in the South began to increase their use of slaves not only for the back-breaking construction of the road but for the routine operation of the line once it was built. The president of the Mississippi Central Rail Road explained that slavery would probably become the dominant means of running and maintaining the railroad. He reported that slaves could be deployed across the system and "could be controlled and directed [sic] at all times be controlled and concentrated whenever wherever an emergency may demand." He admitted that the fifty-four slaves owned by the company represented "a small portion of the number of laborers required by the company," but he expected the company to acquire more each year until "the company becomes the owner of all the labor that may be desired [sic] required for repairs of their road." The deletions and edits were significant. Slaves could indeed be "concentrated" not only "whenever" but "wherever" the company needed them, and the railroad's operations seemed especially conducive to employing slave labor.[19]

Much of the investment that railroad companies made in purchasing slaves would not be entirely apparent until the end of the Civil War, when accounting reconciliation required some kind of statement for the annual reports. In 1865, for example, the Mississippi Central Railroad's annual report contained one line item of note: "Account of C. S. [Confederate States] Bonds and cost of Negroes now free: $585,237." The Nashville and Chattanooga Railroad president was more direct in his 1867 recapitulation of the losses from the war: "We find from the books that there has been invested in negroes, in Georgia, the sum of $154,348 and negroes sold amounting to $32,805.25 leaving negro investment $121, 542.71." This amount, he rather dryly noted, "is now, manifestly, a total loss."[20]

Slavery had taken on new forms with the explosion of railroad building. There was an expectation among white Southerners that the most modernizing technology might be run entirely with slave labor. The promotion of railroads seemed to fit neatly with the idea of the South as an expansive, slaveholding, republican region. Few whites were worried about the compatibility of railroads or industry with slavery. Many thought that the South's natural position could only be enhanced with the arrival of the railroads. In this spirit one delegate to the numerous Southern commercial conventions of the 1850s declared, "Every planter who has a dozen negroes wants a railroad running in front of his house, and every gentleman who has fifty negroes must have one running by his house and another by his kitchen."[21]

The Rush to Modernity

By 1860 the South had constructed not only one of the most extensive rail networks in the world—as we shall see—but also an advanced vision for its economic and social future. It was significant that 75 percent of the total railroad mileage that the South would have at the end of the 1850s had been built during that same decade. Over 8,300 miles of track were laid down in the 1850s rush. Only the states of Ohio, Illinois, Indiana and the rest of the northwest could match this new mileage or boast a similarly rapid growth rate. Two regions—the West and the South—built railroad lines so fast that of the 22,000 new miles in the 1850s they accounted with equal shares for over 17,000 of them.[22]

This feverish railroad building in the 1850s coincided with the rapid transfer of slaves into the southwestern region, and slave prices skyrocketed with the expansion. Slavery, it appeared, could thrive in the western territories and nearly everyone knew it. Between 1840 and 1860, as railroads extended lines westward, Southern slaveholders established themselves in the extreme western reaches where slavery was permitted. Slavery grew fastest in these places in

TABLE 8.1.   Total number of slaves by subregion.

	1840	1850	Change, 1840–1850	1860	Change, 1850–1860
Old South	1,328,603	1,567,052	18%	1,748,273	12%
Cotton South	617,195	897,531	45%	1,203,437	34%
Northern border	457,695	543,098	19%	590,189	9%
Western border	78,175	192,683	146%	408,612	112%

Source: U.S. Historical Census Browser, Geostat, University of Virginia, online at http://fisher.lib.virginia.edu/collections/stats/histcensus/ (accessed October 2010). The Old South is defined as Virginia, North Carolina, South Carolina, Georgia, and Florida; the cotton South includes Alabama, Louisiana, and Mississippi; the northern border states are Delaware, Kentucky, and Tennessee; and the western border states are Arkansas, Missouri, and Texas. Also see Jenny Bourne Wahl, "Stay East, Young Man? Market Repercussions of the Dred Scott Decision," *Chicago-Kent Law Review* 82:1 (2007): 368.

the two decades before 1860 with the number of slaves in the western border states more than doubling from 1840 to 1860 (see table 8.1).

One important consequence of the rush to build railroads in the South was to enhance Southern identity as distinct from the rest of the nation. For the South, the railroads united white Southerners who were separated by vast rural spaces and overcame the region's significant natural barriers. By 1860 the most highly populated regions of the South were linked in ways unimaginable a generation earlier. Only western Virginia, a significant exception, stood out as a major population of white Southerners out of reach of the Southern-oriented rails. In the decades before the 1840s, cities in the South seemed to have little to do with one another: information rarely circulated between them, commodities were traded more with the North, especially New York, Boston, and Philadelphia, and travelers headed out of the region rather than across and within it. But the boom in railroad construction and the emergence of telegraphic communication after 1840 linked the South's cities and created regional networks for shared information, social interaction, and trade. By 1860 people in the smaller cities and towns across the South received their information from the region's larger cities. Even the names of the railroad lines evoked a kind of formal bond or at least a fledgling relationship between distant Southern places: the Memphis and Charleston; the Mississippi Central; the Savannah, Albany & Gulf; the East Tennessee and Virginia.[23]

The different gauges of railroad in the South did not materially hinder this process of unification and common interest. Indeed, the closest study of the development of different gauge systems in the United States reveals precisely how innovative the South was in the decades before 1860. Hardly a recalcitrant and late adopter of the "standard" 4'8.5" gauge, the South experimented with different gauges just as other regions did. The 4'8.5" gauge was steadily losing

TABLE 8.2.   Per capita access to railroad depots and junctions, 1861, for free population (per 10,000 persons).

Region	Total points	Number of Access Points.[1]Estimated percentage of population within 15 miles of junction or depot	
South	1,518	1.856	54.7%
North*	1,636	1.796	62.4%

Source: Historical Geographic Information System database compiled at the Center for Digital Research in the Humanities, University of Nebraska-Lincoln.

1 Access Points reflect the number of junctions and depots per 10,000 residents.
*Selected Northern states here include Pennsylvania, Illinois, Michigan, Ohio, Wisconsin, and Iowa.

its prominence in the 1840s and 1850s to other, wider gauges; by 1860, there were nine major subregions with distinct gauge standards. The period from 1855 to 1865 was the most diverse time in railroad gauge development, with only 17 percent of the entire U.S. railroad network reachable on a common gauge route without a break, either in the North or the South. The development of gauges, it turned out, depended on who the chief engineer was on a project and on what gauges were in use nearby.[24]

By 1861 over 10,000 miles of railroad track linked cities and towns across the South. The region boasted hundreds of junctions, depots, and end points—so many that despite the South's vast geography (compared to much of the North) the level of railroad access for its free population nearly matched Northern states and exceeded them in the number of depots and junctions per capita (see table 8.2).

In a decade the South had vaulted itself into a comparable position with much of the North in its access to railroads and all that they signified. Despite their size and difficult mountainous terrain, the states of Georgia, Tennessee, Maryland, Virginia, and South Carolina led the South in the percentage of free residents living within fifteen miles (a day's journey on an ox-cart) of a railroad depot—all of them with access rates of over 60 percent. Although some Northern states had higher percentages of residents living within this fifteen-mile zone, the South's per capita density of railroad structures (depots and junctions) for its free population was higher than in many Northern states. In Mississippi and South Carolina, for example, there were 3.1 and 4.8 depots per 10,000 free residents, while in Ohio there were 1.7. By this measure, whites in the South could claim by 1861 an extraordinary level of railroad penetration, investment, and accessibility.

The effects of the Southern network were more pervasive than we have imagined. Although the South had previously relied on its extensive river

system for transportation and communication, railroads were what defini-
tively broke the region's geographic barriers. Furthermore, the network was
overlaid on existing river systems and existing roads and turnpike systems.
Plank roads, turnpikes, macadamized roads, and even canals combined with
railroads to create a deep "system." And because steam-powered railroads in
the 1850s required a depot every eight to twelve miles for watering and fu-
eling, the technology created a high level of access, whether the populations
it served were dispersed or concentrated. In this respect New York City had
no greater access to the modern technology than Resaca, Georgia. Moreover,
there were universal limits to the number of tracks and length and number
of cars, further democratizing access. In fact, the Southern white population, because it was dispersed and yet served by widely available railroad
access points, had more direct encounters with the modernity that railroads
brought.

For every state there was a saturation point, a point of diminishing returns,
in the development of railroad mileage and access to the network. Here, too, the
pattern of Southern development was impressive and consequential. Beyond a
certain point each mile of railroad that was added to a network included an
increasingly small percentage of the population. For example, Ohio, one of the
leading states in railroad mileage, had 295 percent more miles of railroad track
than South Carolina in 1860, but only 22 percent more of its population was
serviced by its railroad network. The Southern railroad network served its most
densely populated areas, and, relative to the North, it brought proportionately
more of its residents into contact with the railroads (see figure 8.1).[25]

The pattern was similar across the South: despite the costs and consequences, leading white Southerners saw these projects as modern necessities
for a vibrant, powerful, modern region. A large part of these railroad projects'
appeal was the impression that they would extend the South's slavery-based
civilization, conquer nature, promise economic independence, and enable
physical connections. In the Wiregrass region of Georgia, the Macon and
Brunswick Rail Road got underway in the 1840s. According to a close study by
historian Mark Wetherington, its growth "reflected local support for railroads"
among the elite, who saw it as "one of the building blocks of civil society."
Planters and slaveholders led the effort to bring the railroad into the Wiregrass.
Yeoman farmers, on the other hand, may have feared the railroads as a threat
to their economic independence and stability, suspecting that the railroad
would bring great changes. They knew that wherever the railroad went slaveholding, cotton farming, fence building, and timber cutting followed.[26]

The Wiregrass's commercial activity was transformed in the wake of the
railroad. The number of slaves per farm increased, the number of cotton bales

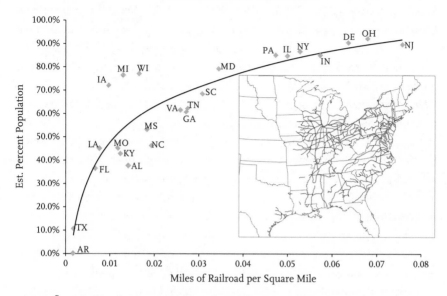

FIGURE 8.1.   Railroad-access correlation logarithmic trend line graph
Source: This graph includes National Historical GIS data from the University of
Minnesota and railroad depot data compiled at the Center for Digital Research in the
Humanities, University of Nebraska, based on original map sources.

per farm doubled. The project's chief engineer, Albert Hall Brisbane, believed
that the railroad was part of a larger commercial struggle with the North and
saw his project in these competitive terms. "Sectional jealousy of the American
states," he wrote in 1849, "is beginning to exhibit itself on the score of comparative wealth." The South could "spare no expense to eclipse" the North in the
race for wealth.[27]

The rush of railroad building prompted Democrats across the South to
recast their Jacksonian-era fears of corporate privilege and power and to use
their state's railroad projects to secure the allegiance of upcountry voters. In
Georgia these Democrats made extravagant claims that the railroad would con-
nect the little town of Brunswick in "direct trade" with Europe. The railroad, in
other words, would bypass the North, free the South, and in the great commercial and economic rivalry taking shape allow Southern planters, large and
small, to dominate the trade.

Expansionists across the South, especially in the Democratic Party, believed
they were in a race with the North and little seemed worth sparing in the contest, even if they had to recast their views of constitutional powers. "We are on
the locomotive expansion," the *Dallas Herald* declared; "The steam is up and

the bell will ring soon; those that don't want to take a ride had better get off. Sonora [Mexico] will be the next watering place." Southern newspapers were filled with these urgent visions. "Railroad mania," as it was sometimes called, swept the region, and Democrats were on the hustings calling for railroad access. There were skeptics, such as South Carolina's senator James Henry Hammond, who wrote a long tract against "railroad mania." Hammond and other Democratic Party detractors, however, objected to state aid for railroads on principle more than to railroads as a modernizing device.[28]

Such conflicts came part and parcel with nearly every railroad project in the South, for not all politicians were sympathetic to the grand schemes of the railroad-planter coalition, especially regarding the state aid these powerful interests repeatedly requested. Most of the opposition came from those strict constructionists and Democrats who in the tradition of Andrew Jackson feared the use of state power to concentrate wealth and capital in the form of a corporation. For the federal transcontinental project these fears were deep-seated, but they trickled down to local and state political debates as well.

Virginia's senator James Murray Mason and South Carolina's congressman Andrew Butler, for example, were leading strict constructionists. They saw congressional efforts to build a transcontinental railroad as an encroachment of the federal government on the power of the states and extrapolated that if a president could choose a route, he could dictate to the states where the route could run and eventually a president could extend his reach to meddle with slavery. This power, they warned, was just a first step in federal authority to control the states. Mason and Butler, followers of John C. Calhoun, fixed their opposition not on the railroad—which they wanted and for which Calhoun had advocated on behalf of the South—but on the excessive exercise of presidential power that the boom mentality might make possible.

The federal government's refusal to consider the Southern route exacerbated North-South relations, especially because many leading white Southerners believed that nature, the landscape itself, favored the South in the race to Mexico, California, and the West. Weather played a role, as heavy snows, bitter cold, and ice blocked more northerly routes through the mountains. Ease of construction and grading were also widely discussed advantages. During the 1858 congressional debates over the location of a proposed transcontinental railroad, Alfred Iverson, Georgia's senator, proposed two routes, one Northern and one Southern, both federally supported, and emphasized the Southern route as the cheapest to build and the most reliable. But Northern congressmen opposed the measure and ignored the arguments for the Southern route's low cost and reliability. This opposition seemed to many white Southern leaders to fly in the face of the obvious natural advantages of the Southern route. After a decade of railroad building in the South designed to break the mountain chain and reshape the geography of the region, the Northern opposition seemed especially galling to white Southern promoters. "We cease almost to be considered as parties having rights," Iverson lamented, echoing the concerns of John C. Calhoun eight years earlier; "Nature itself declares in our favor but her voice is disregarded."[29]

The rush to build railroads in the South led its leaders to constantly recalibrate their region's position relative to the nation's commercial and economic network. As late as 1860 and 1861 the rush was still on. New Southern railroads were coming on line, connecting places never before linked, and adding to the dynamic of sectional examination and measurement. In this respect the 1850s marked a decisive period of change for the white South's identity, as modern ideas, technologies, practices, and institutions were instantiated in repeated sequences across the region. The timetable, the depot platform, the locomotive, and rail bridges and tunnels offered evidence to white Southerners of the mobility and success of their society.[30]

For the white South the transformation of the landscape, the great engineering feats of the railroad companies, and their extensive use of enslaved labor were all tied to the widespread belief, articulated by Iverson, that "nature itself" favored the region. Indeed, nature needed to be conquered and mastered from the malarial swamps of the Tidewater to the craggy passes of the Allegheny Mountains. The effort to take this step required a massive scale of enterprise, state investment, and adaptive forms of slavery. Every Southern state participated in this movement, and, in the context of the newly acquired western territories, the stakes were increasingly significant.[31]

Railroad companies also moved to acquire slaves and use them to extend their lines and man their far-flung networks. As Southern railroad developers adapted slavery into the service of the new technologies, the flexibility of slavery could not have been more apparent, nor its reach more extensive, nor its consequences more alarming for many Northerners. The fastest-growing slaveholding regions of the South were also the fastest-growing railroad regions. It should not seem surprising that the Confederacy had its greatest pull, its greatest adherents, in the regions that railroads penetrated in the 1850s, nor that those places in the South with few railroads—Missouri, Arkansas, western Virginia, western Maryland, eastern Tennessee—remained on the edges of the Confederacy.

The ideas of civilization and progress, what a nation needed to claim modernity, were most strikingly evident in the way white Southerners understood the effects of railroad development. What surprised them was the North's blatant disregard for the underlying geographic advantages that they thought nature had bestowed upon the South. The recent mastery of geography that their railroad building so clearly demonstrated seemed to count for little in the North, and yet the experience gave the white South unprecedented confidence in their modern civilization and slavery's place in it. In this respect the Pacific Railroad Bill and its debates in the 1850s revealed to the white South that Northerners might never respect their region's claim to modern progress.

When Virginia's delegates met for the secession convention in 1861, three railroad directors represented their districts, two of them as outright secessionists. One of them, Thomas Branch of Petersburg, reported on his district's resolution that "negro slaves are property." Another railroad man, William Ballard Preston, however, took a more tempered approach. He did not favor immediate secession and instead pushed throughout the crisis for careful negotiation to achieve clear constitutional guarantees for slavery. Finally, on Tuesday, April 16, 1861, a day after President Lincoln's call for troops to suppress secession in the lower South, William Ballard Preston, a western Virginian, a director of the Virginia and Tennessee Railroad Company, and a holder of eighteen slaves, introduced the Ordinance of Secession in the Virginia Convention. For weeks the floor of the convention had been a junction point for receiving and sending up-to-the-minute information and sparring over the right course of action. Asking for "God's mercy," Preston cautioned that he was not reacting to either "the influence of circumstance or telegraphic information." Instead, his dramatic proposal came forward only after a hand-delivered, hard copy report from Washington, D.C., that confirmed Lincoln's actions.[32]

Despite Preston's reluctance to trust the news over the wires, his motion to secede and the convictions that sustained the white South were possible in large measure because of the region's well-practiced confidence as a modern nation-state. That confidence descended from widely shared experiences with railroads and telegraphs, as symbols of modernity, as carriers of national identity, and as agents for the adaptability and extension of slavery. In this environment of rapid change, both the North and the South staked its society's future on the railroad and what it enabled long before the Civil War. Americans in both regions knew that with secession a modern war between these nations was more than a possibility. That dim recognition was enough to give William Ballard Preston pause, but not nearly enough to stop either him or the Confederates from acting on their national vision.

NOTES

1. My concerns and approaches have been influenced here especially by "actor network theory," as well as by the literature on the social construction of space. Bruno

Latour's views on the modern "constitution" with its separation of Nature and Society, on the importance nonhuman objects as actors, on the idea of a "sociology of associations," and on the mediation among actors in society have been especially important in my thinking about the role of the railroad in Southern society. See Bruno Latour, *Reassembling the Social: An Introduction to Actor Network Theory* (New York: Oxford University Press, 2005), and *We Have Never Been Modern* (Cambridge, Mass: Harvard University Press, 1993). The works on space and modernity include J. Nicholas Entrikin, *The Betweenness of Place: Towards a Geography of Modernity* (New York: Macmillan, 1991), esp. 27–59; Allan Pred, *Making Histories and Constructing Human Geographies: The Local Transformation of Practice, Power Relations, and Consciousness* (Boulder, Colo.: Westview Press, 1990), esp. 126–170; Anthony Giddens, *The Consequences of Modernity* (Cambridge: Polity, 1990). I have also been especially influenced by Peter Onuf and Nicolas Onuf, *Nations, Markets, and War: Modern History and the American Civil War* (Charlottesville: University of Virginia Press, 2006), for their understanding of the South as a nation and of the Civil War as a clash of modern nation-states.

2. On the social construction of technologies, and for a recent account of the social meanings of technology and how people adapt technology to their use, see David Edgerton, *The Shock of the Old: Technology in Global History since 1900* (New York: Oxford University Press, 2006). Edgerton emphasizes a history of "technology in use," rather than invention, and the persistence of old technologies among the modern. He calls the tendency to overemphasize the impact of technology "futurism." Here, Edgerton's view is especially relevant because with railroads the question is how people adjusted to them, adapted, and came to terms with their use and meaning. This is predominately a cultural and social question. Other important works focused on this question include Carolyn Marvin, *When Old Technologies Were New: Thinking about Electric Communication in the Nineteenth Century* (New York: Oxford University Press, 1988), esp. 193–209; and David Nye, *Technology Matters: Questions to Live With* (Cambridge, Mass.: MIT Press, 2006), esp. 46–47. Nye emphasizes that technology is not deterministic and is "unpredictable," often with "no immediate impact."

3. On Douglass, see Lisa Brawley, "Fugitive Nation: Slavery, Travel, and Technologies of American Identity, 1830–1860" (Ph.D. diss., University of Chicago, 1995).

4. William H. Ruffner, *Address to the People of West Virginia Showing that Slavery is Injurious to the Public Welfare, and that it may be Gradually Abolished without Detriment to the Rights and Interests of Slaveholders, By a Slaveholder of West Virginia* (Lexington, Va.: R. C. Noel, 1847). See also William Blair, *Virginia's Private War: Feeding Body and Soul in the Confederacy, 1861–1865* (New York: Oxford University Press, 1998), 18.

5. For analysis along these lines, see Scott Reynolds Nelson, *Iron Confederacies: Southern Railways, Klan Violence, and Reconstruction* (Chapel Hill: University of North Carolina Press, 1999), 16–45 (quotation). For a recent treatment of the South, especially Virginia, as unmodern in its development, see Susan Dunn, *Dominion of Memories: Jefferson, Madison, and the Decline of Virginia* (New York: Basic Books, 2007), esp. 110–112. For a traditional argument along these lines, see Robert C. Black,

Railroads of the Confederacy (Chapel Hill: University of North Carolina Press, 1952), 282–299.

6. Proceedings of the Stockholders of the Louisville, Cincinnati and Charleston Rail-Road Company (Charleston, S.C.: A. E. Miller, 1841), Special Collections, University of Virginia Library, Charlottesville.

7. These figures come from a variety of sources. Exact numbers for railroad ownership of slaves is surprisingly difficult to pin down. The Virginia Central Rail Road leased a dozen slaves in Staunton (Augusta County), Virginia (see *The Valley of the Shadow* project census database at http://valley.lib.virginia.edu/ (accessed October 2010). The online resource http://www.Ancestry.com (accessed September 2010) lists slaveholders but makes no distinction between railroads that hired slaves and those that purchased them, nor do the transcribed names make it possible to search for railroads (which were abbreviated often and cryptically). One of the best (but incomplete) sources online is Tom Blake's "Large Slaveholders of 1860" site at http://freepages.genealogy. rootsweb.ancestry.com/~ajac/ (accessed September 2010), a detailed compilation of many Southern county-level census records on slaveholders. The best records of slave ownership by railroads are the railroad company annual reports. Theodore Kornweibel, Jr., has compiled one of the most detailed accounts of slave numbers on railroads in "Railroads and Slavery," *Railroad History* 34 (Fall-Winter 2003): 34–59.

8. List of company officers and directors taken from Virginia Board of Public Works, *Annual Reports of Railroad Companies* (1859), Charles Kennedy Collection, box 105, Special Collections, University of Nebraska, Lincoln. Slaveholding for individuals compiled and checked against Ancestry.com.

9. Gavin Wright, *Slavery and American Economic Development* (Baton Rouge: Louisiana State University Press, 2006), 48–49. Wright's important argument in this volume explains the significance of the large slaveholders' capacity to dominate new areas and lands by moving enslaved labor quickly and in large numbers into them. Their high rates of return, moreover, help explain the grip that these slaveholders maintained over the institution and, in addition, its significance in the mounting sectional crisis over the western territories. See also Jenny Bourne Wahl, "Stay East, Young Man? Market Repercussions of the Dred Scott Decision," *Chicago-Kent Law Review* 82:1 (2007): 361–391.

10. William Prescott Smith, *The Book of the Great Railway Celebrations of 1857; Embracing a Full Account of the Opening of the Ohio & Mississippi, the Marietta & Cincinnati Railroads, and the Northwestern Virginia Branch of the Baltimore and Ohio Railroad* (New York: D. Appleton & Co., 1858), 86–88.

11. *The Railroad Advocate*, December 16, 1854, January 20, 1855, and January 27, 1855. Colburn's journal was based in the North and offers a different perspective on the industry's view of Southern railroad development from the works of Frederick Law Olmsted. Olmsted's *A Journey in the Seaboard Slave States* (New York: Dix & Edwards, 1856) depicted Southern railroads as badly managed and as ultimately subversive of slavery because of their implicit modernity and culture. "They [railroads] cannot be prevented from disseminating intelligence and stirring thought," Olmsted wrote (quotation, 103).

12. The cost of railroad construction has been a subject of much debate among scholars rightly skeptical of the railroad accounting in this period. Colburn, like many others at the time, used railroad annual reports and state commission data for his basis and admitted that these estimates were rough. The *1860 Census of the United States, Preliminary Report* (U.S. Bureau of the Census, Washington: GPO, 1862), contained detailed construction costs and mileage for each state and railroad and reveals the major discrepancy between Southern and Northern railroad costs per mile. In addition, there are estimates in Dionysius Lardner's *Railway Economy* (London: Taylor, Walton and Maberly, 1850), 403–406. One of the best discussions of this problem is E. R. Wicker, "Railroad Investment Before the Civil War," in *Trends in the American Economy in the Nineteenth Century*, Studies in Income and Wealth 24 (Princeton, N.J.: Princeton University Press, 1960). Wicker states that as a rule New England costs were higher than the South (512). For a full analysis of railroad construction costs, see Albert Fishlow, *American Railroads and the Transformation of the Ante-bellum Economy* (Cambridge, Mass.: Harvard University Press, 1965), 342–347. Fishlow estimates U.S. construction costs at $35,000 per mile. Robert W. Fogel points out that engineers estimated the cost of the Union Pacific construction, for example, at $27,500 per mile; see Robert William Fogel, *The Union Pacific: A Case in Premature Enterprise* (Baltimore: Johns Hopkins University Press, 1960), 57.

13. William F. Askew to Dickenson and Hill, February 13 and 19, 1856; William D. Hix to Moore and Dawson, July 10, 1860; and numerous telegraphic messages, Cornelius Chase Papers, box 6, folders 6 and 10, Library of Congress, Washington, D.C.

14. See William G. Shade, *Democratizing the Old Dominion: Virginia and the Second Party System, 1824–1861* (Charlottesville: University of Virginia Press, 1996). See also Kenneth Noe, *Southwest Virginia's Railroad: Modernization and the Sectional Crisis* (Urbana: University of Illinois Press, 1994), 7–8, 43, 70. For an important analysis of the South's move toward modernization, see John Majewski, *Modernizing a Slave Economy: The Economic Vision of the Confederate Nation* (Chapel Hill: University of North Carolina Press, 2009).

15. See Robert F. Hunter and Edwin L. Dooley, Jr., *Claudius Crozet: French Engineer in America, 1790–1864* (Charlottesville: University of Virginia Press, 1989), 140–160, on the Blue Ridge Tunnel construction, and Robert L. Barrett, "Claudius Crozet," *The National Railway Bulletin, 67*:5 (2002). Claudius Crozet, *A Treatise on Descriptive Geometry: for the Use of the Cadets of the United States Military Academy* (New York: A. T. Goodrich, 1821), and *An Arithmetic for Colleges and Schools* (Richmond: Drinker and Morris, 1848).

16. Claudius Crozet to Board of Public Works, January 4, 1854, Blue Ridge Railroad Correspondence, 1854, no. 216, Library of Virginia, Richmond. On slavery's adaptation to modern industries and settings, especially its legal formulations, see Jenny Bourne Wahl, *The Bondsman's Burden: An Economic Analysis of the Common Law of Southern Slavery* (Cambridge: Cambridge University Press, 1998), 54, 85–90.

17. Kornweibel, "Railroads and Slavery," 34–59.

18. Paul Smith, *Born in Slavery: Slave Narratives from the Federal Writers' Project, 1936–1938*, (Athens) Georgia Narratives, vol. 4, part 3, 336, Federal Writer's Project,

USWPA, Manuscript Division, Library of Congress, American Memory Project, Washington, D.C., http://memory.loc.gov/ammem/snhtml/snhome.html (accessed October 2010).

19. Illinois Central Railroad Company Records, IC 6 M6.51, box 27, folder 666, Newberry Library, Chicago.

20. Mississippi Central Railroad, *Annual Report of the President and Directors* (Holly Springs, Miss., 1855–1860), and Nashville & Chattanooga Railroad Company, *Fifteenth Annual Report of the Directors and Officers of the Nashville & Chattanooga Railroad Company* (Nashville: Roberts, Watterson, & Purvis, 1867), Special Collections, University of Virginia Library, Charlottesville.

21. Richard Nathaniel Griffith Means, "Empire, Progress, and the American Southwest: The Texas and Pacific Railroad, 1850–1882" (Ph.D. diss., University of Southern Mississippi, 2001), 35 (quotation). See esp. Michael John Gagnon, "Transition to an Industrial South, Athens, Georgia, 1830–1870" (Ph.D. diss., Emory University, 1999). Historians have tended to downplay the South's industrial development in these years too much. See the most important close study of the South's manufacturing, and its favorable comparison to the midwestern United States, in Viken Tchakerian, "Productivity, Extent of Markets, and Manufacturing in the Late Antebellum South and Midwest," *Journal of Economic History* 54 (September 1994): 407–525. For an emphasis on Southern industrial development as empty rhetoric, see John McCardell, *The Idea of a Southern Nation: Southern Nationalists and Southern Nationalism, 1830–1860* (New York: W. W. Norton, 1979), 126–127. The major work on the limitations of Southern industry is Fred Bateman and Thomas Weiss, *A Deplorable Scarcity: The Failure of Industrialization in the Slave Economy* (Chapel Hill: University of North Carolina Press, 1981). For a review of the economic arguments about Southern industry, see John Ashworth, *Slavery, Capitalism, and Politics in the Antebellum Republic*, vol. 1: *Commerce and Compromise, 1820–1850* (Cambridge: Cambridge University Press, 1995), esp. 90–100 and 499–509 (appendix). Ashworth emphasizes the importance of slave resistance in shaping the context of Southern industrial development. On railway mileage, see U.S. Interstate Commerce Commission, *Railway Statistics before 1890* (Washington, D.C.: Interstate Commerce Commission, 1932), 2. For an assessment emphasizing the South's seriousness and depth of railroad investment, as well as its significance, see James A. Ward, "A New Look at Southern Railroad Development," *Journal of Southern History* 39 (1973): 409–420. On Virginia and the South's patent activity, see William H. Phillips, "Patent Growth in the Old Dominion: The Impact of Railroad Integration before 1880," *Journal of Economic History* 42 (1992): 398.

22. Mileage data based on Henry V. Poor's *Manual of the Railroads of the United States, for 1868–69,*(New York: H. V. and H. W. Poor, 1868) 20; Bureau of the Census, *1860 Census of the United States, Preliminary Report* (Washington, D.C.: GPO, 1862), 237; and E. R. Wicker, "Railroad Investment Before the Civil War," in *Trends in the American Economy in the Nineteenth Century*, Studies in Income and Wealth 24 (Princeton, N.J.: Princeton University Press, 1960).

23. Benedict Anderson, *Imagined Communities: Reflections on the Origins and Spread of Nationalism* (London: Verso, 1991). Anderson emphasized the importance

of newspapers in cultivating a widely shared national identity. Communication media, especially the telegraph, compounded this effect, as did rapid transportation networks that defied natural barriers. On the South's relative position in its urban systems, see Allen Pred, *Urban Growth and the Circulation of Information: The United States System of Cities, 1790–1840* (Cambridge, Mass.: Harvard University Press, 1973), 295, 170–171, 122. Stephen Kern makes a similar point about the way technology had paradoxical effects: "It is one of the great ironies of the period that a world war became possible only after the world had become so highly united." Stephen Kern, *The Culture of Time and Space, 1880–1918* (Cambridge, Mass.: Harvard University Press, 1983), 270.

24. Douglas J. Puffert, "The Standardization of Track Gauge on North American Railways, 1830–1890," *Journal of Economic History* 60 (December 2000): 933–960. Puffert points out that railroads had every incentive to use the same gauge as the most proximate lines, not necessarily the majority gauge of the system as a whole; in other words, the gauge of the line the railroad will join mattered more than the gauge of the system as a whole. Historians continue to use the South's gauge differences as an explanation for the South's difficulties in the Civil War, despite the fact that the North's gauges were just as mixed. See John Keegan, *The American Civil War: A Military History* (New York: Alfred A. Knopf, 2009), 70.

25. This research was made possible by the Center for Digital Research in the Humanities; data analysis is by C. J. Warwas, GIS specialist and cartographer for the *Railroads and the Making of Modern America Project* (http://railroads.unl.edu [accessed September 2010]). My concern is with passenger access and personal mobility, rather than freight. The closest study of rail and canal and wagon road networks remains Robert W. Fogel, *Railroads and Economic Growth: Essays in Econometric History* (Baltimore: Johns Hopkins University Press, 1964), esp. 79–80 for Fogel's assessment of distance to rail and his use of a forty-mile buffer based on historical sources. We used a fifteen-mile buffer around railroad depots as a day's journey to an access point, because our focus was personal mobility rather than freight shipping. Railroads in the 1850s were significantly more oriented to passenger business than in the later period. The technique for measuring and estimating each county population's railroad access has been modeled on Ian Gregory, "Population Change and Transport in Rural England and Wales, 1825–1911," paper presented at the Association of American Geographers, Boston, 2008 (in possession of the author).

26. Gagnon, "Transition to an Industrial South, 17. Mark Wetherington, *Plain Folk's Fight: The Civil War and Reconstruction in Piney Woods, Georgia* (Chapel Hill: University of North Carolina Press, 2005).

27. A. H. Brisbane, "Detailed Report of General Brisbane, Dated June 30, 1849. Address to Richard Keily, Esq.," in *A Brief Description and Statistical Sketch of Georgia*, by Richard Keily (London: J. Carroll, 1849). This can also be found in Wetherington, *Plain Folk's Fight*, 41.

28. Quoted in Means, "Empire, Progress, and the American Southwest," 52, 59.

29. Iverson quoted in Means, "Empire, Progress, and the American Southwest," 67.

30. For an example, see Annual Report of the Philadelphia, Wilmington, and Baltimore, Railroad (Philadelphia: James A. Bryson, January 9, 1860), Charles Kennedy Collection, Special Collections, University of Nebraska-Lincoln. On the 1850s as a decisive break, see Lacy K. Ford, *The Origins of Southern Radicalism: The South Carolina Upcountry* (New York: Oxford University Press, 1988), 277, 359, 372; Bradley G. Bond, *Political Culture in the Nineteenth-Century South: Mississippi, 1830–1900* (Baton Rouge: Louisiana State University Press, 1995), 110–111. Bond notes that railroads helped unite white Southerners and convey a high degree of economic independence. Indeed, he argues the boom mirrored secessionist sentiments, as the railroad's success gave white Southerners unbounded confidence. For an important explanation of the South's understanding of its modernity, civilization, and nation, see especially Nicholas Onuf and Peter Onuf, *Nations, Markets, and War: Modern History and the American Civil War* (Charlottesville: University of Virginia Press, 2006), 166, 177, 185.

31. Gavin Wright, *Slavery and American Economic Development* (Baton Rouge: Louisiana State University Press, 2006), 48–49.

32. The three railroad directors at the Virginia Constitutional Convention were Thomas Branch of Petersburg, William Ballard Preston of Montgomery, and Lewis E. Harvie of Amelia, although many of the delegates may have been stockholders and involved in railroad promotion. See George H. Reese, ed., *Proceedings of the Virginia State Convention of 1861*, vol. 4 (Richmond: Virginia State Library, 1965), 24. William Freehling suggests that the timing of the completion of the Charleston and Savannah Railroad might have played a decisive role in the secession movement in South Carolina in December 1860. "A modern railroad might seem an ironic engine to further a reactionary revolution," Freehling writes, but the celebration brought Georgians and South Carolinians together at a crucial moment in the secession crisis. William W. Freehling, *The Road to Disunion*, vol. 2: *Secessionists Triumphant, 1854–1861* (New York: Oxford University Press, 2007), 406.

9

Industry and Its Laborers, Free and Slave in Late-Antebellum Virginia

L. Diane Barnes

Blacksmith and German immigrant William H. Tappey arrived in Petersburg, Virginia, during the 1840s, established his own smith works, and settled well into a prosperous life as a skilled laborer in the antebellum South. Within a few years he partnered with Virginia-born pattern maker George L. Lumsden, and together they formed the Southern Foundry, which forged iron to manufacture machines and equipment for the growing industries in the Southside of Virginia, a region that stretched from the James River to the North Carolina line. Both Tappey and Lumsden, like many Petersburg businessmen, made investments in regional development and found slavery useful to their wide-ranging endeavors. The Southern Foundry employed many skilled artisans including molders, blacksmiths, pattern makers, and engineers, and by 1860 it had an annual production valued at $70,000. The foundry proved a model of Southern industrial development and provided employment opportunities for skilled workers in the South's rapidly changing economy. But not all Southern Foundry workers were free and white; among the seventy workers employed in 1860 were a number of slaves who toiled side by side with their white counterparts.[1]

Updating the Debate on Southern Economics

Earlier models exploring the South's economy, such as that of Eugene D. Genovese, have been unable to explain Southern industrial centers like Petersburg. Most, including Fred Bateman and Thomas Weiss's analysis, based their exploration on a wage-labor driven, Northern-derived understanding of industrialization that does not fully consider a mix of free and enslaved labor. The intricate connection between industrial development and labor illustrated in work relations at the Southern Foundry reflects the complicated path to modernity in the late-antebellum upper South, especially after 1840. Modernity brought economic and social mobility, increased specialization, and the division of labor to antebellum America. Across the nation, lives were altered by an increased movement of goods, capital, and ideas that brought more and more localities into connection with regional, national, and even transnational networks of commerce and social organization.[2]

The growth of the Southern Foundry demonstrates the progress of industrialization as Petersburg developed as a modern manufacturing city that produced goods for a regional market, including iron and tobacco. The foundry's owners saw no inherent contradiction in using slave labor to make their industrial pursuit successful. Reexamining the Southern economy, it becomes readily apparent that the South was a region more complicated than the historical debate over its connection to markets and capitalism has allowed. Recent scholarship suggests the alternative consideration that the South was not set apart from the modern world, but that modernity took many paths. Scholars such as Edward Baptist, Anthony Kaye, and Walter Johnson are demonstrating that slavery and capitalism were not at odds, and that slavery actually reinforced industrial development. Southerners may have rejected the North's application of economic theory and development, but they strongly supported liberal values and classical economic theory—along with race-based slavery. In fact, the South's unique path to modernization was shaped exactly by the region's commitment to slavery. As Baptist has argued, the commodification of slave labor was in itself a modern action, noting that "after turning humans into Cuffy, wool and ivory, and fancy maids . . . , perhaps additional commodifications," such as credit, labor power, government services and information, were easy. The Southern Foundry's owners employed such a mix, paying free white workers for their labor time and overseeing the work of slaves, a different but equally valuable commodity. Slavery offered Southern industrialists labor options. Although capital invested in slaves sometimes restricted cash flow, either through the slave market or through the hiring-out process, it was also convertible and could be used to start new businesses and make new profits. Slavery in the hinterland also benefited businesses such as the Southern Foundry, as plantations provided a regional market to consume manufactured goods.[3]

The South's advancing modernity meant acknowledging and adapting to rapid economic change and accommodating traditional social structures, all the while becoming familiar with new social and class tensions. Among the hallmarks of economic change visible in the late antebellum era was the division of labor, the broadening of regional markets, and a link with the plantation economy. In the South, industrialization included both the manufacturing of standard goods such as iron and the processing of agricultural products, such as sugar and tobacco. Industrialization was not a "stage" in a process, as Marxist historians have claimed; rather, as Anthony Kaye has recently suggested, industrialization, as well as biological and mechanical innovation, went hand in hand with the agricultural economy and slavery. Petersburg's development exemplifies this path to modernity. The growth of industry and transportation networks meant that work relations changed as the city's market connections widened rapidly after 1840. Petersburg's location within the Southside plantation belt, however, meant industry was often linked with the agricultural economy.[4]

Especially in states such as Virginia, where after 1840 agriculture became more diversified, industrialization represented a rational response for those seeking economic gain. The assumption that industrialization could only be conducted with free labor, long a central issue in the debate over capitalism, does not hold true.[5] The flexibility and mobility of slave labor were key to the "second slavery" of the antebellum era. In places like Petersburg, agricultural diversification allowed some slaveholders to shift their workforce to new geographic areas and even to industrial work settings that free workers may not have chosen voluntarily. Accompanying Southern industry's burgeoning use of slavery, there was a growing certainty that slavery was compatible with modern innovation.[6] Southern free laborites, such as Tappey and Lumsden, though celebrating the superiority of free and independent labor, supported industrial growth, lobbied for railroads and worked in a climate that often found skilled white, free black, and enslaved labor toiling side-by-side. Indeed, slavery was the single most important distinguishing feature in the industrial world of the Old South.[7] However, instead of setting the region apart from nineteenth-century capitalist development, slavery proved adaptable and was often employed by those reaching toward modernity. As Petersburg clearly demonstrates, it is now apparent that in parts of the upper South, the plantation economy actually bolstered industrial slavery and capitalist development.

As the fourth largest state in the United States, and also claiming the largest slave population until emancipation, Virginia is a particularly interesting setting in which to examine the compatibility of slavery, free labor, and industry. Daniel W. Crofts points out that despite holding the South's largest slave population, antebellum Virginia was actually representative of national trends in economic and social development. He argues that Virginia's agricultural production was not in decline as often stereotyped. Instead, farming shifted from tobacco monoculture to more diversified, less labor-intensive crops. In the late antebellum era, the commonwealth was among the leading states in production of grain, including corn and wheat. Movement toward industrial development also intensified as the annual output of manufactures grew from $30 million in 1840 to $50 million in 1850.[8] Changes in agriculture and the growth of industry linked slavery to both segments of Virginia's economy. David Goldfield was among the first to argue that slavery adapted well to both urbanization and industrial development. More recent scholarship clearly shows that as grain became the major crop on many Virginia plantations, slave owners often leased their surplus laborers to skilled artisans and industrial employers, thereby enhancing industrial development and employment. In contrast to recent statistics put forth by economic historian John Majewski, factories and businesses in Virginia benefited from the diversification of regional plantations. Instead of selling slaves south, many area planters earned a lucrative income leasing their slaves to factories and other industries in Virginia cities such as Richmond, Lynchburg, and Petersburg. Tobacco factories, the largest urban employers, depended almost exclusively on slave labor until the 1850s. Many tobacco manufacturers, or tobacconists, hired their workers from plantation owners in surrounding counties; other industrial employers, including Petersburg's Southern Foundry, also came to rely on slave leasing, especially after slave prices rose in the 1850s.[9]

Adding to Croft's argument, Edward L. Ayers and William A. Link expand the discussion of the connection between slavery and modern growth in late antebellum Virginia. Ayers demonstrates that Augusta County, in the Shenandoah Valley, easily found use for enslaved laborers as its main town of Staunton added a rail connection, macadamized roads, and built gas lighting.[10] Link describes the way that the market economy broadened slaveholding into towns, cities, and industry. He argues that late antebellum "Virginians embraced national notions of business enterprise and public culture. Most were enthusiastic capitalists connected to the outside world and acutely aware of the market revolution."[11] Petersburg's experience adds to this new trend in Southern studies, which collectively show the South as developing a modern capitalist economy compatible with slave labor.

The way slavery was viewed within the industrializing South also impacted the way that free workers viewed their role in the changing society. The free-labor ideology, which encouraged workers to strive for independence and to celebrate the superiority of free labor in contrast to slavery, was not absent from the South. Instead of being a contradiction, slavery stood as an important part of the Southern free-labor ideology: Seeking social mobility, workers believed in working hard, saving their pennies, and eventually purchasing property to demonstrate their independence. In the South reaching the ranks of property holding often mean property (owned or leased) in slave labor.[12] While Michele Gillespie's study of artisans in Georgia found that in the early years of the new republic skilled workers aspired to planter status, the changing nature of the Southern economy after 1820 made that type of mobility less likely. Many free workers, even some African Americans, however, continued to see slaveholding as the means toward upward mobility, a way to increase the profitability of their business establishments and a clear symbol of their success.[13]

The existence of slavery in the South has long been considered an indicator of the region's backwardness, especially when contrasted with the free-labor economy of the North. However, on closer examination, it is possible to build a convincing case that property rights in slaves formed an important element of the South's emerging modernity, representing a tangible and attainable investment for the emerging middle class of businessmen and industrialists. Because Southern political and social institutions protected slavery and tied it to the very fabric of society, it was a wise investment. The income produced from the safe investment in slavery worked to finance industrialization, transportation improvements, agricultural innovation, and government services. At the time of the Civil War, slave property was valued at nearly $3 billion, more than twice the value of all U.S. manufactures, providing a powerful economic motive for its defense.[14]

Slavery was as important to the South's advancing industrialization as it was to the expansion of plantation agriculture. From the colonial era forward, slaves toiled in iron production, sugar manufacture, coal mining, and almost every industrial pursuit.[15] In the 1850s at least 200,000 slaves worked in non-agricultural occupations. In many cases slaves represented direct competition with free labor, but they were crucial to the success of tobacco and iron production as well as coal mining and sugar processing. Robert Starobin was the first to argue convincingly for the compatibility of slavery and industry in the South, suggesting that rather than lessening the control of the slaveholder and weakening the institution, incentives such as pay for overwork were actually an effective means of control. Although other historians have viewed industrial slavery as a more complicated give and take that afforded enslaved workers some control over their work environment, Starobin was correct in asserting that industrial slavery helped to spread slave ownership to many who were not engaged in farming. Especially as slave prices rose in the 1850s, slave hiring extended the reach of the institution to small business owners and artisans.[16] Although the rising value of slaves may have stopped some owners from leasing them into physically dangerous workplaces, the practice continued to thrive in less threatening industries, including tobacco manufacture and blacksmithing, especially once modern insurance policies helped to protect their investment.[17] Many Southern industrialists considered property in slaves to be a reliable investment and necessary to the pursuit of manufacturing in the region.

The experiences of the Southern Foundry's owners help to illustrate the incorporation of slaveholding in business strategies. Although many later immigrants to the antebellum South opposed slavery—especially German immigrants, influenced by the 1848 revolutions in Europe—those who arrived in the South earlier in nineteenth century adapted to the slave society. German-immigrant William H. Tappey had little trouble modifying his image of independence and upward mobility to include owning slaves. Tappey arrived in Petersburg in the 1840s after working in a Richmond foundry for about four years. He established an independent blacksmith's shop and quickly adapted to life in his new homeland and to its peculiar institution. While records indicate that Tappey became a U.S. citizen in 1844, he was clearly a "citizen" of the slave South even earlier. When Tappey first appeared in city tax records in 1843, he already owned two slaves; one was a child, but the other was a man of prime working age. This is not altogether surprising as blacksmiths were among the skilled workers most likely to employ slave labor in their workshops because they required a physical assistant to act as a striker, swinging a sledge hammer on heavy forging operations. Tappey's investment in slave labor yielded the immediate dividend of providing the extra labor needed in his workshop.

Tappey's entrance into the ranks of the slaveholding class of the South marked him as a successful businessman. As James Huston argues, Tappey and other Southern proponents of free labor, "sanctioned private property in Africans."[18] Tappey maintained these two slaves in his household through the establishment of the Southern Foundry; in the 1850s, when slave prices rose exorbitantly, he switched to leasing slaves from plantations surrounding Petersburg. The Southern Foundry partners steadily increased their slaveholdings as their fortunes rose. They invested in slave labor in the same way that other businessmen invested in stocks and bonds, gaining an immediate return on their outlay of cash by employing the slaves' labor. George L. Lumsden also acquired property in slaves, as did a third partner, William Lumsden, who was probably the elder Lumsden's son.[19]

Slavery and Modernity in Context

If, as Edward Baptist and Anthony Kaye have suggested, property in slaves can be considered an indicator of the South's unique path to modernity, it seems likely that other standards used to measure the region's industrial growth also require rethinking. Picking up on statistics first presented by Robert Fogel and Stanley Engerman more than thirty years ago, scholars are now moving toward both comparative and transnational analyses. At a critical era in the evolution of the modern world, nineteenth-century citizens witnessed major changes in social, political, and especially economic structures. Viewing the South through a comparative lens that includes the countries of rapidly industrializing Europe, many of the hallmarks of modernity appear in the antebellum South.[20] Its production of cotton textiles ranked sixth in the world, and Southern manufacturers made inroads into the production of pig iron. Although per capita wealth was well behind the North, if compared to the wider industrializing world, Southern incomes trailed only a small handful of countries and surpassed such nations as Canada, France, the Netherlands, Belgium and the German states.[21] Comparing the South with manufacturing in other slave societies shows a similar superiority, as the South was ahead of Brazil in major industries such as textiles and iron forging.[22] In railroad mileage per capita, the region bore comparison to the North. As William Thomas notes in his chapter in this volume, Southern railroad construction was more extensive and reached significantly more of the region's population than previously believed.[23] Southern railroads reached all of the region's densely populated areas; in some states they actually connected a larger proportion of the population to markets than was true for the North.

Rising production rates and transportation connections served not only to increase profits, but also to foster rationalized government relations, to spur and manage development. State support for internal improvement played an important role in the development of industry, and the ways Southern states approached improvements affected the trajectory of industry.[24] In Petersburg, which was crossed by five railroads, longer lines of communication and connections to wider markets, for example, made it possible for William Tappey and his partner to expand their blacksmith shop into a full-fledged foundry. This experience was likely repeated in numerous industrializing towns across the commonwealth.

As the most populous Southern state, Virginia's approach to internal improvement and economic development influenced transportation and communication flow across the South. Adopting a mixed-enterprise plan for development, Virginians rejected a national program of internal improvements that, in its absence, left much responsibility with individual local capitalists. The creation of the Virginia Board of Public Works in 1820 provided some engineering supervision, but any incorporated transportation project could count on the state for only two-fifths of its funding. Although this was a higher percentage of the overall funding than states offered in other regions, it nevertheless meant that internal improvement projects required individual investment.[25] Virginia businessmen and some state legislators worked diligently to create internal improvements, including railroads and canals, as well as banks that would influence development. In Petersburg, upwardly mobile artisans and industrialists invested in railroads, canal and river improvements and local banks and savings societies. In a common show of support for regional development, Tappey bought shares of the Southside Railroad, which, when completed in 1854, provided a link between Petersburg and Lynchburg.[26]

The South's unique path to industrialization meant that commitment to slave labor was also reflected in urban development. Especially true of Virginia, this guided the commonwealth's ability to attract and foster industrial and commercial development. Cities such as Richmond, Wheeling, and Petersburg bustled with commerce and industry, albeit on a smaller scale than Northern metropolises or cities along the South's seaboard. As John Majewski shows in his comparison of Virginia and Pennsylvania, Virginia's four rivers feeding to the Atlantic made the growth of four smaller cities the most feasible route for development.[27] In 1860, although the second largest city in Virginia after Richmond, Petersburg's population of 18,266 ranked it only forty-ninth in the nation. Despite the importance of ironworks such as the Southern Foundry, the city's growth was most closely linked to the tobacco plantations that populated Virginia's Southside and stretched into the Piedmont of North Carolina. Tobacco factories, which employed unskilled slave and free-black labor to manually prepare plug and chewing tobacco products, formed the most important part of the manufacturing base. Textile milling and iron forging were other important segments of the city's industrial economy. In Petersburg, support for railroad development as well as other industrial concerns, came from municipal funds and from individual small investors such as Tappey who had a financial stake in their success. This investment in development reaped a reward for city industrialists.

As access to markets broadened in the 1840s, Petersburg expanded its industrial base to include eight cotton factories, three flour mills, a paper mill, and a woolen factory. Like the internal improvement projects, small investors drove the growth of these manufacturing concerns and also established two savings and loan corporations that further contributed to industrialization.[28] They bought stock in corporations to ensure that railroads, banks, and manufactures came to their city, but they also bought and leased the labor of slaves. In keeping with the Southern model of industrialization, it was no contradiction to invest in manufactures and slavery simultaneously. Indeed, the path to modernity taken by these cities represents a unique strategy of economic development that incorporated both free and slave labor and saw little contra-diction in placing free and unfree workers side by side.

Southern Labor Tensions

Tappey's rise from a simple blacksmith to an employer and an investor in inter-nal improvement projects suggests that social class and social structures within the Southern economy also need more attention. The region's class structure cannot be described in terms of an exclusive agrarian-urban divide. Since studies now clearly show that the Southern economy was moving toward a fairly complicated modern mix of industry as well as staple crop–based agricul-ture, it stands to reason that two classes of capitalists also emerged. One repre-sented the familiar pattern of wealth-holding in land and slaves, but the other set of capitalists gained their wealth from industrial pursuits and commerce.[29] In a study of South Carolina, Tom Downey argues that although both groups shared a commitment to defending slavery as the significant Southern institu-tion, conflict arose between those committed to agricultural versus commercial interests.[30] Those divisions and disagreements were rooted in the tension between the social relations tied to a planter-dominated political economy and the emerging values of the commercial South. However, the argument that those divisions were tied to antimodernizing impulses may be overstated. In South Carolina, as in Virginia, the planter-centered political economy contin-ued to dominate, but industrialization was gaining ground. Planters opposing measures that helped industry continued to dominate Virginia politics at the state level, but in localities such as Petersburg, the give and take between indus-trialists and planters was growing more fluid, and they often found cooperation to be of mutual benefit.

In the hinterland surrounding Petersburg, most planters embraced the modernizing impulses resulting in internal improvements and industrial growth because facilities such as the Southern Foundry provided much-needed services. The City Point Railroad, completed in 1838, provided a direct link between Petersburg and the nearby James River plantations. Once operating, planters such as Richard Eppes, who owned both Appomattox Manor and Ber-muda Hundred, could reach Petersburg in an hour on the railroad. Eppes often sent trusted slaves via the railroad to conduct business and shipped much of his grain for sale in the city's warehouses.[31] Planters were as likely as business owners to subscribe to internal improvement projects that directly benefited their economic interests, and by the 1850s plantations and industrial pursuits enjoyed an interdependent relationship. Many Virginians grew impatient with the dichotomy between industrial pursuits and farming advocated by the older generation of agrarians.[32] The railroads that brought planters into Petersburg also brought skilled workmen into the hinterland, where they transacted business on a regular basis. Workmen often traveled to regional plantations for on-site jobs. Planters such as Eppes engaged a variety of artisans in this way, but not the Southern Foundry. Instead, for his ironworking needs Eppes often patronized Tappey's main competitor, Uriah Wells.[33]

In exploring the social changes heralded by modernity, it is useful to revisit the emergence of a Southern middle class, closely tied to both commerce and industry. This group included skilled artisans, industrialists, and the commercial men who constituted as much as 10 percent of the region's white male population, while the bulk of the population remained tied to agriculture. It is now clear that the South had an entrepreneurial middle class that supported slavery along with planters, but this middle class also pursued their own distinct interests within the Southern economy. Industrialization and manufacturing both grew out of and served to reinforce the middle class environment.[34] In Petersburg, the middle class was comprised of urban dwellers, but differences between merchants and industrialists were quite fluid. Although Tappey and Lumsden expanded their smith works into a foundry, many other small manufacturers and artisans chose to become merchants instead of expanding their industrial production. For example, gunsmith William Morgan converted his workshop into a mercantile establishment he called the Petersburg Gun and Sporting Store. Small-scale tobacconist John Rowlett took his marketing a step farther, becoming a full-scale commission merchant, eventually advertising in a regional business directory.[35] Whether merchants or industrialists, middle-class Southerners also struggled to define their place in the changing economy. In Petersburg, these tensions were visible in relationships between the owners of the Southern Foundry and their workers.

As the Southern Foundry grew and prospered, Tappey and Lumsden moved into Petersburg's emerging middle class. The iron-forging demands of local industry fostered the foundry's growth; by the middle 1850s, increased operations allowed the completion of large-scale projects, such as building mail cars for the railroad and a steam-powered printing press for a local newspaper.[36] As their business expanded, Tappey and Lumsden became "bosses" to a growing group of wage earners. The seventy molders, blacksmiths, pattern makers, and laborers they employed had little hope of achieving the independence that Tappey knew when he first opened his blacksmith shop in Petersburg. The annual production of $70,000 in iron goods clearly elevated the Southern Foundry's proprietors above the social and economic level of their workforce.[37]

A hallmark of Tappey and Lumsden's social status was their membership in a local fraternal organization, the Petersburg Benevolent Mechanic Association, which served as a collective of businessmen and enterprising master mechanics. Formed in 1825, as a benevolent aid society for artisans, the fraternity was one of the wealthiest organizations in the city and functioned both as a network linking prominent city men and as a source for small business loans to members. George Lumsden joined in 1838, with William Tappey following in 1856. By 1860 both partners held substantial amounts of real and personal property.[38]

Tappey and Lumsden represent one end of the spectrum in the modernizing South. They were characteristic of success in the expanding economy. Other laborers, including free whites and African Americans, did not fare as well. The economic changes that allowed men such as Tappey and Lumsden to move into the developing middle class also made upward mobility and economic independence measured by slave or property ownership increasingly unlikely for others. However, if success is measured by a means other than property ownership, many Southern workers adapted to opportunities in the changing economy. Although Majewski argues that sparse settlement inhibited industrialization and urban growth, the location of Petersburg in the midst of the Southside plantation district gave workers the opportunity to supplement their town earnings with work on area plantations. Many no longer lived with their employers; moreover, although finding their own housing added to their economic burden, it must also have given workers a sense of independence to be free from a master's watchful eye.[39] Workers at the Southern Foundry fit this economic pattern. Their housing arrangements and personal wealth declarations attest to the changing economic reality. More than half of the thirty-three Southern Foundry employees located in the 1850 or 1860 census lived in a boarding house or rented room. None owned any real property, and only one listed a personal estate valued at $100. Another six claimed an estate worth between $20 and $25. Even the Scottish-born foreman, Alexander Steel, lived in a rented room near the foundry.[40] Their lives reflected a precarious balance between the autonomy of living outside their employer's watchful eye and a meager financial situation that prevented ownership of a home or business of their own.

Similar to the advancing age of rural laborers in other areas of the South, the foundry employees' average age was twenty-eight; two-thirds of those reporting their age to 1860 census enumerators were over the age of twenty-five.[41] However, unlike the rural unskilled laborers Charles Bolton studied, the Southern Foundry employees practiced a skilled trade. They were listed as blacksmiths, machinists, molders, pattern makers, and carpenters; however, by

1860, such skills no longer guaranteed a path to owning an independent shop, though they did provide a means to earn a living.[42] Because iron forging was one segment of industry that experienced expansion in the antebellum era, Southern Foundry employees were more likely than skilled workers in other trades to maintain steady employment. Although their position was not as sturdy as those in construction trades, iron forgers' persistence rates (i.e., the number who chose to remain in Petersburg) suggest that they were able to make a living.[43] Only the lucky few who found themselves at the intersection of a variety of special circumstances managed to advance into independence and the emerging Southern middle class. In stark contrast to their employees, foundry partners William Tappey and George Lumsden were quite wealthy by nineteenth-century standards, possibly a reflection of their efforts to suppress workplace racial equality. Although his fortunes was small when compared to wealthy planters, Tappey in 1860 owned real estate valued at $7,000 and claimed a total personal estate value of $15,000. Likewise, Lumsden's real property was worth $4,000 and his total estate claimed a value of $10,000.[44]

Free African Americans and enslaved workers did not fare as well as skilled whites when cities such as Petersburg industrialized. Frank Towers has argued that in cities such as Baltimore and St. Louis politicians and economic elites helped to counteract any common bond that poor whites and blacks might have recognized in the changing economy. He demonstrates how they convinced whites in economic decline that slavery fostered white equality across class lines. This was bolstered by the argument that slavery exempted poor whites from engaging in the lowest form of manual labor.[45] Indeed, census and city directory records do not indicate that the Southern Foundry employed any skilled free blacks. Although the foundry owners did lease slaves on annual contracts from the plantations surrounding Petersburg, it is highly unlikely that these men were skilled ironworkers or tradesmen. While they did not experience the virulent racism that developed in the North after 1830, African Americans in Petersburg struggled to gain equal footing with their white counterparts.[46] Those few free African-American blacksmiths in the city worked independently and not for any of the growing factories or foundries. Whether white or African American, the employees of the Southern Foundry lived in a modern world where their lives were shaped by both the tensions and practices of capitalist development and racial slavery.

The path forged by William Tappey and George Lumsden in Petersburg in the late antebellum era represents one of several emerging modernities. Petersburg and other industrializing cities in the upper South developed on a path distinct from those blazed in other times and places, but it is not fair to count their experience as necessarily "exceptional," as historians have been wont to do when considering the Old South. An immigrant from the German states, Tappey hardly typified the image of the average slaveholder, although he did fit James Oakes's model of artisan-slaveholder who owned just a handful of bondsmen. Tappey's arrival in Petersburg was influenced by the push and pull of global economic, political, and social changes, both in European and American societies. Emblematic of nineteenth-century citizens who believed the rapid change around them meant something special was happening, Tappey embraced change. Together with his partner, Lumsden, he built his blacksmith shop into an industrial complex that employed many men.[47]

Although having iron foundries, tobacco factories, and railroads did not on their own define Petersburg as a modern city, the way that men such as Tappey and Lumsden built their businesses, organized their lives, and related to their workers speaks to their connection with larger networks of commerce and social organization. Even though he came from a society where many opposed the institution of slavery, Tappey quickly adapted to using slave labor because it was a rational way to increase production. This ensured that the people within the walls of the Southern Foundry experienced modernity in diverse ways. While Tappey and Lumsden fashioned themselves as industrialists becoming comfortably situated within an emerging Southern middle class, their workers faced a different reality. For the skilled white workers in the foundry's employ, modernity meant wage labor with little chance for advancement to independence. Most lived in rented houses or roomed in boarding houses, and many sought supplemental employment on the farms and plantations surrounding Petersburg. The enslaved men, whether permanently attached to Tappey and Lumsden or hired on annual contracts, could hardly have helped but resent the way that modernity adapted slavery to fit its new circumstances. As slavery proved easily adjustable to iron forging and other industries, these individuals must have held little hope that the institution that held them in bondage would become obsolete. The tensions that emanated from these different experiences with the nineteenth-century's modern world belies the existence of a harmonious "Old South"; instead, it suggests the antebellum upper South was a complex society that requires more exploration. When viewed in a broader context allowing for changing nuances and global connections brought to the region, historians have much yet to learn about the Old South.

NOTES

1. U.S. Bureau of the Census, "Products of Industry during the Year Ending June 1, 1860," 1860 census, schedule 5, Virginia Eastern Division, City of Petersburg,

National Archives, Washington, D.C. (microfilm); Auction Sales Record Book, 1847–1854, Branch & Company Records, Virginia Historical Society, Richmond.

2. See Eugene D. Genovese, "The Significance of the Slave Plantation for Southern Economic Development," *Journal of Southern History* 28 (November 1962): 422–437; and Fred Bateman and Thomas Weiss, *A Deplorable Scarcity: The Failure of Industrialization in the Slave Economy* (Chapel Hill: University of North Carolina Press, 1981). For recent accounts of Southern industrialization, see Aaron W. Marrs, *Railroads in the Old South: Pursuing Progress in a Slave* Society (Baltimore: Johns Hopkins University Press, 2009); Barbara Hahn, "Making Tobacco Bright: Institutions, Information, and Industrialization in the Creation of an Agricultural Commodity, 1617–1937" (Ph.D. diss., University of North Carolina, Chapel Hill, 2006); Susanna Delfino and Michele Gillespie, eds., *Global Perspectives on Industrial Transformation in the American South* (Columbia: University of Missouri Press, 2005). On the South's liberal values, see James Oakes, *Slavery and Freedom: An Interpretation of the Old South* (New York: W. W. Norton, 1990), esp. chap. 2; on race and modernity, see Zygmunt Bauman, *Modernity and Ambivalence* (Ithaca, N.Y.: Cornell University Press, 1991), 71, 73, 81.

3. Anthony E. Kaye, "The Second Slavery: Modernity in the Nineteenth-Century South and the Atlantic World," *Journal of Southern History* 75 (2009); Walter Johnson, "The Pedestal and the Veil: Rethinking the Capitalism/Slavery Question," *Journal of the Early Republic* 24 (Summer 2004): 299–303; Edward Baptist, "'Cuffy,' 'Fancy Maids,' and 'One-Eyed Men': Rape, Commodification, and the Domestic Slave Trade in the United States," *American Historical Review* 106 (December 2001): 1650 (quote).

4. Stanley L. Engerman, "Southern Industrialization, Myths and Realities," in *Global Perspectives on Industrial Transformation*, 14–19; Gloria Vollmers, "Industrial Slavery in the United States: The North Carolina Turpentine Industry 1849–61," *Accounting, Business & Financial History* 13 (November 2003): 369–392; Anthony E. Kaye, "The Second Slavery: Modernity in the Nineteenth-Century South and the Atlantic World," *Journal of Southern History* 75 (2009): 634.

5. For the early capitalist/precapitalist debate, see James Oakes, *The Ruling Race A History of American Slaveholders* (1982; New York: W. W. Norton, 1998); Eugene D. Genovese, *The Political Economy of Slavery: Studies in the Economy and Society of the Slave South* (1961; repr., New York: Vintage Books, 1967); Elizabeth Fox Genovese and Eugene D. Genovese, *Slavery in Black and White: Class and Race in the Southern Slaveholders' New World Order* (Cambridge: Cambridge University Press, 2008), esp. chap. 6. The debate continues in John Ashworth, *Slavery, Capitalism, and Politics in the Antebellum Republic*, 2 vols. (Cambridge: Cambridge University Press, 1995, 2007); Marc Egnal, *Clash of Extremes: The Economic Origins of the Civil War* (New York: Hill and Wang, 2009), 3–17; John Majewski, *Modernizing a Slave Economy: The Economic Vision of the Confederate Nation* (Chapel Hill: University of North Carolina Press, 2009), 39–45; Mark M. Smith, *Debating Slavery: Economy and Society in the Antebellum South* (Cambridge: Cambridge University Press, 1998); Delfino and Gillespie, *Global Perspectives on Industrial Transformation*.

6. Kaye, "The Second Slavery," 640–641; Gavin Wright, *Slavery and American Economic Development* (Baton Rouge: Louisiana State University Press, 2006), 15.

7. On slavery's adaptability to modernity, see William G. Thomas and Edward L. Ayers, "An Overview: The Differences Slavery Made: A Close Analysis of Two American Communities," *American Historical Review* 108 (December 2003): 1299–1307; William G. Thomas and Edward L. Ayers, "The Differences Slavery Made," http://www2.vcdh.virginia.edu/AHR (accessed October 2010).

8. Daniel W. Crofts, "Late Antebellum Virginia Reconsidered," *Virginia Magazine of History and Biography* 107 (1999): 253–257.

9. David R. Goldfield, *Urban Growth in the Age of Sectionalism: Virginia 1847–1861* (Baton Rouge: Louisiana State University Press, 1977), xxvii, 137; James Irwin, "Exploring the Affinity of Wheat and Slavery in the Virginia Piedmont," *Explorations in Economic History* 25 (1988): 302, 304–315; Wright, *Slavery and American Economic Development*, 113–116; Majewski, *Modernizing a Slave Economy*, 40–42.

10. Edward L. Ayers, *In the Presence of Mine Enemies: War in the Heart of America, 1859–1863* (New York, W. W. Norton, 2003), 17–20.

11. William L. Link, *Roots of Secession: Slavery and Politics in Antebellum Virginia* (Chapel Hill: University of North Carolina Press, 2003), 6–7.

12. James L. Huston, *Calculating the Value of the Union: Slavery, Property Rights, and the Economic Origins of the Civil War* (Chapel Hill: University of North Carolina Press, 2003), 40–41; Gavin Wright, *Old South, New South: Revolutions in the Southern Economy Since the Civil War* (New York: Basic Books, 1986), chap. 2.

13. See Michele Gillespie, *Free Labor in an Unfree World: White Artisans in Slaveholding Georgia, 1789–1860* (Athens: University of Georgia Press, 2000), esp. 1–35; also Michael P. Johnson and James L. Roark, *Black Masters: A Free Family of Color in the Old South* (New York: W. W. Norton, 1984).

14. James L. Huston, "Property Rights in Slavery and the Coming of the Civil War," *Journal of Southern History* 65 (1999): 253–255; Kaye, "The Second Slavery," 633. See also Wright, *Slavery and American Economic Development*, 48–82. For the opposing interpretation, see Bateman and Weiss, *Deplorable Scarcity*; Douglas R. Egerton, "Markets without a Market Revolution: Southern Planters and Capitalism," *Journal of the Early Republic* 16 (1996): 207–221.

15. For early slave employment in iron forging, see John Bezís-Selfa, *Forging America: Ironworkers, Adventurers, and the Industrious Revolution* (Ithaca, N.Y.: Cornell University Press, 2004), 70–90; for the sugar industry, see Richard Follett, *The Sugar Masters: Planters and Slaves in Louisiana's Cane World, 1820–1860* (Baton Rouge: Louisiana State University Press, 2005), 124–127.

16. Huston, *Calculating the Value of the Union*, 99–100; Robert S. Starobin, *Industrial Slavery in the Old South* (New York: Oxford University Press, 1970), 134–135; Ronald L. Lewis, *Coal, Iron, and Slaves: Industrial Slavery in Maryland and Virginia, 1715–1865* (Westport, Conn.: Greenwood Press, 1979), 112–114; Charles Dew, *Ironmaker to the Confederacy: Joseph R. Anderson and the Tredegar Iron Works* (New Haven, Conn.: Yale University Press, 1966), 29–31; Charles Dew, *Bond of Iron: Master and Slave at Buffalo Forge* (New York: W. W. Norton, 1994), 9–12; Barbara Hahn, "Making Tobacco

Bright: Institutions, Information, and Industrialization in the Creation of an Agricultural Commodity, 1617–1937," *Enterprise and Society* 8 (December 2007): 790–798.

17. Wright, *Slavery and American Economic Development*, 73–75; Sharon Ann Murphy, "Securing Human Property: Slavery, Life Insurance, and Industrialization in the Upper South," *Journal of the Early Republic* 25 (Winter 2005): 615–652.

18. Huston, *Calculating the Value of the Union*, 40–41.

19. Personal Property Tax Ledger, 1843, Petersburg, Va., Library of Virginia, Richmond (microfilm); Auction Sales Record Book, 1847–1854, Branch & Company Records, Virginia Historical Society, Richmond; U.S. Bureau of the Census, Population Schedules, Virginia Eastern Division, City of Petersburg, 1860, National Archives, Washington, D.C. (microfilm).

20. C. A. Bayly, *The Birth of the Modern World, 1780–1914: Global Connections and Comparisons* (Malden, Mass.: Blackwell Publishing, 2004), 9–10; for the debate over comparative and transnational approaches, see Peter Kolchin, "The South and the World," *Journal of Southern History* 75 (2009): 565–580.

21. Robert William Fogel and Stanley L. Engerman, *Time on the Cross: The Economics of American Negro Slavery* (New York: W. W. Norton, 1974), 254–255; David L. Carlton and Peter A. Coclanis, *The South, the Nation, and the World: Perspectives on Southern Economic Development* (Charlottesville: University of Virginia Press, 2003), 20–21; Kenneth L. Sokoloff and Viken Tchakerian, "Manufacturing Where Agriculture Predominates: Evidence from the South and Midwest in 1860," *Explorations in Economic History* 34 (1997): 245–246.

22. Richard Graham, "Slavery and Economic Development: Brazil and the United States South in the Nineteenth Century," *Comparative Studies in Society and History* 23 (October 1981): 630–631.

23. See also Marrs, *Railroads in the Old South*, 5–7.

24. Sean Patrick Adams, *Old Dominion, Industrial Commonwealth: Coal, Politics, and Economy in Antebellum America* (Baltimore: Johns Hopkins University Press, 2004), 6–8.

25. John Lauritz Larson, *Internal Improvement: National Public Works and the Promise of Popular Government in the Early United States* (Chapel Hill: University of North Carolina Press, 2001), 94–95; Daniel Walker Howe, *What Hath God Wrought: The Transformation of America, 1815–1848* (New York: Oxford University Press, 2007), 536–537. See also Milton Heath, "North American Railroads: Public Railroad Construction and the Development of Private Enterprise in the South before 1861," *Journal of Economic History* 10, supplement (1950): 4253.

26. Southside Railroad Company, Stock Ledger, Norfolk and Western Railway Archives, Special Collections, Virginia Polytechnic Institute and State University, Blacksburg, 347.

27. Majewski, *A House Dividing*, 145–146.

28. James G. Scott and Edward A. Wyatt, *Petersburg's Story: A History* (Petersburg, Va.: Titmus Optical, 1960), 75, 94–97; "An Act incorporating the Petersburg and Norfolk savings institutions," *Acts of the General Assembly* (Richmond: Thomas Ritchie, 1836), 256–258.

29. For early interpretations of class in the South, see Frank L. Owsley, *Plain Folk of the Old South* (Baton Rouge: Louisiana State University Press, 1949); and more recently, Samuel C. Hyde, Jr., ed., *Plain Folk of the South Revisited* (Baton Rouge: Louisiana State University Press, 1997), ix–xix.

30. Tom Downey, *Planting a Capitalist South: Masters, Merchants, and Manufacturers in the Southern Interior, 1790–1860* (Baton Rouge: Louisiana State University Press, 2006), 5–8.

31. Scott and Wyatt, *Petersburg's Story*, 96; "Trip on the Railroad," *[Petersburg, Va.] American Constellation*, May 25, 1838.

32. Bruce W. Eelman, *Entrepreneurs in the Southern Upcountry: Commercial Culture in Spartanburg, South Carolina, 1845–1880* (Athens: University of Georgia Press, 2008), 51–52; Peter S. Carmichael, *The Last Generation: Young Virginians in Peace, War, and Reunion* (Chapel Hill: University of North Carolina Press, 2005), 39–45.

33. Account Book, 1851–1861, p.1, Richard Eppes Papers, Virginia Historical Society, Richmond.

34. Jonathan Daniel Wells, *The Origins of the Southern Middle Class, 1800–1861* (Chapel Hill: University of North Carolina Press, 2004), 7–14; Frank J. Byrne, *Becoming Bourgeois: Merchant Culture in the South, 1820–1865* (Lexington: University Press of Kentucky, 2006), 8–12; John W. Quist, *Restless Visionaries: The Social Roots of Antebellum Reform in Alabama and Michigan* (Baton Rouge: Louisiana State University Press, 1998), 21–22; Jennifer R. Green, *Military Education and the Emerging Middle Class in the Old South* (Cambridge: Cambridge University Press, 2008), 17–21.

35. *Thomson's Mercantile and Professional Directory* (Baltimore: William Thomson, 1851), 213, 215.

36. Editorial, *[Petersburg, Va.] Daily Southside Democrat*, June 22, 1855; "The City as a Motive Power," *[Petersburg, Va.] Daily Express*, May 2, 1859.

37. U.S. Bureau of the Census, "Products of Industry during the Year Ending June 1, 1860," 1860 census, schedule 5, Virginia Eastern Division, City of Petersburg, National Archives, Washington, D.C. (microfilm).

38. Stuart M. Blumin, *The Emergence of the Middle Class: Social Experience in the American City, 1760–1900* (Cambridge: Cambridge University Press, 1989), 134–136; Mary Ann Clawson, *Constructing Brotherhood: Class, Gender, and Fraternalism* (Princeton, N.J.: Princeton University Press, 1989), 14–15; L. Diane Barnes, *Artisan Workers in the Upper South: Petersburg, Virginia, 1820–1865* (Baton Rouge: Louisiana State University Press, 2008), 186–187; Membership List, Petersburg Benevolent Mechanic Association Papers, 1825–1921, Special Collections, University of Virginia Library, Charlottesville.

39. A similar argument for the liberating qualities of independence is made for Southern single women in Christine Jacobson Carter, *Southern Single Blessedness: Unmarried Women in the Urban South, 1800–1865* (Urbana: University of Illinois Press, 2006), esp. 1–12; Majewski, *Modernizing a Slave Economy*, 41–42.

40. W. Eugene Ferslew, comp., *Second Annual Directory for the City of Petersburg* (Petersburg: George E. Ford, 1860).; and U.S. Bureau of the Census, Population

Schedules, Virginia Eastern Division, City of Petersburg, 1860, National Archives, Washington, D.C. (microfilm).

41. See Charles C. Bolton, *Poor Whites of the Antebellum South: Tenants and Laborers in Central North Carolina and Northeast Mississippi* (Durham, N.C.: Duke University Press, 1994).

42. Bolton, *Poor Whites*, 13–15; see also, Steven Elliott Tripp, *Yankee Town, Southern City: Race and Class Relations in Civil War Lynchburg* (New York: New York University Press, 1997), 30–31.

43. U.S. Bureau of the Census, Population Schedules, Virginia Eastern Division, City of Petersburg, 1860, National Archives, Washington, D.C. (microfilm). An examination of all metal forging workers in Petersburg demonstrates at least 12 percent persisted in the decade before the Civil War.

44. U.S. Bureau of the Census, Population Schedules, Virginia Eastern Division, City of Petersburg, 1860, National Archives, Washington, D.C. (microfilm).

45. Frank Towers, *The Urban South and the Coming of the Civil War* (Charlottesville: University of Virginia Press, 2004), 142–143.

46. For a discussion of the changing nature of race, see James Brewer Stewart, "Modernizing 'Difference': The Political Meanings of Color in the Free States, 1776–1840," *Journal of the Early Republic* 19 (1999): 692–693; Michael O'Brien, *Conjectures of Order: Intellectual Life and the American South, 1810–1860*, 2 vols. (Chapel Hill: University of North Carolina Press, 2004), 1:237.

47. Oakes, *Ruling Race*; Bayly, *Birth of the Modern World*, 10–11.

PART IV

The Blurred Boundaries of Southern Culture

IO

Zion in Black and White: African-American Evangelicals and Missionary Work in the Old South

Charles F. Irons

Maria C. Moore, a wealthy woman of color from Charleston, South Carolina, heard a voice one winter's night in 1848 while she was trying to sleep. Published accounts are not clear about whether she thought the voice was from God or from her deceased husband, but the effect was the same. Moore's husband, Richard Moore, had been a faithful member of the city's Second Presbyterian Church along with his wife, and he had made her promise before his death that she would continue to support foreign missions. "Are you going to forget the cause?" the voice asked. In good conscience, Moore could have insisted—before God and her deceased husband—that she had not forgotten the cause, for she routinely contributed the substantial sum of $30 per year to foreign missions. Convicted by the otherworldly intervention that she must not be doing enough for lost souls the world over, however, Moore immediately sent for her minister, the renowned Thomas Smyth. She then endowed with donations of real estate and bank stock two substantial funds for foreign missions, the "Moore Fund," and a separate, smaller fund designated specifically for Africa.[1]

Maria Moore had more resources than most black Southerners and enjoyed a privileged status as a member of Charleston's colored elite, but she was far from unique in her willingness to sacrifice to extend her church's global reach—or in the racial consciousness that she revealed by designating a portion of her gift specifically for Africa.

In March 1853, the Presbyterian Church's Foreign Missions Board recorded several other gifts from "colored members" marked for Africa in addition to a contribution of $114.44 from "The Moore Fund for African Mission." In Washington, North Carolina, for example, black Presbyterians scraped together $15.58 for the "African Mission," and the Mobile, Alabama, "Colored Missionary Society for Liberia" added $10—each significant donations from communities with characteristically lower incomes than their white counterparts.[2]

The proportion of enslaved donors in each of these instances is impossible to determine, but there is every indication that bondpeople gave from their small, personal accounts for special and regular offerings just as elite women like Moore did.[3] Robert Ryland, pastor of the enormous First African Baptist Church of Richmond, Virginia, estimated that "a congregation of a thousand, worshipping twice on the Lord's Day, will raise a thousand dollars a year without any conscious sacrifice," a standard which his own flock, composed primarily of enslaved persons, met during the 1850s.[4] Black Southerners cooperated with their white coreligionists in supporting both local and international missions.

Historians in recent years have rediscovered modern elements within Southern evangelicalism, particularly in the extent and nature of white Southerners' participation in benevolent work—of which a more rationalized, internationally focused mission movement was the cornerstone. Until the 1990s, scholars had contrasted traditional Southern Protestantism with progressive Northern Protestantism. This earlier scholarship concluded that white Southerners refused, because of their commitment to slavery, to participate in social-reform movements, at least after the 1840s, and that what reform there was aimed to improve individuals rather than society at large.[5] Recently, however, John W. Quist and Beth Barton Schweiger have shown that white Southern evangelicals participated in efforts to transform society as well. They have described religious Southerners, at least those in the region's towns and cities, as both more modern and more like their Northern counterparts.[6]

Even though scholars are learning to appreciate the vibrancy of Southern reform and missionary initiatives, they have thus far concentrated largely on the benevolent work of Southern whites. But black men and women were also sponsors of and participants in reform activity, and interracial interaction characterized Southern evangelical reform as it did other facets of Southern religion, as some recent works have shown.[7] Greater attention to African Americans' cooperation with whites in three key ministries—colonization, the "Mission to the Slaves," and international (African) missions—both adds weight to the emerging redefinition of antebellum Southern Protestantism as modern and reveals new lines of influence that blacks exerted on the development of

Southern evangelicalism. Furthermore, it provides another view of the difficult trade-offs that black Southerners were forced to make within biracial churches as they balanced sometimes-competing desires for racial uplift, personal fulfillment, and the redemption of corrupt social systems.

Nineteenth-century evangelicals in Great Britain and the United States helped to define the concept of modernity when they launched a range of missionary and reform activities in the late eighteenth and early nineteenth centuries. In recent years, anthropologists, scholars of religious studies, and historians have explored how missionaries refined in their encounter with "others" at home and abroad a new understanding of civilization and religion's place in it. Indeed, they have shown that even the twenty-first-century concept of secularism is an artifact from Protestant missions of the nineteenth century.[8] There were emancipatory impulses within the "moral narrative of modernity" which these missionaries told and which scholars have elaborated. As anthropologist Webb Keane put it, modernity was "not only a matter of improvements in technology, economic well-being, or health but [was] also, and perhaps above all, about human emancipation and self-mastery."[9] But a commitment to immediate antislavery was not an essential characteristic of the missionaries' modernity, and some evangelicals used the sliding scale of civilization that avatars of modernity elaborated to justify the indefinite subordination of "backward" peoples.

Maria Moore and other black Southerners who cooperated with whites on religious initiatives confound placement on any continuum of resistance to accommodation. As Erskine Clarke has pointed out, highly churched individuals like Moore were simultaneously "among the most eager to be acculturated" and among the leaders "in the long struggle against the forces of oppression."[10] In a similar vein, scholars of antebellum black nationalism have noted the extent to which (mainly elite Northern) black leaders shared Anglo-Americans' sense of cultural superiority in their attitudes to "uplift" or to the proselytization of enslaved Americans and African natives, even as they proposed schemes to alleviate or eliminate racial oppression.[11] Attention to Southern blacks' mission work, especially to the contributions of enslaved men and women, is important because it shows very real points of shared interest between Southern blacks and whites, interests no less powerful because they were spiritual rather than material in nature. Both Southern black and Southern white evangelicals wanted to rescue others from sin and to bring them within the fold of the church. Both also believed that African Americans would be the key agents in the conversion and redemption of Africa.[12] Despite sharing beliefs and interests with whites, though, black evangelicals did differentiate their participation in benevolent enterprises from that of their white coreligionists.

They tended, like Moore, to direct their offerings to their own congregations or to work in Africa.

White evangelicals, of course, also advanced a distinctive racial agenda through benevolent work, both in their sponsorship of programs that they thought proved slavery's righteousness and in the self-serving ways in which they interpreted the contributions of their black coreligionists. White Southern Methodists in 1848 demonstrated the proslavery function of the Mission to the Slaves, for example, when they cited black converts as a sufficient defense against the slings and arrows of Northern abolitionists. "If our unprovoked accusers think that we could do a *better part than this*, for our slave population, consistently with our obligations as citizens and christians," they challenged, "we shall be most happy to hear from them on the subject."[13]

In 1859, white Presbyterians betrayed in their opportunistic commemoration of Maria Moore's gift the rhetorical value that they placed on black participation in benevolent work. Like other white evangelicals, they considered black cooperation in ministry even more persuasive than black conversion as evidence that black Americans were thriving spiritually in the slave South. For white Presbyterians, Moore's generous gift was too-outstanding an example of black cooperation with whites to allow the world to forget it, and they continued to commemorate it in denominational papers over a decade after she had responded to the voice in the night. In the context of an intensifying sectional crisis, Moore had become a statistic—a data point that Southern whites referenced in order to discredit Northern abolitionist accusations that blacks suffered unjust treatment in Southern churches.

In an attempt to bolster their claims of spiritual equanimity towards black Southerners, the contributors of the 1859 story about Moore added another vignette from Charleston's Second Presbyterian Church that unintentionally highlighted the limits of antebellum interracialism. Second Presbyterian Church had gained prominence in the Mission to the Slaves by sponsoring a flourishing semi-independent Presbyterian congregation for black Charlestonians.[14] The church's representatives boasted in print that out of twenty-four ministers coming out of the church since 1832, "two of these were colored persons." The white writers doubtlessly intended the nurture of two black ministers to be further evidence of black flourishing within Southern evangelicalism, but their boast actually underscored the paucity of outlets for black spiritual leadership under slavery. One of the two black ministers was "settled in Philadelphia and the other [was] abroad." In other words, the same men whom Charleston whites wanted to group with Maria Moore as proof that slavery enhanced the progress of the Gospel among black Americans ultimately needed to leave the South and slavery in order to fulfill their callings![15] Black participation in three benevolent enterprises—colonization, the Mission to the Slaves, and international missions—thus occupied a complex, sometimes contradictory position at the nexus of interracialism, modernity, and evangelicalism.

Colonization

Black Southern evangelicals' participation in international and domestic missions peaked in the late antebellum period, but blacks and whites in the upper South collaborated on an important international project as early as the 1810s: African colonization. From the first evangelical stirrings in the eighteenth century, both black and white evangelicals had plied the Atlantic with their message. After the War of 1812, residents of the United States began to shift the religious currents of the Atlantic eastward.[16] Colonization was part of this outward thrust, as well as an attempt to address the place of black Americans in the republic. Despite the withering criticism that Northern blacks, abolitionists, and many Southern blacks ultimately launched against colonization, a significant cohort of upper South African Americans supported the program for several years after the formation of the American Colonization Society (ACS) in December 1816.

Richmond blacks, led by former slave Lott Cary, actually preempted the ACS by forming in 1815 the "African Baptist Missionary Society." Urban, black Baptists in Virginia (Petersburg African Americans also formed a group) had slightly different goals at the outset than did white members of the ACS, because they emphasized sponsoring missionaries rather than sending colonists—and because, as Cary's correspondence suggests, black Southerners were also much more united in their hope that establishing a settlement in Liberia would provide a route to ending slavery.[17] For expediency's sake, the black-sponsored African Baptist Missionary Society and the white-sponsored ACS merged their agendas in the 1820s, and ministers and families who went out from the commonwealth with the support of both organizations became the most prominent leaders in Liberia.[18] The tension between African Americans' goal of supporting black clerical leaders in Africa and whites' goal of expatriating free black men and women remained, however, accounting for blacks' preference in the late antebellum period for funding African missions over colonization.

Lott Cary embodied the modernizing role of American missionaries. Upon his arrival in Liberia, he became a self-taught physician, a military leader, a successful merchant, and a school teacher, in addition to serving as a missionary and a Baptist minister. Cary, his fellow settlers, and his white partners in the

ACS promoted material, political, and spiritual progress so enthusiastically that scholars have argued over which motivation was primary.[19] This debate obscures the extent to which reform-minded evangelicals in the nineteenth century expected that progress on all three fronts would occur simultaneously and creates an artificial contrast between Cary's secular and religious goals. For Cary, there was no tension between his effort to prosper financially, his urgent insistence that African Americans needed to learn to "conduct the affairs of [their] own in government," or his desire to "preach to the poor Africans the way of life and salvation."[20]

Cary's willingness to accept "the kind & Benevolent aid, of the good Colonization Society" set him apart from many other black Americans who either opposed emigration entirely or simply opposed cooperation with the ACS.[21] Richard Allen, James Forten, David Walker, and other prominent black Northerners rejected colonization on the grounds that white colonizationists wanted to exclude black Americans from the United States and to perpetuate slavery. Walker pleaded with black colonizationists "that the plot is not for the glory of God, but on the contrary the perpetuation of slavery in this country, which will ruin them and the country forever, unless something is immediately done."[22] In terms of his practical program of redeeming enslaved African Americans by redeeming Africa, Cary may have had much in common with black Northern colonizationists like Alexander Crummell, but he and other Southern-born migrants were looking out from slavery and working with slave owners, something which made their orientation towards colonization distinctive.

Whites across the United States praised Cary's success and that of others like him, preferring the example of black colonizationists to the more militant voices rising at home. Soon after Cary's arrival in Liberia, those in the most rarified circles of white Baptist influence began to idealize him as a model African American. At the meeting of the Board of the General Convention in 1825, for example, Baptist leaders passed resolutions praising Cary for his "labors and pious deportment" and rejoiced that "his virtuous deportment has secured to him the high approbation of the American Colonization Society." Whites snatched up Cary's letters home and republished them in periodicals or, after his death in 1828, in hagiographical biographies.[23]

Especially in Virginia, source of over one-third of the migrants to Liberia, white evangelicals remained riveted by the achievements of black men abroad after Cary's death.[24] White evangelicals in the United States continued to lionize individuals such as Joseph Jenkins Roberts, first president of the independent nation from 1848, but they were also attentive to the rank and file. In the fall of 1830, editors of the *Religious Herald*, the most important Baptist paper in the state and arguably in the region, ran at least fourteen different articles on the colonization cause and featured both domestic boosters and African settlers in their pages. Although by 1830 pro-colonization editors focused more attention on white missionaries to Liberia such as Benjamin Rush Skinner, they continued to praise the strivings of African-American settlers. A "friend of missions" reminded readers in early October, "*first*, that among these, are men of intelligence, property, character and integrity—and that these give character to the state of society there; *secondly*, that when these men are translated from the United States to Liberia, they must of necessity feel themselves to be *other men*. No longer are they crushed and parylyzed [sic] under a sense of the inferiority inseparable from a condition, in which, with the FORM of men, they are of necessity without their rights."[25] In other words, immigrants to Liberia like Lott Cary won some supporters by striving so energetically to succeed in terms recognizable to white Americans—by seeking both prosperity and converts.[26]

White evangelicals honored the achievements of black settlers such as Cary in part because they interpreted colonists' achievements as proof of the civilizing and Christianizing effects of slavery. The Maryland Colonization Society was explicit in 1841 about its construction of a narrative of colonization that simultaneously affirmed slavery, honored evangelical blacks, and heralded the progressive (i.e., modernizing) nature of their enterprise. Its officers pledged to keep the story of Liberia's founding generations in the public eye, asking,

> What can be of more intense and thrilling interest in after times,
> than a detail of the progressive steps by which a degraded and
> suffering race of bondsmen and slaves from one of these United
> States, were transported across the Atlantic to the land from which
> their forefathers sprang, and were established as a nation on a
> marked and prominent point of that beautiful land, bearing with
> them the arts, the manners, the government, the religion of the most
> free and independent nation under heaven, to their friends and
> kindred on whom has ever rested the pall of ignorance and
> heathenism?[27]

Emigrants to Liberia thus affirmed white evangelicals' belief in the divine purpose of slavery by trying to civilize and Christianize Africa. Black Americans were not blind to this dynamic, which—along with the high mortality rate— might be one reason that more of them did not leave for Liberia (only about 11,000 sailed between 1820 and 1860).[28]

But thousands of black men and women *did* emigrate and *did* cooperate with officials from the ACS or one of the state colonization societies. Even though these men and women did not believe that their success proved slavery's justice, they celebrated Christian social progress in Africa in terms very similar to those of white colonizationists. When Liberians claimed their independence in 1847, a step that the ACS encouraged because it reduced the society's financial responsibility for the colony, they declared to the world their achievement of progress along the multiple fronts pursued by Lott Cary. "Our numerous and well-attended schools attest our efforts and our desire for the improvement of our children," they proclaimed; and perhaps more importantly, "The native African bowing down with us before the altar of the living God, declares that from us, feeble as we are, the light of Christianity has gone forth."[29] Americo-Liberians tended to emphasize the progress that they were bringing to Africa and Africans, while white colonizationists stressed instead the progress that they had brought to enslaved Africans in America.

Mission to the Slaves

White evangelicals in the South made the conversion of enslaved men and women—the "Mission to the Slaves"—one of the most important benevolent initiatives of the late antebellum period. For most whites, this was an explicitly proslavery enterprise, since every convert proved to them the wisdom of evangelism rather than emancipation. As one editor explained after the division of the Methodist Episcopal Church into Northern and Southern branches in 1844, work among enslaved persons was proof of white Southerners' spiritual integrity: "Query. Which party most strictly conforms to the doctrines and practice of Christ and the Apostles? Those who seek to save the souls of the slave population of the country, or those who strive merely for their freedom?"[30] While some white Southern evangelicals may have preferred the mission because of its emphasis on individual conversion rather than social reformation, several historians have argued that white evangelicals in the antebellum period conceived of the mission as part of a broader effort to preserve and reform slavery *as a social system*.[31] In this way, the proslavery mission was not so much the inverse of Northern reform—that is, a way to stifle change altogether—but its Southern analog, a program for social improvement on terms favorable to slavery.

White Southern evangelicals organized the mission according to the modern practices characteristic of other reforms, though the precise shape of the effort to convert enslaved people varied from denomination to denomination. They founded new societies and/or institutions to recruit and pay missionaries, published catechisms and manuals, held regional conventions, and erected new meetinghouses for enslaved worshippers. Baptists, as befits their historic hostility to centralization, formed regional committees to support the conversion of black Southerners but relied upon individual congregations to execute most of the work. Methodists, on the other hand, formed a central committee to direct missionary work in the neediest districts. W. P. Harrison, an early Methodist historian and apologist for the mission, documented the steady growth of this program throughout the late antebellum period. By 1861, there were 329 separate missions supported by $86,359.20 in annual appropriations.[32]

Black evangelicals faced a dilemma: how could they support the white-run congregations that were an important part of their lives without also supporting the proslavery Mission to the Slaves? In most denominational variations of the mission, white evangelicals subsidized new black congregations until the freshly gathered believers were capable of supporting their churches themselves. Thus, as some blacks recognized, any contribution to the maintenance of an all-black or biracial church was also a de facto contribution to the Mission to the Slaves—because it freed funds for white denominational leaders to subsidize new black congregations.[33]

Black Baptists could at least be confident that any funds that they raised in church would remain within their congregation, since Baptists tended to work through individual congregations to recruit new enslaved members. Evidence from the region's largest African-American church, Richmond's First African Baptist, suggests that most (but not all) worshippers were thus able to overcome their scruples about contributing indirectly to the proslavery mission. In the late 1850s members of the church added to the roughly $1,000 that they collected through offerings another $2,000 from fundraising concerts and rental fees.[34] One of First African Baptist's most famous congregants, Henry "Box" Brown, recognized that white Baptists held the balance of power even in his semi-independent church and therefore questioned the wisdom of giving his allegiance or offering to First African Baptist. There were, in fact, several organic connections between Richmond's black Baptists and the city's white Baptists, who—in an arrangement replicated in urban areas across the South—supervised the First African Church's every worship service, appointed its pastor, and held its sanctuary in trust. This was enough for Brown, who refused in 1848 to sing in any more concerts lest he raise another cent to support proslavery Christianity. In the midst of performing in a Christmas-day fundraiser, Brown and a friend "felt reproved by Almighty God for lending his aid to the cause of slave-holding religion; and it was under this impression he closed his book and formed the resolution which he still acts upon, of never singing again or taking part in the services of a pro-slavery church."[35]

Enslaved and free black Baptists left enough testimony about their discomfort with biracial worship to show that Brown was not alone. William Troy, who became a prominent Baptist minister, remained for years in a congregation in Essex County, Virginia, despite his conviction that Southern churches basely reinforced racial hierarchy. "It was true that I was a member of the church in name," he reminisced from the safety of Canada, "but in reality I was no more so than a horse or a mule."[36] It is not clear, however, how many African Americans had no objections to biracial evangelicalism, how many attended biracial churches despite serious reservations, and how many refused to attend ante-bellum churches altogether because of white churchgoers' complicity in sup-porting the slave regime. Depending upon the method of calculation, the total percentage of black Southerners who attended church on the eve of the Civil War was somewhere between 41 and 54 percent—so many African Americans appear to have overcome whatever scruples they may have had about fellow-ship with proslavery whites.[37] On the other hand, several hundred thousand African Americans did not join a church until after emancipation and ecclesi-astical separation, suggesting that there may have been a significant cohort who refused to join an antebellum church for precisely the reasons cited by Brown and Troy.[38]

Black Methodists, unlike black Baptists, did not have the luxury of imag-ining that all of their offerings stayed within their particular congregations. Southern Methodists funded several missionary enterprises, including "Mis-sions among the People of Color" (the Mission to the Slaves) out of a common fund managed by the denominational "Missionary Society." When black Meth-odists who worshipped at one of the special "mission churches" put money in the offering plate or basket, their funds either went directly to the society or reduced the amount of support that their congregation could expect to receive from it. Many African Americans therefore helped to fund emissaries for the proslavery Mission to the Slaves simply by contributing to their local churches.

Southern Methodists preserved extensive records of white and black con-tributions to the Missionary Society, which make it possible to explore in more detail how black Methodists negotiated this balancing act between support for their congregations and support for a proslavery mission program. The Meth-odist records are not perfect, marred most notably by different accounting con-ventions in different conferences. Nonetheless, the fact that black Methodists, the vast majority of whom were enslaved, raised funds to support both their local churches and larger denominational enterprises is indisputable. African-American support of individual congregations was so pronounced that Harrison felt compelled to offer an explanation; in those "cases, where the slaves them-selves paid their pastors," he reported, "they were given the opportunity by their owners to earn the money for themselves."[39] Though the extra-congregational receipts indicate a marked lack of enthusiasm among black Methodists for

direct contributions to the Mission to the Slaves, some individuals and organizations actively designated their contributions to the general missionary
fund.

Black Methodists as a group did not stint on their local congregations (or
"missions") out of concern that the funds might find their way into the Missionary Society's coffers. In Georgia, officials described several flourishing
black congregations in 1848, a few of which had become fully self-supporting.
In Savannah, for instance, Andrew Chapel began "paying its own expenses"
entirely and was therefore reclassified as a "station" and taken off the Missionary Society's dole. In Athens, a stunningly well-funded body of black Methodists numbering 176 members (and, presumably, several hundred additional
adherents) raised $800 to pay for a new chapel, paid their minister his full
salary of $246.25, and gave $8.08 to the Missionary Society to use at its discre-
tion. It is tempting to read the Athens group's meager contribution to the
state's Missionary Society in contrast to their substantial expenditures at home
as a gauge of black Methodists' disapproval of the work of the society, but there
are enough counter-examples to prevent such a straightforward interpretation.

Black Methodists routinely paid more than the maintenance costs of their
own missions. In Tennessee, for example, officials recorded substantial contributions to the state Missionary Society from nine "coloured" congregations and
one "colored meeting," totaling $887.10. In all, African Americans in the Vol-
unteer State provided roughly one-sixth of the conference's total funds for missions in 1846. In Louisiana, L. Campbell reported of five predominantly black
congregations that "all these missions support themselves" and that they contributed additional money to the general account.[40] In the South Carolina conference (which included portions of North Carolina), Charleston's wealthy free
people of color contributed $60 through the "Free col'd Missionary Society of
Charleston," an amount comparable to contributions from congregations in
Fayetteville, Wilmington, and Columbia but dwarfed by $180.50 from the
Bethel Church.[41]

It is not difficult to see why whites supported the Mission to the Slaves. In
doing so, they defended themselves against charges of inconsistency by white
Northerners, found an outlet for their earnest desire to spread the Gospel, and
gained some control over African-American religious expression. Southern
Methodist bishops placed the evangelization of enslaved people at the center of
their church's mission in their episcopal address at the 1858 General Conference: "The missions to the slaves of the Southern plantations constitute the most
interesting and important field for the missionary operations of the Church,
South," they preached; "We regard these missions as the crowning glory of our
church."[42] Southern white divines of every denomination extrapolated from the

success of the mission to conclude that the peculiar institution itself was ordained of God. In the most widely circulated defense of slavery, for example, Baptist Thornton Stringfellow argued that slavery was "full of mercy," because of the way in which it "has brought within the range of gospel influence, millions of Ham's descendants among ourselves, who but for this institution, would have sunk down to eternal ruin; knowing not God, and strangers to the gospel."[43]

Black Southerners may have declined to support the mission as directly as did whites, but—by the most conservative estimates—they annually contributed tens of thousands of hard-earned dollars to support individual churches. Despite the eloquent testimony of dissenters such as Brown and Troy, most African Americans evidently found enough that was rewarding in their local congregations to support them, notwithstanding any ideological benefit that white evangelicals derived from their campaign to Christianize black Southerners. Perhaps, like African-American Methodist David Smith, black contributors recognized the racial inequality present in their churches but found that biracial worship was nonetheless the most egalitarian experience possible in the antebellum South. Smith complained about unjust treatment of black Methodists and was ultimately so put off by white racism that he helped form the Baltimore wing of the AME Church, but he also recalled moments of extraordinary interracial fellowship. On one memorable day, he "saw the slaves and their owners singing, shouting and praising God together. All seemed to be one in Christ Jesus; there was no distinction as to the rich or poor, bond or free, but all were melted into sweet communion with the spirit and united in Christian fellowship."[44]

Scholars have generally overlooked the modern elements of slave missions and concentrated instead on white evangelicals' role in defending traditional Southern mores.[45] In fact, white evangelicals not only sought to transform Southern society, but they also did so using the latest techniques, upon which they continuously improved by attending conventions and exchanging advice literature. Moreover, whites were not the only supporters of slave missions; black evangelicals directly or indirectly contributed tens of thousands of dollars to the cause. Even the most fundamental practice that set Southern evangelicals apart from their Northern counterparts was thus more modern and biracial than historians have acknowledged.

International (African) Missions

Black evangelicals demonstrated a greater willingness to sponsor missionaries to Africa than missionaries to enslaved men and women within the United

States. There was, to be sure, a close relationship between African colonization and African missions, and some of the most prominent colonists were also missionaries. But there were important institutional and ideological distinctions between colonization and missions as they developed in the final decades of the antebellum period. Most importantly, denominations or denominational missionary societies paid missionaries but not colonists. As a result, missionaries—many of whom *did* support colonization—were nonetheless insulated against some of the criticism that abolitionists leveled against the American Colonization Society. In addition, sponsoring organizations proved willing to appoint black men as missionaries, in part because whites believed that blacks were better able to endure the African climate. Southern Presbyterians and Southern Baptists hired Southern-born African-American missionaries; Daniel Coker of Maryland went on behalf of the African Methodist Episcopal Church; and Methodists and Episcopalians sent Northern blacks.[46]

White evangelicals cast African missions in the same self-congratulatory light as colonization. They believed that their work represented the culmination of a divine plan that featured chattel slavery as an incubator of Christianity and civilization. Thomas Jefferson Bowen, one of the longest-serving white missionaries for the Southern Baptist Convention, rhapsodized in his influential 1857 account of African missions that an impartial observer would be able to

> See millions of civilized negroes in America, better clothed and fed, and more virtuous and happy than the analogous classes of white people in some other countries. He can see tens and hundreds of thousands of evangelical Christians, regenerated men and women, among these blacks, redeemed from the curse of sin in consequence of African slavery. And finally, he can see African colonization and African missions arising from this slavery, and flowing back as a river of light and life upon the African continent.[47]

Black missionaries in the late antebellum period tried to follow Lott Cary's earlier example by bringing both the Gospel and progress to Africa. They shared a commitment to enlighten and improve the religious and civil life in what they regarded as a dark and backwards place. For example, John H. Cheeseman, a black missionary on the Southern Baptist Convention's rolls in Edina, Liberia, believed that education and acculturation were the best ways to open native Africans to the message of the Gospel. Once young Africans learned to live "after American 'fash,' as they term it," then Cheeseman believed that they were "more susceptible of impressions of a religious character."[48] The black Baptist missionaries who served in Liberia embodied in their own lives the tight connection that they perceived between conversion and civilization. John

Day, born free in Virginia and the most important black missionary in Liberia from 1830 through 1859, was at various times chief justice in the Liberian courts and lieutenant governor. Other black Baptist missionaries filled the offices of president and attorney general, among other high-ranking posts.[49] For both whites and blacks, the spread of the Gospel was integral to the progress of American civilization, and African missions allowed for black men to be in the vanguard of the movement. John Saillant has convincingly shown that black missionaries conceived themselves to be "instruments of liberal progress," a characterization that meshed smoothly with triumphalist white narratives of African missions.[50]

Black Southerners supported missions more than colonization in the late antebellum period, probably because their funds went directly to the support of black leaders. From November 1850 through April 1851, the ACS recorded total donations of $13,557.61 (excluding subscriptions to the *African Repository* and annual pledges). Of this amount, only $40 came from black Southerners. Even more telling of black rejection of the ACS were the conditions that members of the Colored Missionary Society of Mobile, the sole African-American donors to the society, attached to their gift. They stipulated that it "be appropriated in equal proportions to the Methodist, the Baptist, the Presbyterian, and the Episcopal Missions in Liberia."[51] For colonization itself, black Southerners did not contribute a penny.

At the same time, African-American evangelicals in the South did give, however modestly, to support missionary work in Africa. Black Baptists who gave to foreign missions typically designated their gifts to the Baptist missionaries, mostly of African descent, who worked in Africa. "Colored members" of twenty Virginia Baptist churches contributed a combined $123.46 to their state's foreign missions board for "African missions" in 1850, in increments no larger than $33 per congregation.[52] For November 1849 through April 1850, black Presbyterians indicated just as decisive a preference for African missions. There are fewer black Presbyterian contributors in the records, only eleven for the same period, but nine of these were for African missions—mostly for the support of H. W. Ellis. Ellis, though the board soon removed him from his post for "charges involving his Christian character," was an inspiration for many black Southerners. The synods of Alabama and Mississippi had purchased him and his family members out of slavery before sending him off as a missionary, directly connecting racial uplift at home and abroad.[53]

Maria Moore may have been unusual for the size of her bequest in late 1848, but she was one of many black evangelicals who desired to contribute to her church's ministries despite her white coreligionists' proslavery convictions. In the late antebellum period, black and white evangelicals may not have always worked side by side, but they at least labored in tandem in very modern efforts to spread the blessings of American civilization and evangelicalism to destitute places at home and abroad. Unlike in the North, where free blacks routinely cooperated with whites who opposed slavery, enslaved and free blacks in the South had little choice other than to work with whites who believed their bondage was divinely appointed. Many black evangelicals were aware that their cooperation with whites made them in some way complicit with white, proslavery Christianity, but they participated selectively enough in benevolence (eschewing slave missions and empowering African-American ministers when possible), to satisfy many of them that the compromise was worth it. In the process, they provided another uncomfortable example of the compatibility of slavery and modernity.

NOTES

1. Second Presbyterian Church Records (Charleston, S.C.), Session Minute Book 1837–1852, January 1849, South Carolina Historical Society, Charleston; "Second Presbyn Church, Charleston," *Central Presbyterian*, June 25, 1859.
On Moore's household, see Larry Kroger, *Black Slaveowners: Free Black Slave Masters in South Carolina, 1790–1860* (Columbia: University of South Carolina Press, 1985), 24–25, 50; U.S. Bureau of the Census, *Fifth Census of the United States, South Carolina* (M19–170), 132.

2. *The Home and Foreign Record of the Presbyterian Church in the United States of America* (Philadelphia: [Presbyterian] Publication House, 1853), 153.

3. Dylan C. Penningroth, *The Claims of Kinfolk: African American Property and Community in the Nineteenth-Century South* (Chapel Hill: University of North Carolina Press, 2003), 45–78.

4. H. A. Tupper, ed., *The First Century of the First Baptist Church of Richmond, Virginia, 1780–1880* (Richmond: Carlton McCarthy, 1880), 272. First African Baptist Church, Minutes 1841–1859, April 17, 1859, February 7, 1858, Library of Virginia, Richmond.

5. John W. Kuykendall, *Southern Enterprize: The Work of National Evangelical Societies in the Antebellum South* (Westport, Conn.: Greenwood Press, 1982), 162–165; Donald Mathews, *Religion in the Old South* (Chicago: University of Chicago Press, 1977), 76–78; Anne Loveland, *Southern Evangelicals and the Social Order, 1800–1860* (Baton Rouge: Louisiana State University Press, 1980), 161–162. For a recent affirmation of this perspective, see Charles Reagan Wilson, *Southern Missions: The Religion of the American South in Global Perspective* (Waco, Tex.: Baylor University Press, 2006), 11.

6. John W. Quist, "Slaveholding Operatives of the Benevolent Empire," *Journal of Southern History* 62:3 (1996): 484; Beth Barton Schweiger, *The Gospel Working Up: Progress and the Pulpit in Nineteenth-Century Virginia* (New York: Oxford University Press, 2000), 4–5; more generally, Daniel Walker Howe, *What Hath God Wrought: The*

Transformation of American, 1815–1848 (New York: Oxford University Press, 2007); Michael O'Brien, *Conjectures of Order: Intellectual Life and the American South, 1810–1860*, 2 vols. (Chapel Hill: University of North Carolina Press, 2004), esp. 1:18.

7. Erskine Clarke, *Dwelling Place: A Plantation Epic* (New Haven, Conn.: Yale University Press, 2005); Paul Harvey, *Freedom's Coming: Religious Culture and the Shaping of the South from the Civil War through the Civil Rights Era* (Chapel Hill: University of North Carolina Press, 2005); Charles Irons, *Origins of Proslavery Christianity: White and Black Evangelicals in Colonial and Antebellum Virginia* (Chapel Hill: University of North Carolina Press, 2008).

8. For the relation between missions and ostensibly "secular" modernity, see Webb Keane, *Christian Moderns: Freedom and Fetish in the Mission Encounter* (Berkeley: University of California Press, 2007), and Janet R. Jakobsen and Ann Pellegrini, introduction to *Secularisms*, ed. Jakobsen and Pellegrini (Durham, N.C.: Duke University Press, 2008), 1–38. For more historical approaches, see Ussama Makdisi, "Reclaiming the Land of the Bible," *American Historical Review* 102 (1997): 680–671; Peter van der Veer, "The Global History of Modernity," *Journal of the Economic and Social History of the Orient* 41 (1998): 285–294; Ryan Dunch, "Beyond Cultural Imperialism," *History and Theory* 41 (2002): 317–325; John Saillant, "Missions in Liberia," in *The Foreign Missionary Enterprise at Home: Explorations in North American Cultural History*, ed. Daniel H. Bays and Grant Wacker (Tuscaloosa: University of Alabama Press, 2003), 13–28; Andrew Witmer, "God's Interpreters: African Missions, Transnational Protestantism, and Race in the United States, 1830–1910" (Ph.D. diss., University of Virginia, 2008).

9. Keane, *Christian Moderns*, 6.

10. Erskine Clarke, *Our Southern Zion: A History of Calvinism in the South Carolina Low Country, 1690–1990* (Tuscaloosa: University of Alabama Press, 1996), 130.

11. Wilson Jeremiah Moses, *The Wings of Ethiopia: Studies in African-American Life* (Ames: Iowa State University Press, 1990); Tunde Adeleke, *Unafrican Americans: Nineteenth-Century Black Nationalists and the Civilizing Mission* (Lexington: University Press of Kentucky, 1998).

12. James Sidbury, *Becoming African in America: Race and Nation in the Early Black Atlantic* (New York: Oxford University Press, 2007); James T. Campbell, *Songs of Zion: The African Methodist Episcopal Church in the United States and South Africa* (Chapel Hill: University of North Carolina Press, 1998); Sylvia M. Jacobs, ed., *Black Americans and the Missionary Movement in Africa* (Westport, Conn.: Greeenwood Press, 1982).

13. *Third Annual Report of the Missionary Society of the Methodist Episcopal Church, South* (Louisville: Morton and Griswold, 1848), 24.

14. Second Presbyterian's sponsorship of this congregation began with a resolution in 1847; see Clarke, *Our Southern Zion*, 190–199.

15. "Second Presbyn Church, Charleston," *Central Presbyterian*, June 25, 1859.

16. Sylvia Frey and Betty Wood, *Come Shouting to Zion: African American Protestantism in the American South and British Caribbean to 1830* (Chapel Hill: University of North Carolina Press, 1998); Jon F. Sensbach, *Rebecca's Revival: Creating*

Black Christianity in the Atlantic World (Cambridge, Mass.: Harvard University Press, 2005); Cedrick May, *Evangelism and Resistance in the Black Atlantic, 1760–1835* (Athens: University of Georgia Press, 2008); Martha Ward, "Where Circum-Caribbean Afro-Atlantic Creoles Met American Southern Protestant Conjurers," in *Caribbean and Southern: Transnational Perspectives on the U.S. South*, ed. Helen A. Regis (Athens: University of Georgia Press, 2006), 124–138.

17. See Lott Cary, "Circular Addressed to the Colored Brethren and Friends in America," ed. John Saillant and reprinted in *Virginia Magazine of History and Biography* 104 (1996): 481–504.

18. Marie Tyler-McGraw, *An African Republic: Black and White Virginians in the Making of Liberia* (Chapel Hill: University of North Carolina Press, 2007), 24, 50.

19. For example, Douglas Egerton, "Averting a Crisis," *Civil War History* 43 (1997): 142–156 (economic); Marie Tyler-McGraw, "'The Prize I Mean is the Prize of Liberty,'" *Virginia Magazine of History and Biography* 97 (1989): 355–374 (political); Irons, *Origins of Proslavery Christianity*, 97–132 (spiritual).

20. Ralph R. Gurley, *Life of Jehudi Ashman, Late Colonial Agent in Liberia* (Washington, D.C.: James C. Dunn, 1835), 148 (appendix); Cary, "Circular Addressed to the Colored Brethren," 495 (quotation); Saillant, "Missions in Liberia," 20.

21. Cary, "Circular to the Colored Brethren," 494.

22. Peter P. Hinks, ed., *David Walker's Appeal to the Colored Citizens of the World* (1829; University Park: Pennsylvania State University Press, 2000), 71.

23. Quotation from James B. Taylor, *Biography of Elder Lott Cary, Late Missionary to Africa* (1837; repr., Documenting the American South, 2001), http://docsouth.unc.edu/neh/taylor/taylor.html (accessed September 2010); see also Cary, "Circular to the Colored Brethren," 504.

24. Eric Burin, *Slavery and the Peculiar Solution: A History of the American Colonization Society* (Gainesville: University Press of Florida, 2005), tables 1–4.

25. *Religious Herald*, August 6–October 29, 1830, esp. "African Mission," September 10, and "A Friend to the Missionary Cause," October 1.

26. See also Bruce Dorsey, "A Gendered History of African Colonization," *Journal of Social History* 34 (2000): 77–103.

27. [James Hall,] opening editorial, *Maryland Colonization Journal*, July 15, 1841.

28. Burin, *Slavery and the Peculiar Solution*, table 2. The total number of migrants, including the postwar period and immigrants to the Maryland Colonization Society's settlements, probably reached 16,000.

29. The Declaration of Independence, "Liberian Constitutions," Trustees of Indiana University, http://onliberia.org/con_declaration.htm (accessed September 2010). See also Moses, *Wings of Ethiopia*, 141–158.

30. "A Crazy Man's Idea," *Richmond Christian Advocate*, June 11, 1846.

31. Drew Gilpin Faust, "Evangelicalism and the Meaning of the Proslavery Argument," *Virginia Magazine of History and Biography* 85 (1977): 3–17; Eugene D. Genovese and Elizabeth Fox-Genovese, "The Divine Sanction of Social Order," *Journal of the American Academy of Religion* 55 (Summer 1987): 211–233; Clarence L. Mohr, *On*

the Threshold of Freedom: Masters and Slaves in Civil War Georgia (Athens: University of Georgia Press, 1986); Clarke, *Our Southern Zion.*

32. W. P. Harrison, *The Gospel among the Slaves: A Short Account of Missionary Operations Among the African Slaves of the Southern States* (Nashville: M.E. Church, South, 1893), 325; Milton Sernett, *Black Religion and American Evangelicalism: White Protestants, Plantation Missions, and the Flowering of Negro Christianity, 1787–1865* (Metuchen, N.J.: The Scarecrow Press and the American Theological Library Association, 1975); Janet D. Cornelius, *Slave Missions and the Black Church in the Antebellum South* (Columbia: University of South Carolina Press, 1999).

33. Across denominations, whites recognized by the late 1840s that the most effective way to add black members to their rolls was to sponsor semi-independent churches. Irons, *Origins of Proslavery Christianity,* 187–189, 200–207.

34. First African Baptist Church, Minutes 1841–1859, September 19, 1858, September 25, 1859, Library of Virginia, Richmond.

35. Henry Brown, *Narrative of the Life of Henry Box Brown* (1851; repr., Documenting the American South, 1999), http://docsouth.unc.edu/neh/brownbox/brownbox.html (accessed September 2010).

36. William Troy, *Hair-breadth Escapes from Slavery to Freedom* (1861; repr., Documenting the American South, 1999), http://docsouth.unc.edu/neh/troy/troy.html (accessed September 2010).

37. Based on the oft-cited figure of 468,000 full members; see Daniel R. Hundley, *Social Relations in Our Southern States* (New York: Henry B. Price, 1860), 297. The range here reflects the difference between two sets of estimates for the ratios of adherents to members—for the low end, see Henry K. Carroll, *Religious Forces of the United States, Enumerated, Classified, and Described on the Basis of the Government Census of 1890* (New York: Christian Literature, 1893), xxxv; for the high end, see Robert Baird, *Religion in America, or An Account of the Origin, Progress, Relation to the State, and Present Condition of the Evangelical Churches in the United States: With Notices of the Unevangelical Denominations* (New York: Harper and Brothers, 1844), 265.

38. Daniel L. Fountain, "Christ in Chains," in *Affect and Power: Essays on Sex, Slavery, Race and Religion in Appreciation of Winthrop D. Jordan,* ed. David J. Libby, Paul Spickard, and Susan Ditto (Jackson: University Press of Mississippi, 2005), 84–104.

39. Harrison, *Gospel among the Slaves,* 311, 318–324.

40. *Third Annual Report of the Missionary Society,* 35, 49, 88–89. The total receipts for the Tennessee Conference were $5,580.35.

41. *Fourth Annual Report of the Missionary Society of the Methodist Episcopal Church, South* (Louisville: Morton and Griswold, 1849), 20.

42. *Journal of the General Conference of the Methodist Episcopal Church, South* (May 1858), 389–402. Issues of this journal from 1854 to 1874 are bound in the Methodist Reading Room, Divinity School Library, Duke University, Durham, N.C.

43. Thornton Stringfellow, *Scriptural and Statistical Views in Favor of Slavery* (1856 [4th ed.]; repr., Documenting the American South, 2000), http://docsouth.unc.edu/church/string/string.html (accessed September 2010).

44. David Smith, *Biography* (1881; repr., Documenting the American South, 1999), http://docsouth.unc.edu/neh/dsmith/dsmith.html#dsmith13 (accessed September 2010).

45. The strongest case for white evangelicals' aversion to modernity may be found in Elizabeth Fox-Genovese and Eugene D. Genovese, *The Mind of the Master Class: History and Faith in the Southern Slaveholders' Worldview* (New York: Cambridge University Press, 2006); for specific reference to the mission's role in preserving a traditional social order, see Eugene D. Genovese, *Roll, Jordan, Roll: The World The Slaves Made* (New York: Vintage Books, 1974), 190.

46. For Coker, see Campbell, *Songs of Zion*, 67–74. The Northern branch of the Methodist Church retained control of African missions after the 1844 division.

47. T. J. Bowen, *Adventures and Missionary Labors in Several Countries in the Interior of Africa from 1849 to 1856* (Charleston, S.C.: Southern Baptist Publication Society, 1857), 61.

48. *Proceedings of the Fifth Biennial Meeting of the Southern Baptist Convention . . . 1855* (Richmond: H. K. Ellyson, 1855), 54.

49. Eddie Stepp, "Interpreting a Forgotten Mission" (Ph.D. diss., Baylor University, 1999), 151–152.

50. Saillant, "Missions in Liberia," 14.

51. *The African Repository*, January–June 1851, sum of contributions. Colored Missionary Society of Mobile appears March 1851, 93.

52. *Minutes of the Virginia Baptist Anniversaries . . . 1850* (Richmond: H. K. Ellyson, 1850), 32–37.

53. *The Home and Foreign Record of the Presbyterian Church . . . 1850* (Philadelphia: [Presbyterian] Publication House, 1850), first six-monthly lists of contributions; for Ellis's downfall (in whites' eyes), *Fifteenth Annual Report of the Board of Foreign Missions of the Presbyterian Church* (New York: For the Board, 1852), 19.

II

The Return of the Native: Innovative Traditions in the Southeast

Andrew K. Frank

In 1831, in the aftermath of the Indian Removal Act, Cherokee editor Elias Boudinot lampooned the American rationale for removing Native Americans from the South. "It has been customary to charge the failure of attempts heretofore made to civilize and christianize the aborigines to the Indians themselves," he explained. "Whence originated the common saying, 'An Indian will still be an Indian.'—Do what you will, he cannot be civilized—you cannot reclaim him from his wild habits— you may as well expect to change the spots of the Leopard as to effect any substantial renovation in his character." The experience of the Cherokees, the largest Indian tribe in the South, demonstrated the fallacy of this racial explanation: "The Cherokees have been reclaimed from their wild habits—Instead of hunters they have become the cultivators of the soil—Instead of wild and ferocious savages, thirsting for blood, they have become the mild 'citizens,' the friends and brothers of the white man—Instead of the superstitious heathens, many of them have become the worshippers of the true God." Rather than merely point to the transformation of Cherokee and other southeastern Indian societies, the editor of the *Cherokee Phoenix* proclaimed that any perceived shortcomings of the Indians resulted from limitations imposed by the United States. Economic, political, and religious changes, he explained, did not entirely satisfy American society.[1] The same government that spent several decades promoting a "civilization plan" to transform Native society now embraced the immutability of the Indian's natural character. As President Andrew Jackson explained in his first annual message to Congress: "Surrounded by the whites with their arts of civilization, which by destroying the resources of the savage doom him to weakness and decay, the fate of the Mohegan, the Narragansett, and the Delaware is fast overtaking the Choctaw, the Cherokee, and the Creek." Removal, Jackson self-servingly explained, was the only way to avoid the destruction of the Indians.[2]

Jackson's detractors—Natives and non-Natives alike—frequently came to different conclusions about southeastern Indians. Although they hardly ignored distinctions between Indians and non-Indians, Boudinot and many others concluded that the transformation of the Native southeast had already demonstrated the potential for Indians to embrace the marketplace and perhaps even live up to Thomas Jefferson's dream that Indians and Americans could "intermix and become one people."[3] By the 1820s, southeastern Indians routinely herded cattle and hogs, engaged in the Atlantic market, pursued English literacy and formal schooling, grew cotton, owned African slaves, hired attorneys to protect their legal claims, centralized their systems of governance, and otherwise embraced various elements that were common in the Old South. They built elegant homes and lavish plantations; constructed toll roads, taverns, steamboats, and ferries; and adopted the clothing of their white neighbors. They wrote new constitutions, codified laws, and organized centralized police forces. Although observers often attributed the greatest changes to so-called mixed-blood Indians, the transformative power of the marketplace touched virtually everyone in the Native southeast. As Reverend Samuel Worcester optimistically proclaimed: "those of mixed blood are generally in the van, the whole mass of the people is on the march."[4]

This chapter revisits this history of the southeastern Indians, tribal peoples who have been too-often excluded from discussions of the "biracial South" or oversimplified as romantically adhering to ancient traditions and stubbornly opposing changes that emanated from Anglo-American society.[5] In recent decades, scholars have complicated these images and have discovered vibrant communities that shaped and were shaped by the larger influences in the American South. Although the choices Natives made were often constrained by events and processes that were not of their choosing, Cherokees, Choctaws, Chickasaws, Creeks, and to a lesser extent Seminoles chose cultural and economic innovations in order to secure their economic and political survival.[6] In other words, they often embraced changes that originated in American society in order to ensure that they would not be subsumed by it. In particular, this chapter explores five changes—the spread of cattle, the rise of cotton production, the proliferation of race slavery, the embrace of schooling and literacy, and the centralization of Native polities.

These often-controversial innovations helped Natives navigate through the tumultuous antebellum era, while making them more dependent on and culturally less distinct from their white neighbors.[7] Cultural innovation, in other words, was both the cause and solution to many of the problems that southeastern Indians faced.

The Eighteenth-Century Southeast

In the eighteenth century, several characteristics united the five largest southeastern tribes into a relatively coherent culture group. Politically, Natives lived in decentralized villages, where individuals who demonstrated the efficacy of their guidance shared and exercised power and authority. Villages operated largely independent of one another, although a range of familial and social ties connected them together. Villages united voluntarily to wage war or make treaties, as leaders lacked centralized polities or coercive power to mandate compliance. Without written languages, laws and lessons were transmitted orally, and treaties with foreign nations were negotiated through interpreters who recorded the "official" versions in English, Spanish, or French.[8]

Socially, a network of clans structured Native communities in the South. Indians presumed that these kinship groups, which structured a range of personal and familial obligations for every member of a community, descended from a natural force or animal. These clans were matrilineal (meaning that children took their familial identity from their mothers only), and households were structured in such a manner that allowed a matrilineage (multigenerational members of the same clan) to live under one roof or in a cluster. Just as importantly, Natives were traditionally matrilocal, meaning that husbands left their families and moved into their wives' homes at marriage, where they were usually surrounded by their wives' female relatives. As a result, women controlled the agricultural fields that surrounded their villages, growing corn, beans, squash and a variety of other crops. For their part, men gathered with members of their clan outside of villages to hunt deer and other animals for their meat and hides.[9] Religiously, southeastern Indians remained largely untouched by Christian missionaries. Despite various missionary efforts, there were few Christian converts in the eighteenth century. Instead, Natives participated in a rich ceremonial life, the center of which was the annual Green Corn Ceremony, and they shared similar rituals, such the purification ceremonies of scratching and the taking of black drink.[10] Economically, the southeastern Indians engaged in trade long before the arrival of Europeans, connecting them with the luxury items and rare materials of distant tribes. The trade of corn and deer occurred within households, serving as a symbolic and practical marital transaction, but basic necessities were largely produced locally.[11]

Around the turn of the nineteenth century, several forces and trends convinced Natives to pursue various social, economic, political, and cultural changes. First, the economic transformation of the American South toward a plantation economy resulted in declining demands for deerskins, a product whose supply dwindled concurrently with the devastation of the region's white-tailed deer population. Second, Natives increasingly faced the land-grab of white American settlers and politicians, a process that intensified as Great Britain, Spain, and France withdrew from the region in the early nineteenth century. This ended the long-standing Native diplomatic practice of playing European powers off of one another in order to secure trade and diplomatic alliances. In the 1830s, the land-grab culminated in the forced removal of approximately fifty thousand Natives to Indian Territory, or what is now Arkansas and Oklahoma. Third, many of the changes were encouraged, magnified, and shaped by religious and cultural missionaries who urged southeastern Indians to embrace "civilization." Indian agent Benjamin Hawkins, for example, spent nearly two decades directing the cultural and political reformation of the southeast from within Creek society. His extensive "plan of civilization," along with the private efforts of countless Moravian, Baptist, and Methodist missionaries, brought new resources and opportunities into Native communities. This plan expedited innovations, though many had begun already and would likely have continued.[12]

Southeastern Indians began to participate in the Atlantic marketplace shortly after the first European traders arrived in the sixteenth century. Initially, the supply of deerskins could not meet the needs of the European leather market, and with this advantage Indians quickly obtained access to a litany of luxuries like mirrors, metal goods, beads, guns, and alcohol.[13] As these goods slowly became necessities, Native families diverted more attention to the hunt and produced less corn and other essentials. The adoption of new technology (especially guns) enabled greater skin harvests and intensified competition between Indians to serve as suppliers. As a result, the deer population plummeted. The resulting scarcity of deerskins in the late eighteenth and early nineteenth centuries accelerated the trend toward market dependence, as women began to join the hunting parties so that they could maximize the number of skins that could be carried by dressing or preparing the skins in the fields. As a result, harvests suffered and hunger and malnutrition spread across Indian country. Missionaries recorded that Native Americans needed to "buy corn" even at "a time of great rain," when they could have "obtain an abundance of bread . . . by . . . cultivat[ing] the earth."[14]

Domesticated Animals

The declining population of deer and dependence on the marketplace led many Indians to augment their livelihoods with various economic pursuits. Many Native men turned to domesticated animals as a logical innovation. Hunting grounds became herding pastures, and herders incorporated domesticated animals in traditionally sanctioned manners. Just as hunters brought deer hides to market and consumed venison at home, herders typically brought hides and some meat to the marketplace and provided their villages with supplies of meat or milk. Indeed, whereas many Indians owned small herds, groups of Indians (either villages or clans) frequently controlled larger herds. At the same time, in the early nineteenth century, Indians maintained many of the cultural norms that shaped their lives when they were hunters. When Choctaw herders died, members of their clan killed the deceased person's cattle, horses, and dogs in accordance with ancient funeral rituals. Choctaws reasoned that the animals "would be equally useful and desirable in the state of being which they enter at death."[15] The switch from hunting to herding also allowed many Indian men to fulfill coming-of-age rituals and otherwise maintain their sense of manhood in a difficult era. The use of feral stocks often mandated that "hunters" spend weeks tracking down their herds. In this manner, free-range techniques resulted in the continuation of the "cow-hunt" deep into the twentieth-century South.[16]

As a result, many Native men transitioned from hunter to herder in the antebellum South. One of the first Seminole leaders, for example, went by the name Cowkeeper because his village controlled vast herds in late-eighteenth-century Florida. During the First (1816–1818) and Second Seminole Wars (1835–1842), the Seminoles' herds became targets for destruction by the U.S Army. At the end of both wars, the United States allowed its Creek allies to augment its own holdings in Georgia with "large droves of cattle . . . captured from the Enemy."[17] Livestock similarly existed throughout the southeastern nations. In 1822, the Choctaws (with a population of roughly fifteen to twenty thousand) owned 43,000 head of cattle, and ownership was widely spread across their society. As it was elsewhere in the Native South, Choctaw herds were proportionally larger than those held by their white neighbors.[18]

The incorporation of livestock into the Native economy resolved some problems and created others. Not surprisingly, American expansion frequently resulted in conflicts over herds. As backcountry settlers and Natives became neighbors, white settlers often ignored the property claims of the Indians, who in turn raided the herds of the white newcomers. For young warriors, raiding and stealing cattle and "committing [other] depredations on property"[19] served both political as well as cultural purposes. While expressing their dissatisfaction with tribal leadership who seemed too eager to acquiesce to American demands, young warriors also demonstrated their manhood at a time of limited hunting and warfare and demonstrated their political defiance to both American and tribal leaders. They also intensified the demands in white society for the removal of the Indians. Only separation could protect the herds of the American backcountry.[20]

When forced removal became a reality for southeastern Indians, livestock both ameliorated and magnified the economic destruction. Although Natives transported many cows and horses on their forced journeys west, the material losses suffered revealed the Indians' immersion in the livestock and market economy. One African-American Cherokee recalled that "the women and children were driven from their homes, sometimes with blows and close on the heels of the retreating Indians came greedy whites to pillage the Indian's homes, drive off their cattle, horses, and pigs."[21] Natives from across the social spectrum left behind a multitude of domesticated animals (breeding sows, chickens, ducks, cows, hogs, and guinea hens), as well as agricultural tools (plows, chains, axes, chisels, hoes, ox yokes, harnesses, and saddles), domestic items (pots and pans, teacups and saucers, silverware, and pewter dishes), the tools of home manufacturing (spinning wheels, looms, and scissors), and luxury items (featherbeds, umbrellas, mirrors, and fur hats). Some Natives even left behind padlocks, one of the most explicit markers of a market-oriented society.[22]

Rather than destroy the Indian's commitment to livestock or the marketplace, the disruptions of removal intensified it. The eastern Cherokee—a group of remnant Indians who resisted removal by either hiding in the less arable hills or staying on privately owned and state-regulated lands—augmented its traditional farming focus by becoming firmly entrenched in animal husbandry. In 1850, the 710 eastern Cherokees owned "516 swine, 416 sheep, 105 cows, 45 oxen, 135 'other cattle.'"[23] For those who were removed to Indian Territory, livestock holdings became widespread and served as a similarly stabilizing force. The western Seminoles, whose population numbered only a few thousand, controlled several herds that were each estimated to exceed ten thousand.[24] In 1835, Baptist missionary Isaac McCoy wrote that the Cherokee and Creek "fields are generally larger, their stocks of cattle greater . . . in proportion to numbers, than we will generally find among whites on the frontiers."[25] Though the size of the herds impressed McCoy and other observers, the free-range practices and vast grazing lands certainly led them to underestimate the antebellum cattle population.[26] Nevertheless, a Chickasaw census from 1846 recorded 14,788 head of cattle for a population of 4,715.[27]

Despite the growing importance of cattle grazing, southeastern Indians also remained committed to the symbolically and economically significant cultivation of corn by Native women. When domesticated animals trampled on or ate from the fields of Indian women, for example, the burden often fell on men to make restitution. In the early nineteenth century, one Moravian missionary proclaimed that "if a Beast comes into the Fields [Natives] shoot it."[28] More than fifty years later, when their cornfields suffered from drought, some Creeks burned the prairies where their cattle grazed as a means of "conjuring for rain."[29] Natives repeatedly sacrificed their interests in cattle to protect their cornfields. In addition, the calendar of the southeastern Indians minimized conflicts between cattle and corn. Indian men captured the free-roaming cattle in spring—after the annual clearing of fields and before the planting. As a result, men could provide agricultural labor when it was needed most, and the sacred work of women continued.[30]

Agricultural Innovations

Southeastern Indians also pursued agricultural innovations in the early nineteenth century. Native peoples, of course, had for centuries developed highly effective techniques for growing and improving their cornfields, incorporating new seeds, irrigation techniques, and tools. By the nineteenth century, this tradition of agricultural innovation led many Indian communities to augment their corn-centered economies with cotton and other crops. The declining value of deerskins and the widespread dispossession of lands, led many market-oriented or dependent Indians to plant cash crops. On the eve of removal, whereas southeastern Native women tended cornfields (as they had for generations), many Native men managed cotton fields worked by African-American slaves.[31]

Several Native Americans (and white men who married Native women) built cotton gins in the heart of Indian country to facilitate and capitalize on this transformation—a change augmented by the contribution of dozens of spinning wheels and looms by Hawkins, the reformist Indian agent. William Claiborne built a cotton gin in the Choctaw nation and tried to monopolize the cotton trade from both Choctaw and Chickasaw villages.[32] Abram Mordecai, similarly, built a gin house near the confluence of the Coosa and Tallapoosa rivers in Alabama.[33] During the Creek Civil War (1813–1814), Mordecai's neighbors, William and Jonathan Pierce, reported the destruction of their gin house, with three cotton machines, a press, 3,600 pounds of ginned cotton, and over 12,000 pounds of cotton seed.[34] As the Pierces learned, in the early 1800s Natives did not uniformly embrace the transition to a cotton culture. Over time, though, opposition to cotton dissipated as it became more widespread. Only about twelve Choctaws, for example, grew cotton at the start the nineteenth century; a few decades later cotton fields and slave laborers were commonplace across the Native southeast. By 1828, one community of Choctaws raised 124,000 pounds of cotton. According to one estimate, a Mississippi plantation with 35 slaves would harvest a similar amount.[35]

After removal, innovations in agriculture continued even as animal husbandry obtained greater importance. This development tended to have a geographic dimension, as some parts of Indian Territory seemed more suitable for herding than other areas. Shortly after their arrival west, for example, some Choctaws established large cotton plantations along the Red River. In neighboring Cherokee society, cotton made similar inroads. In 1853, Agent George M. Butler concluded that "the common people are making slow but steady advances in the science of agriculture; the more enlightened and intelligent portion who have means, live in the same style of the southern gentlemen of easy circumstances."[36]

As with livestock, the rise of cotton production occurred alongside the maintenance of several long-standing traditions. Corn remained an important dietary product, serving as the central element of Native cuisine throughout the nineteenth and twentieth centuries. Corn also remained an essential ritual component—with the Green Corn Ceremony and the Corn Dance continuing into contemporary southeastern society. Just as importantly, Natives maintained gender norms that associated women with fieldwork and men with hunting (and herding). Many Native men, in contrast to women, rejected offers to take wage-labor jobs picking cotton for their white (or Indian) neighbors on the frontier plantations of Alabama and elsewhere. They also tended to avoid working in the fields themselves. Instead, men maintained their masculinity by relying on the labor of their wives or on African slaves.[37]

African Slavery

Although not always connected to the cultivation of cotton, the arrival of African slavery and racial codes also gradually became entrenched among Natives in the early nineteenth century. In this manner, southeastern Indians became even more "civilized" in the eyes of many white Southerners. The owning of slaves had roots in a traditional system of captivity—one largely reserved for war captives and unconnected with manual labor. In the late eighteenth and early nineteenth centuries, southeastern Indians purchased and employed the labor of thousands of African slaves. During the American Revolution, many African slaves took advantage of the chaos of war and escaped to Indian country, while intermarried traders brought others into Native villages. As a result, the free black population among Natives was often larger than the slave population, making the racial connection between Africans and slavery less pronounced in pre-removal Indian villages than elsewhere in the South. The population of slaves among the Indians remained relatively small, especially relative to free blacks. Like elsewhere in the South, ownership was concentrated under a small planter elite, but Native masters often asserted little control over their human property. Many Africans, for example, lived in semi-autonomous villages in Florida, paying tribute to Seminole villages and owners and receiving protection in return. At the other end of the spectrum, the Cherokees embraced slavery. Even there, though, the transition occurred slowly. On the eve of removal, only 207 of the 2,637 Cherokee households (8 percent of a total population of 16,524 Cherokees) owned slaves, and the 1,592 African slaves made up less than one-tenth of the total population living on Cherokee land. Furthermore, most Cherokee slaveholders (83 percent) owned fewer than ten slaves.[38]

The African slave population among the Indians consistently grew in the post-removal era. At first, only a small percentage of Indians owned slaves in the post-removal South, with a handful of owners claiming a majority of the slaves. During the era of removal, slaves constituted a small percentage of the southeastern Indian communities—nearly 10 percent of the total Cherokee population, 4 percent of the Creek, 3 percent of the Choctaw, and an even smaller percentage of the Chickasaw. By 1860, the patterns of slaveholding had changed, and the slave population grew faster than the Indian population. As a significantly greater percentage of Natives became slaveholders, African slaves formed a greater part of Indian society. This resulted from the Cherokees' participation in the internal Southern slave trade, the natural increase of the slave population, inheritance patterns that resulted in the dispersal rather than consolidation of slave communities, and a stagnant Native population that struggled to recover from the devastation of removal. On the eve of the American Civil War, in which the southeastern Indians frequently supported the Confederacy, African slaves constituted 15 percent of the Cherokee population, 18 percent of the Chickasaw, 14 percent of the Choctaw, and 10 percent of the Creek.[39]

With the growth of slavery came a greater association of race and slavery. In 1830, for example, the U.S. agent charged with creating a census for emigrating Creeks concluded that Africans "seem to be in every way identified with these people . . . the only difference is the color."[40] The following decade, the Creeks denied citizenship to anyone, even if born to a Creek mother, who had "more than half African blood."[41] By 1860, southeastern Indians generally lived with strict slave codes that frequently banned manumission and linked blackness and slavery. The marginalization of Africans remained a contentious process throughout the southeast—with matrilineal clan memberships and tribal loyalties occasionally trumping racial identities within communities. At the same time, though, using race within a Native hierarchy allowed many Indians to distinguish themselves from the largest group of nonwhite Southerners and associate themselves as "civilized" members of the American South. In contrast, in the antebellum era, southeastern Indians rarely created racial barriers with white Americans or Natives of mixed white-Indian ancestry. Instead, the Native children of intermarriages with white men—by virtue of their membership in a matrilineal clan—were routinely embraced as Natives and fully incorporated as members of villages and even village or national chiefs. In this manner, Natives secured a nebulous place in a region and nation that was increasingly presumed biracial.[42]

Educational Innovations

As Natives struggled to control the marketplace, they frequently turned to the tools of formal education—especially literacy—to prepare a generation for the emerging economy and the demands of the marketplace. As they did with most elements of white society, Natives rejected the initial offers by missionaries to build schools or educate their children. In the eighteenth century, southeastern Indians routinely turned away missionaries who "so long plagued them with that they no ways understood."[43] By the early nineteenth century, as demands for Native lands increased, Natives actively invited mission schools to their communities. Although many Indians remained suspicious of the missionary efforts, most of the antimissionary energy went toward controlling rather than eliminating their presence. Among the Creeks, for example, in 1822 "Big Warrior, with the advice of his council, [forbade] the missionaries in the nation to preach." Instead, he "allow[ed] them to keep schools for the instruction of his youthful subjects in the various branches of useful learning."[44] Missionaries could teach reading, writing, and gender-appropriate skills. Even as they turned to missionaries for assistance, though, they insisted that women were farmers and men were hunter/herders. Natives withdrew young girls from schools during harvests and took boys out of school during hunting season. Still other family members resisted the teaching of "agriculture and mechanics" to boys or spinning and alien notions of cleanliness to girls.[45]

Although they continued to oppose some of the teachings of the Christian missions and schools, these institutions eventually proliferated in the Native South. For the Choctaws, a Protestant mission school came in 1818. The boarding school accommodated eighty pupils but hardly met the demand, evidenced by the more than three hundred applications it received. Three years later, an additional school opened and a total of 150 Choctaw students attended, while still more attended the distant Choctaw Academy in Kentucky. The Creeks similarly allowed some of their children to attend mission schools, with one reverend concluding that "the progress of the children was as good, as in any school."[46] These schools taught more than reading and the fundamentals of Protestant Christianity: girls were taught skills related to domestic labor (especially spinning cotton and using looms), and boys were taught agricultural and mechanical skills.[47]

Schools proliferated in Indian Territory, where the Cherokees created their own public-education system, opening 126 public schools before 1860. This made the Cherokees potentially more educated than their white neighbors in Arkansas, where approximately 180 chartered private academies and no public school system served a population fifteen to twenty times larger than the Cherokees'.[48] In 1842, the Choctaw General Council created a system of schools that provided separate educational opportunities for men and women and established the Spencer Academy for the future leaders of the Choctaw nation. This satisfied the needs of the Choctaws, who "have at late become anxious that their children should be educated" and insisted that it be done "in their own nation." As a result, many boarding schools became day schools, and Choctaw children attended newly created schools where Native families could oversee and regulate the curriculum.[49] The first missionary school came to the Seminoles in 1848, where they were ministered to by John Bemo, a Seminole who had become a preacher on his earlier travels through New England. Nevertheless, the unbending attitudes toward preexisting spiritual beliefs led Bemo and other missionaries to have difficulty attracting Seminole students.[50]

Although Natives frequently viewed reading and writing with distrust—proclaiming that they would rather "hear the talk themselves"—many of them turned to literacy as a means of protecting tribal interests.[51] Whereas many southeastern leaders learned English to protect their diplomatic interests, the Cherokees created their own alphabet (the syllabary), published a series of books and pamphlets to support their case for self-determination, and released a weekly newspaper. In this manner, Cherokees from disparate villages came to imagine themselves as members of the same nation and sharing similar concerns with neighboring Indians. Outside of the Cherokee nation, the *Cherokee Phoenix* became a widely recognized and innovative voice for Indian rights— giving public voice to the arguments opposed to removal in the late 1820s and 1830s. Established in February 1828, the newspaper and excerpts from it became widely distributed in the United States and Europe in an attempt to "state the will of the majority of our people on the subject of the present controversy with Georgia, and the present removal policy of the United States Government."[52] Not surprisingly, the United States seized the printing press in 1835 in an attempt to repress the opponents of removal.

Legal Innovations

The southeastern Indians' creation of written laws and constitutions may have been their most innovative use of schooling and literacy. Natives codified many of their laws before removal—often as an attempt to counter efforts to deny their political sovereignty and reduce them to private landowners—and all but the Seminoles created constitutions to transform their political structure in the antebellum era. The Choctaws wrote their first constitution in 1826, and the Cherokees ratified theirs in 1827. The Chickasaws and Creeks reformed their nations without constitutions, formalizing the annual meetings of national councils prior to removal, and then reinforcing these changes with constitutions in the 1850s. These constitutions recognized or created bicameral legislatures, national councils, and centralized police forces ("law menders" among the Creeks and "light horsemen" among the Cherokee).[53] Most of these changes diminished the authority of matrilineal clan affiliations and local village autonomy in favor of a centralized state—replacing local clan leaders with centralized chiefs and ending traditional forms of justice with the establishment of courts. Not surprisingly, then, Native women frequently resisted these changes, insisting on the continued use of clan laws alongside male-centered centralized authorities. Creeks maintained kin-based villages as their basic political unit, but other tribes created districts and other innovative structures. In this manner, the five southeastern tribes became centralized nations.[54]

These written laws, often written and supported by literate Indians who attended various schools in the region, frequently supported new economic attitudes and behavior. In 1822, for example, Choctaw chief Hoolatahomba promoted a set of new laws for the Six Towns District in Mississippi. These laws, among many things, criminalized the theft of cattle and the neglect of crops.

The Creeks and Cherokees both made stealing property a crime punishable by the tribe (rather than by individuals or clans), regulated contracts, and otherwise imposed on the centralized state to enforce the laws. Many of the new laws also protected the interests of Native slaveholders. As early as 1818, the Creeks mandated that "if a Negro kill an Indian, the Negro shall suffer death, and if an Indian kill a Negro, he shall pay the owner the value." In 1836, as the U.S. Congress passed the gag rule to squelch discussion of slavery, the Choctaw council banned teaching abolitionist beliefs, prohibited the education of slaves themselves, and criminalized the arming of slaves. Soon after, the Chickasaws followed with a similar set of slave codes. In 1841, the Choctaws declared that freed slaves had to leave the nation. By 1858, the slave code of the Chickasaws included many restrictions that appeared throughout the slave South—they prohibited educating slaves, banned miscegenation, required masters to transport slaves out of the nation upon emancipation, severely punished assistance to runaways, and otherwise established black legal inferiority.[55]

At the same time, legal innovation helped Natives control the changes often associated with the economic and social transformation of the Native South. Several southeastern Indians employed prenuptial agreements as a means of protecting the property rights of intermarried Indian women. Similarly, early-nineteenth-century Creek and Cherokee legislation protected matrilineal inheritance practices, secured women's traditional rights to own land, and otherwise proclaimed the common ownership of lands. Even traditionalists often concluded the necessity of adopting a system of laws to preserve tribal lands.[56] As their legal system transformed from one based on clan obligations to one based on centralization and literacy, educated Native leaders used American law to protect tribal interests. This was especially important as the United States attempted to use the law to effect removal.

The Cherokees' most famous legal maneuvering took place within the American legal system. The Cherokees arranged for legal dignitaries William Wirt and John Sergeant to represent their legal interests. Wirt, a former U.S. attorney general who prosecuted Aaron Burr, and Sergeant, a congressman from Philadelphia who served as the legal advisor to the Second Bank of the United States, were hardly minor legal figures. On the contrary, Cherokee leaders recognized that protecting their sovereignty required learning and even playing by the rules of the same society that was threatening.[57] The use of a legal defense, however, proved futile. Although the Supreme Court recognized the sovereignty of the Cherokees in *Cherokee Nation v. Georgia* (1831) and *Worcester v. Georgia* (1832), no legal justification could halt President Jackson's removal strategy and the subsequent Trail of Tears. Jackson could only maintain his logic for removal—the "savage" Indians had to be removed from the

South in order to make way for "civilization"—by ignoring much of the evidence in front of him.

During the course of the first half of the nineteenth century, the southeastern Indians underwent a transformation that ultimately resulted in their being called the "Five Civilized Tribes." Although this ethnocentric moniker would be eventually taken up as a political tool and source of pride by the Natives themselves, in the antebellum era outsiders repeatedly and favorably measured the "progress" of the southeastern Indians on the terms of white Southern "civilization." As a result, Baptist missionary Roger Williams and many others distinguished "the other class of Indians [that] embraces the Cherokees, Creeks, and some other southern tribes, who have become partially civilized, have instituted governments, and are practicing agriculture and the mechanic arts. These Indians . . . are in a different situation from those at the north."[58] Indeed, many white Americans optimistically concluded that the "the Creeks, Cherokees, Choctaws, and Chickasaws . . . are steadily advancing in civilization, and only require that their rights may be respected by the government, to ensure results much desired by every philanthropist and Christian."[59] In short, in antebellum America, southeastern Natives appeared to be acculturating to the Southern norm.

Despite these optimistic conclusions, southeastern Indians repeatedly demonstrated that embracing innovation and accepting commodities from the marketplace did not necessarily mean accepting the values of American society or deferring to it. Just as white Southerners frequently maintained values that differed from their Northern or European trading partners, southeastern Indians maintained cultural and political distinctions of their own. The emergence of market-oriented behavior did not result in the widespread embrace of American jurisdiction, and cultural changes did not mean political acquiescence. Instead, Natives embraced many traits that were associated with the loaded term "civilization" as a means of surviving regional and national economic and diplomatic trends. Many Indian men pursued the options of the marketplace these became available and as traditional hunting pursuits became less viable. At the same time, many tribes pursued societal changes as a means of resisting the efforts of the United States to dispossess them of their lands and otherwise eradicate tribal sovereignty. Although some Indians contemplated a future as a Native constituent state of the republic, most pursued innovations as attempts to resist the United States rather than join it. James Silk Buckingham recognized as much in 1842: "As these Indians . . . made some advances in civilization . . . they were exceedingly averse to moving, and rejected all offers made to them."[60] It should be no surprise then, that the racial lines that separated Indians from white Americans became clarified in the years that their cultures converged. Members of both Native and Southern societies recognized their own necessities of drawing lines and defining their communities.

NOTES

1. *Cherokee Phoenix*, November 12, 1831.

2. Andrew Jackson, "First Annual Message to Congress," in *A Compilation of the Messages and Papers of the Presidents*, ed. James D. Richardson (1829; repr., Washington, D.C.: Bureau of National Literature, 1897), 2:458.

3. Thomas Jefferson to Benjamin Hawkins, February 18, 1803, in *The Works of Thomas Jefferson*, ed. Paul Leicester Ford, 12 vols. (New York: G. P. Putnam's Sons, 1892–1899), 7:214.

4. Samuel Worcester to William S. Codey, March 15, 1830, in *Christian Register* (April 24, 1830): 67.

5. James Taylor Carson, "'The Obituary of Nations': Ethnic Cleansing, Memory, and the Origins of the Old South," *Southern Cultures* 14 (Winter 2008): 6–31.

6. James Taylor Carson advocated the term "innovative," rather than "progressive" or "acculturated," in *Searching for the Bright Path: The Mississippi Choctaws from Prehistory to Removal* (Lincoln: University of Nebraska Press, 1999), esp. 71, 87–88.

7. Opposition to these innovations manifested themselves most explicitly during the Creek Civil War (1813–1814). See Claudio Saunt, *A New Order of Things: Property, Power, and the Transformation of the Creek Indians, 1733–1816* (New York: Cambridge University Press, 1999).

8. Joshua Piker, *Okfuskee: A Creek Indian Town in Colonial America* (Cambridge, Mass.: Harvard University Press, 2004); Tyler Boulware, "'Rim of the Gap': Negotiating Identity on the Southern Colonial Frontier" (Ph.D. diss., University of South Carolina, 2005).

9. Theda Perdue explores the importance of clan and gender identities in *Cherokee Women: Gender and Culture Change, 1700–1835* (Lincoln: University of Nebraska Press, 1999).

10. Charles Hudson, *The Southeastern Indians* (Knoxville: University of Tennessee Press, 1976).

11. Cameron B. Wesson, *Households and Hegemony: Early Creek Prestige Goods, Symbolic Capital, and Social Power* (Lincoln: University of Nebraska Press, 2008), 22–57; Kathryn Holland Brand, *Deerskins and Duffels: The Creek Indian Trade with Anglo-America, 1685–1815* (Lincoln: University of Nebraska Press, 1996).

12. Bernard W. Sheehan, *Seeds of Extinction: Jeffersonian Philanthropy and the American Indian* (Chapel Hill: University of North Carolina Press, 1973); Clara Sue Kidwell, *Choctaws and Missionaries in Mississippi, 1818–1918* (Norman: University of Oklahoma Press, 1995).

13. Richard White, *Roots of Dependence: Subsistence, Environment, and Social Change among the Choctaws, Pawnees, and Navajos* (Lincoln: University of Nebraska Press, 1983); James Merrell, *The Indian's New World: Catawbas and their Neighbors from*

European Contact Through the Era of Removal (Chapel Hill: University of North Carolina Press, 1989), 4–91.

14. Joyce B. Phillips and Paul Gary Phillips, eds., *The Brainerd Journal: A Mission to the Cherokees, 1817–1823* (Lincoln: University of Nebraska Press, 1998), 33–34.

15. James Taylor Carson, "Native Americans, the Market Revolution, and Culture Change: The Choctaw Cattle Economy, 1690–1830," *Agricultural History* 71 (1997): 12.

16. John Solomon Otto, "Open-Range Cattle-Ranching in South Florida: An Oral History," *Tampa Bay History* 8 (Fall/Winter 1986): 27. Even when herds were easily found, Natives often stalked their animals in order to perform cultural rituals. See Perdue, *Cherokee Women*, 121–123.

17. John K. Mahon, ed., "The Journal of A. B. Meek and the Second Seminole War, 1836," *Florida Historical Quarterly* 38 (April 1960): 313, 315; Andrew Jackson to David B, Mitchell, July 8, 1818, Panton Leslie Papers, reel 21 (microfilm), Florida State University Library, Tallahassee.

18. In antebellum Alabama, the cattle population closely approximated the state's total human population. See Brooks Blevins, *Cattle in the Cotton Fields* (Tuscaloosa: University of Alabama Press, 1998), 167.

19. Benjamin Hawkins to Wade Hampton, August 26, 1811, in *Letters, Journals and Writings of Benjamin Hawkins*, ed. C. L. Grantz, 2 vols. (Savannah, Ga.: Beehive Press, 1980), 2:590.

20. Carson, "Native Americans, the Market Revolution, and Culture Change," 1–18; Terry G. Jordan, *North American Cattle-Ranching Frontiers: Origins, Diffusion, and Differentiation* (Albuquerque: University of New Mexico Press, 1993), 182–183.

21. Eliza Whitmire, in *The American Slave: A Composite Autobiography*, ed. George Rawick, 19 vols. (Westport, Conn.: Greenwood Press, 1972), 12:380–381.

22. Mary Young, "The Cherokee Nation: Mirror of the Republic," *American Quarterly* 33 (Winter 1981): 516–517.

23. John R. Finger, *The Eastern Band of Cherokees, 1819–1900* (Knoxville: University of Tennessee Press, 1984), 70.

24. William W. Savage, "Indian Ranchers," in *Ranch and Range in Oklahoma*, ed. Jimmy M. Skaggs (Oklahoma City: Oklahoma Historical Society, 1978), 34.

25. Isaac McCoy to Lewis Cass, March 6, 1832, 23rd Congress, 1st sess., S. Doc. 512 (1833), 3:343.

26. U.S. Office of Indian Affairs, *Annual Report of the Commissioner of Indian Affairs* (Washington D.C.: GPO, 1843), 343.

27. Henry R. Schoolcraft, *Historical and Statistical Information Respecting the History, Condition, and Prospects of the Indian Tribes of the United States*, 6 vols. (Philadelphia: Lippincott & Grambo, 1851–1857), 1:498.

28. "Bro. Martin Schneider's Report of his Journey to the Upper Cherokee Towns," in *Early Travels in the Tennessee Country 1540–1800*, ed. Samuel Cole Williams (Johnson City, Tenn.: Watauga Press, 1928), 261.

29. "Indian Superstitions," *Christian Secretary* (November 29, 1850): 1.

30. Richard A. Sattler, "Cowboys and Indians: Creek and Seminole Stock Raising, 1700–1900," *American Indian Culture and Research Journal* 22 (1998): 79–99.

31. Daniel H. Usner, Jr., "American Indians on the Cotton Frontier: Changing Economic Relationships with Citizens and Slaves in the Mississippi Territory," *Journal of American History* 72 (September 1985): 297–317.

32. Adam Rothman, *Slave Country: American Expansion and the Origins of the Deep South* (Cambridge, Mass.: Harvard University Press, 2005), 57.

33. Albert James Pickett, *History of Alabama and Incidentally of Georgia and Mississippi, from the Earliest Period*, 2 vols. (Charleston, S.C.: Walker and James, 1851), 2:190.

34. Richard S. Lackey, ed., *Frontier Claims in the Lower South* (New Orleans: Polyanthos, 1977), 35.

35. Carson, *Searching for the Bright Path*, 81; White, *Roots of Dependence*, 129; Duane Champagne, *Social Order and Political Change: Constitutional Governments among the Cherokee, the Choctaw, the Chickasaw, and the Creek* (Stanford, Calif.: Stanford University Press, 1992), 146–148; John Hebron Moore, *The Emergence of the Cotton Kingdom in the Old Southwest: Mississippi, 1770–1860* (Baton Rouge: Louisiana State University Press, 1988), 9.

36. Butler, quoted in William G. McLoughlin, *After the Trail of Tears: The Cherokees Struggle for Sovereignty, 1839–1880* (Chapel Hill: University of North Carolina Press, 1994) 59.

37. Carson, *Searching for the Bright Path*, 81–82.

38. Theda Perdue, *Slavery and the Evolution of Cherokee Society, 1540–1866* (Knoxville: University of Tennessee Press, 1979), 58. By contrast, about 36 percent of white Southerners owned slaves in 1830 and slaves comprised nearly the same percent of the region's population. Equally contrasting, in 1850, almost 27 percent of slaveholders owned ten or more slaves. John B. Boles, *Black Slaveholders, 1619–1869* (Lexington: University Press of Kentucky, 1984), 107.

39. Fay A. Yarbrough, *Race and the Cherokee Nation: Sovereignty in the Nineteenth Century* (Philadelphia: University of Pennsylvania Press, 2008), 42, 116; Claudio Saunt, "The Paradox of Freedom: Tribal Sovereignty and Emancipation during the Reconstruction of Indian Territory," *Journal of Southern History* 70 (February 2004): 64–65. The population of Africans among the Seminoles eludes scholars.

40. Quotation in Daniel F. Littlefield, *Africans and Creeks: From the Colonial Period to the Civil War* (Westport, Conn.: Greenwood Press, 1979), 112.

41. Quotation in Gary Zellar, *African Creeks: Estelveste and the Creek Nation* (Norman: University of Oklahoma Press, 2007), 40.

42. For a discussion of the debate over race in the Native southeast, see Theda Perdue, "Race and Culture: Writing the Ethnohistory of the Early South," *Ethnohistory* 51 (Fall 2004): 701–723; Claudio Saunt, Barbara Krauthamer, Tiya Miles, Celia E. Naylor, and Circe Sturm, "Rethinking Race and Culture in the Early South," *Ethnohistory* 53 (Spring 2006): 399–405.

43. Quotation in Henry T. Malone, *Cherokees of the Old South* (Athens: University of Georgia Press, 1956), 96.

44. *Niles Weekly Register*, August 3, 1822.

45. Andrew K. Frank, *Creeks and Southerners: Biculturalism on the Early American Frontier* (Lincoln: University of Nebraska Press, 2005), 67.

46. "Notes furnished A. J. Pickett by the Rev. Lee Compere of Mississippi," April 6, 1848, Albert James Pickett Manuscripts, Alabama Department of Archives and History, Montgomery.

47. Carolyn Thomas Foreman, "The Choctaw Academy," *Chronicles of Oklahoma* (December 1928): 453–480.

48. Edgar Wallace Knight, *Public Education in the South* (Boston: Ginn and Company, 1922), 97–98.

49. "Tribes of Indians West of the Mississippi," *The Friend; a Religious and Literary Journal* (January 27, 1844): 17; Valerie Lambert, *Choctaw Nation: A Story of American Indian Resurgence* (Lincoln: University of Nebraska Press, 2007), 36.

50. Jack M. Schultz, *The Seminole Baptist Churches of Oklahoma: Maintaining a Traditional Community* (Norman: University of Oklahoma Press, 1999), 46–47.

51. Quoted in Saunt, *New Order of Things*, 189.

52. *Cherokee Phoenix*, February 21, 1828.

53. Lambert, *Choctaw Nation*, 44.

54. Champagne, *Social Order and Political Change*, 87–123, 176–190.

55. Clara Sue Kidwell, *The Choctaws in Oklahoma: From Tribe to Nation, 1855–1870* (Norman: University of Oklahoma Press, 2007), xv, 5. Creek Agency Records, McIntosh Papers, Laws of the Creek Nation, June 12, 1818, David B. Mitchell Papers, Newberry Library, Chicago; Laws of the Muscogee Nation, March 1824, Antonio J. Waring, Jr., Papers, Georgia Historical Society, Savannah; Littlefield, *Chickasaw Freedmen: A People without a Country* (Westport, Conn.: Greenwood Press, 1980), 13.

56. Frank, *Creeks and Southerners*, 131; Yarbrough, *Race and the Cherokee Nation*, 29–31; Rennard Strickland, *Fire and the Spirits: Cherokee Law from Clan to Court* (Norman: University of Oklahoma Press, 1975), 41.

57. Jill Norgren, "Lawyers and the Legal Business of the Cherokee Republic in Courts of the United States, 1829–1835," *Law and History Review* 10 (Autumn 1992): 256.

58. *Baptist Missionary Magazine* 10 (December 1830): 362–363.

59. M., "Our Indian Tribes," *New York Observer and Chronicle* (April 6, 1854): 109.

60. James Silk Buckingham, *Slave States of America* (1842; repr., New York: Negro Universities Press, 1968), 521.

12

Sex, Self, and the Performance of Patriarchal Manhood in the Old South

Craig Thompson Friend

James Henry Hammond was a despicable man. In 1829, with little wealth but much ambition, the twenty-one-year-old South Carolinian pursued Catherine Fitzsimmons—a plain, socially awkward, and fatherless heiress—against her family's wishes. He wed her two years later, but he did not love her, openly expressing his philosophy of marriage: "Women were made to breed—men to do the work of this world. As a toy for recreation, and one soon tires of any given one for this, or as bringing wealth and position, men are *tempted* to marry them and the world is kept peopled." Upon taking control of Catherine's dowry, he came to own hundreds of slaves, allowing nearly eighty to die over the next decade through either mistreatment or neglect. He sexually abused several female slaves, including Sally Johnson, whom he purchased (along with her infant daughter, Louisa) specifically to be his mistress. He fathered several children with Sally before replacing her with Louisa when the girl turned twelve years old.[1]

Hammond also sexually molested four nieces, the daughters—ages twelve to nineteen—of his wife's sister and her husband. As he justified in his diary, "all of them rushing on every occasion to my arms and covering me with kisses, lolling on my lap, pressing their bodies almost into mine, wreathing their limbs with mine, encountering warmly every portion of my frame, and permitting my hands to stray unchecked over every part of them and to rest without the slightest shrinking of it, in the most secret and sacred regions."[2] When his improprieties became known, his brother-in-law worked tirelessly to undermine Hammond's political career. None of the girls ever married, their reputations and psyches warped by the incidents. Hammond expected Catherine to remain faithful throughout, and she overlooked the episodes with the nieces and with Sally Johnson, even bearing him another child. Not until Hammond refused to forego Louisa's bed did his wife leave, although she eventually returned.

For over a century, Hammond has featured frequently in Southern histories. In book after book, he shows up as an agricultural reformer, politician, and always very vocal proponent of slavery and the Southern way of life. Moreover, historians use Hammond as a symbol of antebellum Southern manhood, finding in his interactions with women and men, black and white, a series of symbols and performances that enjoin multiple traditions of patriarchy, honor, and mastery. Yet, when historians have examined Hammond's psychopathology—specifically, the sexual and gendered ways through which he constructed his masculine Self—they have concluded, as did Carol Blesser, that "in almost every respect James Henry Hammond seems to have resembled nothing less than a monster." On the face of it, Hammond *was* a monster, a product of a premodern ideal of the white, colonizing, "predatory male" who believed he had full liberty to act on his hormonal impulses, even to the point of rape and molestation.[3]

Why are historians so taken with Hammond? Clearly, we have fallen into a trap that Daniel Boorstin once labeled "the Law of the Survival of the Self-Serving": "are we victims, willingly or not, of a Casanova syndrome that puts us at the mercy of the most articulate boasters of the past?" After all, when Hammond confessed in his diary about his intimacy with his nieces—concluding with his plea, "Am I not after all entitled to some, the smallest portion of, credit for not going further?"—to whom was he appealing if not us, his voyeurs and judges? Every time Hammond wrote in his diary, penned a letter, and recorded plantation transactions in his business ledgers, he constructed his patriarchal Self with an audience in mind. Have we too readily accepted his voice as representative of antebellum white Southern manhood? I submit that, when it comes to issues of manhood and the sexual Self, the answer is yes.[4]

What is at stake here is not the psychopathology of one individual but rather the character of white, patriarchal masculinity in the Old South, of which Hammond was both typical and atypical. He was uncommonly intense in his passion for the elite South and the mythmaking required to sustain it, including his 1858 "Mudsill" Speech in which, upon proclaiming "Cotton *is* King," he justified slavery by arguing that white and black lower classes worked as menial laborers so that the upper class could be freed to advance the Southern way of life. Simultaneously, he was recognized by thousands among the white laboring classes almost as one of their own—"the people's candidate," as the *Charleston Evening News* proclaimed, who became governor of South Carolina, and a U.S. congressman and senator. Neither were Hammond's physical and sexual indulgences atypical, though his eagerness to commit them to the written record certainly was. Most Southern white men expected similar sexual license, but few matched Hammond's braggadocio.[5]

Thirty years ago, consideration of the Southern patriarchal Self was unimagined. The poststructuralist work of Michel Foucault was just emerging onto the academic scene, and Southern masculinity studies were unknown. Historians studied what men *did*, not how they understood themselves. When, in 1982, Bertram Wyatt-Brown published *Southern Honor: Ethics and Behavior in the Old South*, he established honor as the primary formative force in Southern white manhood. Wyatt-Brown uncovered honor as a series of symbols, rules, and expectations drawn from Protestant and classical influences, a code increasingly outdated in early national America, clashing with the rationalism, restraint, and respectability sought by a commercializing middle-class culture. Emotion rather than reason drove Southern manhood: Southern men immortalized valor through vengeance, exalted individual will, and defended reputations through duels and vigilantism. For Wyatt-Brown, fighting, hospitality, and gambling evinced a specific, honor-driven mentality of Southern manhood. By considering *how* Southern men thought of themselves and *why* they did so, *Southern Honor* dramatically altered the historiographic landscape of Southern gender history.[6]

Conceptually, however, the honor paradigm relied on an essentialist notion of gender differences that would come under attack. For example, Wyatt-Brown characterized male lust as "simply a recognized fact of life. To repress natural impulse was to defy nature itself, leading to prissiness and effeminacy. Outright libertinism also suggested unmanly self-indulgence and inner weaknesses. But a healthy sex life without regard to marriage was quite in order." Essentialism employs biological impulses and functions to define manhood and womanhood. Male lust? Why it's merely what men's biology drives them to do. When James Henry Hammond proclaimed that "women were made to breed," his was an essentialist definition of gender; and so too was the vigorous, "natural," male (hetero)sexuality in Wyatt-Brown's honor-laden South.[7]

Essentialism was the predominant way of thinking about gender until the rise of women's history in the 1970s and 1980s. Concerned about essentialism's consequences for women's equality, many women's historians argued that gender is culturally constructed rather than biologically grounded. Joan Scott complained about the scholarship of the day: "whether domination comes in the form of the male appropriation of the female's reproductive labor or in the sexual objectification of women by men, the analysis rests on physical difference," an approach that "assumes a consistent or inherent meaning for the human body—outside social or cultural construction—and thus the ahistoricity of gender itself." In other words, by limiting understanding of gender to men's biological ability to physically dominate and to women's reproductive capabilities (and by judging all gendered relations along that continuum), scholars contributed to continued repression of women.[8]

Catherine Clinton's *The Plantation Mistress* (1983) exemplified this push away from essentialist definitions of gender and toward cultural construction. "White men in the Old South were compulsively preoccupied with deference and authority," explained Clinton: "Their egos were poised on a precarious pinnacle of honor. Sex in this context, much as in Victorian England, had melodramatic elements; force, potential if not explicit, took center stage. . . . As a result, ante-bellum patriarchs simultaneously emasculated male slaves, dehumanized female slaves, and desexualized their own wives." Instead of acting out of biological impulses and functions, Clinton's white Southern men sought to dominate sexual and reproductive systems on their plantations out of deep-seated fears about losing their own authority and virility, fears created and perpetuated by the cultural constructions of slavery and patriarchy.[9]

Throughout the late 1980s and 1990s, historians moved in new historiographic directions, including new postmodern methodologies that broke free from essentialism and joined with women's history to inspire the new field of gender history. Over two decades of women's history had created a rich and deep historiography of how Southern black, white, and Indian women acted upon ideas of womanhood, but the student of history would have thought these different women lived in different Souths. As Clinton lamented in 1994, "How can we accomplish anything by depicting unintegrated parallel lives?" The same may have been asked of gender history: how could gender scholars integrate their subjects' lives into a more complete picture of Southern gender if, beyond Wyatt-Brown's *Southern Honor*, there was no historiography for Southern manhood to match the abundance of work on Southern womanhood? A true gender history required greater understanding of men and masculinity, a historiographic limitation keenly understood by the earliest masculinity scholars. In her analysis of American masculinity, Gail Bederman challenged scholars "to study the historical ways different ideologies about manhood develop, change, are combined, amended, contested—and gain the status of truth." She encouraged a more discursive construction of masculinity in which manhood is multivalent, regularly reenacted, and unsettled. "I don't see manhood as either an intrinsic essence [essentialism] or a collection of traits, attributes, or sex roles [cultural construction]," Bederman explained, "Manhood . . . is a continual, dynamic process."[10]

There is no reason to imagine that Old South manhood, too, was not continually dynamic, even among elite white men who peopled the planter class. We have had a very static notion of those patriarchs because patriarchy itself is often portrayed as unchanging and constant. In this regard, Clinton's interpretation was as problematic as Wyatt-Brown's in that Clinton's descriptors for patriarchy—"old," "entrenched," and "bedrock"—reiterated an unchanging nature of Southern patriarchy, as did Wyatt-Brown's characterization of Southern honor as "ancient," "primal," and "prehistoric." As exciting as their works were, these historians persisted in portraying manhood, in Scott's words, as "epiphenomenal, providing endless variations on the unchanging theme of a fixed gender inequality."[11]

Consider the historical narrative with which we currently work: Shaped by Old World feudalism and monarchy, patriarchy became the primary form of manhood in colonial America, pervading law, religion, family, and politics. The democratic impulses of the American Revolution collided with patriarchy, as Michael Kimmel explained, because "it freed the sons from the tyranny of the despotic father." Even as new models of manhood—like the self-made man— appeared in the industrializing North, in the agrarian South, aristocratic conceptions of manhood persisted primarily because of slavery. Southern patriarchs became "anxious" in the late eighteenth and early nineteenth centuries and willingly compromised privilege to retain hegemony. "In the age of 'sensibility' patriarchy was being sentimentalized into paternalism," concluded Rhys Isaac. But paternalism was just a kinder and more insidious form of patriarchal power, as Eugene Genovese exposed in his analysis of the expectations and obligations between planters and their dependents. This narrative portrays Southern patriarchy as abnormally stable, static, and reactionary over two and a half centuries, notably evolving only once and not very dramatically into paternalism. If we accept, however, that masculinity is always developing and changing, being contested by, amended by, and combining with other ideas of manhood, then we can begin to imagine the dynamism of elite Southern white manhood in the Old South. When we look at any given Southern patriarch, even Hammond, we do not see manhood realized but rather a man *becoming*.[12]

Southern patriarchy was performative, meaning that the ideal did not just set standards for masculinity but participated in constructing that reality. As historian Steven Stowe explained, elite actions like dueling or epistolary courtship were affairs "of theater and ideology; it *happened* and it *explained* what happened." Advice literature like *Lord Chesterfield's Advice to His Son* provided the theatrical scripts on becoming such a man, and one cannot overstate the

Southern upper class's obsession with Chesterfield. "There are so many polite reflections and useful lessons that no man can be well accomplished either in mind or body but with their perusal," proclaimed John Ramsey of North Carolina. But as historian Michael Curtin has elaborated, Chesterfield believed it "the duty of the rich and the enlightened to support the myths by which public order was maintained"—recall Hammond's Mudsill Speech—and his letters "appeared to represent manners at their most cynical, expedient, and immoral light." Chesterfieldian manhood encouraged the individual to use institutions and people for his own ends: "There is hardly anybody good for every thing, and there is scarcely anybody who is absolutely good for nothing." Historians have demonstrated time and again how Hammond and other Southern patriarchs exploited slavery, marriage, academies and universities, the market, the law, and everyone around them for their own manly advancements.[13]

Yet, since they were humans and not just actors, Southern patriarchs struggled with Chesterfield's advice. What Laura Edwards has argued for Southern law—that it "continually asserted the power of white manhood" precisely because "that power was neither complete nor stable in practice"—was true for all structures in which patriarchs and patriarchs-in-training operated. From the law to slavery, families to churches, courtship to marriage, duels to politics, *becoming* occurred within rigid and very public institutional venues that created tension between personal satisfaction and public expectations—between what one was and what one thought the performative script dictated he be. Consider, for example, Cyrus Stuart. The orphaned son of a blacksmith, Stuart attended a South Carolina academy, read Chesterfield, and aspired to become a Southern patriarch. He understood the ideal before him, but he failed in the testing. He experienced conflict in the academy, was rebuffed in courtship, stumbled in oration, was unable to overcome self-doubt, and failed to separate illusion from reality. He pursued a planter's daughter, hoping courtship and marriage would elevate him to patriarchal manhood (as it had for Hammond), but alas: "I thought I could insinuate myself into her favour, this I only hoped, for none ever had a better nack of hoping than I have." One need only peruse Stuart's and other aspiring patriarchs' diaries and letters to find the repressed emotions, compulsive insistence on manliness, and obsession with self-control. More established men like Hammond confessed in their later years that they found the ideal hollow and unfulfilling: "My life is a blank, all daily sorrows aggravated by my follies." Even younger men, however, sensed the lie: "I seem happy & cheerful & hopeful," reflected North Carolinian Henry Craft, "What a liar the *seeming* is." *Seeming* is not *becoming: seeming* is performance, and in many ways the patriarchal Self was always performing the scripts.[14]

So when a wave of modernizing forces—democracy, individualism, indus-trialization, consumerism, evangelicalism, romanticism, sentimentalism—crashed against the South in the late eighteenth and early nineteenth centuries, Southern patriarchal performance responded in order to sustain the sense of entitlement and self-aggrandizement that characterized their eighteenth-century aristocratic script. Over the past fifteen years, a flurry of historical scholarship has drawn attention to these forces, the most powerful of which was the market economy. For example, Diane Barnes explored how industrial-ization facilitated social ambition and mobility among Petersburg, Virginia, artisans and laborers. Such self-made men, striving to achieve the type of respectability promoted by the patriarchal ideal, ideologically (and awkwardly) blended their commitment to free labor with a commitment to slavery. Other historians have found comparable scenarios among the Creeks, Choctaws, and other Native Southern peoples. As an expanding market economy offered refinement to those beyond the upper classes, planter-class hegemony faced gradual diffusion, requiring responses from the patriarchy. John Mayfield dem-onstrated how the consequential strain on Southern patriarchal manhood became a central theme of regional literature in which writers like William Gilmore Simms and Johnson Jones Hooper mocked self-made aspirations. Beyond literature, patriarchs developed a rhetoric of mastery that appealed to yeoman farmers who controlled small worlds, binding the two classes in common political interest. White Southern patriarchs reacted, as Ted Ownby noted, by "self-consciously" constructing masculinity to resist "interference from outside the region." The educational process became a way to "manufac-ture" men. In her study of military academies, Jennifer Green concluded that military education dictated the rules of Southern patriarchy to an emerging middle class; likewise, Lorri Glover has shown how education and refinement pushed elite white boys into reactionary civic roles and racial stances.[15]

Sentimentalism and an accompanying emphasis on affectation also swept into the Old South. Patriarchy faced a modernizing childhood in which preteen whites were freed from labor, educated, increasingly viewed as innocents, and pampered with love. Correspondingly, women had to become more affectively and physically available to meet the emotional and material demands of chil-drearing. Family sizes grew smaller; sibling relationships grew more intense; children became more distinct from adults in appearances and activities. More affectionate and intimate families strengthened the nuclear family at the expense of extended kinship. New expectations of mutual love and companion-ship eroded more traditional concerns over lineage, property, and control. Anya Jabour's work on William and Elizabeth Wirt's companionate marriage, for example, demonstrates how emotional fulfillment and romantic love offered alternative models of marriage to those based on male domination and female submission. And as evangelicalism put new expectations on masculinity, including an attack on those "licit vices" so commonly associated with Southern patriarchy, men faced greater moral pressures from churchgoing wives.[16]

Despite the Chesterfieldian script, these modernizing forces required every Southern patriarch to negotiate his *becoming* against his *seeming*, pitting his Self against his performance. Southern patriarchs' diaries regularly reflect this contest: a dispassionate persona simply records thoughts on the weather, local politics, a recently read book, or business transactions without any hint of personal investment, because the scripts of manhood required him to think of those things; an emotional persona wrestles with love, lust, family, courtship, paternal responsibilities, and other demands of manhood. Consequently, in comparison to the dispassionate voice, the emotional investment in manhood always comes off as overly dramatic. "I think that I am too ambitious," opined Cyrus Stuart, "ever to be successful in my under takings, yet I will endeavour to acquire that equinimity of temper which is absolutely necessary to make a great man." Mississippian Henry Hughes pleaded with God: "Please help me. Push me on. I am half frightened. I am not. It is true. I must be the Greatest mortal man that can be; I must be the best mortal man that can be. I am God's Favorite."[17]

The most intimate realm in which negotiation between Self and performance took place was sexuality. Just as they were to be physically aggressive and emotionally restrained in the public sphere, men were to exhibit similar qualities sexually. Failure to meet one of these qualities required exaggeration of the other. In the public realm, for example, when emotions could not be controlled, physicality and aggression were often amplified—duels, slave whippings, crimes of passion. In the household, uncontrolled emotions often resulted in physical abuse and forced sex with wives and slaves. Consider, for example, William Byrd II's employment of sexual power to assert his masculine authority in a moment of emotional discordance: "In the afternoon my wife and I had a little quarrel which I reconciled with a flourish. Then she read a sermon in Dr. Tillotson to me. It is to be observed that the flourish was performed on the billiard table." Although Byrd lived in the early eighteenth century, he subscribed to the same type of advice literature as antebellum planters would, with the same emphasis on performance as a gentleman. And so, on the billiard table—a very male space—he won the quarrel and reestablished husband over wife by "flourishing" her, a refined term that relates more about his satisfaction in his gentlemanly performance than the act itself.[18]

At its core, Chesterfieldian advice was misogynistic, casting women as persons to be used rather than as people to love: "Every man and his wife hate each other cordially, whatever they may pretend, in public, to the contrary. The husband wishes his wife at the devil, and the wife certainly cuckolds her husband." Still, marriage was key to both *seeming* and *becoming* a man. In an 1826 letter, Jeff Withers mocked James Henry Hammond's eagerness to find a wife: "And you'll 'be damn-d if you don't marry'?" Hammond did find that wife, and Catherine Fitzsimmons provided him the things he needed to become a Southern patriarch—a plantation from which he could perform patriarchal manhood and a wife through which he could perform patriarchal sex. "To get children, it is true, fulfills a department of social & natural duty," he responded to Withers, but if Catherine meant anything more to Hammond emotionally, it is difficult to discern. As Steven Stowe recognized, Hammond was "cruelly incisive about the dynamics of romantic wishfulness: at its core was an awkward dichotomy of woman as transcendent lover and honest helper, an uneasy union of passion and utility."[19]

Patriarchs-in-training were early introduced to sex as performance; and because in many cases the act was with female slaves, they quickly learned the relationship of power to sex. "The men of the South especially are more indelicate in their thoughts and tastes than any European people," noted one British commentator in 1842, "and exhibit a disgusting mixture of prudery and licentiousness combined, which may be regarded as one of the effects of the system of slavery, and the early familiarity with vicious intercourse to which it invariably leads." That "early familiarity" was what nearly every planter's son experienced in the slave quarters when he "became a man." That "early familiarity" licensed Robert Newsom of Missouri, after his wife's death, to purchase Celia to serve as his mistress. For five years, with the silent acquiescence of his daughters who dared not challenge their father's actions, Newsom repeatedly raped Celia by whom he fathered two children. One night, Celia, wearied and angered by that "early familiarly," bludgeoned Newsom to death before burning his body in the fireplace. That "early familiarity" led another slave woman, suspecting that her master intended to rape her, to flee into the woods pursued by bloodhounds. "He catched her and hit her in de head wid something like de stick de police carry, she bleed like a hog and he made her have him," remembered the woman's niece. That "early familiarity" underlay Anna Matilda King's demands of her planter husband upon a female friend's suicide: "Think you not that your sex is too blame? There are too many faithless husbands." Southerners' essentialist understanding of the reproductive purpose of the human body and sexual intercourse framed the way they thought of men, but it also granted men sexual license as the more physically powerful gender. Southern society even institutionalized patriarchal sexual liberty to the degree that it recognized an appropriate moment for male infidelity: the "gander months," the late term of pregnancy when husbands pursued sex outside marriage.[20]

In most cases, intercourse with female slaves was a different type of performance, one to affirm power more than potency. As Southern sons realized in the slave quarters and Byrd asserted on the billiard table, sex related to more than reproductive desires. In the 1970s, French philosopher Michel Foucault argued that "deployments of power are directly connected to the body—to bodies, functions, physiological processes, sensations, and pleasures." Sex is a form of power, and patriarchs could wield their masculine authority almost without restraint.[21]

Hence, patriarchs had to protect their masculine power from the male Other on the plantation: the black male whose sexual actions they believed they needed to suppress or surpass. On the auction block or when occasionally punished, black men were stripped and exposed. Since masculine power was invested in the phallus, visibility of slaves' penises contributed to assumptions about sexually charged black men, in contrast to the white patriarchal penis, which remained hidden from view and therefore supposedly controlled. Slave men bragged of their sexual potency and freedom, highlighting the importance they placed on male sexual veracity and colliding with patriarchs' own sense of sexual virility as a tenet of manhood. Some historians have suggested that patriarchs used slavery to emasculate black men by reducing them to dependents, but patriarchs also actively sought to diminish black manhood by denying male slaves' sexual access to female slaves (including wives), raping female slaves, and even publically denigrating black male sexuality. One common minstrel song performed in blackface included the lyrics:

> Nigger, put down that jug,
> Touch not a single drop.
> I hab gin him many a hug
> And dar you luff him stop.
> I kissed him two three times,
> And den I suck him dry
> Dat jug, he's none but mine
> So dar you luff him lie.

By mocking and even converting black male sexual prowess into male-male intimacy, white performers counteracted the imagined power of the black phallus. The Other is so often a reflection of the Self, however, and patriarchs interpreted black male sexual prowess through an assumption that slaves—as men—were just as boundless in their sexual appetites as white men were allowed to be.[22]

When a white plantation woman gave birth to a visibly mulatto child, not only did racial lines blur but the child challenged patriarchal manhood because a child's legal status followed the mother. Children of black men and white women not only violated the equation of blackness with slavery, but they existed independent of Southern patriarchy. Sadly but tellingly, in trials concerning black males accused of raping poor or working-class women, many patriarchs (who restricted sexual contact between black men and white women on their own plantations) demanded their accused slaves be forgiven and returned to them, whether it was rape or not. Continually asserting the power of white manhood, the law often forgave black rapists of unruly women, in effect acknowledging the common bond between black and white men—the boundless male sexual appetite.[23]

In contrast, when white men had mulatto children with enslaved black women, the children could easily be hidden (and consequently ignored) with their mothers in the slave community, seamlessly assuming dependent roles as slaves. The South's judicial patriarchy regulated its black and white women's sexual relations not only as a means of social control but as a way to strengthen male authority over the household. Men also acted in personal and immediate ways to assert that authority. When a white man "flourished" his wife, he asserted his gendered authority; when he raped a slave woman, he declared gender, class, and racial dominance. In neither case was the act exclusively an attack on one woman. Indirectly, it made a statement to the entire household, where wives, children, female and male slaves provided an audience to the patriarch's sexual power.[24]

Not surprisingly, if we look at dreams—where no audience existed and men were freed from performance—we find patriarchs emotional, anxious, and confused. Cyrus Stuart dreamt: "O! delicious thought, I lay my neck upon her arms, and put my arm around her and reveled there with sweet kisses on her rudy lips, until We were both overcome by Morpheus. Yet, I woke alone, isolated, and still in celibacy." "I had her in my arms, in arms which pressed her convulsively, frantically to my bosom . . ." recorded Mississippian Harry St. John Dixon,

> My soul was on fire, my brain was dizzy with excitement. I was
> strangely enthralled, and my feelings defy words. My vile hand felt
> its way to the sacred grotto of love. Then my arm should have been
> severed from my body. It was unendurable—nature's pent up
> substance flowed from me as I stood. I thought, "it is over," but it
> was not. As the flood was subsiding, I found myself lying almost
> senseless between her downy thighs, wallowing in a deluge of illicit

love. . . . I was pursued by my mother. We still travelled on foot, and
she spoke of our iniquity lamentably. . . .

Dreams relate sex not as power but as uncontrolled passion, feelings commonly associated more with emerging patterns of romantic love than with
Chesterfieldian gentlemanliness. Yet, both men had imbibed Chesterfield
well: unconsciously, at least, their recountings concluded with disappointment,
loss, and loneliness, as Chesterfield had warned would come from romantic
wishfulness.[25]

There was still hope for Stuart and Dixon because emotional restraint and
sexual aggression could be learned, but another quality of patriarchal sexuality
was assumed to be innate—that sex should be between a man and a woman.
Successful sexual performances demonstrated potency through the conception
of children. In this regard, procreation had as much to do with confirmation of
masculinity as it did with intimacy, signifying the performative nature of sex as
an important instrument in *seeming* the patriarchal Self.

We should not overlook, then, sex as power among men. Same-gender sexuality was clearly antithetical to Southerners' conceptualization of the reproductive purpose for sex. Still, the act was not beyond comprehension. Minstrel
songs about performing fellatio on a whisky jug reveal how audiences were in
on the joke. Most historians have been reluctant to explore same-gender physicality in the Old South, however, and this is most evident in the case of James
Henry Hammond and his "long fleshen pole."

Two years before Hammond courted Catherine Fitzsimmons, he received
a couple of letters from his law school roommate, Thomas Withers. "I feel
some inclination to learn whether you yet sleep in your Shirt-tail," Withers
wrote, "and whether you yet have the extravagant delight of poking and punching a writhing Bedfellow with your long fleshen pole—the exquisite touches of
which I have often had the honor of feeling? . . . Sir, you roughen the downy
Slumbers of your Bedfellow—by such hostile—furious lunges as you are in the
habit of making at him—when he is least prepared for defence against the
crushing force of a Battering Ram." Withers may have been "hardly referring to
overt homosexual behavior," as historian Drew Faust insisted. In fact, Withers
continued that "unless thou changest former habits in this particular, thou wilt
be represented by every future Chum as a nuisance," suggesting that even if
Hammond did poke Withers in bed, it was likely an incidental and unwelcomed
consequence of the nineteenth-century practice of men bundling together
when cold or in cramped accommodations. But Faust concluded that even such
harmless physicality was not what Withers meant either: instead, she employed
a *reductio ad absurdum*, arguing the ridiculousness of Hammond's obsession

with aggressive Southern patriarchy by associating it with the untenable possibility of same-gender intimacy. Apparently, inconceivable to Faust is the notion
that two men who became prime examples of heteronormative Southern patriarchy would have compromised that sexual identity in their youth.[26]

Historians' reluctance to read the episode as same-gender physicality must
be partially attributed to an unreflective acceptance of essentialist definitions of
male and female. That continuum of gender leaves no room for variability
except as deviance; and because it assumes the eventual triumph of the male/
female binary, it subordinates everything that is not heteronormative. Wyatt-
Brown, for example, did not mention same-gender sexuality once in *Southern
Honor*. When considering the "three broad categories in the realm of sexual
ill-conduct," he listed male fornication, adultery, and varieties of miscegenation—all of which are described as socially problematic but nonetheless heterosexual. Orlando Paterson took Wyatt-Brown to task for this exclusion: "I draw
attention to this not out of intellectual fashion, but simply because anyone
acquainted with the comparative ethnohistory of honorific cultures will be
immediately struck by it. Homosexuality is pronounced in such systems, both
ancient and modern. Southern domestic life most closely resembles that of the
Mediterranean in precisely those areas which are most highly conducive to
homosexuality. Does the author's silence imply its absence in the pronounced
male bonding of the Old South?" At least Wyatt-Brown just remained silent;
Faust not only dismissed the possibility that Withers and Hammond were
sexually intimate, but concluded that Withers, who wrote so imaginatively and
descriptively about the episode, actually viewed same-gender intimacy as
absurd. Carol Blesser insisted that any suggestion of same-gender relations
between Withers and Hammond results "from a rather tortured reading of
passages"—although it seems rather evident that any dismissal of that possibility requires an even more tortured argument. After all, Withers was not
inclined to employ innuendo in his letters: when he penned, for example,
"Southeasterly breezes doth make my cock stand as furious as a stud's," he
literally meant that the lofting smells from a house of ill repute southeast of his
tenement room gave him an erection! We cannot assume that, in the pre-
Freudian nineteenth century, before categories of homosexuality and heterosexuality existed, intimate same-gender sexuality did not exist merely because
it did not neatly fit the essentialist norms of the era.[27]

So, let us trust Withers's words: Hammond poked him, even if just incidentally. Withers's openness to discussing the episode relates the exclusive
power of masculine sexuality. Historian Martin Duberman argued that because
the Old South existed in "one of those rare 'liberal interregnums' in our history
when the body could be treated as a natural source of pleasure and 'wanton'

sexuality viewed as the natural prerogative—the exemplification even—of 'manliness,'" sexual intercourse between Withers and Hammond was plausible. After all, male sexuality was supposedly boundless. Extending that natural prerogative to male-male relationships raises interesting questions about homosociality, the sexual performance of power, and an emerging, modern discourse of natural oppositions that elevated white male heteronormativity as the fulfillment of American civilization.[28]

Until the mid- to late-nineteenth century, language exchanged in male homosocial friendships was often indistinguishable from the idiom and images of love relationships. "With you I could speak of everything—Love, Ambition, Life and all things and all feelings of my heart were known to you," wrote another of Hammond's academy friends. Since affection was allowed, friendships could be intimate while not sexual. "Must we then be so long separate?" opined Daniel Baker to a friend in Georgia, "shall one sweet interview be allowed us in all that time?—'tis painfull to think of it, will not our former intimacy be forgotten? . . . shall we long for a friendly and tender and sweet embrace?"[29]

But where was the line between homosocial intimacy and homoerotic interests drawn? At dinner in 1860, Harry St. John Dixon and a friend bantered:

> "Harry, they tell us your p[enis] is harder than your head. Is it so?"
> "Do you judge others by yourself?"
> "They tell me this, I speak from hearsay."
> "Oh! Well what they tell you may be true—it is possible."

The phrasing is curious: the original question was not meant to imply Dixon's stubbornness (which would have been stated: "Is your head harder than your penis?") but rather to suggest Dixon's unrestrained sexuality. So too did Withers allude to Hammond's sexual power. In a second letter, Withers continued his interest in Hammond's phallus: "I fancy, Jim, that your *elongated protuberance*—your fleshen pole—your *turgeus inguen* [swollen groin]—has captured complete mastery over you—and I really believe, that you are charging over the pine barrens of your locality, braying, like an ass, at every she-male you can discover."[30]

If Withers's complaint had been that Hammond inadvertently screwed his chums—either literally or figuratively—in his reckless pursuit of Southern masculinity, why now characterize those men (including himself) as "she-males," gendered aberrations who compromised their manly, power-filled sexual roles and therefore confused genders? Men commonly depicted other men as feminine in order to challenge their authority, particularly in the nineteenth century as definitions of masculine and feminine grew more rigid. The practice was most public in the political sphere. For fifteen years, James Buchanan lived with William Rufus King, an Alabama senator and briefly vice-president of the United States. During those years, Andrew Jackson called King "Miss Nancy" and "Aunt Fancy," and Tennessee's governor referred to the two as "Buchanan and his wife." In 1802, Charles Cotesworth Pinckney of South Carolina faced public ridicule in the *Richmond Examiner* as "Miss *Charlotte* Cotesworth PINCKNEY," and the paper repeatedly referred to him as "she."[31]

Part of the modernization of America and the South, however, was more rigid delineation of natural oppositions—free/slave, white/black, domesticity/ patriarchy, masculine/feminine—that projected onto others specific racial, gendered, and sexual attributes differentiating "us" from "them." While "she-male," "miss," and "aunt" could serve as markers of gendered Others, suggesting effeminacy as a way of signifying weakness, their use was far more nuanced. Although "miss" signified a young unmarried woman, it also indicated a kept woman, a concubine that a man used in lieu of a wife for sexual satisfaction. "Aunt" could represent familiarity with and respect for an older woman, often a relative, but the term also referred to someone who provided sex outside of marriage. Similarly, use of "she-" as a feminizing qualifier had been employed since the seventeenth century. By the mid-nineteenth century, Webster's *Dictionary* (1860) defined it as "female, representing sex; as, a *she*-bear; and *she*-cat" . . . or *she*-male. Whatever Withers and others intended by their use of such words, the possibility for double entendre was there and certainly purposeful, raising doubts about the individual's sexuality. In a society in which male-female sex predominated, patriarchs struggled to grasp how some men did not meet the expectations of manly, heteronormative sexuality. Beyond suggesting feminine qualities, "she-male," "miss," "aunt" recast the male body to imply sexual passivity. What is interesting here, then, is that in his letters Withers relinquished his masculine Self by conceding sexual power and privilege to Hammond who *became* the dominant male in their relationship because he *seemed* the more sexually powerful: poking, punching, lunging, crushing, braying.[32]

Hammond and his contemporaries lived in a world awkwardly situated between the premodern and the modern. In premodern America, gender and sexuality were diverse: historians have uncovered cross-dressing, sodomy, beastiality, sadomasochism, gender-bending, intercourse with the Devil, child molestation, and homosexuality. (Apparently, Duberman's "liberal interregnum" was not so rare after all!) Such acts were at times "similar to other sinful acts, that all individuals could be capable of" and at other times were "distinct and unusual," according to historian Thomas A. Foster. In either case, such acts did not lead to identification as abnormal, as would happen in the modern era, when the construction of a rigid male-female binary would lead to such judgments.[33]

Traces of premodern America's gendered and sexual diversity lingered in the Old South, but by the late antebellum period, the social context for gender and sexuality was changing. White Southern patriarchs lived under constant criticism from the North and Europe for their "peculiar institution." Even as they characterized blacks as uncivilized, white Southerners were critiqued as backward and vulgar. As historian Jeanne Boydston described, "the embrace of a modern trope of gender was part of a historically situated discourse that allowed them to divide the world into natural oppositions that bolstered their own brutal domination even as it redeemed them as the fulfillment of idealized civilizations." In other words, in order to respond to modern critiques and define themselves as modern, over the course of the mid- to late-nineteenth century, white Southern men embraced oppositions that situated them as dominant racially (white/black), in gendered terms (male/female), and sexually (heterosexual/homosexual).[34]

From our twenty-first-century perspective, we wonder why Withers in 1826 did not express shame over being poked by Hammond. Elements of the pre-modern remained in their increasingly modern world. Whatever had happened between the two—incidental sexual contact or more purposeful sexual intimacy—did not identify either as abnormal. In the absence of a language about homosexual and heterosexual behavior, Withers interpreted the episode as one of power, specifically manly dominance. Premodern Americans had constructed masculinity as a status more than as a gender; indeed, instead of defining manhood in opposition to womanhood as modern Americans would, they defined it in opposition to childhood and, more specifically, to those who were childlike—dependents. Hammond's sexual interactions with his wife, nieces, slaves, and Withers demonstrate how sex was one device employed by white men in the incessant contest of *seeming* and *becoming*, providing a way to establish power over others—women, men, black, white—and ultimately, to demonstrate manliness.[35]

NOTES

1. James Henry Hammond to Harry Hammond, December 20, 1852, Papers of James Henry Hammond, South Caroliniana Library, University of South Carolina, Columbia (hereafter cited as SCL).

2. Entry for December 9, 1846, James Henry Hammond Diary, SCL.

3. Carol Blesser, ed., *Secret and Sacred: The Diaries of James Henry Hammond, a Southern Slaveholder* (New York: Oxford University Press, 1988), xii.

4. Daniel Boorstin, "The Historian: 'A Wrestler with the Angel,'" *New York Times Book Review*, September 20, 1987.

5. Drew Gilpin Faust, *James Henry Hammond and the Old South: A Design for Mastery* (Baton Rouge: Louisiana State University Press, 1982), 338, 346.

6. Bertram Wyatt-Brown, *Southern Honor: Ethics and Behavior in the Old South* (New York: Oxford University Press, 1982), 20.

7. Ibid., 295.

8. Joan Scott, "Gender: A Useful Category of Analysis," *American Historical Review* 91 (December 1986): 1059.

9. Catherine Clinton, *The Plantation Mistress: Woman's World in the Old South* (New York: Pantheon Books, 1983), 221–222.

10. Catherine Clinton, *Half Sisters of History: Southern Women and the American Past* (Durham, N.C.: Duke University Press, 1994), 4; Gail Bederman, *Manliness and Civilization: A Cultural History of Gender and Race in the United States, 1880–1917* (Chicago: University of Chicago Press, 1995), 7. On masculinity studies, see Bryce Traister, "Academic Viagra: The Rise of American Masculinity Studies," *American Quarterly* 52 (June 2000): 274–304.

11. Faust, *James Henry Hammond and the Old South*; Clinton, *Plantation Mistress*; Wyatt-Brown, *Southern Honor*; Scott, "Gender," 1067.

12. Michael Kimmel, *Manhood in America: A Cultural History* (New York: Free Press, 1996), 48; Jay Fliegelman, *Prodigals and Pilgrims: The American Revolution Against Patriarchal Authority, 1750–1800* (New York: Cambridge University Press, 1982); Rhys Isaac, *The Transformation of Virginia, 1740–1790* (New York: W.W. Norton, 1982), 309; Kathleen M. Brown, *Good Wives, Nasty Wenches, and Anxious Patriarchs* (Chapel Hill: University of North Carolina Press, 1996), 323; Eugene D. Genovese, *Roll Jordon Roll: The World the Slaves Made* (New York: Random House, 1976), 4–7.

13. Steven M. Stowe, *Intimacy and Power in the Old South: Ritual in the Lives of the Planters* (Baltimore: Johns Hopkins University Press, 1987), 46; John Ramsey to Thomas Jones, May 26, 1810, Thomas Williamson Jones Papers, Southern Historical Collection, University of North Carolina, Chapel Hill; Michael Curtin, "A Question of Manners: Status and Gender in Etiquette and Courtesy," *Journal of Modern History* 57 (September 1985): 404; *The Letters of Philip Dormer Stanhope, Earl of Chesterfield: Letters on Education* (London: Richard Bentley, 1847), 100.

14. Laura F. Edwards, "Law, Domestic Violence, and the Limits of Patriarchal Authority in the Antebellum South," in *Gender and the Southern Body Politic*, ed. Nancy Bercaw (Jackson: University Press of Mississippi, 2000), 66; entry for February 24, 1828, Cyrus Stuart Diary, Special Collections, Clemson University Library, Clemson, S.C. (hereafter cited as CU); Craig Thompson Friend, "Belles, Benefactors, and the Blacksmith's Son: Cyrus Stuart and the Enigma of Southern Gentlemanliness," in *Southern Manhood: Perspectives on Masculinity in the Old South*, ed. Craig Thompson Friend and Lorri Glover (Athens: University of Georgia Press, 2004), 92–122; entry for July 3, 1845, Hammond Diary, SCL; entry for June 26, 1848, Henry Craft Diary, Craft,

Fort, and Thorne Family Papers, Southern Historical Collection, University of North Carolina, Chapel Hill.

15. L. Diane Barnes, *Artisan Workers in the Upper South: Petersburg, Virginia, 1820–1865* (Baton Rouge: Louisiana State University Press, 2008); Greg O'Brien, *Choctaws in a Revolutionary Age, 1750–1830* (Lincoln: University of Nebraska Press, 2005); John Mayfield, *Counterfeit Gentlemen: Manhood and Humor in the Old South* (Gainesville: University Press of Florida, 2009); Stephanie McCurry, *Masters of Small Worlds: Yeoman Households, Gender Relations, and the Political Culture of the Antebellum South Carolina Low Country* (New York: Oxford University Press, 1995); Ted Ownby, "Southern Manhood," in *American Masculinities: A Historical Encyclopedia*, ed. Bret E. Carroll (Thousand Oaks, Calif.: SAGE, 2003), 429; Jennifer R. Green, *Military Education and the Emerging Middle Class in the Old South* (New York: Cambridge University Press, 2008); Lorri Glover, *Southern Sons: Becoming Men in the New Nation* (Baltimore: John Hopkins University Press, 2007).

16. Daniel Blake Smith, *Inside the Great House: Planter Family Life in Eighteenth-Century Society* (Ithaca, N.Y.: Cornell University Press, 1980); Christine Heyrman, *Southern Cross: The Origins of the Bible Belt* (New York: Alfred A. Knopf, 1997); Anya Jabour, *Marriage in the Early Republic: Elizabeth and William Wirt and the Companionate Ideal* (Baltimore: Johns Hopkins University Press, 1998).

17. Entry for March 19, 1828, Stuart Diary, Special Collections, CU; entry for December 21, 1851, Henry Hughes Diary, published in *Princes of Cotton: Four Diaries of Young Men in the South, 1848–1860*, ed. Stephen Berry (Athens: University of Georgia Press, 2007), 286.

18. Richard Godbeer, "William Byrd's 'Flourish': The Sexual Cosmos of a Southern Planter," in *Sex and Sexuality in Early America*, ed. Merril D. Smith (New York: New York University Press, 1998), 135–162.

19. *Letters of Philip Dormer Stanhope*, 72; Withers to James Henry Hammond, September 24, 1826, and James Henry Hammond to Harry Hammond, December 20, 1852, Papers of James Henry Hammond, SCL; Kenneth A. Lockridge, "Colonial Self-Fashioning: Paradoxes and Pathologies in the Construction of Genteel Identity in Eighteenth-Century America," in *Through a Glass Darkly: Reflections on Personal Identity in Early America*, ed. Ronald Hoffman, Mechal Sobel, and Fredrika J. Teute (Chapel Hill: University of North Carolina Press, 1997), 274–339; Stowe, *Intimacy and Power in the Old South*, 83.

20. J. S. Buckingham, *The Slave States of America*, 2 vols. (London: Fisher, Son, & Co., 1842), 2:241; Melton A. McLaurin, *Celia, a Slave: A True Story* (New York: Avon Books, 1991); Annie Young, in *The WPA Oklahoma Slave Narratives*, ed. T. Lindsey Baker and Julie P. Baker (Norman: University of Oklahoma Press, 1996), 13; Anna Matilda King to Thomas Butler King, June 20, 1849, Thomas Butler King Papers, Southern Historical Collection, University of North Carolina, Chapel Hill.

21. Michel Foucault, *The History of Sexuality*, vol. 1, trans. R. Hurley (New York: Penguin Books, 1978), 12; Judith Butler, *Gender Trouble: Feminism and the Subversion of Identity* (New York: Routledge, 1990).

22. Brenda E. Stevenson, *Life in Black and White: Family and Community in the Slave South* (New York: Oxford University Press, 1996), 241; *Christy's Ram Horn*, 76–77, quoted in Alexander Saxton, "Blackface Minstrelsy and Jacksonian Ideology," *American Quarterly* 27 (March 1975): 11–12.

23. Martha Hodes, *White Women, Black Men: Illicit Sex in the Nineteenth-Century South* (New Haven, Conn.: Yale University Press, 1997), 96; Victoria E. Bynum, *Unruly Women: The Politics of Social and Sexual Control in the Old South* (Chapel Hill: University of North Carolina Press, 1992); Diane Miller Sommerville, *Rape and Race in the Nineteenth-Century South* (Chapel Hill: University of North Carolina Press, 2004).

24. Michael Grossberg, *Governing the Hearth: Law and the Family in Nineteenth-Century America* (Chapel Hill: University of North Carolina Press, 1985), 300; Angela Davis, "Reflections on the Black Woman's Role in the Community of Slaves," *Black Scholar* 2 (December 1971): 12–13.

25. Entry for May 13, 1828, Stuart Diary, Special Collections, CU; entry for April 4, 1860, Harry St. John Dixon Diary, published in Berry, ed., *Princes of Cotton*, 140–141; Mechal Sobel, *Teach Me Dreams: The Search for Self in the Revolutionary Era* (Princeton, N.J.: Princeton University Press, 2000), chap. 4.

26. Faust, *James Henry Hammond and the Old South*, 19n18; Jeff Withers to Hammond, May 15, 1826, Papers of James Henry Hammond, SCL.

27. Blesser, *Secret and Sacred*, 5; Thomas Jefferson Withers to James Henry Hammond, May 4, 1826, Papers of James Henry Hammond, SCL; Wyatt-Brown, *Southern Honor*, 294; Orlando Paterson, review of *Southern Honor*, in *Reviews in American History* 12 (March 1984): 29.

28. Martin Duberman, "'Writhing Bedfellows' in Antebellum South Carolina: Historical Interpretation and the Politics of Evidence," in *Carryin' On in the Lesbian and Gay South*, ed. John Howard (New York: New York University Press, 1997), 23; Jeanne Boydston, "Gender as a Question of Historical Analysis," *Gender and History* 20 (November 2008): 574.

29. H. W. Hilliard to James Henry Hammond, April 21, 1826, Papers of James Henry Hammond, SCL; Daniel Baker to George Palmes, October 5, 1811, George E. Palmes Papers, Special Collections, Duke University, Durham, N.C.

30. Entry for July 6, 1860, Dixon Diary, published in Berry, *Princes of Cotton*, 137; Withers to Hammond, September 24, 1826, Papers of James Henry Hammond, SCL.

31. Jean H. Baker, *James Buchanan* (New York: Henry Holt & Co., 2004), 25–26; *Richmond Examiner*, October 2, 1802.

32. Mechal Sobel, "The Revolution in Selves: Black and White Inner Aliens," in Hoffman, Sobel, and Teute, *Through a Glass Darkly*, 172; Noah Webster, *An American Dictionary of the English Language* (Springfield, Mass.: George and Charles Merriam, 1860), 1020.

33. Thomas A. Foster, "Introduction: Long Before Stonewall," in *Long Before Stonewall: Histories of Same-Sex Sexuality in Early America*, ed. Thomas A. Foster (New York: New York University Press, 2007), 8. For examples of the sexual and gendered diversity of premodern America, see Mary Beth Norton, *Founding Mothers and Fathers: Gendered Power and the Formation of American Society* (New York: Knopf,

1996); Catherine Clinton and Michele Gillespie, eds., *The Devil's Lane: Sex and Race in the Early South* (New York: Oxford University Press, 2002); Richard Godbeer, *Sexual Revolution in Early America* (Baltimore: John Hopkins University Press, 2004); Clare Lyons, *Sex among the Rabble: An Intimate History of Gender and Power in the Age of Revolution, 1730–1830* (Chapel Hill: University of North Carolina Press, 2006); and the many essays in Foster, *Long Before Stonewall*.

34. Boydston, "Gender as a Question of Historical Analysis," 574; Foster, "Introduction," 8.

35. Michael Kimmel, *Manhood in America: A Cultural History* (New York: The Free Press, 1996), 81. Also see Norton, *Founding Mothers and Fathers*, chap. 3.

PART V

The Long View of the Old South

13

Counterpoint: What If Genovese Is Right?: The Premodern Outlook of Southern Planters

Marc Egnal

What if Eugene Genovese is right? In *The Political Economy of Slavery* (1965) Genovese argues that the "premodern quality of the Southern world was imparted to it by its dominant slaveholding class," adding, "the planters, in truth, grew into the closest thing to feudal lords imaginable in a nineteenth-century bourgeois republic."[1] Judging the South to be "premodern" and ascribing a quasi-feudal mind-set to the slave lords is a decidedly unfashionable view. Most scholars today dismiss such assertions, viewing the planters as profit maximizers, with the same outlook as Northern entrepreneurs. To be sure, many writers concede that the South was less wealthy than the North, but contend the differences between the two regions were of degree not kind.[2]

This essay supports Genovese and takes issue with the prevailing view. But first, it is important to understand exactly what Genovese, and this chapter, argue. For Genovese, the "premodern" outlook was defined by a series of dichotomies. Such a society was agricultural rather than industrial. It was hierarchical rather than democratic. And it was rural rather than urban. Premodern planters sought to accumulate wealth, but never in ways that might undermine traditional relationships. Furthermore, Genovese does not view the South as uniformly premodern. He notes the progress made in manufacturing and discusses agricultural reform in Virginia and Maryland. Genovese contends only that the dominant planter class resisted those developments, laboring (successfully for the most part) to preserve a "premodern" South.

This chapter elaborates that hypothesis. It argues that a powerful group of slave lords opposed change and kept the culture of most Southern states aligned with older values. In part, this argument emerges from the geography of the South. Modernizing trends were most striking in the border states, while planter control was greatest in the Deep South. Indeed, even in the cotton states patterns of trade, settlement, and cultivation created crucial divisions between those resisting and those accepting change. And in part, the argument is political. Slave owners turned to legislative measures—spirited resolutions and, ultimately, secession—to counter economic trends they found so unsettling. To be sure, Northern actions triggered the decision to declare an independent state; but the planters' fears were immeasurably heightened by their awareness that modernizing trends were undermining the world they valued.

I/

The planters' hierarchical society was threatened by three broad, overlapping, changes: urbanization, the weakening of slavery in the border states, and the growth of manufacturing.

Slave lords distrusted the rise of cities for several reasons. To begin with, planters denounced the urban economy's increasing reliance on free labor, including both free blacks and a swelling, restless immigrant population. The weakening grip of slavery on the Southern cities is striking. In the eighteen largest Southern towns—the urban places with a population over 10,000—the percentage of slaves declined from 1850 to 1860 (or in the case of Wilmington, Delaware, which was slave-free, remained the same). On the eve of the Civil War, slaves constituted less than 8 percent of the population of the five largest Southern cities: Baltimore, St. Louis, New Orleans, Louisville, and Washington, D.C.

Planters regarded the towns, with their growing free populations, as a large, alien intrusion into their rural society. Although the South was far less urbanized than the North, the numbers in Southern centers remain noteworthy. Taken together, the eighteen largest towns in the slave states housed 949,196 people in 1860. Their average slave population of 9.4 percent made this urban world less dependent on forced labor than all Southern states except Delaware.

The slaveholders, with their strength in the rural counties, made clear their opposition to trends that were gradually transforming the larger towns into free-labor economies. The legislatures of Maryland and Virginia illustrate those efforts. An unfair apportionment gave the planters control of the Maryland assembly. In 1830, southern Maryland, home to the state's largest slaveholders, had 60 percent of the seats, even though it could claim only 35 percent of the white population. In 1832 planters pushed through a law ordering the deportation of freed slaves and setting aside $200,000 to develop a colony in Africa. Baltimore employers (and others in northern Maryland) ignored the decree, its penalties, and the incentives for colonization. Free blacks played too important a role in the local economy to be exiled. These servants provided a flexible workforce and helped keep down the wages of white workers. Similarly, Virginia cities defied the restrictive laws that the Virginia assembly passed in the wake of the 1831 Nat Turner rebellion. Curfews were not enforced, nor was the decree stating that freed blacks had to leave Virginia within twelve months of their manumission.[3]

Defying coercive legislation and driven by economic self-interest, city dwellers relied more and more on a free workforce. The growth of Baltimore, the South's largest city, is a good example. The town had long boasted extensive connections with the North. During the colonial era, the Susquehanna River brought Pennsylvania grain to Baltimore for milling. The Baltimore & Ohio Railroad (B & O), chartered in 1828, expanded upon canal, river, and ocean links with the free states. As a result of these ties, Baltimore grew as an industrial city—one that increasingly depended on a skilled, free workforce. The town's population soared from 81,000 in 1830 to 169,000 in 1850 and 212,000 in 1860. At mid-century it was the largest city in the South and the second largest in the nation. Gradually, Baltimore businessmen directed their wealth from flour milling to new enterprises, including metalworking and textiles. On the west side of the city, the B & O established the Mount Clare depot and machine shops, which came to employ a thousand people. Still more operatives were involved in producing finished clothing, the city's premier industry. Ironworkers, shipbuilders, carpenters, merchants, and clerks swelled the city's population. Slaves, denied education and excluded from apprenticeships, were ill suited for this urban labor market. Baltimoreans emancipated their slaves, relying on the freed blacks for a significant portion of their workforce—despite the measures adopted by the legislature.[4]

Similar economic developments weakened slavery in Virginia cities. By 1850 almost all African Americans in Wheeling and most in Alexandria were free. In Norfolk County and several nearby districts, the proportion of free blacks rose strikingly, reflecting individual decisions of masters rather than any concerted movement. Many employers in Richmond, facing growing but erratic demands for labor, shifted from purchasing slaves to hiring them. These bondsmen often received wages and the freedom to live where they pleased, leaving observers to fret about the consequences of such liberality.[5]

More broadly, Southern cities shifted away from slavery both because of the "push" of the new artisanal industries, which spurned bound workers, and the "pull" of a countryside that drew slaves from the towns. Even in the 1840s—a difficult decade for many planters—the proportion of slaves in the urban population dropped. During that decade, however, that percentage did not fall as uniformly or as sharply as it did in the 1850s, when agricultural prosperity drove up the price for field hands. In other words, the "pull" factor accelerated the decline of urban slavery in the 1850s—but was not the only cause of that drop. Similarly, the gender imbalance in most urban slave populations, with women outnumbering men, suggests that men were drawn off for farmwork. Only in Richmond, where male slaves forged iron and processed tobacco, were there significantly more men. Richmond perhaps illustrates the adaptability of urban slavery. But it should also be emphasized that even in Richmond the proportion of slaves in the town population declined in the 1840s and again in the 1850s.[6]

Planters disliked urbanization because of another troubling development: the increasing ties between these towns and the North. Like Baltimore, Virginia cities were drawn into the Northern commercial orbit. In the late eighteenth and early nineteenth centuries, Richmond and Norfolk were bustling independent entrepôts, boasting a thriving overseas trade. In 1815, when New York accounted for 19 percent of U.S. exports, Richmond and Norfolk together shipped 12 percent of the total. However, overseas shipments from the Old Dominion dropped precipitously, so that by 1840 the two Virginia ports handled only 3 percent of all exports and in 1860 only 1 percent. The two Virginia cities lacked the financiers, merchants, and rich hinterland that allowed the great ports to flourish. (Meanwhile, New York's foreign trade soared to 36 percent of all exports in 1860.) In place of sending their goods overseas, Virginians increasingly directed their wares to Northern cities. Richmond tobacco was forwarded to New York shippers, who sent the casks to Europe and to retailers throughout the United States. Garden crops, destined for New York tables, became the chief export of Norfolk. Most flour milled at Alexandria was sent to Baltimore, Philadelphia, and New York. The industrial products produced in Wheeling, which was located on the Ohio River near Pittsburgh, were sold primarily in the North. States' rights advocate George Fitzhugh commented acidly, "Trade very easily effects now what conquest did formerly."[7]

The planters championing states' rights condemned the cities for their moderation on sectional issues. The leanings of the towns were clear even before the mid-century crisis. By the mid-1840s most urban places in the South were bastions of the Whig Party; and as a rule, Southern Whigs proved more cautious than Southern Democrats in defending slavery. The presence of

Northern traders reinforced this leaning. One correspondent told Southern rights leader John C. Calhoun in 1849: "The cities all of them are becoming daily more & more unsound & uncertain & all for the same reason; the infusion of Northerners & Foreigners amongst them & their influence is being felt in the interior[?]."[8]

The urbanites' lack of enthusiasm for Southern rights was striking in the years before the Civil War. In 1854 a South Carolina editorialist noted: "Every city is destined to be the seat of free-soilism. It is unconsciously making its appearance in Charleston, and it is destined to increase with every fresh arrival of European immigrants."[9] St. Louis showed its loyal colors, electing a Free-Soil congressman in 1856 and a Republican in 1860, and giving a plurality of votes to Lincoln. A German editor remarked, "St. Louis has the character of a free state, a virtual enclave in this region of slavery."[10] Baltimore too set itself against secession. Businessmen signed two pro-Union petitions, one in December 1860 with thirteen hundred names, and another the following January with five thousand names. Southern rights spokesman J. D. B DeBow complained: "Baltimore must be counted not for us but against us. We must deal with her as with the other Northern cities, all sectional enemies who are assailing our domestic peace and property."[11] In Kentucky no county provided as many volunteers for the Union army as Jefferson, which contained Louisville. New Orleans showed the same leanings. Although John Breckinridge, the Southern Democratic presidential candidate, swept the Deep South in 1860, he fared poorly in the Crescent City. He ran a dismal third in the city's polls, with only 24 percent of the ballots, well behind the two unionist candidates, Constitutional Unionist John Bell (48 percent) and Northern Democrat Stephen Douglas (28 percent).[12]

To be sure, Southern cities were never monolithic in their political leanings. The St. Louis and Baltimore merchants who focused on the Southern market typically supported the campaigns of the fire-eaters. Irish immigrants in the larger towns often applauded states' rights orators, delighting in their racist attacks on Free-Soilers and Republicans. Charleston, South Carolina, was a storm center of the Southern rights movement. Acknowledging those exceptions, it remains clear that Southern towns, including most in the Deep South, proved a force for moderation.[13]

II/

Planters felt threatened by a second broad development: the decline of slavery in the border states. Between 1830 and 1860 each decennial census showed that slaves made up an ever-smaller proportion of the populations in Delaware, Kentucky, Maryland, and Missouri.

The decline was particularly worrisome because it was accompanied, in each border state, by proposals that slavery be abolished. To be sure, those who questioned the "peculiar institution" were always a minority. None of the suggestions, even for gradual emancipation, came to fruition before the Civil War. But the very fact that prominent individuals raised such daring proposals unsettled the slave lords.

In two public gatherings in 1849, Kentuckians courageously criticized slavery. In April over 150 delegates, including both Whig leader Henry Clay and his outspoken cousin, Cassius Marcellus Clay, attended an emancipation convention at Frankfort. Speakers denounced bondage and proposed plans for freeing slaves, although no actions resulted. Delegates to the constitutional convention held at the end of the year presented similar critiques. "We have at hand a Convention to revise the Constitution," one observer told Calhoun, "& gradual emancipation reared its head with the Northern party." Again change was voted down, but most Kentuckians recognized that a vocal minority favored a legislated end to the "peculiar institution."[14]

Similar sentiments were voiced in Delaware and Maryland. In 1803 and again in 1847 the Delaware assembly came close to adopting a plan for gradual emancipation. Only the actions of the state senate, mirroring the wishes of Sussex County (where most of the larger plantations were located), prevented the measure from becoming law. Still, James Hammond of South Carolina could justly observe that Delaware was "no southern or slave state."[15] Although no conventions or legislative initiatives promoted emancipation in Maryland, many citizens accepted that slavery was on the road to extinction. "I assume that we of the South," Baltimorean J. H. Alexander remarked in 1848, "are no ways desirous of extending and perpetuating Slavery *per se* and for its own sake; and that we are even ready and willing to do away with the whole Institution *if we could afford it.*"[16]

Planters in the Deep South responded to the weakening of slavery in the border states by urging secession before the corrosive acid of change spread to their states as well. In the "first secession crisis" of 1849–1851, slave lords pointed to the decline of forced labor in the Northern tier of states as a strong reason for severing ties with the free states. "How long will Maryland, Western Virginia, Kentucky, Eastern Tennessee and even the Western part of No. Carolina feel it is their interest to retain slaves?" Governor David Johnson of South Carolina asked in 1848. "They are already unproductive as laborers & their sympathy would not weigh a feather against their interest & their prejudices in another scale."[17] The following year South Carolinian Marcus Hammond told his brother James that Southerners should "break up" the Union before, "Ky., Md., Mo. & Tennessee draw off." The transformation of the border states raised the chilling specter of the collapse of the entire slave system.[18]

III/

Planters denounced a third broad trend that threatened their hierarchical society: the growth of manufacturing. The proliferation of factories in larger cities and craft enterprises in smaller ones challenged the slave lords in several ways. One problem was the danger posed by the industrial workforce. Employing this group in large numbers, whether white or black, posed risks to a society that demanded quiescent whites and closely watched slaves.

Christopher Memminger, South Carolina lawyer, legislator, and later treasurer of the Confederacy, noted the dangers of relying on white workers rather than slaves. He asked, "Drive our negro mechanics and all sorts of operatives from our Cities, and who must take their place?" His answer: "The same men who make the cry in the Northern Cities against the tyranny of Capital—and there as here would drive all before them all who interfere with them—and would soon raise hue and cry against the Negro, and be hot Abolitionists—and every one of those men have a vote."[19] Such views persuaded Richmond ironmaster Joseph Anderson to replace white workers with slaves after a strike in 1847 closed his foundry. In the 1850s, strikes in Baltimore, St. Louis, Louisville, and New Orleans exacerbated planter concerns about white laborers.[20]

Planters were equally worried about turning servants into operatives. Industrial slaves could not be subjected to the same strict regime as field workers. To a remarkable degree, industrialists who employed slaves had to provide incentives, either in the form of pay for "overwork" or additional holiday time. But those rewards, which went far beyond the incentives offered field workers, created problems. One slave owner, who withdrew his laborers from service, explained: "I regret having to adopt this course but you will upon a moments reflection, see the impolicy of keeping amongst a gang of negroes a portion to be more favored than the rest. It would prevent all just and efficient discipline."[21] James H. Hammond of South Carolina agreed. He noted in 1849, "Whenever a slave is made a mechanic, he is more than half freed, and soon becomes, as we too well know, and all history attests, with rare exceptions, the most corrupt and turbulent of his class."[22]

Planters also worried that Southern manufacturers might join the crusade for higher tariffs and challenge one of slave society's fundamental tenets: free trade. Even the stirrings of artisan production in the northern districts of states like South Carolina, Georgia, and Alabama appeared worrisome. One observer remarked in 1860,

> How long would it be after disunion before we should have the
> same hungry manufacturing population infesting the upper part of
> So. Ca., Cherokee Georgia, Tennessee, North Carolina . . . and even
> the upper portion of Alabama—why not five years would elapse
> before they would be setting their looms on every stream in these
> locations under the impulse of occupation and the introduction of
> numbers. . . . A few years more and you would have a strong party of
> our own people in favour of a protective Tarriff, and advocating all
> those extravagant expenditures for Internal Improvements, and
> nearer home we shall be compelled to fight that same battle which
> has continued in the present Union since 1824.[23]

The hostility of the Southern elite to manufacturing was evident in the actions of legislatures and in the policies of public and private institutions. Sean Adams's study of coal production in Virginia and Pennsylvania illustrates how planters and their allies hindered industrialization. In 1810 coal from the Richmond, Virginia, basin dominated the market in the eastern United States. By contrast, Pennsylvania anthracite was labeled "stone coal" and considered unusable. But by 1860 the picture was reversed: Pennsylvania now produced 78 percent of the nation's coal, while Virginia, despite rich deposits in both the east and west, was reduced to a peripheral role, supplying only 2.4 percent of national consumption.

The explanation for these divergent paths did not lie in the resource endowment of the two states. Both had large coalfields. Rather it reflected the very different role played by the dominant groups. Pennsylvania's lawmakers provided corporate charters on favorable terms and subsidized the canals and railroads that moved the heavy fuel. By contrast, Virginia lawmakers placed more restrictions on incorporation and refused to improve waterways. Moreover, the planters who controlled the James River Company charged miners higher fees than farmers. Virginia also had no counterpart to Philadelphia's Franklin Institute, which mounted a successful campaign to market anthracite.[24]

States' rights advocates wanted manufacturing to play at most a minor role. Few went as far in condemning enterprise as John Forsythe, the editor of the *Columbus Times*. In 1850 Forsythe declared: "I would to God we had fewer miles of railroad, fewer millions invested in manufactures and stocks, fewer proofs of enterprise, and thrift and money-making, and more of that chivalry of Georgia, of the olden time, which, on more than one occasion, has interposed her sovereignty to check the usurpations of the federal government."[25] Most politicians, of all persuasions, favored railroads. Some Southern rights leaders accepted a subordinate role for manufacturing. They acknowledged that the occasional textile mill or armory could help the South become more self-reliant. But states' rights leaders condemned the spread of "manufacturing as a system"; industrialization neither could be nor should be the path of Southern development.[26]

Economic historians who view the slave lords as profit-maximizers argue that rational self-interest explains the opposition to manufacturing and comparatively low levels of production. Staple production, they suggest, simply paid better. Such an argument might be valid for the eighteenth-century South. Slaves worked longer days and had a higher "labor force participation rate" than whites, since most black women worked outside the home while most white women did not.

But in the nineteenth century, planters favored agriculture and shunned industry *despite* higher returns from manufacturing. Artisans, benefiting from the division of labor and specialized tools, and operatives, assisted by machinery, generated higher profits than field slaves. Using manufacturing census returns, Fred Bateman and Thomas Weiss show that the average profitability of all Southern industries in 1850 was 25 percent and in 1860, 28 percent. Still-higher returns came from boot-and-shoe-making; the fabrication of tin, sheet iron, and copper; and the production of wagons and carriages. By comparison, plantations provided only single-digit earnings. Although industry outperformed agriculture, wealthy slaveholders shunned manufacturing. Only 6 percent of wealthy slaveholders invested in manufacturing. Less than 15 percent of industrialists in the South belonged to the slaveholding elite. Bateman and Weiss conclude that it seems "plausible to accept the view espoused by Eugene Genovese and others: that the opportunities existed [in the South] and were known, but that investors chose to ignore them."[27]

IV/

While urbanization, the decline of slavery, and the growth of manufacturing unsettled many planters, the impact of these developments must be kept in perspective. Before 1860 these trends did not turn a traditional society into a modern one. The impact of these changes was greatest in the border states, and their influence was least felt where wealthy planters remained strongest: the Deep South.

Urbanization was focused in the border area. Four of the top five cities in the South were located there, while fully one-fifth of the population in this region lived in towns. Except for Louisiana, the other Southern states had less than 10 percent of their population in towns of 2,500 or more. Indeed, in six states (Arkansas, North Carolina, Mississippi, Florida, Tennessee, and Texas) town dwellers accounted for less than 5 percent of the total, and of this group only Tennessee boasted a city of 10,000 or more. More generally, the South, excluding the border areas, lagged far behind the North. Maryland was the only Southern state more than 30 percent of the population urbanized. By contrast, five Northern states (Rhode Island, Massachusetts, New York, New Jersey, and Pennsylvania) surpassed that mark, and two (Massachusetts and Rhode Island) had urban majorities. New York alone boasted as many cities of 10,000 or more as the entire South.

Similarly, the steady decline of slavery evident in the border states was rarely repeated elsewhere in the South. Outside of the four border states, only Virginia (which included in its boundaries the future border state of West Virginia), Louisiana, and Florida exhibited a similar steady declension. Several states—Arkansas, Tennessee, Alabama, and Texas—increased their percentage of slaves in every census year. Most states showed a rising proportion of slaves from 1830 to 1860..

Finally, manufacturing lagged in the slave states, and particularly in the Deep South. In 1860 the South contained the bottom nine states in the union for per capita manufactures (Florida, North Carolina, Tennessee, Georgia, South Carolina, Alabama, Texas, Mississippi, Arkansas). All of these states produced finished goods worth less than $1,800 per person. That group of nine included all the states of the Deep South, except for Louisiana, whose output, thanks to the sugar industry and the artisans of New Orleans, was just slightly higher. By contrast, the top eight manufacturing states were Northern, each creating products worth over $9,000 per person. Among the slave states, only Maryland and Delaware compared favorably to the less wealthy Northern states.[28]

Clearly, by 1860 modernizing trends had an impact on the South. But apart from the border states and a few scattered enclaves, the slave South still remained its old self. It was overwhelmingly rural, dependent on a growing slave population, and focused on agriculture rather than manufacturing.

V/

Although critics urged the leading planters to accept the forces for change, these slave lords firmly rejected all such suggestions. Instead, following the logic of their commitment to premodern values, they vigorously opposed the rise of an urban, diversified, free-labor society; and when their efforts to stifle change appeared doomed, they led their states out of the union.

These traditional-minded planters, however, faced considerable opposition within the South. The border states spurned the proposals of states' rights leaders in the 1840s and 1850s and rejected secession in 1860–1861. Upper South politicians were divided during these decades: some individuals championed the states' rights movement, but others strongly dissented. And while Southern nationalists carried the day in the Deep South, a sizeable minority disagreed with them and applauded the new commercial developments. Sorting out who stood on the two sides of this divide deepens any analysis of the battle over modernization. A brief essay, such as this one, can only sketch the broad outlines of this division. My book, *Clash of Extremes: The Economic Origins of the Civil War*, provides a fuller discussion, surveying a range of evidence, including the votes in state elections and Congress, and presenting a series of maps documenting these splits.[29]

To begin with, in the upper South the defenders of traditional society typically hailed from the districts with the largest plantations and the highest concentrations of slaves, such as the tobacco-growing counties of eastern Virginia and North Carolina. Early in the century these districts elected lawmakers such as John Randolph and Nathaniel Mason; in the decades before the Civil War, they selected equally strong-minded individuals such as Robert M. T. Hunter, James M. Mason, and Abraham Venable. These individuals denounced manufacturing, urban growth, tariffs, and federal outlays for internal improvements. They called for a limited central government that would confine its activities to measures such as keeping new western territories open to slavery and capturing fugitive slaves.

Representatives of the small farmers opposed these states' rights planters. But because the South remained a deferential society, the split was never strictly along class lines. Where large plantations predominated, most small farmers voted for their wealthy neighbors. Only in the areas with few slaves and few plantations—for example, western Virginia and eastern Tennessee—did small farmers and their spokesmen openly challenge the great planters. Townsfolk and some of the business interests in the upper South also criticized the designs of the slave lords.

The most outspoken, numerous, and influential defenders of traditional society resided in the Deep South—but they too had to deal with determined opponents. Some historians suggest that the conflict in the cotton states resembled the clashes in the upper South, with small farmers pitted against planters.[30] But the evidence does not support that simple dichotomy. Rather, the most important line of division in the Deep South was a geographical one.

The citizenry in the northern part of states like South Carolina, Georgia, Alabama, and Mississippi were more sympathetic to manufacturing and the creation of a diversified economy, while representatives from the southern districts in those states were the most vehement in denouncing change. This fissure divided both planters and yeomen.

Citizens in the cotton states split along these geographical lines for several reasons. One was the different origins of the inhabitants. Settlers in the northern districts typically had migrated from the upper South and had ties of kinship with states to the north. Those in the southern districts arrived from settlements in South Carolina and Georgia. Patterns of commerce reinforced this division, as a growing overland trade, which exchanged cotton for finished goods, gradually integrated the northern districts into the national economy. Differences in crop choices strengthened the split. Wheat cultivation, which fostered a society of towns and craft industry, flourished in the northern districts but not in the southern ones.

To be sure, circumstances varied from state to state, with local conditions modifying these generalizations. In Louisiana crop choices helped dictate loyalties: sugar planters depended on government protection and applauded a central government that levied tariffs and encouraged local industry. Overland trade had little impact on politics in Florida, the one Deep South state that did not border the upper South. In Texas relatively few planters joined the wheat-growing small farmers in protesting the plans of the secessionists. South Carolina remained more unified and harbored fewer moderates than the other states. Neverthless, divisions shaped by settlement, trade, and crops were evident in all the cotton states, as was a vigorous debate over modernization.

Politicians from the northern districts of South Carolina, Georgia, Alabama, and Mississippi (and kindred spirits in the other Deep South states) demonstrated courage in standing up to the states' right majority and in applauding the new commercial trends. James Alcorn, a Whig planter who resided in northern Mississippi, exemplified these leaders. A follower of Henry Clay, he argued that the future of the South lay in a broad program of economic development, not in a rush to secession. Alexander Stephens, a northern Georgia planter and lawyer, contended that the South would fare better within a growing union than outside of it. James Orr, head of the South Carolina National Democrats, also argued for economic diversification not separation. "The first step to be taken," he explained in 1855, "to reinvigorate our decaying prosperity, and to develop our exhaustless resources, is for our planters and farmers to invest the whole of the nett profits on agricultural capital in some species of manufacturing; the field is broad and inviting, and but little has yet been occupied."[31]

Many townsfolk shared the outlook of these landholders and made clear their receptivity to modernizing currents. Newspapers based in the larger centers often boosted new crops and industry. For example, the *Mobile Advertiser* suggested that cotton planters "instead of investing their surplus capital in negroes and lands, [should] invest it in manufactures, and draw around and among them in every neighborhood of the South an industrious, thriving, laboring white population to *consume* their surplus products and manufacture their staple."[32]

These townsfolk, planters, and small farmers made certain that in the Deep South the debate over modernization was always a discussion and never simply a monologue. During the "first secession crisis," of 1849–1851, spokesmen from the northern districts and their allies resisted call for secession, and they rehearsed the same arguments again in 1860–1861. Lincoln's election, however, weakened the forces advocating diversification rather than independence. Once secession occurred, almost all the moderates "went with their state," often accepting high offices in the Confederacy.

The dominant group in the Deep South, the ones who championed secession and who fought modernization—and who shaped the path taken by Southern society—came from the southern districts. These were the individuals least involved in overland trade, least likely to raise crops other than cotton, and least inclined to promote local manufacturing. Although opposed by the small farmers and planters in the northern counties, these slave lords drew strong support from the poorer farmers in the southern reaches. The deep fissures within the yeomanry would remain evident during the war and Reconstruction.

The states' rights leaders insisted time and again that regional prosperity depended on fresh soils and a cash crop raised by slaves. They contended that approaches to growth based on manufacturing or agricultural diversification inevitably must fail. U.S. senator and future Confederate president Jefferson Davis was among the most outspoken advocates of this credo. "Without mountain slopes, and mountain streams to furnish water power," he explained in 1846, "without coal mines permanently to supply large amounts of cheap fuel at any locality, we cannot expect, in competition with those who enjoy either or both of these advantages, ever to become a manufacturing people. We must continue to rely, as at present, almost entirely upon our exports."[33] Davis often returned to this theme. During the Panic of 1857, he rejoiced in the strengths of the Southern way. "Ours was an agricultural people, and in that consisted their strength," he told an audience in Jackson, Mississippi. "Their prosperity was not at the mercy of such a commercial crisis as the one with which the country had just been visited. Our great staple was our safety."[34]

More broadly, Southern rights leaders extolled their traditional way of life, distinguishing it from the destructive commercial spirit of the North. In 1855 Alabama fire-eater William Lowndes Yancey expounded on the differences between the North and South: "The climate, soil and productions of these two grand divisions of the land, have made the character of their inhabitants. Those who occupy the one are cool, calculating, enterprising, selfish and grasping; the inhabitants of the other, are ardent, brave and magnanimous, more disposed to give than to accumulate, to enjoy ease rather than labor."[35] Mississippi radical John F. H. Claiborne remarked: "Sedentary and agricultural, we cherish the homesteads and laws of our ancestors, and live among the reminiscences of the past."[36]

Louis Wigfall, the South Carolinian who became a leader of Texas's secession movement, affirmed similar values, sharply distinguishing the South from modern, industrializing societies. "We are an agricultural people," he announced in May 1861. "We are a primitive but a civilized people. We have no cities—we don't want them. . . . We want no manufactures; we desire no trading, no mechanical or manufacturing classes. As long as we have our rice, our sugar, our tobacco, and our cotton, we can command the wealth to purchase all we want from those nations with which we are in amity, and lay up money besides."[37]

Given this mind-set, secession was the logical response for the slave lords as they witnessed the mounting threats to their way of life. In their minds, reform was never an option. For this dominant group of planters, slavery was more than a means of production. Slavery defined a social hierarchy with the bondmen and bondwomen at the bottom and the great slave lords at the pinnacle. By protecting slavery, they were protecting the world they knew. Henry Benning, the secessionist commissioner that Georgia sent to Virginia in February 1861, presented the case succinctly. "What was the reason that induced Georgia to take the step of secession?" he asked. "This reason may be summed up in a single proposition. It was a conviction, a deep conviction on the part of Georgia, that a separation from the North was the only thing that could prevent the abolition of her slavery."[38] Robert Barnwell Rhett, editor of the *Charleston Mercury*, warned his readers that "the issue before the country is the extinction of slavery. No man of common sense, who has observed the progress of events, and who is not prepared to surrender the institution, with the safety and independence of the South, can doubt that the time for action has come—now or never."[39]

This same antimodern outlook, the same determination to defend older ways, was embodied in the Constitution of the Confederate States of America, adopted in March 1861. That charter forbade all tariffs "laid to promote or foster

any branch of industry." It barred all "internal improvement intended to facilitate commerce"—a prohibition that delighted fire-eaters like Barnwell Rhett.
His newspaper, the *Charleston Mercury*, rejoiced: "Internal improvements, by
appropriations from the treasury of the Confederate States is therefore rooted
out of the system of Government the Constitution establishes."[40]

In deciding for secession, these planters responded to several threats. The
rise of the Republican Party and its decision to block the spread of slavery was
the most serious problem—and the immediate cause of the war. But this group
of slave lords also recognized that modernizing trends—the growth of Southern cities, the decline of slavery in the border South, and the rise of manufacturing—also posed long-term challenges to their existence. These developments
made clear that unless the planters remained masters in their own house, they
could not survive.

In sum, Genovese is right: The leading planters had a premodern outlook,
and that ideology dominated politics, particularly in the Deep South. The powerful forces for change, unmistakable by the middle of the nineteenth century,
did not dissuade these autocrats. Instead, the incipient forces for modernization made them more determined to defend their traditional view of society,
even to the point of breaking up the union.

NOTES

[Readers will notice that Marc Egnal does not adopt the same interpretive framework
as the other contributors to this anthology. His essay is intended as a counterpoint to
interpretations of the Old South as modern-minded. As such this contribution seeks to
further debate on reinterpreting the history of the antebellum South.]—Ed.

1. Eugene Genovese, *The Political Economy of Slavery: Studies in the Economy &
Society of the Slave South* (New York: Pantheon Books, 1965), 3, 31. Also see Genovese,
The World the Slaveholders Made: Two Essays in Interpretation (1968; repr., Middletown,
Conn.: Pantheon Books, 1988), vi; Elizabeth Fox-Genovese and Eugene D. Genovese,
The Mind of the Master Class: History and Faith in the Southern Slaveholders' Worldview
(New York: Cambridge University Press, 2005), 3, and the introduction to *Political
Economy of Slavery*, 2nd ed. (Middletown, Conn.: Pantheon Books, 1989).

2. Robert Whaples, "Where Is There Consensus Among American Economic
Historians? The Results of a Survey on Forty Propositions," *Journal of Economic History*
55 (1995): 139–154.

3. J. H. Alexander to Calhoun, July 31, 1848, in *The Papers of John C. Calhoun*, ed.
Robert L. Meriwether et al., 28 vols. (Columbia: University of South Carolina Press,
1959–2003), 25:643; William W. Freehling, *The Road to Disunion*, vol. 1: *Secessionists at
Bay, 1776–1854* (New York: Oxford University Press, 1990), 197–202, 204.

4. Frank Towers, *The Urban South and the Coming of the Civil War* (Charlottesville: University of Virginia Press, 2004), 8, 22–24, 39–60, 95; Barbara J. Fields,

Slavery and Freedom on the Middle Ground: Maryland during the Nineteenth Century (New Haven, Conn.: Yale University Press, 1985), 40–62; Marc Egnal, *Divergent Paths: How Culture and Institutions Have Shaped North American Growth* (New York: Oxford University Press, 1996), 14–18.

5. Freehling, *Road to Disunion: Secessionists at Bay*, 123–135; Jonathan D. Martin, *Divided Mastery: Slave Hiring in the American South* (Cambridge, Mass.: Harvard University Press, 2004), 179–195; Midori Takagi, *"Rearing Wolves to Our Own Destruction": Slavery in Richmond, Virginia, 1782–1865* (Charlottesville: University of Virginia Press, 1999), 71–80, 96–123; Richard Wade, *Slavery in the Cities: The South, 1820–1860* (New York: Oxford University Press, 1964), 242–252.

6. U.S. Bureau of the Census, *Compendium of the Enumeration of the Inhabitants and Statistics of the United States*: (Washington, D.C.: T. Allen, 1841); *The Seventh Census of the United States, 1850* (Washington, D.C.: Robert Armstrong, 1853); *Population of the United States in 1860* (Washington, D.C.: GPO, 1864), online at http://www.census.gov/prod/www/abs/decennial (accessed October 2010). See also Wade, *Slavery in the Cities*, 28–40.

7. David R. Goldfield, *Urban Growth in the Age of Sectionalism: Virginia, 1847–1861* (Baton Rouge: Louisiana State University Press, 1977), xi–xxiv, 2–21, 182–201, 228–247, 235 (quotation).

8. Augustus Fisher[lue?] to Calhoun, September 24, 1848, Henry Conner to Calhoun, January 12, 1849, Joseph W. Lesesne to John C. Calhoun, September 12, 1847, *Papers of John C. Calhoun*, 26:63, 26:211, 24:552; J. Mills Thornton III, *Politics and Power in a Slave Society: Alabama, 1800–1860* (Baton Rouge: Louisiana State University Press, 1978), 42; D. Clayton James, *Antebellum Natchez* (Baton Rouge: Louisiana State University Press, 1968), 164–165; Towers, *Urban South*, 78–79; Lacy K. Ford, Jr., *Origins of Southern Radicalism: The South Carolina Upcountry, 1800–1860* (New York: Oxford University Press, 1988), 167–170; Marc Egnal, *Clash of Extremes: The Economic Origins of the Civil War* (New York: Hill and Wang, 2009), 198–199, 289–292. President John Tyler (1790–1862)was one of the last, prominent states' rights Whigs.

9. Quoted in John Majewski, *Modernizing a Slave Economy: The Economic Vision of the Confederate Nation* (Chapel Hill: University of North Carolina Press, 2009), 100.

10. Quoted in Towers, *Urban South*, 188.

11. *DeBow's Review* (1856), quoted in Towers, *Urban South*, 31.

12. Towers, *Urban South*, 192–197; Egnal, *Clash of Extremes*, 176, 183–187; Roger W. Shugg, *Origins of Class Struggle in Louisiana: A Social History of White Farmers and Laborers during Slavery and After, 1840–1875* (Baton Rouge: Louisiana State University Press, 1939), 157–168; John M. Sacher, *A Perfect War of Politics: Parties, Politicians, and Democracy in Louisiana, 1824–1861* (Baton Rouge: Louisiana State University Press, 2003), 259–290.

13. Towers, *Urban South*, 170–178, 185–192; William J. Evitts, *A Matter of Allegiances: Maryland from 1850 to 1861* (Baltimore: Johns Hopkins University Press, 1971), 170–171.

14. Nathan Gaither to Calhoun, December 2, John Custis Darby to Calhoun, December 4, 1848, *Papers of John C. Calhoun*, 26:145, 26:155; Freehling, *Road to Disunion: Secessionists at Bay*, 467–471.

15. Freehling, *Road to Disunion: Secessionists at Bay*, 197, 207–209, 473 (quotation).

16. J. H. Alexander to Calhoun, July 31, 1848, *Papers of John C. Calhoun*, 25:643; Freehling, *Road to Disunion: Secessionists at Bay*, 197–209; William W. Freehling, *The Road to Disunion: Secessionists Triumphant, 1854–1861*, 2 vols. (New York, 2007), 2: 175, 281, 438, 499–501.

17. David Johnson to Calhoun, October 18, 1848, *Papers of John C. Calhoun*, 26:98.

18. Marcus Hammond to James Hammond, December 17, 1849, quoted in Freehling, *Road to Disunion: Secessionists at Bay*, 474; Egnal, *Clash of Extremes*, 166–168, 179–202.

19. C. G. Memminger to J. H. Hammond, April 28, 1849, quoted in Robert S. Starobin, *Industrial Slavery in the Old South* (New York: Oxford University Press, 1970), 210. I have added the question mark for clarity.

20. Genovese, *Political Economy of Slavery*, 232–233; Towers, *Urban South*, 37–71; Charles B. Dew, *Ironmaker to the Confederacy: Joseph R. Anderson and the Tredegar Iron Works* (New Haven, Conn.: Yale University Press, 1966), 22–26; Takagi, "*Rearing Wolves to Our Own Destruction,*" 81–84.

21. Starobin, *Industrial Slavery*, 103, 111; Ira Berlin, *Many Thousands Gone: The First Two Centuries of Slavery in North America* (Cambridge, Mass.: Harvard University Press, 1998), 269–277; Eugene Genovese, *Roll, Jordan, Roll: The World the Slaves Made* (New York: Vintage Books, 1974), 566–584; William A. Link, *Roots of Secession: Slavery and Politics in Antebellum Virginia* (Chapel Hill: University of North Carolina Press, 2003), 88–91.

22. Genovese, *Political Economy of Slavery*, 182, 225 (quotation); Wade, *Slavery in the Cities*, 143–179, 242–266.

23. Daniel H. Hamilton to William Porcher Miles, January 23, 1860, Charleston, S.C., William Porcher Miles Papers, Southern Historical Collection, University of North Carolina, Chapel Hill.

24. Sean Patrick Adams, *Old Dominion, Industrial Commonwealth: Coal, Politics, and Economy in Antebellum America* (Baltimore: Johns Hopkins University Press, 2004), passim.

25. John Forsythe to "Gentlemen of Charleston," September 12, 1850, in John W. DuBose, *The Life and Times of William Lowndes Yancey*, 2 vols. (1892; repr., New York: Peter Smith, 1942), 2:426.

26. Genovese, *Political Economy of Slavery*, 180–239; William H. Pease and Jane H. Pease, *The Web of Progress: Private Values and Public Styles in Boston and Charleston, 1828–1843* (New York: Oxford University Press, 1985), 18–20, 40–53, 222–224; Majewski, *Modernizing a Slave Economy*, 81–107.

27. Fred Bateman and Thomas Weiss, *A Deplorable Scarcity: The Failure of Industrialization in the Slave Economy* (Chapel Hill: University of North Carolina Press, 1981), 99–127, 113 (quotation). For a contrasting viewpoint, see David L. Carlton and

Peter A. Coclanis, *The South, the Nation, and the World: Perspectives on Southern Economic Development* (Charlottesville: University of Virginia Press, 2003), 73–83, 163–178; Robert W. Fogel and Stanley L. Engerman, *Time on the Cross: The Economics of American Negro Slavery* (Boston: Little, Brown, 1974), 254–257; Gavin Wright, "Cheap Labor and Southern Textiles before 1880," *Journal of Economic History* 39 (1979): 655–680.

28. Data drawn from U.S. Bureau of the Census, *The Eighth Census*, vol. 3: *Manufactures of the United States in 1860* (Washington, D.C.: GPO, 1865). Scott P. Marler, "Merchants and the Political Economy of Nineteenth-Century Louisiana: New Orleans and Its Hinterlands" (Ph.D. diss., Rice University, 2007), 54–101, shows that New Orleans merchants were far more interested in investing in real estate than in manufacturing or railroads.

29. The following discussion of divisions within the South is drawn from Egnal, *Clash of Extremes*, 150–202, 258–306.

30. For example, Michael P. Johnson, *Toward a Patriarchal Republic: The Secession of Georgia* (Baton Rouge: Louisiana State University Press, 1977).

31. James L. Orr, "Development of Southern Industry," *DeBow's Review* 19:1 (July 1855): 1–22, 11–12 (quotation); Egnal, *Divergent Paths*, 63–68.

32. *[Mobile] Advertiser*, November 27, 1848, quoted in Larry K. Menna, "Southern Whiggery and Economic Development: The Meaning of Slavery in a National Context," in *The Meaning of Slavery in the North*, ed. David Roediger and Martin H. Blatt, (New York: Garland Publishers, 1998), 64; Menna, "Embattled Conservatism: The Ideology of the Southern Whigs" (Ph.D. diss., Columbia University, 1991), 230.

33. Davis to the People of Mississippi, July 13, 1846, *The Papers of Jefferson Davis*, ed. Haskell M. Monroe, Jr., and James T. McIntosh, 10 vols. (Baton Rouge: Louisiana State University Press, 1971–1999), 3:5.

34. Davis, Speech at Jackson, November 4, 1857, *Papers of Jefferson Davis*, 6:157.

35. Yancey, Speech at Columbus, Georgia, 1855, in DuBose, *William Lowndes Yancey*, 1:301.

36. J. F. H. Claiborne, *Life and Correspondence of John A. Quitman*, 2 vols. (New York: Harper & Brothers, 1860), 2:273; Egnal, *Divergent Paths*, 21–32, 87–101.

37. Quoted in Majewski, *Modernizing a Slave Economy*, 144. Majewski, who argues that the South was indeed a modern society, has a different reading of this quotation, which was given to a reporter for the *Times* of London. Majewski suggests that Wigfall presented these views to gain British support for the Confederacy.

38. Henry Benning, secessionist commissioner of Georgia, to Virginia convention, February 18, 1861, online at http://civilwarcauses.org/benningva.htm (accessed October 2010); Egnal, *Clash of Extremes*, 258–286.

39. *Charleston Mercury*, November 3, 1860, quoted in *Southern Editorials on Secession*, ed. Dwight L. Dumond (1931; repr., Gloucester, Mass.: Peter Smith, 1964), 204; Laura A. White, *Robert Barnwell Rhett: Father of Secession* (1931; repr., Gloucester, Mass.: Peter Smith, 1965), 135–190; Eric H. Walther, *The Fire-Eaters* (Baton Rouge: Louisiana State University Press, 1992), 147–156; Robert Barnwell Rhett, Jr., to William Porcher Miles, April 7, 1858, January 29, 1860, March 28, 1860, April 17,

1860, William Porcher Miles Papers, Southern Historical Collection, University of North Carolina, Chapel Hill.

40. Constitution of the Confederate States, March 11, 1861, online at http://avalon.law.yale.edu/19th_century/csa_csa.asp (accessed December 2010); *Charleston Mercury* quoted in Majewski, *Modernizing a Slave Economy*,146.

14

The American Civil War, Emancipation, and Reconstruction on the World Stage

Edward L. Ayers

Americans demanded the world's attention during their Civil War and Reconstruction. Newspapers around the globe reported the latest news from the United States, as one vast battle followed another, as the largest system of slavery in the world crashed into pieces, as American democracy expanded to include people who had been enslaved only a few years before.[1]

Both the North and the South appealed to the global audience. Abraham Lincoln argued that his nation's Civil War "embraces more than the fate of these United States. It presents to the whole family of man, the question, whether a constitutional republic, or a democracy . . . can, or cannot, maintain its territorial integrity." The struggle, Lincoln said, was for "a vast future," a struggle to give all men "a fair chance in the race of life."[2]

Confederates claimed that they were also fighting for a cause of worldwide significance: self-determination. Playing down the centrality of slavery to their new nation, white Southerners built their case for independence on the right of free citizens to determine their own political future.[3]

People in other nations could see that the massive struggle in the United States embodied conflicts that had been appearing in different forms throughout the world. Defining nationhood, deciding the future of slavery, reinventing warfare for an industrial age, reconstructing a former slave society—all these played out in the American Civil War.

By no means a major power, the United States was nevertheless woven into the life of the world. The young nation touched, directly and indirectly, India and Egypt, Hawaii and Japan, Russia and Canada, Mexico and Cuba, the Caribbean and Brazil, Britain and France. The country was still very much an experiment in 1860, a representative government stretched over an enormous space, held together by law rather than by memory, religion, or monarch. The American Civil War, played out on the brightly lit stage of a new country, would be a drama of world history. How that experiment fared in its great crisis— regardless of what happened—would eventually matter to people everywhere.

More obviously than most nations, the United States was the product of global history. Created from European ideas, involvement in Atlantic trade, African slavery, conquest of land from American Natives and European powers, and massive migration from Europe, the United States took shape as the world watched. Long before the Civil War, the United States embodied the possibilities and contradictions of modern Western history.

Slavery was the first, most powerful, and most widespread kind of globalization in the first three centuries after Columbus. While colonies came and went, while economies boomed and crashed, slavery relentlessly grew—and nowhere more than in the United States. By the middle of the nineteenth century, the slave South had assumed a central role on the world stage. Cotton emerged as the great global commodity, driving factories in the most advanced economies of the world. The slaves of the South were worth more than all the railroads and factories of the North and South combined; slavery was good business and shrewd investment.

While most other slave societies in the hemisphere gradually moved toward freedom, the American South moved toward the permanence of slavery. Southerners and their Northern allies, eager to expand, led the United States in a war to seize large parts of Mexico and looked hungrily upon the Caribbean and Central America. Of all the slave powers—including the giants of Brazil and Cuba, which continued to import slaves legally long after the United States—only the South and its Confederacy fought a war to maintain bondage.[4]

Ideas of justice circulated in global intercourse just as commodities did, and those ideas made the American South increasingly anomalous as a modern society built on slavery. Demands for universal freedom came into conflict with ancient traditions of subordination. European nations, frightened by revolt in Saint Domingue (Haiti) and elsewhere and confident of their empires' ability to prosper without slavery, dismantled slavery in their colonies of the Western Hemisphere while Russia dismantled serfdom.

Black and white abolitionists in the American North, though a tiny despised minority, worked with British allies to fight the acceptance of slavery in the United States. A vision of the South as backward, cruel, and power-hungry gained credence in many places in the North and took political force in the Republican Party. The global economy of commodities and ideology, demanding cotton while attacking slavery. put enormous and contradictory strains on the young American nation.[5]

Meanwhile, a new urge to define national identity flowed through the Western world in the first half of the nineteenth century. That determination took quite different forms. While some people still spoke of the universal dreams of the French and American revolutions, of inalienable attributes of humankind, others spoke of historical grievance, ethnic unity, and economic self-interest. Many longed for new nations built around bonds of heritage, imagined and real.[6]

White Southerners, while building their case for secession with the language of constitutions and rights, presented themselves as a people profoundly different from white Northerners. They sought sanction for secession in the recent histories of Italy, Poland, Mexico, and Greece, where rebels rose up against central powers to declare their suppressed nationhood, where native elites led a "natural, necessary protest and revolt" against a "crushing, killing union with another nationality and form of society."[7]

As the South threatened to secede, the Republicans, a regional party themselves, emphasized the importance of union for its own sake, the necessity of maintaining the integrity of a nation created by legal compact. It fell to the United States, the Republicans said, to show that large democracies could survive internal struggles and play a role in world affairs alongside monarchies and aristocracies.[8]

Once it became clear that war would come, the North and the South seized on the latest war-making strategies and technologies. From the outset, both sides innovated at a rapid pace and imported ideas from abroad. Railroads and telegraphs extended supply lines, sped troop reinforcements, and permitted the mobilization of vast armies. Observers from Europe and other nations watched carefully to see how the Americans would use these new possibilities. The results were mixed. Ironclad ships, hurriedly constructed, made a difference in some Southern ports and rivers, but were not seaworthy enough to play the role some had envisioned for them. Submarines and balloons proved disappointments, unable to deliver significant advantages. Military leaders, rather than being subordinated by anonymous machinery, as some expected, actually became more important than before, their decisions amplified by the scale of their armies and the speed of communication and transport.[9]

The scale and drama of the Civil War that ravaged America for four years, across an area larger than the European continent, fascinated and appalled a jaded world. A proportion of the population equal to five million people today died, and the South suffered casualties at a rate equal to those who would be decimated in Europe's mechanized wars of the twentieth century.

The size, innovation, and destructiveness of the American Civil War have led some, looking back, to describe it as the first total war, the first truly modern war. Despite new technologies and strategies, however, much of the Civil War remained old-fashioned. The armies in the American Civil War still moved vast distances on foot or with animals. The food soldiers ate and the medical care they received showed little advance over previous generations of armies. The military history of the Civil War grew incrementally from world history and offered incremental changes to what would follow. Although, late in the war, continuous campaigning and extensive earthen entrenchments foreshadowed World War I, Europeans did not grasp the deadly lesson of the American Civil War: combining the tactics of Napoleon with rapid-fire weapons and trenches would culminate in horrors unanticipated at Shiloh and Antietam.[10]

Diplomacy proved challenging for all sides in the American crisis. The fragile balance of power in Europe and in the empires centered there limited the range of movement of even the most powerful nations. The Confederacy's diplomatic strategy depended on gaining recognition from Great Britain and France, using cotton as a sort of blackmail, but European manufacturers had stockpiled large supplies of cotton in anticipation of the American war. British cartoonists, sympathetic to the Confederacy, ridiculed Abraham Lincoln at every opportunity, portraying him as an inept bumpkin—until his assassination, when Lincoln suddenly became sainted. Overall, the North benefited from the inaction of the British and the French, who could have changed the outcome and consequences of the war by their involvement.[11]

Inside the United States, the change unleashed by the war was as profound as it was unexpected. Even those who hated slavery had not believed in 1861 that generations of captivity could be ended overnight and former slaves and former slaveholders left to live together. The role of slavery in sustaining the Confederacy through humbling victories over the Union created the conditions in which Abraham Lincoln felt driven and empowered to issue the Emancipation Proclamation. The Union, briefly and precariously balanced between despair and hope, between defeat and victory, was willing in 1862 to accept that bold decision as a strategy of war and to enlist volunteers from among black Americans.[12]

The nearly 200,000 African Americans who came into the war as soldiers and sailors for the Union transformed the struggle. The addition of those men, greater in number than all the forces at Gettysburg, allowed the Union to build its advantage in manpower without pushing reluctant Northern whites into the draft. The enlistment of African Americans in the struggle for their own freedom ennobled the Union cause and promised to set a new global standard for the empowerment of formerly enslaved people. The world paid admiring attention to the brave and disciplined black troops in blue uniforms.[13]

The destruction of American slavery, a growing system of bondage of nearly four million people in one of the world's most powerful economies and most dynamic nation-states, was a consequence of world importance. Nowhere else besides Haiti did slavery end so suddenly, so completely, and with so little compensation for former slaveholders.[14] Had the United States failed to end slavery in the 1860s, the world would have felt the difference. An independent Confederate States of America would certainly have put its enslaved population to effective use in coal mines, steel mills, and railroad building, since industrial slavery had been employed before secession and became more common during wartime. Though such a Confederacy might have found itself stigmatized, its survival would have meant the evolution of slavery into a new world of industrialization. The triumph of a major autonomous state built around slavery would have set a devastating example for the rest of the world, an encouragement to forces of reaction. It would have marked the repudiation of much that was liberating in Western thought and practice over the preceding two hundred years.[15]

Driven by the exigencies of war, Northern ideals of color-blind freedom and justice, so often latent and suppressed, suddenly if briefly bloomed in the mid-1860s. The radical Republicans sought to create a black male American freedom on the same basis as white male American freedom: property, citizenship, dignity, and equality before the law. They launched a bold Reconstruction to make those ideals a reality, their effort far surpassing those of emancipation anywhere else in the world. The white South resisted with vicious vehemence, however, and the Republicans, always ambivalent about black autonomy and eager to maintain their partisan power, lost heart after a decade of bitter, violent, and costly struggle in Reconstruction. Northern Democrats, opposing Reconstruction from the outset, hastened and celebrated its passing.[16]

If former slaves had been permitted to sustain the enduring political power they tried to build, if they had gone before juries and judges with a chance of fair treatment, if they had been granted homesteads to serve as a first step toward economic freedom, then Reconstruction could be hailed as a turning point in world history equal to any revolution. Those things did not happen, however.

The white South claimed the mantle of victim, of a people forced to endure an unjust and unnatural subordination. They won international sympathy for generations to follow through films such as *Birth of a Nation* and *Gone With the Wind*, which viewed events through the eyes of sympathetic white Southerners. Reconstruction came to be seen around the world not as the culmination of freedom but as a mistake, a story of the dangers of unrealistic expectations and failed social engineering. Though former slaves in the American South quietly made more progress in landholding and general prosperity than former slaves elsewhere, the public failures of Reconstruction obscured the progress black Southerners wrenched from the postwar decades.[17]

When the South lost its global monopoly of cotton production during the Civil War, governments, agents, and merchants around the world responded quickly to take the South's place and to build an efficient global machinery to supply an ever-growing demand in the world market. As a result, generations of black and white sharecroppers would compete with Indian, Brazilian, and Egyptian counterparts in a glutted market in which hard work often brought impoverishment. The South adapted its economy after the war as well. By the 1880s, the South's rates of urban growth, manufacturing, and population movement kept pace with the North—a remarkable shift for only twenty years after losing slavery and the Civil War—but black Southerners were excluded from much of the new prosperity.[18]

The destruction of slavery, a major moral accomplishment of the U.S. Army, of Abraham Lincoln, and of the enslaved people themselves, would be overshadowed by the injustice and poverty that followed in the rapidly changing South, a mockery of American claims of moral leadership in the world. Black Southerners would struggle, largely on their own, for the next one hundred years. Their status, bound in an ever-tightening segregation, would stand as a rebuke to the United States in world opinion. The postwar South and its new system of segregation, in fact, became an explicit model for South Africa. That country created apartheid as it, like the American South, developed a more urban and industrial economy around racial subordination.

Some people around the world were surprised that the United States did not use its enormous armies after the Civil War to seize Mexico from the French, Canada from the English, or Cuba from the Spanish. Conflict among the great powers on the European Continent certainly opened an opportunity, and the United States had expanded relentlessly and opportunistically throughout its history. Few Americans, though, had the stomach for new adventures in the wake of the Civil War. The fighting against the American Indians on the Great Plains proved warfare enough for most white Americans in the 1870s and 1880s.[19]

The United States focused its postwar energies instead on commerce. Consolidated under Northern control, the nation's economy proved more formidable than ever before. The United States, its economic might growing with each passing year, its railroad network and financial systems consolidated, its cities and towns booming, its population surging westward, its mines turning out massive amounts of coal and precious minerals, its farms remarkably productive, and its corporations adopting new means of expansion and administration, became a force throughout the world. American engineers oversaw projects in Asia, Africa, and Latin America. American investors bought stock in railroads, factories, and mines around the globe. American companies came to dominate the economies of nations in Latin America.[20]

Americans became famous as rich, energetic, and somewhat reckless players amid the complexity of the world. As the Civil War generation aged, younger men looked with longing on possible territorial acquisitions in their own hemisphere and farther afield. They talked openly of proving themselves, as their fathers and grandfathers had, on the battlefield. Some welcomed the fight against the Spanish and the Filipinos as a test of American manhood and nationalism. The generation that came of age in 1900 built monuments to the heroes of the Civil War but seldom paused to listen to their stories of war's horror and costs.

The American Civil War has carried a different meaning for every generation of Americans. In the 1920s and 1930s leading historians in a largely isolationist United States considered the Civil War a terrible mistake, the product of a "blundering generation." After the triumph of World War II and in the glow of the Cold War's end, leading historians interpreted the Civil War as a chapter in the relentless destruction of slavery and the spread of democracy by the forces of modernization over the forces of reaction. Recently, living through more confusing times, some historians have begun to question straightforward stories of the war, emphasizing its contradictory meanings, unfulfilled promises, and unintended outcomes.[21]

The story of the American Civil War changes as world history lurches in unanticipated directions and as people ask different questions of the past. Things that once seemed settled now seem less so. The massive ranks, fortified trenches, heavy machinery, and broadened targets of the American Civil War once seemed to mark a step toward the culmination of "total" war. But the wars of the twenty-first century, often fought without formal battles, are proving relentless and boundless, "total," in ways the disciplined armies of the Union and Confederacy never imagined.[22] Nations continue to come apart over ancient grievances and modern geopolitics, the example of the United States notwithstanding. Coerced labor did not end in the nineteenth century, but instead has mutated and adapted to changes in the global economy. "A fair chance in the race of life" has yet to arrive for much of the world.

The great American trial of war, emancipation, and Reconstruction mattered to the world. It embodied struggles that would confront people on every continent, and it accelerated the emergence of a new global power. The American crisis, it was true, might have altered the course of world history more dramatically, in ways both worse and better, than what actually transpired. The war could have brought forth a powerful and independent Confederacy based on slavery, or it could have established with its Reconstruction a new global standard of justice for people who had been enslaved. As it was, the events of the 1860s and 1870s in the United States proved momentous for generations to follow around the world.

NOTES

1. For other portrayals of the Civil War in international context, see David M. Potter, "Civil War," in *The Comparative Approach to American History*, ed. C. Vann Woodward (New York: Basic Books, 1968), 135–145; Carl N. Degler, "One Among Many: The Civil War in Comparative Perspective," 29th Annual Robert Fortenbaugh Memorial Lecture (Gettysburg: Gettysburg College, 1990); Robert E. May, ed., *The Union, the Confederacy, and the Atlantic Rim* (West Lafayette, Ind.: Purdue University Press, 1995); Peter Kolchin, *A Sphinx on the American Land: The Nineteenth-Century South in Comparative Perspective* (Baton Rouge: Louisiana State University Press, 2003).

My view of the workings of world history has been influenced by C. A. Bayly, *The Birth of the Modern World, 1780–1914: Global Connections and Comparisons* (Malden, Mass.: Blackwell, 2004). Bayly emphasizes that "in the nineteenth century, nation-states and contending territorial empires took on sharper lineaments and became more antagonistic to each other at the very same time as the similarities, connections, and linkages between them proliferated" (2). By showing the "complex interaction between political organization, political ideas, and economic activity," Bayly avoids the teleological models of modernization, nationalism, and liberalism that have dominated our understanding of the American Civil War.

2. Lincoln quoted in James M. McPherson, *Abraham Lincoln and the Second American Revolution* (New York: Oxford University Press, 1992), 28.

3. The seminal work is Drew Gilpin Faust, *The Creation of Confederate Nationalism: Ideology and Identity in the Civil War South* (Baton Rouge: Louisiana State University Press, 1988). For an excellent synthesis of the large literature on this topic, see Anne Sarah Rubin, *A Shattered Nation: The Rise and Fall of the Confederacy, 1861–1868* (Chapel Hill: University of North Carolina Press, 2005).

4. For a useful overview, see Robert W. Fogel, *Without Consent or Contract: The Rise and Fall of American Slavery* (New York: W. W. Norton, 1989).

5. David Brion Davis, *Slavery and Human Progress* (New York: Oxford University Press, 1984); Davis, *The Problem of Slavery in the Age of Revolution, 1770–1823* (Ithaca, N.Y.: Cornell University Press, 1975); Davis, *Inhuman Bondage: The Rise and Fall of Slavery in the New World* (New York: Oxford University Press, 2006).

6. For helpful overviews of the global situation, see Steven Hahn, "Class and State in Postemancipation Societies: Southern Planters in Comparative Perspective," *American Historical Review* 95 (February 1990): 75–99, and Hahn, *A Nation Beneath Our Feet: Black Political Struggles in the Rural South from Slavery to the Great Migration* (Cambridge, Mass.: Harvard University Press, 2003).

7. Quoted in Faust, *Creation of Confederate Nationalism*, 13.

8. There is a large literature on this subject, not surprisingly. A useful recent treatment is Susan-Mary Grant, *North Over South: Northern Nationalism and American Identity in the Antebellum Era* (Lawrence: University Press of Kansas, 2000). Peter Kolchin also offers penetrating comments on nationalism in *Sphinx on the American Land*, 89–92.

9. Brian Holden Reid, *The American Civil War and the Wars of the Industrial Revolution* (London: Cassell, 1999), 211–213; John E. Clark, Jr., *Railroads in the Civil War: The Impact of Management on Victory and Defeat* (Baton Rouge: Louisiana State University Press, 2001); Robert G. Angevine, *The Railroad and the State: War, Politics, and Technology in Nineteenth-Century America* (Stanford: Stanford University Press, 2004).

10. For a range of interesting essays on this subject, see Stig Forster and Jorg Nagler, eds., *On the Road to Total War: The American Civil War and the German Wars of Unification, 1861–1871* (Cambridge: The German Historical Institute and Cambridge University Press, 1997).

11. See D. P. Crook, *The North, the South, and the Powers, 1861–1865* (New York: John Wiley and Sons, 1974); R. J. M. Blackett, *Divided Hearts: Britain and the American Civil War* (Baton Rouge: Louisiana State University Press, 2001); James M. McPherson, *Crossroads of Freedom: Antietam* (New York: Oxford University Press, 2002); May, *Union, the Confederacy, and the Atlantic Rim;* and Charles M. Hubbard, *The Burden of Confederate Diplomacy* (Knoxville: University of Tennessee Press, 1998).

12. See Allen C. Guelzo, *Lincoln's Emancipation Proclamation: The End of Slavery in America* (New York: Simon and Schuster, 2004).

13. See Joseph T. Glatthaar, *Forged in Battle: The Civil War Alliance of Black Soldiers and White Officers* (New York: Free Press, 1990).

14. See Leon Litwack, *Been in the Storm So Long: The Aftermath of Slavery* (New York: Vintage, 1979), and the major documentary collection edited by Ira Berlin, Leslie S. Rowland, and their colleagues, sampled in *Free At Last: A Documentary History of Slavery, Freedom, and the Civil War* (New York: The New Press, 1992).

15. See Davis, *Slavery and Human Progress*, for a sweeping perspective on this issue.

16. The classic history is Eric Foner, *Reconstruction: America's Unfinished Revolution, 1863–1877* (New York: Harper and Row, 1988). I have offered some thoughts on Reconstruction's legacy in "Exporting Reconstruction" in my *What Caused the*

Civil War? Reflections on the South and Southern History (New York: W. W. Norton, 2005).

17. On the legacy of Reconstruction, see David W. Blight, *Race and Reunion The Civil War in American Memory* (Cambridge, Mass: Harvard University Press, 2001).

18. For a fascinating essay on the South's loss of the cotton monopoly, see Sven Beckert, "Emancipation and Empire: Reconstructing the Worldwide Web of Cotton Production in the Age of the American Civil War," *American Historical Review* 109 (December 2004): 1405–1438. On South Africa, see John W. Cell, *The Highest Stage of White Supremacy: The Origins of Segregation in South Africa and the American South* (Cambridge: Cambridge University Press, 1982), and George Fredrickson, *White Supremacy: A Comparative Study in American and South African History* (New York: Oxford University Press, 1981).

19. See the discussion in the essays by Robert E. May and James M. McPherson in May, *Union, the Confederacy, and the Atlantic Rim.*

20. For the larger context, see Eric J. Hobsbawm, *The Age of Empire, 1875–1914* (New York: Pantheon, 1987), and Bayly, *Birth of the Modern World.*

21. I have described this literature and offered some thoughts on it in the essay "Worrying About the Civil War" in my *What Caused the Civil War?*

22. Reid, *American Civil War,* 213.

Afterword

Michael O'Brien

Modernity is old, though how old is obscure. In 1860 Jacob Burckhardt claimed that it was born in Italy during the fourteenth century, when "the *subjective* . . . asserted itself [and] man became a spiritual *individual*." A few intellectual historians think that it began in the early seventeenth century, perhaps most evidently in the dense pages of Thomas Hobbes, where many medieval beliefs were demolished and "the sheer multiplicity of human moral opinions" were turbulently pondered with that skepticism that earlier Michel Montaigne had more calmly displayed. Others prefer the late seventeenth century, when there was a sharper quarrel between ancient and modern knowledge, and it became important to contradistinguish Lucretius and Isaac Newton, by way of describing how modern dwarves were standing on the shoulders of ancient giants.[1] Social and economic historians interested in cities, markets, and domesticity lean towards the middle to late eighteenth century for the break, though historians of the Enlightenment like that moment, too. A diehard few say that nothing decisive happened until the mid-nineteenth century, when Charles Darwin and Karl Marx spoke, when a sense of movement and crisis had become habitual and even desirable. Hence, give or take about four hundred years bartered between friends and enemies, modernity is old—or old enough.

The modern sensibility has been haunted by *before* and *after*. It has especially liked revolutions, which might be used as turning points— the Scientific Revolution, the Industrial Revolution, the American

Revolution, the French Revolution. So, *before* they believed the earth was the center of the universe; *after* they discovered it revolved around the sun. *Before* they lived immemorial lives on farms; *after* they sweated at factory benches and lived wandering urban lives on asphalt roads. *Before* they trusted in kings and God; *after* they believed in democracy and man. These dramas of old and new simplified narrative. Newton felt an apple bounce off his head, Arkwright invented the spinning frame, Jefferson scratched the word *inalienable*, Robespierre rose to speak, Darwin walked on the Galapagos—these were nicely bounded stories, tidily explaining *before* and *after*. The stories acquired labels: the Asiatic mode of production, feudalism, Renaissance, capitalism, freedom, premodern, postmodern, *gemeinschaft*, and *gesellschaft*.

To be sure, there have been awkward people, unconvinced about labels and unsure that much turned at the turning points. Believers in the Jewish, Christian, and Islamic God curiously declined to die away and still insist that burning bushes on Mount Sinai long ago matter to a Los Angeles suburb. Alexis de Tocqueville perversely suggested that the fall of the Bastille changed little in French lives. Thomas Kuhn ingeniously questioned whether science was more than a series of ultimately indemonstrable paradigms, convincing only for the nonce.[2] Everyone and his mother (perhaps even Condorcet's mother) have doubted the reality of progress, because it did not sit with their religion or their data sets or the stench of rotting Cambodian flesh. Still, even skeptics have habitually accepted the story line of transition from ancient, to medieval, to modern; they just said it happened here not there, slowly not quickly, incompletely not utterly. As Edmund Burke once said about matters "incapable of exact definition": "Though no man can draw a stroke between the confines of day and night, yet light and darkness are upon the whole tolerably distinguishable."[3] True enough, though it is hard to know whether as moderns we are in the light or the dark, when one contemplates conservatives who think modernity a disaster and tradition a blessing, progressives who think modernity a blunder and greater change a blessing, and liberals who mostly like what we have but are vague about the location of the light switch.

These are what the philosophers call metanarratives, very large stories, preferably told with words and phrases possessed of Teutonic capital letters— the Human Condition, the Old Testament, Romanticism, the Founding Fathers. The postmodernists say we live in a time of incredulity about metanarratives, but we probably do not, because it is hard to let go of the sense that the world is intelligible.[4] Still, there is an itching discomfort about seeing a long sweep in history, an unease that tends to express itself in a selective decoupling of the great stories and the small stories. Once everything fitted together, or so *they* said—the people for whom it came to seem that everything did not fit together.

Once there had been patterns, everything had a place in the order of things, there was a "chain of being." So everything in a single place implied everything everywhere else; a "little postage stamp of native soil" in Mississippi, as described by William Faulkner, might encompass humanity.[5] Now we tell smaller stories, while implying that something larger is implied, something seldom articulated. Connections grow shadowy. The stabbing finger of certainty has been replaced by the Gallic shrug, the raised eyebrow, the diffident frown or smile.

In these metanarratives, the American South has had its place. Of course, everywhere *was* deemed to have a place on the continuum of transformation, whether it was La Vendée (behind the times because opposed to the French Revolution), Brussels (up with the times for industrializing early), London (leading the times because the metropolis of a great modern empire), or Los Angeles (ahead of the times for being home to Hollywood and being choked with traffic). These placings were unstable, depending on how the transition was defined and who was the definer, and the historical reputation of societies has slid up and down the scale, as intellectual trends have varied or political economies fluctuated. The South has slid around more than most. In the eighteenth century, many Americans and western Europeans believed the English plantation societies below the Chesapeake to be in the vanguard of politics and economics; in the late nineteenth century and for nearly a hundred years to follow, most presumed that the South was retrograde, because failing to keep up with industrialization and urbanization; today, the scholarly consensus would probably be that the southeastern states of the United States are in the middle of the pack, as far as modernity goes, perhaps behind Shanghai and Abu Dhabi, presumably ahead of Istanbul and Detroit, probably on a par with New Delhi and São Paulo. Often cold economic judgments about per capita incomes, these not infrequently have also been moral judgments, if it was presumed (as the Massachusetts politician and abolitionist Charles Sumner did presume) that economics and virtue were interrelated and that material progress was a predicate for moral progress—or even that moral progress (as the Quakers presumed) was a predicate for material progress.

As the essays in this book frequently remind us, these have been comparative judgments, explicit or implicit. Retrograde or progressive compared to what? Was South Carolina in 1750 to be judged by the standards of Bath, Barbados, or (as Voltaire half-whimsically might have preferred) Canton? Was Alabama in 1900 to be coupled with Massachusetts unfavorably, the Transvaal equivalently, or Haiti favorably? Was the South in 1950 only answerable to American standards, because nationality was all that mattered, or should it have been considered as a region, comparable to other regions, whether American (the Midwest) or not (Andalusia)? Or should it have been compared to other staple-crop plantation economies with oil, like Venezuela? And, if the last was the right intellectual strategy, considering that not all parts of the South had plantations and fewer had oil, did it make sense to compare the South, in toto, with anything? Was it not more coherent to disaggregate the region and compare, say, Louisiana with Cuba, because both grew sugar?

The business of sliding the South up and down has required a negotiation with what the South has come to define as its significant moments of *before* and *after*. For a Southerner before 1861, this meant the settlement in Jamestown and the American Revolution; by 1880, she had to add the Civil War and perhaps Reconstruction; in 1980, the civil rights movement. So, for us, there are four moments which need adjustment, if you wish to concoct a metanarrative of Southern history. The historian is free to deny sharp discontinuity, to say that C. Vann Woodward was wrong to denounce what he called "continuitarianism" and instead opt for the Tocquevillean analysis, which elides the *ancien régime* and the *nouvelle régime*, but the historian needs to explain why this is a plausible intellectual strategy.[6]

All these are difficult matters, intelligently debated in the essays of this book and not susceptible of a definitive conclusion. One thing is clear, at least to me. There is what many antebellum Southerners thought about themselves, and there is what modern scholars think now about antebellum Southerners. The latter must take account of the former, but historicism does believe, if shyly, that historical actors can misunderstand themselves or grasp only fragments of their reality, more accessible to the leisured consideration of historians, who can trawl through diaries, collate census data, and even utilize theoretical perspectives and words unavailable to the once living, now dead. This ill-fitting is no reproach to historians, since history is not a transcription but an interpretation, intended to serve what the historian imagines to be her times and his audience. Naturally, historians like to think that they close the gap between present and past, that the ill-fitting is kept to a minimum, that we add something but do not repress anything of significance. This is probably an illusion, but serviceable.

So, if a literate white male Southerner of 1850 were available for questioning and was asked about the issues debated in this book, what would he answer? (What she would have answered would be only subtly different.) And, if a modern historian were available, as he is, what would she claim the antebellum Southerner ought to have answered, if that Southerner was apprised of the historical evidence adduced by these essays? It might go roughly like this, with first the question, second the response from 1850, and third the response from now.

Are you modern?

1850: Yes.

2010: It depends what you mean by "modern"—certainly, the South has a variation of modernity.

Do you live in a progressive society?

1850: Yes.

2010: It depends what you mean by "progressive—but, probably so, upon the understanding that change and improvement are not identical and that there can be a mix of progress and retrogression.

How do you compare with the North?

1850: In some ways, better—a sounder social and democratic system, a purer religion, a more discriminating scholarship, less crime. But in others, worse—a lower standard of literacy, worse schools and colleges, an overdependence on outsiders for our wealth, a weak publishing industry.

2010: This is a comparison of limited usefulness.

Are there other societies, then, to which you bear comparison?

1850: Yes, though you need to know that the South is the best part of the United States, which is better than any European society, itself better than the degraded Catholics and mongrels of Latin America—as for Africa, it is barbaric, while Asia is an inert despotism.

2010: This is an interesting question—we are more advanced than other slave societies like Brazil, less urbanized than England, but more developed than France, Prussia, or Italy.

Is the South a nation?

1850: A few among us think it is becoming so, but I do not.

2010: Many of us think it is.

Are you an expansive people?

1850: Yes, God has given us all of the American continent.

2010: Yes, alas, because we will pay a heavy price for our greed.

Does slavery mean you are less modern, less progressive, or less likely to expand?

1850: Of course not.

2010: Of course not, unfortunately.

Will your world be better in a hundred years' time?

1850: Yes.

2010: Probably not.

Do you belong to a global economic order?

1850: I do not know what you mean.

2010: Yes.

Are you transnational?

1850: Say what?

2010: Probably so.

Postcolonial?

1850: Excuse me, ma'am?

2010: Intermittently

Imperial?

1850: Oh, yes.

2010: Oh, yes.

Several differences will be apparent, but three are striking. The first is that the Southerner of 1850 was more self-confident than we might think justified by his historical condition and was more sure of progress, superiority, and mastery. The second is that, superficially, he had a more restricted frame of cultural and theoretical reference. That is, he saw the South as in a lineal descent from European cultures, while transcending them, and would have found it fairly unintelligible to be asked to compare his society with other settler or colonial societies, let alone with "developing" countries. Third, obviously, he was oblivious of categories only later invented—postcolonialism, transnationalism, globalism. In truth, it is not that his frame was more restricted, just different. Certain questions, of little interest to many recent historians, he would have expected to be asked: How does the South compare to Periclean Athens? How does Southern slavery differ from the bondage of the ancient Israelites? How does original sin influence democracy? When will Caucasians inherit the earth?[7] Most pertinently, he would be astonished that his interviewer would find it of value to have other interviews, with the planter's wife, his slave, and the Irish navvy digging a canal in the next county. (Come to think of it, the planter would be surprised to be interviewed at all, since the genre did not exist in 1850.)

One implication of the view from 2010 is that sharp discontinuity in Southern history seems to be mistrusted. In such skepticism, this volume of essays conforms to a wider trend. The historians of the colonial period are less impressed with 1607 and Jamestown; more interested in other colonial regimes. earlier (Spanish, French) and later (Dutch); more struck with the cross-fertilizations of European and Indian cultures; a little bored with the idea that arriving at 1776 is what most matters. As is shown here, the historians of the nineteenth century see the roots of the New South greatly evident in the Old South, not only in the sense that urban and industrial modernity can be seen before 1861, but that the unfree labor relations of 1850 and 1900 are not as different as William Lloyd Garrison and Alexander Stephens imagined and hoped. The historians of race relations since the 1870s have flattened out the old dramatic narrative—bewildering changes in the 1880s and 1890s, a long period of rigid stasis, the uplifting implosion of segregation in the 1950s and 1960s, a new moral order later—and prefer to see more change earlier, less change later, mixed and inconclusive results insistently.

No doubt, some of this stance arises from our muddled times. The last half century, for Americans, has not been remarkable for discontinuities of dramatic historical moment. But I think that the explanation runs deeper than muddled times. Nothing is more striking in these essays, as in recent American historiography, than their interest in the global, the transnational, and the comparative. The consequences of this interest are many and need further discussion, but one effect seldom noticed is that the attempt to bring so many perspectives, so many places, so many cultures, so many events into a conversation has the effect of making any one perspective, place, culture, or event less singular and dramatic. Look at a photograph of a single face (say, that of John C. Calhoun), enlarge it, look closely at the nose, the eyebrows, the ears—ears always look odd, don't they? Do this, and a face cannot fail to look peculiar, singular, exceptional. That is what Southern historians used to do when they wrote Southern history. Place a second face next to the first (say, Wendell Phillips), and it is, if anything, easier to see peculiarity. But add a third (William Gladstone), a fourth (Mohatma Gandhi), a fifth (Julius Nyrere), a sixth (Simone

Bolivar), a seventh (Mary Wollstonecraft), an eighth (Olaudah Equiano), then a hundred more from the Americas, then a thousand more from Asia and Africa, and no face looks odd at all.

Still, it helps to makes a few distinctions. Some terms deployed in this book ("global," "transnational," "comparative") need to be distinguished. If one takes the definition of "global history" ventured by Christopher Bayly, one means that "historical trends and sequences of events, which have been treated separately in regional or national histories, can be brought together," and that there was an "interconnectedness and interdependence of political and social changes across the world well before the supposed onset of the contemporary phase of 'globalization' after 1945."[8] This insists that the shifting experiences of Bengali peasants, Southern slaves, and Frankfurt bankers, being interconnected, had consequences for each other; hence, the historian of American slavery is inadequately informed if she knows nothing of Bengali peasants and Frankfurt bankers. The idea of the "transnational" sits fairly comfortably beside "global," not least by keeping the "regional" or "national" at arm's length. Historians of transnationalism are stringently insistent, however, that there are movements and patterns of people, goods, and ideas which are little explicable by the boundaries of the nation-state, though these movements might be (or might not be) influenced by state power, when, where, and if that power has existed as a compulsion, a suggestion, or a gesture. As a method of analysis, however, comparative history works differently. Although it is not formally opposed to the intellectual logics of the global and transnational historian, it prefers to delineate reasonably stable structures that might usefully be compared, in order to denote differences and similarities. The units of analysis should be neither so different nor so similar that comparison is pointless, just middlingly analogous. In principle, these units might be almost anything, if they have occurred historically—marriage patterns, systems of corporate law, visions of the Apocalypse—but, in practice, comparative historians drawn to Southern history have most liked to compare social formations (Russian serfdom and Southern slavery, Southern segregation and South African apartheid) and the tensions between nationalism and regionalism (the American Civil War, the Risorgimento).[9] The upshot is that the strategies of global/transnational historians and comparative historians widely differ. The former like to take what seem to be still points ("the United States," "Mexico," "Poland"), set them in motion, and observe whether motion forms patterns. The latter take motion and freeze it.

While engaged with the global and transnational, the intellectual preferences displayed in this volume evidence a greater attraction for the comparative. In the Bayly manner, they are disposed to disaggregate regionalism, because several essayists stress that their part of the South does not map precisely onto other parts of the South. But the contributors are most interested in how Southern cities might compare to, for example, Prussian ones, but less interested in whether the Prussian economy influenced the Southern economy (which a global historian would examine) or what happened when Prussians appeared in Kentucky (which a transnational historian would notice). My guess is that this incomplete preference for the comparative over the global/transnational may be inevitable for any set of American historians who are sensitive to the recent expansion of interest in what is non-American, but who retain a stake in keeping the South as a more-or-less discrete subject matter. This is so because a thoroughgoing global or transnational history, which happened to take an interest in the Old South, would only be interested in a few Southern things, some of the time. Slavery and the slave trade, yes, but not Appalachian homesteads. Irish migrants in Savannah, yes, but not theologians in Louisville. The defect of global history's virtue is that it offers what Niall Ferguson has called "distance-annihilating synthesis."[10] That is, the global historian flies like an hawk or a CIA drone over the world's surface and mostly notices what is large or what moves. But much in history is small and keeps still, and is no less important for that.

One last thought, arising from what (to my eye) is the most original argument of this book. As several essayists and the introduction explain, the proposition that the Old South was a modern society has been gathering pace for some decades in sundry historical works, including my own.[11] Except for a few obtuse observers, not usually historians, no one claimed that the antebellum South lacked some elements of modernity. No modern society, after all, does lack for premodern elements, even now. Nineteenth-century Britain had the great metropolis of London and any number of factories and macadamized roads, but it also had Scottish crofters. The issue was whether modern elements in the South were determinative or marginal. For Eugene Genovese and Elizabeth Fox-Genovese, they were marginal. As the latter elegantly put it, the South was "in but not of the transatlantic capitalist world." That is, slavery might produce cotton to be exported to the quintessential engine of early industrial modernity, the Lancashire cotton mill, but the internal social relations and values of the South were little touched by this relationship and remained "precapitalist."[12] The external was modern, the internal premodern. For some of us who participated in this debate, it was a puzzle how this discordance was possible, and the debate sometimes felt like those arguments that once rent the early Christian world over the nature of the Trinity. Was God, Christ, and the Holy Spirit *homoousion* (of one essence) or *heteroousion* (of different essences)? Genovese was firmly of the *heteroousion* persuasion, upon the strict understanding that, if slavery was the God of the Southern world, Christ and the Holy Spirit did not matter much. In truth, everyone accepted the premise of *heteroousion*, and the argument was over whether the second and third members of the Trinity were less, as much, or more important.

It is my impression that this book moves us closer to *homoousion*. In part, this is because it does more with the second and third members of the Trinity, those elements of the Southern world that were not plantations—Southern cities, Native Americans, railroads, industry. In part, it is because several essayists make a strong case that slavery itself, for masters and slaves alike, was soaked in modernity. Thereby the gap between the internal and external is starkly reduced. The implications are, of course, troubling. One reason *heteroousion* was appealing was that, if you believe we live a modern world and that slavery was incompatible with modernity, then slavery could safely be considered as irretrievable. Whatever its shortcomings, modernity was supposed to have driven a stake through slavery's heart—it was over—it would never come back. But, to quote from essays in this volume, if slaves were "commercial savvy," if slave traders were "merchants of the first order," if "the fastest-growing slaveholding regions of the South were also the fastest-growing railroad regions," if "in parts of the upper South, the plantation economy actually bolstered industrial slavery and capitalist development," and if slavery "was often employed by those reaching toward modernity," do we moderns not have a potential problem?

NOTES

1. Jacob Burckhardt, *The Civilization of the Renaissance in Italy*, 2 vols. (1860; repr., New York: Harper & Row, 1958), 1:143; Richard Tuck, *Hobbes* (Oxford: Oxford University Press, 1989), 115; on *la querelle des anciens et des modernes*, see Joseph M. Levine, *The Battle of the Books: History and Literature in the Augustan Age* (Ithaca, N.Y.: Cornell University Press, 1991).

2. Alexis de Tocqueville, *The Ancien Regime and the French Revolution*, trans. Stuart Gilbert (1856; repr., London: Collins, 1966); Thomas S. Kuhn, *The Structure of Scientific Revolutions*, 2d ed. (1962; repr., Chicago: University of Chicago Press, 1967).

3. Edmund Burke, "Thoughts on the Causes of the Present Discontents," in *The Works of Edmund Burke*, vol. 1 (Boston: Little, Brown, 1869), 477.

4. See Jean François Lyotard, *The Postmodern Condition: A Report on Knowledge* (Minneapolis: University of Minnesota Press, 1984).

5. James B. Meriwether and Michael Millgate, eds., *Lion in the Garden; Interviews with William Faulkner, 1926–1962* (New York: Random House, 1968), 255.

6. See C. Vann Woodward, *Thinking Back: The Perils of Writing History* (Baton Rouge: Louisiana State University Press, 1986), 59–79.

7. Some of these questions are, however, addressed in Elizabeth Fox-Genovese and Eugene D. Genovese, *The Mind of the Master Class: History and Faith in the Southern Slaveholders' Worldview* (Cambridge: Cambridge University Press, 2005), and

Elizabeth Fox-Genovese and Eugene D. Genovese, *Slavery in White and Black: Class and Race in the Southern Slaveholders' New World Order* (Cambridge: Cambridge University Press, 2008).

8. C. A. Bayly, *The Birth of the Modern World, 1780–1914: Global Connections and Comparisons* (Malden, Mass.: Blackwell, 2003), 1.

9. See Peter Kolchin, *Unfree Labor: American Slavery and Russian Serfdom* (Cambridge, Mass.: Harvard University Press, Belknap, 1987); George M. Fredrickson, *White Supremacy: A Comparative Study of American and South African History* (New York: Oxford University Press, 1981); Don H. Doyle, *Nations Divided: America, Italy, and the Southern Question* (Athens: University of Georgia Press, 2002); Enrico Dal Lago and Rick Halpern, eds., *The American South and the Italian Mezzogiorno: Essays in Comparative History* (New York: Palgrave, 2002). For a recent discussion, see Peter Kolchin, "The South and the World," *Journal of Southern History* 75 (August 2009): 565–580.

10. This is from Ferguson's blurb on the paperback edition of Bayly's book, *The Birth of the Modern World*.

11. "The long debate about whether the Old South was an anachronistic, seignorial society or a variant of modern capitalism is approaching a consensus on the latter": Anthony E. Kaye, "The Second Slavery; Modernity in the Nineteenth-Century South and the Atlantic World," *Journal of Southern History* 75 (August 2009): 628.

12. Elizabeth Fox-Genovese, *Within the Plantation Household: Black and White Women in the Old South* (Chapel Hill: University of North Carolina Press, 1988), 98; on "precapitalism," see Eugene D. Genovese and Elizabeth Fox-Genovese, *The Fruits of Merchant Capital: Slavery and Bourgeois Property in the Rise and Expansion of Capitalism* (New York: Oxford University Press, 1983).

Conclusion: The Future of the Old South

L. Diane Barnes, Brian Schoen, Frank Towers

What to make of the Old South in light of the current generation of scholarship? This question haunts the essays in this volume and the larger field of Southern history. Characterizations of the antebellum South as tradition-bound and provincial seem more open to question than in the past, whereas comparisons of the Old South to places beyond the North and considerations of its history in global dimensions fit more comfortably with the historical consciousness of today. In our time, the global interconnections of American life figure prominently as does the recognition that countries once viewed as "developing" or "third world" now claim markers of modernity that had formerly been reserved for the "developed" nations of the "first world." Further removed from the horrors of two massive world wars and freed from the reductionist tendencies prevalent during the Cold War, twenty-first-century historians are also less likely to embrace the stark dichotomies—liberalism vs. fascism, capitalism vs. communism, progressivism vs. traditionalism—that defined twentieth-century scholarship. At the same time, multiculturalism and revolutions in gender identity and family organization in the last decades of the twentieth century have, along with important historiographic developments, raised the possibility that the heterogeneity of the way we live now has resulted from a diversity of ways of living in the past.

Our polyglot understanding of a pluralistic past is reshaping the questions that define new Southern scholarship. In place of studies that asked if the Old South was an advancing society or in retreat, similar to the North or different, engaged with the world or closed off from it, historians now tend to ask how Southerners engaged modernity, what sectionalism meant to Americans, and in what ways did transnational flows of people, goods, and ideas cross into a South with less clearly defined boundaries than we previously thought. The essays in this volume allow the region to stand as a constituent element in America's future that sits alongside and interlinked with the North, the West, and the world. The people of the Old South voluntarily entangled themselves in the expansion of the market and the culture of capitalism; slavery was a flexible system of labor control adaptable to industrial settings; Southerners paid close attention to international events and many of them came from or traveled to the world outside slavery's borders.

Rather than the great exception to modern progress, the Old South might now be understood as one of several building blocks of American modernity. As the essays herein suggest, the Old South, considered as the sum of its diverse parts, modernized—albeit on terms unlike those of the North. Those terms made for critical differences between the sections, but they did not place the North necessarily ahead of the South on the road to the future. Going forward, perhaps, it is the trace of some, but by no means all, of America's future in the Old South rather than the region's embodiment of a doomed-to-die past that will be more intriguing to the historical imagination.[1]

Of course, searching for a definitive answer to broad historical questions is itself illusory, given the nature of the sources, which are neither transparent nor self-evident, and the diversity of opinion that is inherent to scholarly inquiry. Looking through wider and less monochromatic lenses, recent scholarship on Southern history expands the ground for historical inquiry and debate rather than fielding a rival argument designed to run over the same pathways covered by its predecessors. Remapping the antebellum South in this way enables us to see under-explored pathways and discover new topographic features previously difficult or impossible to detect because of the narrower questions asked. Immigrant manufacturers like William Tappey and free-black reformers like Maria Moore emerge as individuals worthy of study rather than remain ignored as exceptions to an unspoken rule. Conceiving of the Old South as a nonperipheral part of nineteenth-century modernity also allows us to understand well-known features of the region (cities, plantations, and Native Americans) in fresh ways and as shaped by, rather than set apart from, the complicated and increasingly global processes of the day. By reframing questions and using different historical tools, the slave states, as depicted in this volume, remain a distinct region, but not one that was exceptional to the main currents of American or world history.

To understand more about what this altered interpretive terrain says about the Old South, scholars might pursue several avenues of further research that draw on the global and the local and reconsider the South's influence on the nineteenth-century world. In light of the enhanced appreciation for the Old South's participation in global processes, historians will continue to benefit from comparative analysis, a method for studying Southern history that has done much to sharpen our understanding by drawing out similarities and differences between places.[2] Southerners—regardless of their race, gender, creed, or class—did precisely that; however, as Peter Kolchin reminds us, they had multiple points of reference, and to "generalize about the southerness of these southerners is indeed a Herculean task."[3] For example, examinations of Indian-white interaction might usefully be compared and contrasted with similar developments within Latin American nations and ever-expanding interracial European empires. In addition to continued comparisons within the Atlantic world, a heightened awareness of the significance of Asia—both in today's world and in nineteenth-century globalization—suggest great promise lies in broadening our comparative reference points to include the diverse societies of the Pacific rim.[4]

A related way of looking at the Old South is to place its history into what David Brion Davis calls the "broader view." Treating the conflicts of the slave South within global battles over slavery and freedom helps to lift the struggles fought on Old South plantations beyond the marginal subfield of southern history.[5] This perspective is expressed in new scholarship that sees slavery as a national problem, emancipation as a hemispheric struggle, and the Southern planters as "a part of the master class of the Americas."[6] Considering material modernity, the broader view makes us aware of how international developments, and Southerners' cognizance of them, shaped regional political economy, industrial slavery, and geopolitical calculations.[7] In addition, knowing that Southerners participated in intellectual, cultural, and religious trends that were transnational in nature permits us the opportunity to reintegrate regional history into a larger world history in a way that will help enlighten both.[8]

Another approach explores the changes of the nineteenth century through the lens of their interplay within the Old South. How did Southerners adapt to aspects of industrialism and accelerated international trade? What reception did Victorian culture find in the slave states? How did the rising tide of nationalism shape Southern politics—black, white, and Native American? Historians who have begun to ask these questions have found a diversity of industrial practices,[9] a thriving railroad network,[10] a vibrant middle class,[11] slaves in contact with resistance movements in Africa and elsewhere in the Americas,[12] and slaveholding politicians absorbed in Europe's revolutions.[13] There remains much work to do, however. For example, despite Harold Woodman's, Peter

Coclanis's, and David L. Carleton's models and appeals for more scholarship, we know comparatively little about how planters, factors, merchants, and farmers created and financed local, national, and international trade.[14] Answers to broader sets of questions like these will likely reconfigure how we understand the interrelationships formed within the South.

In this sense, an increased emphasis on the "big picture" should not displace the local studies, which have, quite often, offered the most interesting windows into Southern history. Instead, more consciously situating Southern farms, cities, and plantations within broader worlds (rather than defining them as outside of them) allows us to better explain the interconnectedness between town and country and between those localities and the world economy upon which their residence often depended. Advances in computer technology and digital history allow for precisely this type of approach, enabling us to better assemble and interpret information about specific localities—like the Valley of the Shadow Project has done for Augusta County, Virginia—but also, as David Eltis's slave database indicates, to track relationships and patterns across space and time.[15]

The recent historiographic emphasis on the Old South as modern and interconnected also begs a rethinking of other critical issues in U.S. history. In making the Old South one of several of modernity's nineteenth-century midwives, scholars necessarily destabilize the North and western Europe's familiar position as the forebearers of everything from middle-class families to big business. Such a perspective also recasts some well-known differences between the sections that factored into the Civil War's causes and outcome. How should historians who conceive of the Old South as sharing many of the same modernizing trends that swept the North explain the Civil War? Nothing in this volume disputes the fact that in 1861, the free states had more of many modern things that nations need to win wars. The North had more people who filled out a bigger wartime army; more factories that supplied that army with more and deadlier weapons; more trains, ships, and draft animals to transport all those troops and supplies to the front; more cities to house the people and the factories and to coordinate the traffic. All that "more" contributed to Union victory in the Civil War, and it is tempting to interpret that balance of resources as the product of a southern mindset opposed to the modern things that helped the North win. Without gainsaying these differences, other measures of modernity counterbalanced these aspects of Northern superiority. In short, as Edward Ayers has suggested elsewhere, "modernity was a shared catalyst between North and South, a shared medium, a necessary precondition for anything like the war that began in 1861."[16] As this volume indicates, by some important measures of antebellum political economy, Southerners counted themselves ahead of their sectional rivals rather than behind. Up to the election of Abraham Lincoln in 1860, American presidents had supported slavery's steady expansion westward, and Southern slaveholders had exercised much more power in the federal government than was proportional to their tiny share of the U.S. electorate. Southern slaveholders also made more money than most other Americans and used that superiority to create dependent relationships with their less-wealthy countrymen. An improved understanding of slavery's reach into the political economy of both sections—of the ways that Northern free-labor capitalism and Southern slave-labor capitalism were comingled—might better illuminate the revolutionary aspects of Northerners' decision to elect a Republican who vowed to put slavery on the road to extinction.[17] The tenacity with which white Southerners fought and died for the Confederacy strongly suggests that a modern nationalist sensibility had taken root in the South. Similarly, the modernizing impulses of the Old South help explain the centralizing policies of the Confederacy as more continuous with the prewar era and less a product of wartime emergency.[18] If the Southerners who helped start the Civil War and determine its outcome were as deeply enmeshed in modernity as their opponents, we must reassess a prevailing narrative that minimizes agency and views the crisis as the inevitable result of two diverging societies: a North that portended the future and a South clinging to the past.

Beyond the Civil War, the revised picture of the Old South suggests continuities stretching into the late nineteenth century that are harder to see if the Civil War is regarded as a fundamental break. Antebellum Southerners provided blueprints for the New South's railroads, towns, and mills as well as its "cosmopolitan-minded" racism and its mix of free and forced labor. And, as Steve Hahn has argued, black Southerners' efforts to carve out a separate space from whites can be understood as a thread of African-American politics stretching back to slavery rather than as a new agenda devised after the defeat of liberal, integrationist ideals in Reconstruction.[19]

In this vein, the future that had some, but not all, of its roots in the Old South reached beyond 1900. In the twentieth and twenty-first centuries commentators consistently juxtaposed the apparent end of Southern distinctiveness against the backdrop of the tradition-bound, parochial Old South. Removing that prop promotes a reevaluation of what accounts for the unique dynamics of Southern politics, culture, and racial conflicts. That reevaluation may provide a better appreciation for the national and global dimensions of what too often has been written off as a Southern problem from which the rest of the country, and the world, are exempt.

Perhaps the most discomforting perspective gained by looking at the Old South as a contributor to the present and future is the context it provides for twentieth- and twenty-first-century systems of human coercion that if not called slavery nonetheless approximate it. Slavery's legal abolition stands as perhaps the greatest human rights achievement in world history, but as Seymour Drescher notes in reference to Soviet gulag and Nazi slave labor, "the second quarter of the twentieth century . . . offered traumatic reminders that devastating forms of mass coerced labor could still reemerge anywhere." Recent estimates put the number of people "entrapped in servile conditions for part or all of their lives" at between ten and thirty million people worldwide. Fortunately, heads of state and their publics now oppose rather than sanction slavery and, unlike the world in 1800, those living free of slavery far outnumber those in bondage. Still, slavery, the most troubling aspect of the Old South, cannot easily be consigned to the forever-gone past. Because slavery was part of the future that the Old South's leaders sought to create, understanding its entanglement in making our modern present is vital to explaining abolition's victories won and battles ongoing.[20]

This brief foray into ways of thinking about the future of the Old South encourages a critique and reevaluation of what the antebellum slave states were and what they left in their wake. Yet whatever future the Old South has in academic writing, the idea of it as the exception to American modernity will likely endure in popular culture because the themes of Southern traditionalism and provincialism play an enduring, vital role in the ways Americans understand themselves a nation. Nonetheless, historians have a role to play in offering alternatives to received wisdom; and if this volume can help to refine collective understanding of the South's place in making the modern world, then it will have succeeded in its goal.

NOTES

1. Laura F. Edwards, "Southern History as U.S. History," *Journal of Southern History* 75 (August 2009): 563–564.

2. Recent examples of comparative historians' sophisticated approach to the Old South include Stanley L. Engerman, *Slavery, Emancipation and Freedom: Comparative Perspectives* (Baton Rouge: Louisiana State University Press, 2007); David Brion Davis, *Inhuman Bondage: The Rise and Fall of Slavery in the New World* (New York: Oxford University Press, 2006); Enrico Dal Lago, *Agrarian Elites: American Slaveholders and Southern Italian Landlords, 1815–1861* (Baton Rouge: Louisiana State University Press, 2005); Peter Kolchin, *A Sphinx on the American Land: The Nineteenth Century South in Comparative Perspective* (Baton Rouge: Louisiana State University Press, 2003); Don H. Doyle, *Nations Divided: America, Italy, and the Southern Question* (Athens: University of Georgia Press, 2002).

3. Kolchin, *Sphinx on the American Land*, 49.

4. Peter A. Coclanis, "Lee's Lieutenants: The American South in Global Context," paper delivered at The Historical Society, 2010 Conference, June 3, 2010,

Washington, D.C.: and "Atlantic World or Atlantic/World?" *William and Mary Quarterly* 63 (October 2006): 725–742.

5. David Brion Davis, "Looking at Slavery from Broader Perspectives," *American Historical Review* 105 (April 2000): 455.

6. Matthew Pratt Guterl, *American Mediterranean: Southern Slaveholders in an Age of Emancipation* (Cambridge, Mass.: Harvard University Press, 2008), 6 (quotation); Laura Jarnagin, *A Confluence of Transatlantic Networks: Elites, Capitalism, and Confederate Migration to Brazil* (Tuscaloosa: University of Alabama Press, 2008); Edward Rugemer, *The Problem of Emancipation: The Caribbean Roots of the American Civil War* (Baton Rouge: Louisiana State University Press, 2008); Gerald Horne, *The Deepest South: The United States, Brazil, and the African Slave Trade* (New York: New York University Press, 2007).

7. Peter A. Coclanis, "Globalization before Globalization: The South and the World to 1950," in *Globalization and the American South*, ed. James C. Cobb and William Stueck (Athens: University of Georgia Press, 2005), 25; Sven Beckert, "Emancipation and Empire: Reconstructing the Worldwide Web of Cotton Production in the Age of the American Civil War," *American Historical Review* 109 (December 2004): 1405–1438; Daniel Rood, "Industrial Epistemologies: A Social History of Knowledge in the Slaveholding Atlantic World, 1830–1860" (Ph.D. diss., University of California, Irvine, 2010).

8. For example, see Michael O'Brien, *Rethinking the South: Essays in Intellectual History* (Baltimore: Johns Hopkins University Press, 1988); and O'Brien, *Conjectures of Order: Intellectual Life in the American South, 1810–1860*, 2 vols. (Chapel Hill: University of North Carolina Press, 2004).

9. Angela Lakwete, *Inventing the Cotton Gin: Machine and Myth in Antebellum America* (Baltimore: Johns Hopkins University Press, 2003); Susanna Delfino and Michele Gillespie, eds., *Global Perspectives on Industrial Transformation in the American South* (Columbia: University of Missouri Press, 2005); Barbara Hahn, "Making Tobacco Bright: Institutions, Information, and Industrialization in the Creation of an Agricultural Commodity, 1617–1937" (Ph.D diss., University of North Carolina, Chapel Hill, 2006); L. Diane Barnes, *Artisan Workers in the Upper South: Petersburg, Virginia, 1820–1865* (Baton Rouge: Louisiana State University Press, 2008).

10. Aaron W. Marrs, *Railroads in the Old South: Pursuing Progress in a Slave Society* (Baltimore: Johns Hopkins University Press, 2009); William G. Thomas, *Railroads and the Making of America: A Digital History Project*, online at http://railroads.unl.edu/ (accessed October 2010); Kenneth W. Noe, *Southwest Virginia's Railroad: Modernization and the Sectional Crisis* (Urbana: University of Illinois Press, 1994).

11. Jonathan Daniel Wells, *The Origins of the Southern Middle Class, 1860–1861* (Chapel Hill: University of North Carolina Press, 2004), 8, 10; Jennifer R. Green, *Military Education and the Emerging Middle Class in the Old South* (New York: Cambridge University Press, 2008); Frank J. Byrne, *Becoming Bourgeois: Merchant Culture in the South, 1820–1865* (Lexington: University Press of Kentucky, 2006).

12. Sylviane A. Diouf, *Dreams of Africa in Alabama: The Slave Ship* Clotilda *and the Story of the Last Africans Brought to America* (New York: Oxford University Press, 2007); Eric Robert Taylor, *If We Must Die: Shipboard Insurrections in the Era of the Atlantic Slave Trade* (Baton Rouge: Louisiana State University Press, 2006); Alfred N. Hunt, *Haiti's*

Influence on Antebellum America: Slumbering Volcano in the Caribbean (Baton Rouge: Louisiana State University Press, 2006); Gwendolyn Midlo Hall, *Slavery and African Ethnicities in America: Restoring the Links* (Chapel Hill: University of North Carolina Press, 2005).

13. Timothy Mason Roberts, *Distant Revolutions: 1848 and the Challenge to American Exceptionalism* (Charlottesville: University of Virginia Press, 2009); Robert E. Bonner, *Mastering America: Southern Slaveholders and the Crisis of American Nationhood* (New York: Cambridge University Press, 2009); Paul D. H Quigley, "Patchwork Nation: Sources of Confederate Nationalism, 1848–1865" (Ph.D. diss., University of North Carolina, Chapel Hill, 2006).

14. Harold D. Woodman, *King Cotton and Its Retainers: Financing and Marketing the Cotton Crop of the South, 1800–1925* (1960; repr., Columbia: University of South Carolina, 1990), xv; David L. Carlton and Peter A. Coclanis, *The South, the Nation, and the World: Perspectives on Southern Economic Development* (Charlottesville: University of Virginia Press, 2003).

15. See the websites by Edward L. Ayers, *The Valley of the Shadow: Two Communities in the American Civil War*, http://valley.lib.virginia.edu/ (accessed October 2010); and David Eltis, *The Trans-Atlantic Slave Trade Database*, http://www.slavevoyages.org/tast/index.faces (accessed October 2010).

16. Edward Ayers, *What Caused the Civil War? Reflections on the South and Southern History* (New York: W. W. Norton, 2005), 142.

17. Don E. Fehrenbacher, *The Slaveholding Republic: An Account of the United States Government's Relations to Slavery* (New York: Oxford University Press, 2002); Leonard L. Richards, *The California Gold Rush and the Coming of the Civil War* (New York: Alfred A. Knopf, 2007); Leonard L. Richards, *The Slave Power: The Free North and Southern Domination, 1780–1860* (Baton Rouge: Louisiana State University Press, 2000); David L. Lightner, *Slavery and the Commerce Power: How the Struggle Against the Interstate Slave Trade Led to the Civil War* (New Haven, Conn.: Yale University Press, 2006); Robin L. Einhorn, *American Taxation, American Slavery* (Chicago: University of Chicago Press, 2006); James L. Huston, *Calculating the Value of the Union: Slavery, Property Rights, and the Economic Origins of the Civil War* (Chapel Hill: University of North Carolina Press, 2003).

18. Robert E. Bonner, "Proslavery Extremism Goes to War: The Counterrevolutionary Confederacy and Reactionary Militarism," *Modern Intellectual History* 6:2 (2009): 261–285; John Majewski, *Modernizing a Slave Economy: The Economic Vision of the Confederate Nation* (Chapel Hill: University of North Carolina Press, 2009); Harold S. Wilson, *Confederate Industry: Manufacturers and Quartermasters in the Civil War* (Jackson: University Press of Mississippi, 2002); Mark E. Neely, *Southern Rights: Political Prisoners and the Myth of Confederate Constitutionalism* (Charlottesville: University of Virginia Press, 1999).

19. Michael W. Fitzgerald, *Splendid Failure: Postwar Reconstruction in the American South* (Chicago: Ivan R. Dee, 2007); Steven Hahn, *A Nation Under Our Feet: Black Political Struggles in the Rural South form Slavery to the Great Migration* (Cambridge, Mass.: Harvard University Press, 2003).

20. Seymour Drescher, *Abolition: A History of Slavery and Antislavery* (New York: Cambridge University Press, 2009), 455, 460 (quotation).

Index